Mobile
Communications

Jochen H. Schiller

Mobile Communications

▲▲ Addison-Wesley

An imprint of **PEARSON EDUCATION**

Harlow, England · London · New York · Reading, Massachusetts · San Francisco · Toronto · Don Mills, Ontario · Sydney ·
Tokyo · Singapore · Hong Kong · Seoul · Taipei · Cape Town · Madrid · Mexico City · Amsterdam · Munich · Paris · Milan

PEARSON EDUCATION LIMITED

Head Office:
Edinburgh Gate
Harlow CM20 2JE
Tel: +44 (0)1279 623623
Fax: +44 (0)1279 431059

London Office
128 Long Acre
London WC2E 9AN
Tel: +44 (0)207 447 2000
Fax: +44 (0)207 240 5771

Website: www.awl.com/cseng

First Published in Great Britain 2000

© Pearson Education Limited 2000

ISBN 0 201 39836 2

The right of Jochen Schiller to be identified as author of
this work has been asserted by him in accordance with
the Copyright, Designs, and Patents Act 1988.

British Library Cataloguing-in-Publication Data
A catalogue record for this book is available from the British Library.

Library of Congress Cataloging in Publication Data
Applied for.

10 9 8 7 6 5 4 3 2 1

Text design by barker/hilsdon @ compuserve.com
Typeset by Pantek Arts, Maidstone, Kent
Printed and bound in Great Britain by Biddles Ltd, Guildford

The publishers' policy is to use paper manufactured from sustainable forests.

To my students

Contents

About the author

Jochen Schiller received his Diploma and PhD (Dr.-Ing.) degrees in computer science from the University of Karlsruhe, Germany. During his research visit at Uppsala University, Sweden, he worked within the European HIPPARCH project and industry co-operations dealing with Quality of Service (QoS) provisioning for large-scale WWW servers.

Current research at the Institute of Telematics, University of Karlsruhe, is focused on telecommunications in traffic systems, feedback mechanisms for QoS architectures and mobile communications. Additionally, Dr Schiller is an Assistant Professor in the areas of computer networks, especially mobile communications, at the University of Karlsruhe, one of the leading technical universities in Europe, and he also teaches at Uppsala University, Sweden. He is a member of IEEE and GI and acts as consultant for several companies in the networking and communication business.

Preface

We are experiencing exponential growth rates in mobile communication systems, increasing mobility awareness in society, and deregulation of former monopolized markets. While traditional communication paradigms deal with fixed networks, mobility raises a new set of questions, techniques, and solutions. For many countries, mobile communication is the only solution due to the lack of an appropriate fixed communication infrastructure. The trends mentioned above create an ever-increasing demand for well-educated communication engineers who understand the developments and possibilities of mobile communication. What we see today is only the beginning. There are many new and exciting systems currently being developed in research labs. The future will see more and more mobile devices, the merging of classical voice and data transmission technologies, and the extension of today's Internet applications (e.g., the world wide web) onto mobile and wireless devices. New applications and new mobile networks will bring ubiquitous multimedia computing to the mass market; radios, personal digital assistants (PDAs), laptops and mobile phones will converge and many different functions will be available on one device.

This book is an introduction to the field of mobile communications and focuses on digital data transfer. The book is intended for use by students of EE or CS in computer networking or communication classes, engineers working with fixed networks who want to see the future trends in networking, as well as managers who need a comprehensible overview in mobile communication. The reader requires a basic understanding of communication and a rough knowledge of the Internet or networking in general. While resources are available which focus on a particular technology, this book tries to cover many aspects of mobile communications from a computer science point of view. Furthermore, the book points out common properties of different technical solutions and shows the integration of services and applications well-known from fixed networks into networks supporting mobility of end systems and wireless access. If the reader is interested in more detailed information regarding a certain topic, he or she will find many pointers to research publications or related web sites.

Teachers may find this book useful for a course which follows after a general data communication or computer networking class. The book can also replace parts of more general courses if it is used together with other books covering fixed networks or aspects of high-speed networks. It should be straightforward to teach a mobile networking class using this book together with the course material provided online via the following link:

http://www.telematik.informatik.uni-karlsruhe.de/~schiller/

The material comprises all of the figures, over 370 slides in English and German as PDF and PowerPoint™ files, a list of all acronyms, and many links to related sites. Additionally, the questions included in the book can provide a good self-test for students.

This book addresses people who want to know how mobile phone systems work, what technology will be next in satellite communication, and how mobility will influence applications, security, or networks. Engineers working in fixed networks can see paths of migration towards mixed fixed/mobile networks.

The book follows a 'tall and thin' approach. It covers a whole course in mobile communication, from signals, access protocols, up to application requirements and security, and does not stress single topics to the neglect of others. It focuses on digital mobile communication systems, as the future belongs to digital systems such as CDMA, GSM, DECT, DAB. New and important topics in the higher layers of communication, like the wireless application protocol (WAP), are included.

Chapter 1 introduces the field of mobile and wireless communication, presents a short history and challenges for research, and concludes with a market vision which shows the potential of mobile technology. Chapter 2 follows the classical layers of communication systems and explains the basics of wireless technology from a computer science point of view. Topics in this chapter are signal propagation, multiplexing, and modulation. Profound electrical engineering knowledge is not required, however it is necessary to comprehend the basic principles of wireless transmission to understand the design decisions of higher layer communication protocols and applications. Chapter 3 presents several media access schemes and motivates why the standard schemes from fixed networks fail if used in a wireless environment.

Chapters 4–8 present different wireless communication systems and may be read in any order. All systems have in common that they involve wireless access to a network and that they can transfer arbitrary data between communication partners. Chapter 4 comprises global system for mobile communications (GSM) as today's most successful public mobile phone system, cordless phone technology, trunked radios, and the future development with universal mobile telecommunications system (UMTS). Satellite systems are covered in chapter 5, while chapter 6 discusses digital broadcast systems such as digital audio broadcasting (DAB) which can be one component of a larger communication system providing end-users with mass data. Wireless LANs as replacement for cabling inside buildings are presented in chapter 7. Examples are IEEE 802.11, HIPERLAN, and Bluetooth. Chapter 8 focuses on wireless ATM, i.e., the extension of the asynchronous transfer mode (ATM) technology into the wireless domain. A special feature of wireless ATM is the provisioning of quality of service (QOS), i.e., the system can give guarantees for, such as bandwidth or error rates.

Chapter 9 mainly presents Mobile IP, the extension of the Internet protocol (IP) into the mobile domain. Ad hoc networks with their requirements for specific routing protocols are also covered. The subsequent layer, the transport layer, is covered in chapter 10. This chapter discusses several approaches of adapting the current transmission control protocol (TCP), which is well-known from the Internet, to the special requirements of mobile communication systems. Finally, chapter 11 presents the new wireless application protocol (WAP) standard that enables wireless and mobile devices to use the world wide web (WWW) from today's fixed Internet.

The book is based on a course taught at the University of Karlsruhe. The course typically consists of 14 lectures of 90 minutes each. Over 150 students have already used the material compiled for this book, which, remember is available online.

You are encouraged to send any comments regarding the book or course material to schiller@computer.org. Finally, I hope you enjoy reading the book and forgive me for simplifications I have used to avoid blurring the big picture of mobile communications. Many such details may change as research and standards evolve over time.

Acknowledgements

First of all I want to thank the numerous students from my Mobile Communications courses who pushed me towards writing this book by requesting more information regarding wireless and mobile communication. The students' questions and answers were a great help to shaping the contents.

Many of my colleagues at the University of Karlsruhe gave generously of their intellect and time, reading, commenting, and discussing the chapters of the book. I am especially grateful to Marc Bechler, Stefan Dresler, Jochen Seitz, and Günter Schäfer. I want to thank Hartmut Ritter for his support by taking over some of my daily routine work. I also had help from Verena Rose and Elmar Dorner during the early stages of the course material.

For many insightful comments to the book I thank Per Gunningberg from Uppsala University, Sweden. I am profoundly grateful to Angelika Rieder and Kerstin Risse for their help in polishing the copy, particularly my English – without their help it would not be as easy to read.

I thank the Addison-Wesley team in the UK for all their support during the making of the book, special thanks to Penelope Allport, Alison Birtwell and Steve Temblett.

Last, but definitively not least, I want to thank the head of the Institute of Telematics, Prof. Gerhard Krüger, for giving me the freedom and support to set up the Mobile Communications course in an inspiring environment.

Introduction

1

What will **computers** look like in ten years, in the next century? No wholly accurate prediction can be made, but as a general feature, most computers will certainly be **portable**. How will users **access** networks with the help of computers or other communication devices? An ever-increasing number without any wires, i.e., **wireless**. How will people spend much of their time at work, during vacation? Many **people** will be **mobile** – already one of the key characteristics of today's society. Think, for example, of an aircraft with 800 seats. Modern aircraft already offer limited network access to passengers, and aircraft of the next generation will offer easy Internet access. In this scenario, a mobile network moving at high speed above ground with a wireless link will be the only means of transporting data to and from passengers. Furthermore, think of cars with Internet access and billions of embedded processors that have to communicate with for instance cameras, mobile phones, CD-players, headsets, keyboards, intelligent traffic signs and sensors.

Before presenting more applications, definitions of the terms 'mobile' and 'wireless' as used throughout this book should be given. There are two different kinds of mobility: user mobility and device portability. **User mobility** refers to a user who has access to the same or similar telecommunication services at different places, i.e., the user can be mobile, and the services will follow him or her. Examples for mechanisms supporting user mobility are simple call-forwarding solutions known from the telephone or computer desktops supporting roaming (i.e., the desktop looks the same no matter which computer a user uses to log into the network).

With **device portability**,[1] the communication device moves (with or without a user). Many mechanisms in the network and inside the device have to make sure that communication is still possible while it is moving. A typical example for systems supporting device portability is the mobile phone system, where the system itself hands the device from one radio transmitter (also called a base station) to the next if the signal becomes too weak. Most of the scenarios described in this book contain both user mobility and device portability at the same time.

With regard to devices, the term **wireless** is used. This only describes the way of accessing a network or other communication partners, i.e., without a wire. The wire is replaced by the transmission of electromagnetic waves through 'the air' (although wireless transmission does not need any medium).

A communication device can thus exhibit one of the following characteristics:

- **Fixed and wired:** This configuration describes the typical desktop computer in an office.
- **Mobile and wired:** Many of today's laptops fall into this category; users carry the laptop from one hotel to the next, reconnecting to the company's network via the telephone network and a modem.
- **Fixed and wireless:** This mode is used for installing networks, e.g., in historical buildings to avoid damage by installing wires, or at trade shows to ensure fast network setup.
- **Mobile and wireless:** This is the most interesting case. No cable restricts the user, who can roam between different wireless networks. Most technologies discussed in this book deal with this type of devices and the networks supporting them.

The following section highlights some application scenarios predestined for the use of mobile and wireless devices. An overview of some typical devices is also given. The reader should keep in mind, however, that the scenarios and devices discussed only represent a selected spectrum, which will change in the future. As the market for mobile and wireless devices is growing rapidly, more devices will show up, and new application scenarios will be created. A short history of wireless communication will provide the background, briefly summing up the development over the last 200 years. Section 1.3 shows wireless and mobile communication from a marketing perspective. While there are already millions of users of wireless devices today, the market potential is still enormous.

Section 1.4 shows some open research topics resulting from the fundamental differences between wired and wireless communication. Section 1.5 presents the basic reference model for communication systems used throughout this book. This chapter concludes with an overview of the book, explaining the 'tall and thin' approach chosen. Tall and thin means that this book covers a variety of different aspects of mobile and wireless communication to provide a complete picture. Due to this broad perspective, however, it does not go into the details of each technology and systems presented.

1.1 Applications

Although wireless networks and mobile communications can be used for many applications, particular application environments seem to be predestined for their use. Some of them will be enumerated in the following sections – it is left to you to imagine more.

1.1.1 Vehicles

Tomorrow's cars will comprise many wireless communication systems and mobility aware applications. Music, news, road conditions, weather reports, and other broadcast information is received via digital audio broadcasting (DAB) with 1.5 Mbit/s. For personal communication, a global system for mobile communications (GSM) phone might be available offering voice and data connectivity with 384 kbit/s. For remote areas satellite communication can be used, while the current position of the car is determined via global positioning system (GPS). Additionally, cars driving in the same area build a local ad hoc network for fast information exchange in emergency situations or to help each other keeping a safe distance. In case of an accident, not only will the airbag be triggered, but also an emergency call to a service provider informing ambulance and police. Cars with this technology are already available. Future cars will also inform other cars about accidents via the ad hoc network to help them slow down in time, even before a driver can recognize the accident. Buses, trucks, and trains are already transmitting maintenance and logistic information to their home base, which helps to improve organization (fleet management), and thus save time and money.

Figure 1.1 shows a typical scenario for mobile communications with many wireless devices. Networks with a fixed infrastructure like cellular phones (GSM, UMTS) will be interconnected with trunked radio systems (TETRA) and wireless LANs (WLAN). Additionally, satellite communication links can be used. The networks between cars and also inside a car will more likely work in an ad hoc fashion. Wireless pico networks inside a car can comprise PDAs, laptops, or mobile phones, e.g., connected with each other using the Bluetooth technology.

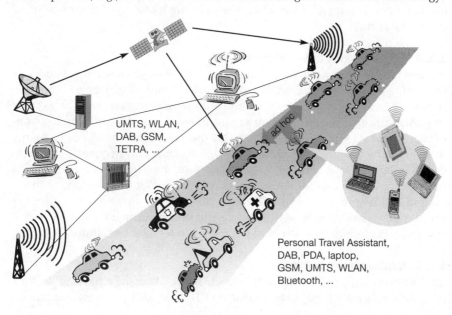

UMTS, WLAN, DAB, GSM, TETRA, ...

ad hoc

Personal Travel Assistant, DAB, PDA, laptop, GSM, UMTS, WLAN, Bluetooth, ...

Figure 1.1
A typical application of mobile communications: road traffic

This first scenario shows, in addition to the technical content, something typical in the communication business – many **acronyms**. This book contains and defines many of these. If you get lost with an acronym, please check appendix A, which contains the complete list.

Think of similar scenarios for air traffic or railroad traffic. Different problems can occur here due to speed. While aircraft typically travel at up to 900 km/h, current trains up to 350 km/h, many technologies cannot operate if the relative speed of a mobile device exceeds, e.g., 250 km/h for GSM or 100 km/h for AMPS. Only some technologies, like DAB work up to 900 km/h.

1.1.2 Emergencies

Just imagine the possibilities of an ambulance with a high-quality wireless connection to a hospital. After an accident, vital information about injured persons can be sent to the hospital immediately. There, all necessary steps for this particular type of accident can be prepared or further specialists can be consulted for an early diagnosis. Furthermore, wireless networks are the only means of communication in the case of natural disasters such as hurricanes or earthquakes. In the worst cases only decentralized, wireless ad hoc networks survive. The breakdown of all cabling not only implies the failure of the standard wired telephone system, but also the crash of all mobile phone systems requiring base stations!

1.1.3 Business

Today's typical travelling salesman needs instant access to the company's database: to ensure that files on his or her laptop reflect the actual state, to enable the company to keep track of all activities of their travelling employees, to keep databases consistent etc. With wireless access, the laptop can be turned into a true mobile office.

1.1.4 Replacement of wired networks

In some cases, wireless networks can also be used to replace wired networks, as for remote sensors, for tradeshows, or in historic buildings. Due to economic reasons, it is often impossible to wire remote sensors in cases such as weather forecast, earthquakes detection, or environmental information. Wireless connections, e.g., via satellite, can help in this situation. Tradeshows need a highly dynamic infrastructure, but cabling takes a long time and frequently proves to be too inflexible. Many computer fairs, therefore, use WLANs as a replacement for cabling. Other cases for wireless networks are computers, sensors, or information displays in historical buildings, where it is crucial not to add more cabling than necessary to avoid the destruction of valuable walls or floors. Wireless access points in a corner of the room can represent a solution.

1.1.5 Infotainment and more

Internet everywhere? Not without wireless networks! Imagine a travel guide for a city. Static information might be loaded via CD-ROM, DVD, or even at home via the Internet. But wireless networks can provide up-to-date information at any appropriate location. The travel guide might tell you something about the history of a building (knowing via GPS where you are), downloading information about a concert in the building at the same evening via a local wireless network. You may choose a seat, pay via electronic cash,

and send this information to a service provider. Another growing field of wireless network applications lies in entertainment and games in order to enable, e.g., ad hoc gaming networks as soon as people meet to play together.

1.1.6 Location dependent services

Many research efforts in mobile computing and wireless networks try to hide the fact that the network access has been changed (e.g., from mobile phone to WLAN or between different access points) or that a wireless link is more error prone than a wired one. Many chapters in this book give examples: Mobile IP tries to hide the fact of changing access points by redirecting packets but keeping the same IP address (see section 9.1), and many protocols try to improve link quality using encoding mechanisms or retransmission so that applications made for fixed networks still work.

In many cases, however, it is important for an application to 'know' something about the location or it might be that the user needs location information for further activities. Several services that might depend on the actual location can be distinguished:

- **Follow-on services:** The function of forwarding calls to the current user location is well-known from the good old telephone system. Wherever you are, just transmit your temporary phone number to your phone and it redirects incoming calls.[2] Using mobile computers, a follow-on service could, for instance, offer the same desktop environment wherever you are around the world. All e-mail would automatically be forwarded, all changes to your desktop and documents stored, at a central location at your company. If someone wanted to reach you using a multimedia conferencing system, this call would then also be forwarded to your current location.

- **Location aware services:** Imagine you wanted to print a document sitting in the lobby of a hotel using your laptop. If you drop the document over the printer icon, where would you expect the document to be printed? Certainly not by the printer in your office! But without additional information about your environment, this might be the only thing you can do. Therefore, services are needed that provide information about the capabilities of your environment. For instance, there could be a service in the hotel announcing that a standard laser printer is available in the lobby, a colour printer in a hotel meeting room etc. In return, your computer might then transmit your personal profile to your environment, so that the hotel can charge you with the printing costs.

- **Privacy:** The two service classes listed above immediately raise the question of privacy. You might not want video calls following you to dinner, but maybe you would want important e-mails to be forwarded. So there might be locations and/or times when you want to exclude certain services from reaching you, thereby telling the caller that you do not want to be disturbed. Furthermore, although you want to utilize location dependent services, you might not want the environment to know exactly who you are. Imagine a hotel monitoring all guests and selling these profiles to companies for advertisements.

- **Information services:** While walking around in a city you could always use your wireless travel guide to 'pull' information from a service, e.g., 'Where is the next Mexican restaurant to my current position?' But a service could also actively 'push' information on your travel guide, e.g., that the Mexican restaurant just around the corner has a special taco offer.

- **Support services:** Finally, many small additional mechanisms can be integrated to support a mobile device. Intermediate results of calculations, state information, or cache contents could 'follow' the mobile node through the fixed network. As soon as the mobile node reconnects, all information is available again. This helps to reduce access delay and traffic within the fixed network. The alternative would be a central location for user information and a user accessing this information through the (possibly large and congested) network all the time as it is typically done today.

1.1.7 Mobile and wireless devices

Even though many mobile and wireless devices are already available, we will see many more in the future. There is no precise classification of such devices, by size, shape, weight, or computing power. Currently, laptops are considered to be the upper end of the mobile device range.[3] The following list gives some examples of mobile and wireless devices graded by increasing performance (CPU, memory, display, input devices etc.).

- **Sensor:** A very simple wireless device is represented by a sensor transmitting state information. An example for such a sensor could be a switch sensing the office door. If the door is closed, the switch transmits this state to the mobile phone inside the office and the mobile phone will not accept incoming calls. Thus, without user interaction the semantics of a closed door is applied to phone calls.

- **Embedded controllers:** Many appliances already contain a simple or sometimes more complex controller. Keyboards, mice, headsets, washing machines, coffee machines, hair dryers and TV sets are just some examples.

Why not have the hair dryer as a simple mobile and wireless device (from a communication point of view) that is able to communicate with the mobile phone? Then the phone could switch off the dryer as soon as the phone starts ringing – that would be a nice application!

- **Pager:** As a very simple receiver, a pager can only display short text messages, has a tiny display, and cannot send any messages. Pagers can even be integrated into watches.
- **Mobile phones:** The traditional mobile phone only had a simple black and white text display and could send/receive voice or short messages. Today, however, mobile phones migrate more and more toward PDAs. Mobile phones with full colour graphic display, touch screen, and Internet browser are available.
- **Personal digital assistant:** PDAs typically accompany a user and offer very simple versions of office software (calendar, note-pad, mail). The typical input device is a pen, with built-in character recognition translating hand-writing into characters. Web browsers and many other software packages are already available for these devices.
- **Palmtop/pocket computer:** The next step toward full computers are pocket computers offering tiny keyboards, colour displays, and simple versions of programs found on desktop computers (text processing, spread sheets etc.).
- **Notebook/laptop:** Finally, laptops offer more or less the same performance as standard desktop computers, use the same software, the only technical difference being size, weight, and the ability to run on a battery.

The mobile and wireless devices of the future will be more powerful, less heavy, and comprise new interfaces to the user and to new networks. However, one big problem which has not been solved yet, is the energy supply. The more features are built into a device, the more power it needs. The higher the performance of the device, the faster it drains the batteries (assuming the same technology). Furthermore, wireless data transmission consumes a lot of energy.

Although the area of mobile computing and mobile communication is developing rapidly, the devices typically used today still exhibit some major drawbacks compared to desktop systems in addition to the energy problem. Interfaces have to be small enough to make the device portable. Thus, smaller keyboards are used, which are frequently clumsy for typing due to their limited key size. Furthermore, small displays are often useless for graphical display, and a higher resolution of the display does not help as the limiting factor is the resolution capacity of the human eye. Therefore, these devices have to use new ways of interacting with a user, such as, e.g., touch sensitive displays and voice recognition.

Mobile communication is greatly influenced by the merging of telecommunication and computer networks. We cannot say for certain what the telephone of the future will look like, but it will most probably be a computer. Even today, telephones and mobile phones are far from the simple 'voice transmission devices' they were in the past.[4] Developments like 'voice over IP' and the general trend toward packet-oriented networks enforce the metamorphosis of telephones. While no-one can predict the future of communication devices precisely, it is quite clear, that there will still be many fixed systems, complemented by a myriad small wireless computing devices all over the world.

1.2 A short history of wireless communication

For a better understanding of today's wireless systems and developments, a short history of wireless communication is presented in the following section. This cannot cover all inventions but highlights those that have contributed fundamentally to today's systems.

The use of light for wireless communications reaches back to ancient times. In former times, the light was either 'modulated' using mirrors to create a certain light on/light off pattern ('amplitude modulation') or, for example flags were used to signal code words ('amplitude and frequency modulation', see chapter 2). The use of smoke signals for communication is mentioned by Polybius, Greece, as early as 150 BC. Using light and flags for wireless communication remained important for the navy until radio transmission was introduced. But even today a sailor has to know some codes represented by flags if all other means of wireless communication fail.

It was not until the end of the 18th century, when **Claude Chappe** invented the optical telegraph (**1794**), that long-distance wireless communication was possible. Almost until the end of the following century optical telegraph lines were built.

Wired communication started with the first commercial telegraph line between Washington and Baltimore in 1843, and **Alexander Graham Bell's** invention and marketing of the telephone in 1876 (others tried the marketing before but did not succeed, e.g., **Philip Reis**, 1834–1874, discovered the telephone principle in **1861**). In Berlin, a public telephone service was available in **1881**, the first regular public voice and video service (multimedia!) was already available in 1936 between Berlin and Leipzig.

All optical transmission systems suffer from the high frequency of the carrier light. As every little obstacle shadows the signal, rain and fog make communication almost impossible. Furthermore, at that time it was not possible to focus light as efficiently as can be done today by means of a laser. Therefore, wireless communication did not really take off until the discovery of electromagnetic waves and the development of equipment to modulate them. It all started with **Michael Faraday** (and about the same time **Joseph Henry**) demonstrating electromagnetic induction in 1831 and **James C. Maxwell** (1831–79) laying the theoretical foundations for electromagnetic fields with his famous equations (**1864**). Finally, **Heinrich Hertz** (1857–94) was the first to demonstrate through an experiment the wave character of electrical transmission through space[5] (**1886**), thus proving Maxwell's equations. Today the unit Hz reminds us of this discovery. **Nikola Tesla** (1856–1943) soon increased the distance of electromagnetic transmission.

The name which is most closely connected with the success of wireless communication is certainly that of **Guglielmo Marconi** (1874–1937). He gave the first demonstration of wireless telegraphy in **1895** using long wave transmission with very high transmission power (> 200 kW). The first transatlantic transmission followed in 1901. Only six years later, in **1907**, the first **commercial transatlantic connections** were set up. Huge base stations using up to thirty 100 m high antennas were needed on both sides of the Atlantic Ocean. Around that time, the first **World Administration Radio Conference (WARC)** took place, coordinating the worldwide use of radio frequencies. The first **radio broadcast** took place in **1906** when **Reginald A. Fessenden** (1866–1932) transmitted voice and music for Christmas. In 1915, the first wireless voice transmission was set up between New York and San Francisco. The first **commercial radio station** started in **1920** (KDKA from Pittsburgh). But still, sender and receiver needed huge antennas and high transmission power.

This changed fundamentally with the discovery of **short waves**, again by Marconi, in **1920**. In connection with wireless communication, short waves have the advantage of being reflected at the ionosphere. This way it was now possible to send short radio waves around the world bouncing at the ionosphere – this technique is still used today. The invention of the electronic **vacuum tube** in **1906** by **Lee DeForest** (1873–1961) and **Robert von Lieben** (1878–1913) helped to reduce the size of sender and receiver. Vacuum tubes are still used, e.g., for the amplification of the output signal of a sender in today's radio stations. One of the first '**mobile**' **transmitters** was on board a Zeppelin in **1911**. Finally, as early as **1926**, the first **telephone in a train** was available on the Berlin-Hamburg line. Wires parallel to the railroad track worked as antenna. The first **radio for cars** was **commercially** available in **1927** ('Philco Transitone'), indeed in 1922 the 18-year-old George Frost from Chicago had integrated a radio into a Ford Model T.

Nineteen twenty-eight was the year of many field trials for **television broadcasting**. **John L. Baird** (1888–1946) transmitted TV across the Atlantic and demonstrated **colour TV**, the station **WGY** (Schenectady, NY) started **regular TV broadcasts** and the first **TV news**. The first **teleteaching** started in **1932** from the **CBS** station W2XAB. Up to then, all wireless communication used amplitude modulation (see section 2.6), which offered relatively poor quality due to interference. One big step forward in this respect was the invention of **frequency modulation** in **1933** by **Edwin H. Armstrong** (1890–1954). Both fundamental modulation schemes are still used for today's radio broadcasting with frequency modulation resulting in a much better quality. By the early 1930s, many radio stations were already broadcasting all over the world.

After the second world war many national and international projects in the area of wireless communications were triggered off. The first network in Germany was the analog A-Netz from 1958, using a carrier frequency of 160 MHz. Connection setup was only possible from the mobile station, no hand-over, i.e., changing of the base station, was possible. Back in 1971 this system had a coverage of 80 per cent and 11,000 customers. It was not until 1972 that the B-Netz followed in Germany, using the same 160 MHz. As a new feature, this network offered the possibility to initiate the connection setup from a station in the fixed telephone network. However, the current location of the mobile receiver had to be known. This system was also available in Austria, The Netherlands, and Luxembourg. The B-Netz had 13,000 customers in 1979 in West Germany and needed a heavy sender and receiver, typically built into cars.

At the same time, the northern European countries of Denmark, Finland, Norway, and Sweden (the cradle of modern mobile communications) agreed upon the **nordic mobile telephone (NMT)** system. The analog NMT uses a 450 MHz carrier and is still the only available system for mobile communication in some very remote places (NMT at 900 MHz followed in 1986). Several other national standards evolved and finally in the early 1980s Europe had more than a handful of different, completely incompatible analog mobile phone standards. In accordance with the general idea of a European Union, the European countries decided to develop a pan-European mobile phone standard in **1982**. The new system should use a new spectrum at 900 MHz and allow roaming[6] throughout Europe. Furthermore, it should be fully digital and offer voice and data service. The **'Groupe Spéciale Mobile' (GSM)** was founded for this new development.

At almost the same time (**1983**) the US system **advanced mobile phone system (AMPS)** started (EIA, 1989) AMPS is an analog mobile phone system working at 850 MHz. Telephones at home went wireless with the standard **CT1 (cordless telephone)** in **1984**, that followed its predecessor **CT0** from **1980**. As the digital systems were not yet available, more analog standards followed, such as the German C-Netz at 450 MHz with analog voice transmission. Now hand-over between 'cells' was possible, the signalling system was digital in accordance with the trends in fixed networks (SS7), and automatic localization of a mobile user within the whole network was supported. This network is still in use today, mainly due to its coverage of almost 100 per cent. The services offered apart from voice transmission are fax, data transmission via modem, X.25, and electronic mail. **CT2**, the successor of CT1, was embodied into British Standards published in **1987** (DTI, 1987) and later adopted by ETSI for Europe (ETS, 1994). CT2 uses the spectrum at 864 MHz and offers a data chan-nel at a rate of 32 kbit/s.

The early 1990s marked the beginning of **fully digital systems**. In **1991**, ETSI adopted the standard **digital european cordless telephone (DECT)** for digital cordless telephony (ETSI, 1998). DECT works at a spectrum of 1880–1900 MHz with a range of 100–500 m. One hundred and twenty duplex channels can carry up to 1.2 Mbit/s for data transmission. Several more new features, such as voice encryption and authentication are built-in. The system supports several 10,000 users/km^2 and is used in more than 40 countries around the world. Today, DECT has been renamed **digital enhanced cordless telecommunications** for marketing reasons and to reflect the capabilities of DECT to transport multimedia data streams. Finally, after many years of discussions and field trials, **GSM** was standardized in a document of more than 5,000 pages in **1991**. This first version of GSM, now called **global system for mobile communication**, works at 900 MHz and uses 124 full-duplex channels. GSM offers full international roaming, automatic location services, authentication, encryption on the wireless link, efficient interoperation with ISDN systems, and a relatively high audio quality. Furthermore, a short message service with up to 160 alphanumeric characters, fax group 3, and data services at 9.6 kbit/s have been integrated. Depending on national regulations, one or several providers can use the channels, different accounting and charging schemes can be applied etc. However, all GSM systems remain compatible. Providers in more than 130 countries have adopted the GSM standard at 900 MHz worldwide.

It was soon discovered that the analog AMPS in the US and the digital GSM at 900 MHz in Europe are not sufficient for the high user densities in cities. While in the beginning in the US no new spectrum was allocated for a new system, in Europe a new frequency band at 1800 MHz was chosen. The effect was as follows. In the US different companies developed different new, more bandwidth-efficient technologies to operate side-by-side with AMPS in the same frequency band. This resulted in three incompatible systems, the analog narrowband AMPS (IS-88, (TIA, 1993a)), and the two digital **TDMA** (IS-136, (TIA, 1996)) and **CDMA** (IS-95, (TIA, 1993b)) systems. The Europeans agreed upon the use of GSM in the 1800 MHz spectrum, currently supported by more than a dozen countries. These GSM-1800 networks (also known as **DCS 1800**, digital cellular system) operate with a better voice quality and smaller cells, and thus are better adapted to business use in big cities. Nowadays, GSM is also available in the US as GSM-1900 (also called **PCS 1900**) using spectrum at 1900 MHz like the newer versions of the TDMA and CDMA systems.

Europeans believe in standards, while the US believes in market forces – GSM is one of the few examples where the approach via standardization worked. Thus, while Europe has one common standard, and while roaming is possible even to Australia or Singapore, the US still struggles with many incompatible systems. However, the picture is different if it comes to more data communication-oriented systems like local area networks. Many proprietary wireless local area network systems already existed when back in **1996** ETSI standardized the High Performance Radio Local Area Network (HIPERLAN). This is a family of standards and recommendations. HIPERLAN type 1 should operate at 5.2 GHz and offer data rates of up to 23.5 Mbit/s. Further types have been specified with type 4 going up to 155 Mbit/s at 17 GHz. However, although coming later than HIPERLAN in **1997**, the IEEE standard **802.11** looks like the winner for local area networks. It works at the licence-free Industrial,

Science, Medical (ISM) band at 2.4 GHz and infrared offering 2 Mbit/s (up to 10 Mbit/s with special solutions). Although HIPERLAN has better performance figures, no products are presently available while many companies offer 802.11 compliant equipment.

Nineteen ninety-eight finally marked the beginning of mobile communication using satellites with the **Iridium** system (Iridium, 1998). While up to this time satellites basically worked as a broadcast distribution medium or could only be used with big and heavy equipment, Iridium marks the beginning of small and truly portable mobile satellite telephones including data service. Iridium consists of 66 satellites in low earth orbit and uses the 1.6 GHz band for communication with the mobile phone. Secondly, in 1998 the Europeans agreed on the **universal mobile telecommunications system** (UMTS) as the European proposal for the International Telecommunication Union (ITU) **IMT-2000 (international mobile telecommunications)**. UMTS combined GSM technology with the more bandwidth-efficient CDMA solutions.

The IMT-2000 recommendations define a common, worldwide framework for future mobile communication at 2 GHz (ITU, 1998). This includes, e.g., a framework for services, the network architecture including satellite communication, strategies for developing countries, requirements of the radio interface, spectrum considerations, security and management frameworks, and different transmission technologies.

An overview of some of the networks described above is given in Figure 1.3. This diagram shows the development of cellular systems and cordless phones in Europe together with satellites and LANs. The current trend is a unification of at least some of the technologies toward IMT-2000 for global mobile communication and some kind of a **mobile broadband system (MBS)** for local wireless communication with much higher bandwidth and additional quality of service features. The dates shown in the figure typically indicate the start of service (i.e., the systems have been designed, invented, and tested earlier). The systems behind the acronyms will be explained in the following chapters (cellular and cordless phones in chapter 4, satellites in chapter 5, WLANs in chapters 7 and 8).[7]

1.3 A market for mobile communications

The current growth rates in wireless communication show the huge market potential of these technologies. More and more people use mobile phones, wireless technology is built into many cars, wireless data services are available in many regions, and wireless local area networks are used in many places.

Figure 1.4 shows the increasing numbers of subscribers to mobile phone services worldwide (GSM Data, 1998).[8] This figure shows the tremendous growth rates, especially in countries outside the three big regions, the Americas, Europe, and Japan. This effect will be mainly due to the introduction of more and more mobile phone services in Asia.

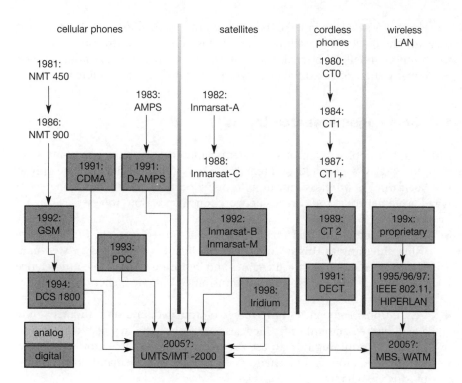

Figure 1.3
Overview of some wireless communication systems

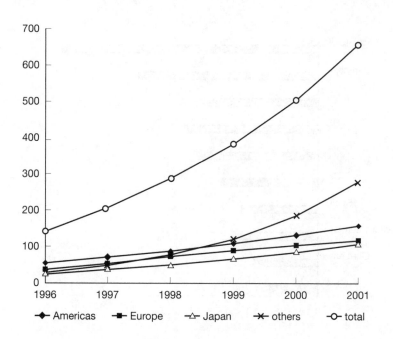

Figure 1.4
Mobile phone service subscribers worldwide (in millions)

Figure 1.5 shows the market penetration of mobile phones in 1998. In this diagram, the potential for selling more phones in many countries and the trend toward more mobile phones all over the world is clearly visible. Countries such as Germany and France exhibited growth rates of 40 per cent or more in 1998.

1.4 Some open research topics

Although this book explains many systems supporting mobility and many solutions for wireless access, a lot still remains to be done in the field. We are only at the beginning of wireless and mobile networking. The differences between wired, fixed networks and wireless networks open up various topics:

- **Interference:** Radio transmission cannot be protected against interference using shielding as this is done in coaxial cable or shielded twisted pair. Thus, for example, electrical engines and lightning cause severe interference and result in higher loss rates for transmitted data or higher bit error rates respectively.
- **Regulations:** Frequencies have to be co-ordinated, and unfortunately, only a very limited amount of frequencies is available. One research topic would involve determining how to use the frequencies available more efficiently, e.g., by new modulation schemes (see chapter 2) or demand-driven multiplexing (see chapter 3).

Figure 1.5
Market penetration of mobile phones per 100 people (1998)

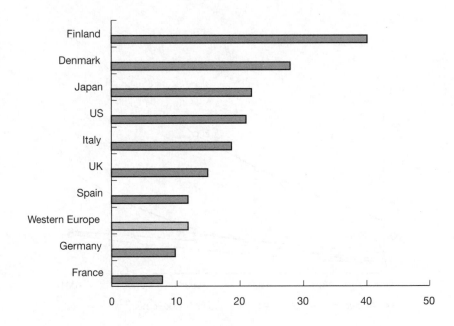

- **Low bandwidth:** Although they are continuously increasing, transmission rates are still very low for wireless devices compared to desktop systems. Local wireless systems reach some Mbit/s while wide area systems only offer some 10 kbit/s. One task would involve adapting applications used with high-bandwidth connections to this new environment so that the user can continue using the same application when moving from the desktop outside the building.
- **High delays, large delay variation:** A serious problem for communication protocols used in today's Internet (TCP/IP) is the big variation in link characteristics. In wireless systems, delays of several seconds can occur, and links can be very asymmetrical (i.e., the links offer different service quality depending on the direction to and from the wireless device).
- **Lower security, simpler to attack:** Not only can portable devices be stolen more easily, but the radio interface is also prone to the dangers of eavesdropping. Thus, wireless access always has to include encryption, authentication, and other security mechanisms.
- **Shared medium:** Radio access is always realized via a shared medium. As it is impossible to have a separate wire between a sender and each receiver, different competitors have to 'fight' for the medium. Although many different medium access schemes have been developed, many questions are still unanswered, for example how to provide quality of service efficiently.

1.5 A simplified reference model

This book follows the **basic reference model** used in the field of communication for structuring communication systems (Tanenbaum, 1996). It is recommended that readers who are unfamiliar with the basics of communication networks look up the relevant sections in the literature recommended (Halsall, 1996), (Keshav, 1997). Figure 1.6 shows a personal digital assistant (PDA) which provides an example for a wireless and portable device. This PDA communicates with a base station in the middle of the picture. The base station consists of a radio transceiver (sender and receiver) and an interworking unit connecting the wireless link with the fixed link. Finally, on the right-hand side, the communication partner of the PDA, a conventional computer, is shown.

Underneath each network element (such as PDA, interworking unit, computer), the figure shows the **protocol stack** implemented in the system according to the reference model. **End-systems**, such as the PDA and computer in the example, need a full protocol stack comprising the application layer, transport layer, network layer, data link layer, and physical layer. Applications on the end-systems communicate with each other using the lower layer services. **Intermediate systems**, such as the interworking unit, do not necessarily need all of the layers. Figure 1.6 only shows the network, data link, and physical layers. As (according to the basic reference model) only entities at the same level

Figure 1.6
Simple network and
reference model used in
this book

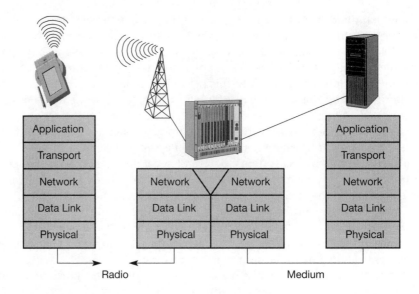

communicate with each other (i.e., transport with transport, network with network), the end-system applications do not notice the intermediate system
directly in this scenario. The following paragraphs explain the functions of each
layer in more detail in a wireless and mobile environment.

- **Physical layer:** This lowest layer in a communication system is responsible
  for the conversion of a stream of bits into signals that can be transmitted
  on the sender side. The physical layer of the receiver then transforms the
  signals back into a bitstream. For wireless communication, the physical
  layer is responsible for frequency selection, generation of the carrier frequency, signal detection (although heavy interference may disturb the
  signal), modulation of data onto a carrier frequency and (depending on the
  transmission scheme) encryption. These features of the physical layer will
  mainly be discussed in chapter 2 and will furthermore be mentioned for
  each system separately in the appropriate chapters.
- **Data link layer:** The main tasks of this layer include accessing the medium,
  multiplexing of different data streams, correction of transmission errors,
  and synchronization (i.e., detection of a data frame). Chapter 3 will discuss
  different medium access schemes and a small section about the specific data
  link layer used in the systems presented is combined in each respective
  chapter. Altogether, the data link layer is responsible for a reliable point-to-
  point connection between two devices or a point-to-multipoint connection
  between one sender and several receivers.
- **Network layer:** This third layer is responsible for routing packets through a
  network or establishing a connection between two entities over many other

intermediate systems. Important topics are addressing, routing, device location, and handover between different networks. Chapter 9 presents several solutions for the network layer protocol of the Internet (the Internet Protocol IP). The other chapters also contain sections about the network layer as routing is necessary in most cases.

- **Transport layer:** This layer is used in the reference model to establish an end-to-end connection. Topics like quality of service, flow and congestion control are relevant, especially if the transport protocols known from the Internet, TCP and UDP, are to be used over a wireless link.

- **Application layer:** Finally, the applications (complemented by additional layers that can support applications) are situated on top of all transmission-oriented layers. Topics of interest in this context are service location, support for multimedia applications, adaptive applications that can handle the large variations in transmission characteristics, and also wireless access to the world wide web using a portable device. One of the most demanding applications is video, Bahl (1998) shows problems and solutions.

A general research topic for wireless communication is its influence on the human body. Up to now it has not been clear if and to what extent electromagnetic waves transmitted from wireless devices can influence organs. Microwave ovens and WLANs both operate at the same frequency of 2.4 GHz. However, the radiation of a WLAN is very low (e.g., 1 W) compared to a microwave oven (e.g., 800 W inside the oven). But more studies are needed to understand the effects of long-term low-power radiation (Lin, 1997).

1.6 Overview

The whole book is structured in a bottom-up approach as shown in Figure 1.7. **Chapter 2** presents some basics about wireless transmission technology. Topics covered include frequencies used for communication, signal characteristics, antennas, signal propagation, several fundamental multiplexing and modulation schemes. This chapter requires neither profound knowledge of electrical engineering nor does it explore all details about the underlying physics of wireless communication systems. The aim is rather to help the reader understand many design decisions in the higher layers of mobile communication systems.

Chapter 3 presents a broad range of media access technologies. Starting with an explanation why media access technologies from fixed networks often cannot be applied to wireless networks, the chapter shows special problems of wireless terminals accessing 'space' as the common medium. The chapter shows access methods for different purposes, such as wireless mobile phones with a central base station that can control the access, or completely decentralized ad hoc networks without any dedicated station. This chapter shows how the multiplexing schemes of chapter 2 can now be used for accessing the medium.

Figure 1.7
Overview of the
book's structure

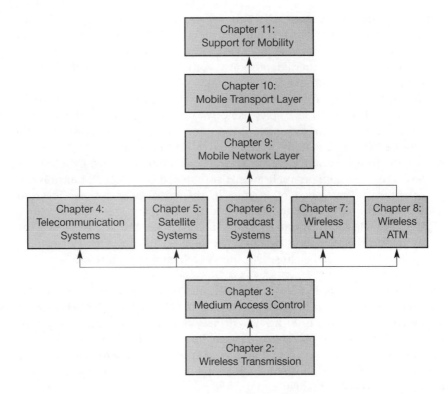

Special focus lies on code division multiple access (CDMA), which is one of the important access methods of the future. Further topics are variants of Aloha and reservation schemes known from satellite networks.

After chapter 3, the reader can select any of the chapters from 4 to 8. These present selected wireless transmission systems using the basic technologies shown in chapters 2 and 3 and offer a data transport service to higher layers. **Chapter 4** covers wireless communication systems originating from the telecommunication industry and standardization bodies. On the one hand GSM, which is currently one of the most successful digital mobile phone systems worldwide, and on the other digital enhanced cordless telecommunications (DECT), an example for a local wireless telecommunication system. The chapter presents standards, frequencies, services, access methods, and the architecture of the systems. Furthermore, it shows the migration from voice orientation toward packet transmission. UMTS as one candidate for future mobile systems concludes the chapter.

Chapter 5 gives a basic introduction to satellite communication. Again, the myriad technical details are not of interest, but the potential of satellite systems to exchange data worldwide. A relatively young field of wireless communication, digital broadcast systems, is covered in **chapter 6**. Broadcast systems allow only unidirectional data distribution but can offer new services that come along with digital radio (digital audio broadcasting, DAB) and digital television digital video broadcasting (DVB). For these systems, the ability to distribute arbitrary multimedia data using standard formats known from the Internet is an extremely important design factor. DAB is currently one of the few systems that is able to transmit multimedia data streams to vehicles with speeds of up to 900 km/h. Most other mobile systems fail at speeds above 100 km/h.

Chapter 7 presents three examples of wireless LANs, i.e., the extension of today's fixed local area networks into the wireless domain. The examples presented are the standards IEEE 802.11 and HIPERLAN, as well as the emerging Bluetooth system. After a general introduction to the design goals of wireless LANs, physical layer, medium access control layer, and services of all three LANs are presented. In this chapter, a comparison of the different approaches taken for IEEE 802.11 and HIPERLAN is of particular interest. While the first system offers only best-effort traffic at a moderately low bit rate of 2 Mbit/s, the latter tries to give quality of service (QoS) guarantees and to achieve a relatively high bandwidth of more than 23 Mbit/s. However, while many IEEE 802.11 compliant products are available, no HIPERLAN product has been released yet. Several products with proprietary solutions and new standardization efforts even reach 10 Mbit/s with 802.11 products. Bluetooth is different for it was primarily designed for short range ad hoc networking using very cheap hardware and offers only some kbit/s (as replacement for infrared).

Chapter 8 focuses on a more advanced topic, namely WATM. ATM as fixed network technology offers a broad range of QoS guarantees. This was one of the reasons to start the development of wireless ATM systems. The chapter describes the ATM reference model with its layers, interoperation with fixed ATM networks, and further efforts toward broadband radio access networks (BRAN). However, up to now, the future role of wireless ATM networks is not at all obvious.

Chapter 9 presents solutions for a mobile network layer. This layer can be used on top of different transmission technologies as presented in chapters 4 through 8. While mobile IP is the main topic of the chapter, it discusses also mechanisms such as the dynamic host configuration protocol (DHCP) and routing in ad hoc networks. Because IP is clearly dominating data communication networks (it is the basis for the Internet), it is only natural to extend this protocol to the mobile domain. The chapter discusses the problems associated with IP and mobility and shows some solutions. From chapter 9 onwards the term 'mobility' is used more often, because it does not matter for higher layer protocols if the mobility is supported by wireless transmission technologies or if the user has to plug-in a laptop wherever she or he currently is. The problems of interrupted connections and changing access points to the network remain almost identical.

In order to work with well-known applications from the Internet, e.g., file transfer or remote login, a user might need a reliable end-to-end communication service as provided by the transmission control protocol (TCP). Therefore,

chapter 10 focuses on changes needed for TCP so it can be used in a mobile environment. It is shown that today's TCP fails if it is not adapted or enhanced. Several solutions are discussed and compared. Each solution exhibits specific strengths and weaknesses, so up to now there is no standard for a 'Mobile TCP'.

All mobile networks are worthless without applications using them. **Chapter 11** shows problems with current applications as they are known from fixed networks and presents some new developments. Among other topics, it deals with file systems. Here consistency in a distributed system brings about major problems. How is consistency to be maintained in the case of disconnection? Is it better to deny access to data if consistency cannot be granted? The chapter presents systems dealing with these problems.

The big topic in today's Internet is the world wide web (WWW), the logical structure made by multimedia documents and hyperlinks. In connection with the WWW, the problems can be summarized as follows: the WWW of today assumes connections with higher bandwidth, desktop computers with a lot of memory, a powerful CPU, high-resolution graphics, and dozens of plug-ins installed. Mobile devices have scarce energy resources, therefore less powerful CPUs and less memory. Furthermore, these devices have to be portable, and consequently input devices are very limited and displays are of a low resolution, not to mention the hi-fi capabilities. This obvious mismatch between two technologies, both with exponential growth rates, has resulted in a variety of solutions for bringing them together. One recent approach in this respect, the wireless application protocol (WAP), which is supported by many companies, is explained in more detail.

Many important security aspects will be explained together with the technology in all chapters. Security mechanisms are important in all layers of a communication system. Different users, even different nations, have different ideas about security. However, it is quite clear that a communication system transmitting personal information through the air must offer special security features to be accepted. Companies do not want competitors to listen to their communication and people often do not like the idea that their neighbour might hear their private conversation as is possible with older analog cordless phone systems. Wireless systems are especially vulnerable in this respect due to air interface. No wire-tapping is needed to listen in a data stream. Therefore, special encryption methods should be applied to guarantee privacy. Further security mechanisms are authentication, confidentiality, anonymity, and replay protection.

For each chapter the reader can find review exercises and references at the end of the chapter. A complete list of acronyms used throughout the chapters and the index conclude the book.

1.7 Review exercise

1 Discover the current numbers of subscribers for the different systems. As mobile communications boom, no printed number is valid for too long!

1.8 References

Bahl, S. (1998) 'Supporting digital video in a managed wireless network', *IEEE Communications Magazine*, 36, (6).

Department of Trade and Industry (1987) *Performance Specification: Radio equipment for use at fixed and portable stations in the cordless telephone service*, MPT 1334.

Electronic Industries Association (1989) *Mobile land station compatibility specification*, ANSI/EIA/TIA Standard 553.

ETSI (1994) *Common air interface specification to be used for the interworking between cordless telephone apparatus in the frequency band 864.1 MHz to 868.1 MHz, including public access services*, European Telecommunications Standards Institute, I-ETS 300 131 (1994–11).

ETSI (1998) *Digital Enhanced Cordless Telecommunications (DECT), Common Interface (CI)*, European Telecommunications Standards Institute, EN 300 175, V1.4.1 (1998–02).

GSM Data, Intel Corporation (1998) http://www.gsmdata.com/.

Halsall, F. (1996) *Data communications, computer networks and open systems*. Addison-Wesley.

Iridium Corporation (1998) http://www.iridium.com/.

International Telecommunication Union (ITU) (1998) *International Mobile Telecommunications*, set of recommendations, http://www.itu.int/imt/.

Keshav, S. (1997) *An engineering approach to computer networking*, Addison-Wesley.

Lin, J.C. (1997) 'Biological aspects of mobile communication fields', (series of articles), *Wireless Networks*, J.C. Baltzer, 3 (6).

Tanenbaum, A. (1996) *Computer Networks*, Prentice-Hall.

Telecommunications Industries Association (TIA) (1993a) *Mobile station land station compatibility specification for dual-mode narrowband analog cellular technology*, Interim Standard 88.

Telecommunications Industries Association (1993b) *Mobile station base station compatibility standard for dual-mode wideband spread spectrum cellular systems*, Interim Standard 95.

Telecommunications Industries Association (1996) *800 MHz TDMA cellular radio interface mobile station base station compatibility*, Interim Standard 136A.

Wireless transmission 2

This book focuses more on higher layer aspects of mobile communications, the computer science element, than the radio and transmission aspects, the electrical engineering part. Therefore, this chapter introduces only those fundamental aspects of wireless transmission which are necessary for understanding the problems of higher layers and the complexity needed to handle transmission impairments. Wherever appropriate, the reader is referred to literature giving deeper insight into the topic. To avoid too many details blurring the overall picture, this chapter sometimes simplifies the real world characteristics of wireless transmission.

While transmission over different wires typically does not cause interference, this is an important topic in wireless transmission. Therefore, the frequencies used for transmission are all regulated. The first section gives a general overview of these frequencies. The following sections recall some basic facts about signals, antennas, and signal propagation. The varying propagation characteristics create particular complications for radio transmission, frequently causing transmission errors. Multiplexing is a major design topic in this context, because the medium is always shared. Multiplexing schemes have to ensure low interference between different senders.

In order to transmit digital data via certain frequencies, modulation is needed. A separate section of this chapter presents standard modulation schemes that will reoccur together with the wireless communication systems presented in chapters 4 to 8. In the next section, a discussion of spread spectrum, a special transmission technique that is more robust against errors, follows. A short introduction into cellular systems concludes this chapter.

2.1 Frequencies for radio transmission

Radio transmission can take place using many different frequency bands. Each frequency band exhibits certain advantages and disadvantages. Figure 2.1 gives a rough overview of the frequency spectrum that can be used for data transmission. The figure shows frequencies starting at 300 Hz and going up to over 300 THz.

Figure 2.1 Frequency
spectrum

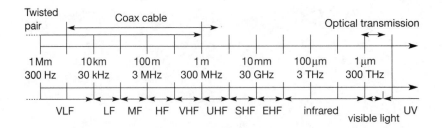

Figure 2.1 Frequency spectrum

Directly coupled to the frequency is the wavelength λ via the equation:

$$\lambda = c/f,$$

where c ≅ 3·10^8 m/s (the speed of light in vacuum) and f the frequency. For traditional wired networks, frequencies of up to several hundred kHz are used with twisted pair copper wires, while frequencies of several hundred MHz are used with coaxial cable (new coding schemes work with several hundred MHz even with twisted pair copper wires). Then again, fibre optics are used for frequency ranges of several hundred THz, but here one typically refers to the wavelength which is, e.g., 1500 µm, 1350 µm etc. (infrared).

Radio transmission starts at several kHz, the **very low frequency (VLF)** range. These are very long waves. Waves in the **low frequency (LF)** range are used by submarines, because they can penetrate water and can follow the earth's surface. Some radio stations still use these frequencies, e.g., between 148.5 kHz and 283.5 kHz in Germany. The **medium frequency (MF)** and **high frequency (HF)** ranges are typical for transmission of hundreds of radio stations either as amplitude modulation **(AM)** between 520 kHz and 1605.5 kHz, as short wave **(SW)** between 5.9 MHz and 26.1 MHz, or as frequency modulation **(FM)** between 87.5 MHz and 108 MHz. The frequencies limiting these ranges are typically fixed by national regulation and, thus, vary from country to country. Short waves are typically used for (amateur) radio transmission around the world, enabled by reflection at the ionosphere. Transmit power is up to 500 kW – which is quite high compared to the 1 W of a mobile phone.

As we move to higher frequencies, the TV stations follow. Conventional analog TV is transmitted in ranges of 174-230 MHz and 470-790 MHz using the very high frequency **(VHF)** and ultra high frequency **(UHF)** bands. In this range, digital audio broadcasting (DAB) takes place as well (223-230 MHz and 1452-1472 MHz) and digital TV is planned (470-862 MHz), reusing some of the old frequencies for analog TV. UHF is also used for mobile phones with analog technology (450-465 MHz), the digital GSM (890-960 MHz, 1710-1880 MHz), digital cordless telephones following the DECT standard (1880-1900 MHz) and many more. VHF and especially UHF allow for small antennas and relatively reliable connections for mobile telephony.

Super high frequencies (SHF) are typically used for directed microwave links (approx. 2-40 GHz) and fixed satellite services in the C-band (4 and 6 GHz), ku-band (11 and 14 GHz), or ka-band (19 and 29 GHz). Some systems are planned in the **extremely high frequency (EHF)** range which comes close to infrared. All radio frequencies are regulated in order to avoid interference, e.g. the German regulation covers 9 kHz to 275 GHz.

The next step into higher frequencies involves optical transmission, which is not only used for fibre optical links but also for wireless communications. **Infrared (IR)** transmission is used for directed links, e.g., to connect different buildings via laser links. The most widespread IR technology, infrared data association (IrDA), uses wavelengths of approximately 850-900 nm to connect laptops, PDAs etc. Finally, visible light has been used for wireless transmission for thousands of years. While light is not very reliable due to interference, it is nevertheless useful due to built-in human receivers.

2.1.1 Regulations

As the examples in the previous section have shown, radio frequencies are scarce resources. Additionally, many national (economic) interests make it hard to find common, worldwide regulations. The International Telecommunications Union (ITU) located in Geneva is responsible for worldwide coordination of telecommunication activities (wired and wireless). ITU is a sub-organization of the UN. The ITU Radiocommunication sector (ITU-R) handles standardization in the wireless sector, thus also frequency planning (formerly known as Consultative Committee for International Radiocommunication, CCIR).

To have at least some success in worldwide coordination and to reflect national interests, the ITU-R has split the world into three regions: **Region 1** covers Europe, the Middle East, countries of the former Soviet Union, and Africa. **Region 2** includes Greenland, North- and South America, and **region 3** comprises the Far East, Australia, and New Zealand. Within these regions national agencies are responsible for further regulations, e.g. the Federal Communications Commission (FCC) in the US, or several nations have a common agency such as European Conference for Posts and Telecommunications (CEPT) in Europe. While CEPT is still responsible for the general planning, many tasks have been transferred to other agencies (thus confusing anybody following the regulation process). For example, the European Telecommunications Standards Institute (ETSI), is responsible for standardization and consists of national standardization bodies, public providers, manufacturers, user groups, and research institutes.

To achieve at least some harmonization, the ITU-R holds periodic conferences, the World Radio Conference (WRC), to discuss and decide frequency allocations for all three regions. This harmonization is obviously a difficult task since many regions or countries may have already installed a huge base of a certain technology and will, therefore, be reluctant to change frequencies just for the sake of harmonization. But harmonization is needed as soon as satellite communication is used. Satellites, especially the new generation of low earth orbiting satellites (see chapter 5) do not 'respect' national regulations, but operate worldwide.

Table 2.1 gives some examples for frequencies used for (analog and digital) mobile phones, cordless telephones, and wireless LANs for countries in the three regions. Older systems like Nordic Mobile Telephone (NMT) are not available all over Europe, and sometimes they have been standardized with different national frequencies. The newer (digital) systems are compatible throughout Europe (standardized by ETSI).

While older analog **mobile phone** systems like NMT or its derivatives at 450 MHz are still available, Europe is heavily dominated by the common fully digital **GSM** (see chapter 4.1) at 900 MHz and 1800 MHz (also known as DCS1800, Digital Cellular System). In contrast to Europe, the US FCC allowed several cellular technologies in the same frequency bands around 850 MHz. Starting from the analog advanced mobile phone system (AMPS), this led to the co-existence of several solutions, such as dual mode mobile phones supporting digital time division multiple access (TDMA) service and analog AMPS according to the standard IS-54. Furthermore, all digital TDMA phones according to IS-136 (also known as NA-TDMA, North American TDMA) and digital code division multiple access (CDMA) phones according to IS-95 have been developed. Thus, the US did not adopt a common mobile phone system but waited for market forces to decide. This led to many islands of different systems, and consequently full coverage, as in Europe, is not available in the US. The long discussions about pros and cons of TDMA and CDMA also promoted the worldwide success of GSM. GSM is available in over 120 countries, a user can roam with the same mobile phone from Zimbabwe, via Uzbekistan, Sweden, Singapore, Tunisia, Russia, Italy, Greece, Germany, China, Belgium to Austria.

Another system, the personal digital cellular (PDC), formerly known as Japanese digital cellular (JDC) was established in Japan. The first mobile phones covering all systems around the world were announced for late 1999.

Similar to mobile phone standards, many different **cordless telephone** standards exist around the world. However, this wide variety is not as problematic as the mobile phone standard diversity. Some older analog systems such as cordless telephone (CT1+) are still in use, but frequently digital technology has been introduced for cordless telephones as well. Examples include **CT2** as the first digital cordless telephone introduced in the UK, digital enhanced cordless telecommunications (**DECT**) as a European standard (see chapter 4.2), personal access communications system (PACS) and PACS-Unlicensed Band (**PACS-UB**) in the US, as well as personal handyphone system (PHS) as replacement for the analog Japanese cordless telephone (**JCT**) in Japan. Mobile phones covering, e.g., DECT and GSM are already available.

Finally, the area of **WLAN** standards is of special interest for wireless, mobile computer communication on a campus or in buildings. Here the com-

	Europe	US	Japan
Mobile phones	**NMT** 453-457 MHz, 463-467 MHz; **GSM** 890-915 MHz, 935-960 MHz; 1710-1785 MHz, 1805-1880 MHz	**AMPS, TDMA,** **CDMA** 824-849 MHz 869-894 MHz; **GSM, TDMA,** **CDMA** 1850-1910 MHz, 1930-1990 MHz	**PDC** 810-826 MHz, 940-956 MHz, 1429-1465 MHz, 1477-1513 MHz
Cordless telephones	**CT1+** 885-887 MHz, 930-932 MHz; **CT2** 864-868 MHz; **DECT** 1880-1900 MHz	**PACS** 1850-1910 MHz, 1930-1990 MHz; **PACS-UB** 1910-1930 MHz	**PHS** 1895-1918 MHz; **JCT** 254-380 MHz
Wireless LANs	**IEEE 802.11** 2400-2483 MHz; **HIPERLAN 1** 5176-5270 MHz	**IEEE 802.11** 2400-2483 MHz	**IEEE 802.11** 2471-2497 MHz

Table 2.1
Examples for
frequency
allocations

puter industry developed products within the licence-free **ISM** band, of which the most attractive is located at 2.4 GHz and is available for licence-free operation almost everywhere around the world (with national differences limiting frequencies, transmit power etc.). The most widespread standard in this area is **IEEE 802.11**, which is discussed in chapter 7. The European wireless LAN standard **HIPERLAN 1** operates at 5.2 GHz, but up to now it has not been clear where this frequency band will be available.

Many more frequencies have been assigned for trunk radio (e.g., trans European trunked radio (TETRA), 380-400 MHz, 410-430 MHz, 450-470 MHz – depending on national regulations), paging services, Terrestrial Flight Telephone System (TFTS), 1670-1675 MHz and 1800-1805 MHz), satellite services etc. Furthermore, new frequency allocations are planned, e.g., for universal mobile telecommunications system (UMTS) at 1885-2025 MHz and 2110-2200 MHz. Higher frequencies are of special interest for high bit-rate transmission, although these frequencies face severe shadowing by many obstacles. Licence-free bands at 5.7, 17.2, 24 and even 61 GHz are under consideration.

2.2 Signals

Signals are the physical representation of data. If users of a communication system want to exchange data, this is only possible through the transmission of signals. Layer 1 of the ISO/OSI basic reference model is responsible for the conversion of data, i.e., bits, into signals and vice versa (Halsall, 1996).

Signals are functions of time and location. Signal parameters represent the data values. The most interesting types of signals for radio transmission are **periodic signals**, especially **sine waves** as carriers. (The process of mapping of data onto a carrier is explained in 2.6.) The general function of a sine wave is:

$$g(t) = A_t \sin(2\pi f_t t + \varphi t)$$

Signal parameters are the **amplitude** A, the **frequency** f, and the **phase shift** φ. The amplitude as a factor of the function g may also change over time, thus A_t, see section 2.6.1. The frequency f expresses the periodicity of the signal with the period $T=1/f$. (In equations, ω is frequently used instead of $2\pi f$.) The frequency f may also change over time, thus f_t, see section 2.6.2. Finally, the phase shift determines the shift of the signal relative to the same signal without a shift. An example for shifting a function is shown in Figure 2.2. This figure shows a sine function without a phase shift and the same function, i.e., same amplitude and frequency, with a phase shift φ. Section 2.6.3 shows how shifting the phase can be used to represent data.

Sine waves are of special interest, as it is possible to construct every periodic signal g by using only sine and cosine functions according to a fundamental equation of **Fourier**:

$$g(t) = \frac{1}{2}c + \sum_{n=1}^{\infty} a_n \sin(2\pi n f t) + \sum_{n=1}^{\infty} b_n \cos(2\pi n f t)$$

Figure 2.2
Time domain
representation of a
signal

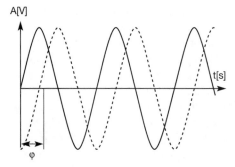

A[V]

t[s]

φ

In this equation the parameter c determines the **Direct Current (DC)** component of the signal, the coefficients a_n and b_n are the amplitudes of the nth sine and cosine function. The equation shows that an infinite number of sine and cosine functions is needed to construct arbitrary periodic functions. However, the frequencies of these functions (the so-called **harmonics**) increase with a growing parameter n and are a multiple of the **fundamental frequency** f. But the bandwidth of any medium, air, cable, transmitter etc. is limited and, thus, there is an upper limit for the frequencies. In reality it is, therefore, enough to consider a limited number of sine and cosine functions to construct periodic functions – all real transmitting systems exhibit these bandwidth limits and can never transmit arbitrary periodic functions. For us it is sufficient to know that we can think of transmitted signals as composed of one or many sine functions. The following illustrations always represent the example of one sine function, i.e., the case of a single frequency.

A typical way to represent signals is the time domain (see Figure 2.2). Here the amplitude A of a signal is shown versus time (time is mostly measured in seconds s, amplitudes can be measured in, e.g., volt V). This is also the typical representation known from an oscilloscope. As already mentioned, a phase shift can also be shown in this representation.

Representations in the time domain are problematic if a signal consists of many different frequencies (as the Fourier equation indicates). In this case, a better representation of a signal is the **frequency domain** (see Figure 2.3). Here the amplitude of a certain frequency part of the signal is shown versus the frequency. Figure 2.3 only shows one peak and, thus, the signal consists only of a single frequency part (i.e., it is a single sine function). Arbitrary periodic functions would have many peaks, known as frequency spectrum of a signal, a tool to display frequencies is a spectrum analyzer. Fourier transformations are a mathematical tool for translating from the time domain into the frequency domain and vice versa (using the inverse Fourier transformation).

A third way to represent signals is the **phase domain** as shown in Figure 2.4. This representation, also called phase state diagram, shows the amplitude M of a signal and its phase φ in polar coordinates. (The length of the vector represents the amplitude, the angle the phase shift.) The x-axis represents a phase of 0 and is also called **In-Phase (I)**. A phase shift of 90° or $\pi/2$ would be a point on the y-axis, called **Quadrature (Q)**.

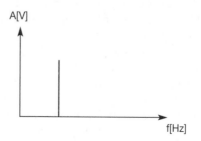

Figure 2.3
Frequency domain representation of a signal

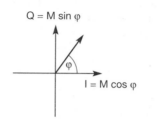

Figure 2.4
Phase domain representation of a signal

2.3 Antennas

As the name wireless already indicates, this communication mode involves 'getting rid' of wires and transmitting signals through space without guidance. We do not need any 'medium' (such as an ether) for the transport of electromagnetic waves. But somehow we have to couple the energy from the transmitter to the outside world and, in reverse, from the outside world to the receiver. This is exactly what **antennas** do. Antennas couple electromagnetic energy to and from space to and from a wire or coaxial cable (or any other appropriate conductor).

A theoretical reference antenna is the **isotropic radiator**, a point in space radiating with equal power in all directions, i.e., all points with equal power are located on a sphere with the antenna as its centre. Thus, the **radiation pattern** is symmetric in all directions (see Figure 2.5).

However, such an antenna does not exist in reality. Real antennas all exhibit **directive effects**, i.e., the intensity of radiation is not the same in all directions from the antenna. The simplest real antenna is a thin, centre fed **dipole**, also called Hertzian dipole, as shown in Figure 2.6 (right-hand side). The length of the dipole is not arbitrary, but, for example, half the wavelength λ of the signal to transmit results in a very efficient radiation of the energy. If mounted on the roof of a car, the length of λ/4 is efficient.

A λ/2 dipole has a uniform or **omnidirectional** radiation pattern in one plane and a figure eight pattern in the other two planes as shown in Figure 2.7. This type of antenna can only overcome environmental challenges by boosting the power level of the signal. Challenges could be mountains, valleys, buildings etc.

If an antenna is positioned, e.g., in a valley or between buildings, an omnidirectional radiation pattern is not very useful. In this case, **directional antennas** with certain fixed preferential transmission and reception directions can be used. Figure 2.8 shows the radiation pattern of a directional antenna with the main lobe in direction of the x-axis. A special example of directional antennas is constituted by satellite dishes.

Directed antennas are typically applied in cellular systems as presented in section 2.8. Several directed antennas can be combined on a single pole to construct a **sectorized antenna**. A cell can be sectorized into, for example, three or six sectors, thus enabling frequency reuse as explained in section 2.8. Figure 2.9 shows the radiation patterns of these sectorized antennas.

Figure 2.5
Radiation pattern
of an ideal
isotropic radiator

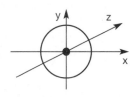 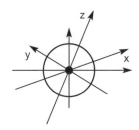

Two or more antennas can also be combined to improve reception by counteracting the negative effects of multipath propagation (see section 2.4.3). These antennas, also called **multi-element antenna arrays**, allow different diversity schemes. One such scheme is **switched diversity** or **selection diversity**, where the receiver always uses the antenna element with the largest output. **Diversity combining** constitutes a combination of the power of all signals to produce gain. Therefore, the phase is first corrected (cophasing) to avoid cancellation. As shown in Figure 2.10, different schemes are possible. On the left, two λ/4 antennas are combined with a distance of λ/2 between them on top of a ground plane. On the right, three standard λ/2 dipoles are combined with a distance of λ/2 between them. Spacing could also be in multiples of λ/2.

Figure 2.6
Simple antennas

A more advanced solution is provided by **smart antennas** which combine multiple antenna elements with signal processing to optimize the radiation/reception pattern in response to the signal environment. These antennas can adapt to changes in reception power, transmission conditions and many signal propagation effects as discussed in the following section.

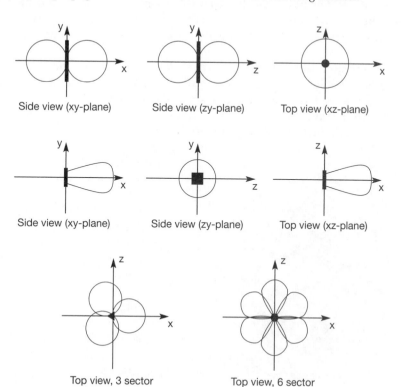

Figure 2.7
Radiation pattern of a simple dipole

Figure 2.8
Radiation pattern of a directed antenna

Figure 2.9
Radiation patterns of sectorized antennas

Figure 2.10
Diversity antenna
systems

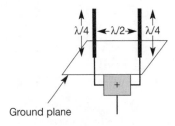
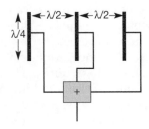

Figure 2.10
Diversity antenna
systems

Ground plane

2.4 Signal propagation

Like wired networks, wireless communication networks also have senders and receivers of signals. However, in connection with signal propagation, these two networks exhibit considerable differences. In wireless networks, the signal has no wire to determine the direction of propagation, whereas signals in wired networks only travel along the wire (which can be a twisted pair copper wires, a coax cable, but also a fibre etc.). As long as the wire is not interrupted or damaged, it typically exhibits the same characteristics at each point. Thus, one can precisely determine the behaviour of a signal travelling along this wire, e.g., received power depending on the length. For wireless transmission, this predictable behaviour is only valid in a vacuum, i.e., without matter between the sender and the receiver. Then the situation would be as follows (Figure 2.11):

- **Transmission range:** Within a certain radius around the sender transmission is possible, i.e., a receiver receives the signals with an error rate low enough to be able to communicate and can also act as sender.
- **Detection range:** Within a second radius, detection of the transmission is possible, i.e., the transmitted power is large enough to differ from background noise. However, the error rate is too high to establish communication.

Figure 2.11
Ranges for transmission,
detection, and
interference of signals

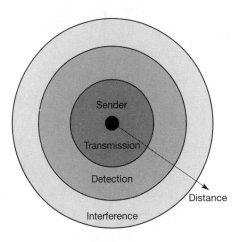

- **Interference range:** Within a third radius which is even larger, the sender may interfere with other transmission by adding to the background noise. A receiver will not be able to detect the signals, but the signals may disturb other signals.

This simple and ideal scheme led to the notion of **cells** around a transmitter as briefly discussed in section 2.8. However, real life does not happen in a vacuum, radio transmission has to contend with our atmosphere, mountains, buildings, moving senders and receivers etc. The three circles referred to above will be bizarrely-shaped polygons in reality, with their shape being time and frequency dependent. The following paragraphs discuss some problems arising in this context, thereby showing the differences between wireless and wired transmission.

2.4.1 Path loss of radio signals

In free space radio signals propagate as light does (independently of their frequency), i.e., they follow a straight line (besides gravitational effects). If such a straight line exists between a sender and a receiver it is called **line-of-sight (LOS)**. If no matter exists between the sender and the receiver (i.e., if there is a vacuum), the signal still experiences the **free space loss**. The received power P_r is proportional to $1/d^2$ with d being the distance between sender and receiver (**inverse square law**). The reason for this phenomenon is quite simple. Think of the sender being a point in space. The sender now emits a signal with a certain energy. This signal travels away from the sender at the speed of light as a wave with a spherical shape. If there is no obstacle, the sphere continuously grows with the sending energy equally distributed over the sphere's surface. This surface area s grows with the increasing distance d from the centre according to the equation $s = 4\pi d^2$.

Even without any matter between sender and receiver, additional parameters are important. The received power also depends on the wavelength and the gain of receiver and transmitter antennas. As soon as there is any matter between sender and receiver, the situation becomes more complex. Most radio transmission takes place through the atmosphere and, thus, signals travel through air, rain, snow, fog, dust particles, smog etc. While the **path loss** or **attenuation** does not cause too much trouble for short distances, e.g., for LANs (see chapter 7), the atmosphere heavily influences transmission over long distances, such as satellite transmission (see chapter 5). Even mobile phone systems are influenced by weather conditions such as heavy rain. Rain can absorb much of the radiated energy of the antenna (this effect is used in a microwave oven to cook), and thus communication links may break down as soon as the rain sets in.

Depending on the frequency, radio waves can also penetrate objects. Generally the lower the frequency is, the better the penetration will be. Long waves can be transmitted through the oceans to a submarine while high frequencies can even be blocked by a tree. The higher the frequency, the more the behaviour of the radio waves resemble that of light, a phenomenon which is clear if one considers the spectrum shown in Figure 2.1.

2.4.2 Additional signal propagation effects

As discussed in the previous section, signal propagation in free space always follows a straight line like light does. But in real life, we rarely have a line-of-sight between sender and receiver of radio signals. Mobile phones are typically used

Figure 2.12
Blocking (shadowing)
and reflection of waves

Figure 2.12
Blocking (shadowing)
and reflection of waves

in big cities with skyscrapers, on mountains, inside buildings, while driving through an alley etc. Then several effects occur in addition to the attenuation caused by the distance between sender and receiver, which are again very much frequency dependent.

An extreme form of attenuation is **blocking** or **shadowing** of radio signals due to large obstacles (see Figure 2.12, left side). The higher the frequency of a signal, the more it behaves like light. Thus, even smaller obstacles like a simple wall, a truck on the street, or trees in an alley may block the signals. Another effect is the **reflection** of signals as shown on the right side of Figure 2.12. If an object is large compared to the wavelength of the signal, e.g., huge buildings, mountains, or the surface of the earth, the signal is reflected. The reflected signal is not as strong as the original, as objects can absorb some of the signal's power. Reflection helps transmitting signals as soon as no LOS exists. This is the standard case for radio transmission in cities or mountain areas. Signals transmitted from a sender may bounce off the walls of buildings several times before they reach the receiver. The more often the signal is reflected, the weaker it becomes.

While shadowing and reflection are caused by objects much larger than the wavelength of the signals (and demonstrate the typical 'particle' behaviour of radio signals), the following two effects exhibit the 'wave' character of radio signals. If the size of an obstacle is in the order of the wavelength or less, then waves can be **scattered** (see Figure 2.13, left side). An incoming signal is scattered into several weaker outgoing signals. In school experiments, this is typically demonstrated with laser light and a very small opening or obstacle, but here we have to take into consideration that the typical wavelength of radio transmission for, e.g., GSM or AMPS is in the order of some 10 cm. Thus, many objects in the environment can cause these scattering effects. Another effect is

Figure 2.13
Scattering and
diffraction of waves

diffraction of waves. As shown on the right side of Figure 2.13, this effect is very similar to scattering. Radio waves will be deflected at an edge and propagate in different directions. The result of scattering and diffraction are patterns with varying signal strength depending on the location of the receiver.

2.4.3 Multipath Propagation

Together with the direct transmission from a sender to a receiver, the propagation effects mentioned in the previous section lead to one of the most severe radio channel impairments, called **multipath propagation**. Figure 2.14 shows a sender on the left and one possible receiver on the right. Radio waves emitted by the sender can either travel along the straight line, or they may be reflected at a large building, or scattered at smaller obstacles. This simplified figure only shows three possible paths for the signal. In reality many more paths are possible. Due to the finite speed of light, signals travelling along different paths with different lengths arrive at the receiver at different times. This effect (caused by multipath propagation) is called **delay spread**: the original signal is spread due to different delays of parts of the signal. This delay spread is a typical effect of radio transmission, because no wire guides the waves along a single path as in the case of wired networks (however, a similar effect, dispersion, is known for high bit-rate optical transmission over multimode fibre, see Halsall 1996). Notice that this effect has nothing to do with possible movements of the sender or receiver. Typical values for delay spread are up to 3 µs in cities. GSM, for example, can tolerate up to 16 µs of delay spread, i.e., somewhat more than 3 km path difference.

What are the **effects** of this delay spread on the signals representing the data? The first effect is that a short impulse will be smeared out into a broader impulse, or rather into several weaker impulses. In Figure 2.14 only three possible paths are shown and, thus, the impulse at the sender will result in three smaller impulses at the receiver. For a real situation with hundreds of different paths, this implies that a single impulse will result in many weaker impulses at the receiver. Each path has a different attenuation and, thus, the received pulses have different power. Some of the received pulses will be too weak even to be detected (i.e., they will appear as noise).

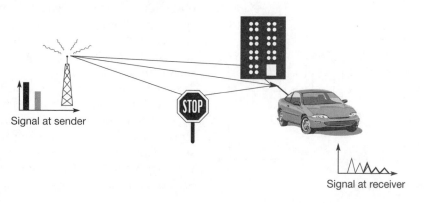

Signal at sender

STOP

Signal at receiver

Figure 2.14
Multipath
propagation and
intersymbol
interference

Now consider the second impulse shown in Figure 2.14. On the sender side, both impulses are separated. At the receiver, both impulses interfere, i.e., they overlap in time. Now consider that each impulse should represent a symbol, and that one or several symbols could represent a bit. The energy intended for one symbol now spills over to the adjacent symbol, an effect which is called **intersymbol interference (ISI)**. The higher the symbol rate to be transmitted, the worse the effects of ISI will be, as the original symbols are moved closer and closer to each other. ISI limits the bandwidth of a radio channel with multipath propagation (which is the standard case). Due to this interference, the signals of different symbols can cancel each other leading to misinterpretations at the receiver and thus causing transmission errors.

In this case, knowing the channel characteristics can be a great help. If the receiver knows the delays of the different paths (or at least the main paths the signal takes), it can compensate for the distortion caused by the channel. The sender may first transmit a training sequence known by the receiver. The receiver then compares the received signal to the original **training sequence** and programs an **equalizer** that compensates for the distortion (Wesel, 1998).

While ISI and delay spread already occur in the case of fixed radio transmitters and receivers, the situation is even worse if receivers or senders or both move. Then the channel characteristics change over time, and the paths a signal can travel along vary. This effect is well known (and audible) with analog radios while driving. The power of the received signal changes considerably over time. These quick changes in the received power are also called **short term fading**. Depending on the different paths the signals take, these signals may have a different phase and cancel each other as shown in Figure 2.15. The receiver now has to try to constantly adapt to the varying channel characteristics, e.g., by changing the parameters of the equalizer. However, if these changes are too fast, such as driving on a highway through a city, the receiver cannot adapt fast enough and, thus, the error rate of transmission increases dramatically.

An additional effect shown in Figure 2.15 is the **long term fading** of the received signal. This long term fading, here shown as the average power over time, is caused by, for example, varying distance to the sender or more remote

Figure 2.15
Short term and long
term fading

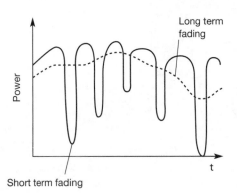

obstacles. Typically, senders can compensate for long term fading by increasing/decreasing sending power so that the received signal always stays within certain limits.

There are many more effects influencing radio transmission which will not be discussed in detail. One is, for example, the **Doppler shift** caused by a moving sender or receiver. While this effect is audible for acoustic waves already at low speed, this is also a topic for radio transmission from or to fast moving transceivers. Examples for such transceivers could be satellites (see chapter 5) – there Doppler shift causes random frequency shifts. The interested reader is referred to Anderson (1995) for more information about the characteristics of wireless communication channels. For the present it will suffice to know that multipath propagation limits the maximum bandwidth due to ISI and that moving transceivers cause additional problems due to varying channel characteristics.

2.5 Multiplexing

Multiplexing is not only a fundamental mechanism in communication systems but also in everyday life. Multiplexing describes how several users can share a medium with minimum or no interference. One example from everyday life are highways with several lanes. Many users (car drivers) use the same medium (the highways) with hopefully no interference (i.e., accidents). This is possible due to the provision of several lanes (space division multiplexing) separating the traffic. In addition, different cars use the same medium (i.e., the same lane) at different points in time (time division multiplexing).

While this simple example illustrates our everyday use of multiplexing, the following examples will deal with the use of multiplexing in wireless communications. Mechanisms controlling the use of multiplexing and the assignment of a medium to users (the traffic regulations), are discussed in chapter 3 under the aspect of medium access control.

2.5.1 Space division multiplexing

For wireless communication, multiplexing can be carried out in four dimensions: **space**, **time**, **frequency**, and **code**. In this field, the task of multiplexing is to assign space, time, frequency, and code to each communication channel with a minimum of interference and a maximum of medium utilization. The term communication channel here only refers to an association of sender(s) and receiver(s) that want to exchange data. Characteristics of communication channels (e.g., bandwidth, error rate) will be discussed together with certain technologies.

Figure 2.16 shows six channels k_i and introduces a three dimensional coordinate system. This system shows the dimensions of code c, time t and frequency f. For this first type of multiplexing, **space division multiplexing** (SDM), the (three dimensional) space s_i is also shown. Here space is represented via circles indicating the interference range as introduced in Figure 2.11. How is the separation of the different channels achieved? The channels k_1 to k_3 can be mapped onto the three 'spaces' s_1 to s_3 which clearly separate the channels and prevent the interference ranges from overlapping. The space between the interference range is sometimes called **guard space**. Such a guard space is needed in all four multiplexing schemes presented.

Figure 2.16
Space division
multiplexing (SDM)

Channels k_i

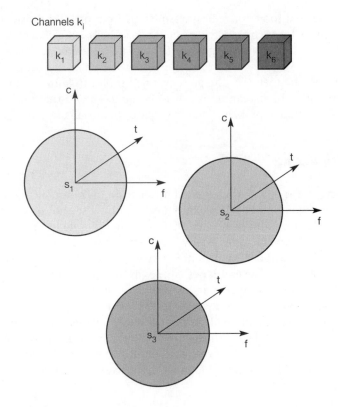

For the remaining channels (k_4 to k_6) three additional spaces would be needed. In our highway example this would imply that each driver had his or her own lane. Although this procedure clearly represents a waste of space, this is exactly the principle used by the old analog telephone system: each subscriber is given a separate pair of copper wires to the local exchange. In wireless transmission, SDM implies a separate sender for each communication channel with a wide enough distance between senders. This multiplexing scheme is used, for example, at FM radio stations where the transmission range is limited to a certain region – thus many radio stations around the world can use the same frequency without interference. Using SDM, obvious problems arise if two or more channels were established within the same space, for example, several radio stations want to broadcast in the same city. Then, one of the following multiplexing schemes must be used (frequency, time, or code division multiplexing).

2.5.2 Frequency division multiplexing

Frequency division multiplexing (FDM) describes schemes to subdivide the frequency dimension into several non-overlapping frequency bands as shown in Figure 2.17. Each channel k_i is now allotted its own frequency band as indicated.

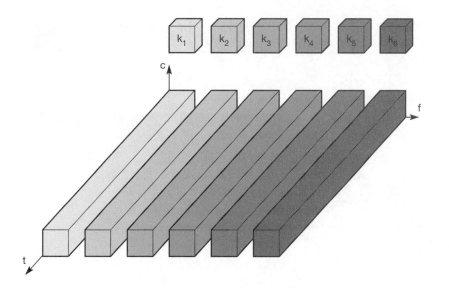

Figure 2.17
Frequency division
multiplexing (FDM)

Senders using a certain frequency band can use this band continuously. Again, **guard spaces** are needed to avoid frequency band overlapping (also called **adjacent channel interference**). This scheme is used for radio stations within the same region, where each radio station has its own frequency. This very simple multiplexing scheme does not need a complex co-ordination between sender and receiver, the receiver only has to tune in to the specific sender.

However, this scheme also exhibits disadvantages. While radio stations broadcast 24 hours a day, mobile communication typically takes place for only a few minutes a day. Assigning a separate frequency for each possible communication scenario would thus be a tremendous waste of (scarce) frequency resources. Additionally, the fixed assignment of a frequency to a sender makes the scheme very inflexible and limits the number of senders.

2.5.3 Time division multiplexing

A more flexible multiplexing scheme for typical mobile communications is **time division multiplexing (TDM)**. Here a channel k_i is given the whole bandwidth for a certain amount of time, i.e., all senders use the same frequency but at different points in time (see Figure 2.18). Again, **guard spaces**, which now represent time gaps, have to separate the different periods when the senders use the medium. In our highway example, this would refer to the gap between two cars. If two transmissions overlap in time, this is called co-channel interference. (In the highway example, interference between two cars results in an accident.) To avoid this type of interference, precise synchronization between different senders is necessary. This is clearly an disadvantage of the scheme, as all senders need precise clocks or, alternatively, a way to distribute a synchronization signal to all senders has to be found. Additionally, for a receiver tuning in to a sender

Figure 2.18
Time division
multiplexing (TDM)

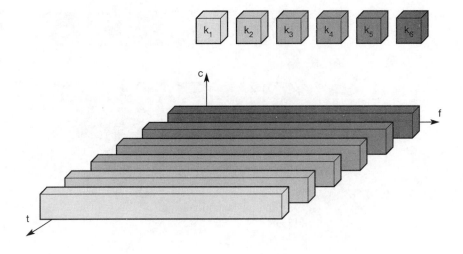

now does not involve adjusting the frequency but listening at exactly the right
point in time. However, this scheme is quite flexible as one can assign more
sending time to senders with a heavy load and only less sending time to senders
with a light load.

Frequency and time division multiplexing can be combined, i.e., a channel
k_i can use a certain frequency band for a certain amount of time as shown in
Figure 2.19. Now guard spaces are needed both in the time and in the frequency
dimension. This scheme is more robust against frequency selective interference,
i.e., interference in a certain small frequency band. A channel may use this band
only for a short period of time. Additionally, this scheme provides some (weak)
protection against tapping, as in this case the sequence of frequencies a sender
uses has to be known to listen in to a channel. The mobile phone standard GSM
uses this combination of frequency and time division multiplexing for transmission between a mobile phone and a so-called base station (see chapter 4.1).

A disadvantage of this scheme is again the necessary co-ordination between
different senders. Now one has to control the sequence of frequencies and the
time of changing to another frequency. Two senders will interfere as soon as
they select the same frequency at the same time. However, if the frequency
change (also called frequency hopping) is fast enough, the periods of interference may be so small that, depending on the coding of data into signals, a
receiver can still recover the original data. (This technique is discussed in section 2.7.2.)

2.5.4 Code division multiplexing

While SDM and FDM are well known from the early days of radio transmission
and TDM is used in connection with many applications, **code division multiplexing (CDM)** is a relatively new scheme in commercial communication

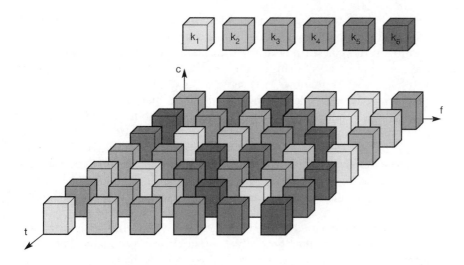

Figure 2.19
Frequency and time
division multiplexing
combined

systems. First used in military applications due to its inherent security features (together with spread spectrum techniques, see section 2.7), it is now also introduced in many civil wireless transmission scenarios (explained in more detail in section 3.5). Figure 2.20 shows how all channels k_i use the same frequency at the same time for transmission. Separation is now achieved by assigning each channel its own 'code', **guard spaces** are realized by using codes with the necessary 'distance' in code space, e.g., **orthogonal codes**. The technical realization of CDM is discussed in section 2.7 and chapter 3 together with the medium access mechanisms. An excellent book dealing with all aspects of CDM is Viterbi (1995).

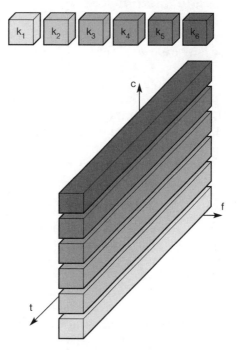

Figure 2.20
Code division
multiplexing (CDM)

The typical everyday example of CDM is a party with many participants from different countries around the world. Many participants establish communication channels, i.e., they talk to each other, using the same frequency range (approx. 300–6000 Hz depending on a person's voice) at the same time. If everybody speaks the same language, SDM is needed to be able to communicate (i.e., standing in groups, talking with limited transmit power). But as soon as another code, i.e., another language, is used, one can tune in to this language and clearly separate communication in this language from all the other languages. (The other languages appear as background noise.) This example explains why CDM has built-in security: if the language is unknown, the signals can still be received, but they are useless. By using a secret code (or language), a secure channel can be established in a 'hostile' environment. (At parties this may cause some confusion.) Guard spaces are also of importance in this illustrative example. Using, e.g., Swedish and Norwegian does not really work; the languages are too close. But, for example, Swedish and Finnish are 'orthogonal' enough to separate the communication channels.

The main advantage of CDM for wireless transmission is the good protection against interference and tapping. Different codes have to be assigned, but code space is huge compared to the frequency space and, thus, assigning individual codes to each sender typically does not cause problems. The main disadvantage of this scheme is the relatively high complexity of the receiver (see section 3.5). A receiver has to know the code and must separate the channel with user data from the background noise composed of other signals and environmental noise. Additionally, a receiver must be precisely synchronized with the transmitter to apply the decoding correctly.

2.6 Modulation

Section 2.2 introduced the basic function of a sine wave which already indicates the three basic modulation schemes:

$$g(t) = A_t \sin(2\pi f_t t + \varphi_t)$$

This function has three parameters, amplitude A_t, frequency f_t, and phase φ_t which may be varied in accordance with data or another modulating signal. For **digital modulation**, which is the main topic in this section, digital data (0 and 1) is translated into an analog signal (baseband signal). Digital modulation is required if digital data has to be transmitted over a medium that only allows for analog transmission. One example for wired networks is the old analog telephone system – to connect a computer to this system a modem is needed. The modem then performs the translation of digital data into analog signals and vice versa. Digital transmission is used, for example, in wired local area networks or within a computer (Halsall, 1996). In wireless networks, however, digital transmission cannot be used. Here, the binary bitstream has to be translated into an analog signal first. The three basic methods for this translation are **amplitude shift keying (ASK)**, **frequency shift keying (FSK)**, and **phase shift keying (PSK)**. These will be discussed in more detail in the following sections.

Apart from the translation of digital data into analog signals, wireless transmission requires an additional modulation, an **analog modulation**, that shifts the centre frequency of the baseband signal generated by the digital modulation up to the radio carrier. Digital modulation, e.g., translates a 1 Mbit/s bit-stream into a baseband signal with a bandwidth of 1 MHz. There are several reasons why this baseband signal cannot be directly transmitted in a wireless system:

- **Antennas:** As shown in section 2.3, an antenna must be the order of magnitude of the signal's wavelength in size to be effective. For the 1 MHz signal in the example this would result in an antenna some hundred metres high, which is obviously not very practical for handheld devices. With 1 GHz, antennas a few centimetres in length can be used.
- **Frequency division multiplexing:** Using only baseband transmission, FDM could not be applied. Analog modulation shifts the baseband signals to different carrier frequencies as required in 2.5.2. The higher the carrier frequency the more bandwidth is available for many baseband signals.
- **Medium characteristics:** Path-loss, penetration of obstacles, reflection, scattering, and diffraction – all the effects discussed in section 2.4 depend heavily on the wavelength of the signal. Depending on the application, the right carrier frequency with the desired characteristics has to be chosen: long waves for submarines, short waves for handheld devices, very short waves for directed microwave transmission etc.

As for digital modulation, three different basic schemes are known for analog modulation: **amplitude modulation (AM)**, **frequency modulation (FM)**, and **phase modulation (PM)**. The reader is referred to Halsall (1996), and Stallings (1997) for more details about these analog modulation schemes.

Figure 2.21 shows a (simplified) block diagram of a radio transmitter for digital data. The first step is the digital modulation of data into the analog baseband signal according to one of the schemes presented in the following sections. The analog modulation then shifts the centre frequency of the analog signal up to the radio carrier. This signal is then transmitted via the antenna.

The receiver (see Figure 2.22) receives the analog radio signal via its antenna and demodulates the signal into the analog baseband signal with the help of the known carrier. This would be all that is needed for an analog radio tuned in

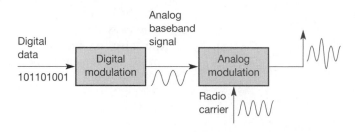

Figure 2.21
Modulation in a transmitter

Figure 2.22
Demodulation and
data reconstruction
in a receiver

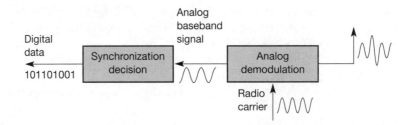

to a radio station. (The analog baseband signal would constitute the music.) For digital data, another step is needed. Bits or frames have to be detected, i.e., the receiver must synchronize with the sender. How synchronization is achieved, depends on the digital modulation scheme. After synchronization, the receiver has to decide if the signal represents a digital 1 or a 0, thus reconstructing the original data.

The digital modulation schemes presented in the following sections differ in many issues, such as **spectral efficiency** (i.e., how efficiently the modulation scheme utilizes the available frequency spectrum), **power efficiency** (i.e., how much power is needed to transfer bits – which is very important for portable devices that are battery dependent), and **robustness** to multipath propagation, noise, and interference (Wesel, 1998).

2.6.1 Amplitude shift keying

Figure 2.23 illustrates **amplitude shift keying (ASK)**, the most simple digital modulation scheme. The two binary values, 1 and 0, are represented by two different amplitudes. In the example, one of the amplitudes is 0 (representing the binary 0). This simple scheme only requires low bandwidth, but is very susceptible to interference. Effects like multipath propagation, noise, or path loss heavily influence the amplitude. Thus, in a wireless environment, a constant amplitude cannot be guaranteed. Therefore, ASK is typically not used for wireless radio transmission. However, the wired transmission scheme with the highest performance, namely optical transmission, uses ASK. Here, a light pulse may represent a 1, while the absence of light represents a 0. The carrier frequency in optical systems is some hundred THz. ASK can also be applied to wireless infrared transmission, using a directed beam or diffuse light (see chapter 7, wireless LANs).

Figure 2.23
Amplitude shift
keying (ASK)

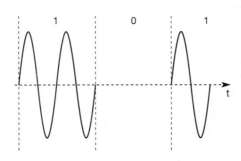

2.6.2 Frequency shift keying

A modulation scheme often used for wireless transmission is **frequency shift keying (FSK)** (see Figure 2.24). The simplest form of FSK, also called **binary FSK (BFSK)**, assigns one frequency f_1 to the binary 1 and another frequency f_2 to the binary 0. A very simple way to implement FSK is to switch between two oscillators, one with the frequency f_1, the other with f_2, depending on the input. To avoid sudden changes in phase special frequency modulators with **continuous phase modulation, (CPM)** can be used.[9]

A simple way to implement demodulation is by using two band-pass filters, one for f_1 the other for f_2. A comparator can then compare the signal levels of the filter outputs and can decide which of them is stronger. FSK needs a larger bandwidth compared to ASK but is much less susceptible to errors.

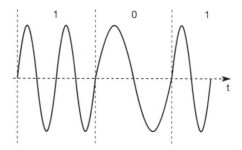

Figure 2.24
Frequency shift keying (FSK)

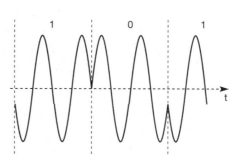

Figure 2.25
Phase shift keying (PSK)

2.6.3 Phase shift keying

Finally, **phase shift keying (PSK)** uses shifts in the phase of a signal to represent data. Figure 2.25 shows a phase shift of 180° or π as the 0 follows the 1 (the same happens as the 1 follows the 0). This simple scheme, shifting the phase by 180° each time the value of data changes, is also called **binary PSK (BPSK)**. A simple implementation of a BPSK modulator could multiply a frequency f with +1 if the binary data is 1 and with –1 if the binary data is 0.

In order to correctly receive the signal, the receiver must synchronize in frequency and phase with the transmitter. This can be done using a **phase lock loop (PLL)**. Compared to FSK, PSK is more resistant to interference, but receiver and transmitter are also more complex.

2.6.4 Advanced frequency shift keying

A famous FSK scheme used in many wireless systems is **minimum shift keying (MSK)**. MSK is basically BFSK without abrupt phase changes, i.e., it belongs to CPM schemes. Figure 2.26 shows an example for the implementation of MSK. In a first step, data bits are separated into even and odd bits, the duration of each bit being doubled. The scheme also uses two frequencies: f_1, the lower frequency, and f_2, the higher frequency, with $f_2 = 2f_1$.

Figure 2.26
Minimum shift
keying (MSK)

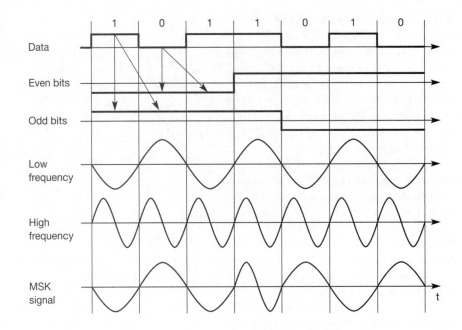

According to the following scheme, the lower or higher frequency is chosen (either inverted or non-inverted) to generate the MSK signal:

- If the even and the odd bit are both 0, then the higher frequency f_2 is inverted (i.e., f_2 is used with a phase shift of 180°).
- If the even bit is 1, the odd bit 0, then the lower frequency f_1 is inverted. This is the case, e.g., in the 5th to 7th columns of Figure 2.26.
- If the even bit is 0 and the odd bit is 1, as in column 1 to 3, f_1 is taken without changing the phase.
- Finally, if both bits are 1 then the original f_2 is taken.

Altogether, a high frequency is always chosen if even and odd bits are equal, the signal is inverted if the odd bit equals 0. This scheme avoids all phase shifts in the resulting MSK signal.

Adding a so-called Gaussian lowpass filter to the MSK scheme results in **Gaussian MSK (GMSK)**, the digital modulation scheme for many European wireless standards (see chapter 4 for GSM, DECT, section 7.4 for HIPERLAN). The filter reduces the large spectrum needed by MSK.

2.6.5 Advanced phase shift keying

The simple PSK scheme can be improved in many ways. The basic BPSK scheme only uses one possible phase shift of 180°. The left side of Figure 2.27 shows BPSK in the phase domain (which is typically the better representation compared to the time domain in Figure 2.25). The right side of Figure 2.27 shows **quadrature PSK (QPSK)**, one of the most common PSK schemes. Here, higher bit rates can be achieved for the same bandwidth by coding two bits into one phase shift. Alternatively, one can reduce the bandwidth and still achieve the same bit rates as for BPSK.

QPSK (and other PSK schemes) can be realized in two variants. The phase shift can always be relative to a **reference signal** (with the same frequency). If this scheme is used, a phase shift of 0 means that the signal is in phase with the reference signal. A QPSK signal will then exhibit a phase shift of 45° for the data 11, 135° for 10, 225° for 00, and 315° for 01 – with all phase shifts being relative to the reference signal. The transmitter 'selects' parts of the signal as shown in Figure 2.28 and concatenates them. To reconstruct data, the receiver has to compare the incoming signal with the reference signal. One problem of this scheme involves producing a reference signal at the receiver. Transmitter and receiver have to be synchronized very often, e.g., by using special synchronization patterns before user data arrives or via a pilot frequency as reference.

One way to avoid this problem is to use **differential QPSK (DQPSK)**. Here the phase shift is not relative to a reference signal but relative to the phase of the previous two bits. In this case, the receiver does not need the reference signal but only compares two signals to reconstruct data. DQPSK is used in the US wireless technologies IS-136 and PACS and in the Japanese PHS.

One could now think of extending the scheme to more and more angles for shifting the phase. For instance one can think of coding 3 bits per phase shift using 8 angles. Additionally, the PSK scheme could be combined with ASK as is done for example in **quadrature amplitude modulation (QAM)** for standard 9,600 bit/s modems (Figure 2.29). Here, three different amplitudes and 12 angles are combined coding 4 bits per phase/amplitude change.

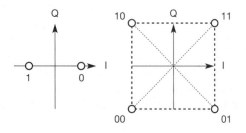

Figure 2.27
BPSK and QPSK in the phase domain

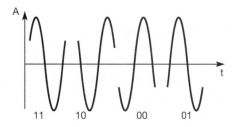

Figure 2.28
QPSK in the time domain

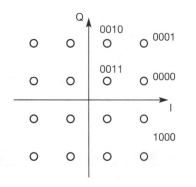

Figure 2.29
Quadrature amplitude modulation

Problems occur for wireless communication in case of noise or ISI. The more 'points' are used in the phase domain, the harder it is to separate them. DQPSK has been proven as one of the most efficient schemes under these considerations (Wesel, 1998).

2.6.6 Multicarrier modulation

A special modulation scheme that stands somewhat apart from the others is **multicarrier modulation (MCM)**, also called **orthogonal frequency division multiplexing (OFDM)** or **coded OFDM (COFDM)** in the context of the European digital radio system DAB (see section 6.3). The main attraction of MCM is its good ISI mitigation property. As explained in section 2.4.3, higher bit rates are more vulnerable to ISI. MCM splits the high bit rate stream into many lower bit rate streams, each stream being sent using an independent carrier frequency. If, for example, n symbols/s have to be transmitted, each subcarrier transmits n/c symbols/s with c being the number of subcarriers. One symbol could, for example represent 2 bit as in QPSK. DAB, for example, uses between 192 and 1,536 of these subcarriers.

Using this scheme, frequency selective fading only influences some subcarriers, and not the whole signal, which constitutes an additional benefit of MCM. Typically, MCM transmits symbols with guard spaces between single symbols or groups of symbols. This helps the receiver to handle multipath propagation. More details about the implementation of MCM can be found in Wesel (1998), ETSI (1997) and in section 6.3.

2.7 Spread spectrum

As the name implies, **spread spectrum** techniques involve spreading the bandwidth needed to transmit data. Spreading the bandwidth has several advantages. The main advantage of these techniques is the resistance to **narrowband interference**. In Figure 2.30, diagram i) shows an idealized narrowband signal from a sender of user data (here power P versus frequency f). The sender now spreads the signal in step ii), i.e., converts the narrowband

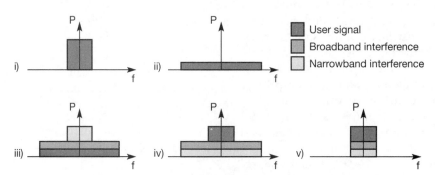

Figure 2.30
Spread spectrum:
spreading and
despreading

signal into a broadband signal. The energy needed to transmit the signal, i.e., the area shown in the diagram, is the same, but it is now spread over a larger frequency range. Thus, the power level of the signal can be much lower than that of the original narrowband signal. This power level of the user signal can even be as low as the background noise. This makes it difficult to distinguish the user signal from the noise and thus hard to detect it.

During transmission, narrowband and broadband interference add to the signal in step iii). The receiver now knows how to despread the signal, converting the spread user signal into a narrowband signal again, while spreading the narrowband interference and leaving the broadband interference. In step v) the receiver applies a bandpass filter to cut off frequencies left and right of the narrowband signal. Finally, the receiver can reconstruct the original data because the power level of the user signal is high enough, i.e., the signal is much stronger than the remaining interference. The following sections show how spreading is performed.

Just as spread spectrum helps to deal with narrowband interference for a single channel, it can be used for several channels. Consider a situation as shown in Figure 2.31. Six different channels use FDM for multiplexing. This means that each channel has its own narrow frequency band for transmission. Between each frequency band a guard space is needed to avoid adjacent channel interference. As mentioned in section 2.5.2, this method requires careful frequency planning. Additionally, Figure 2.31 depicts a certain channel quality. This channel quality is frequency dependent and is a measure for interference at this frequency. Channel quality also changes over time – the diagram only shows a snapshot at one moment. Depending on receiver characteristics, it could be the case that channels 1, 2, 5, and 6 can be received while the quality of channels 3 and 4 is too bad to reconstruct transmitted data. Narrowband interference destroys the transmissions of channel 3 and 4. However, this illustration only represents a snapshot and the situation could be completely different at the next moment. All in all, communication may be very difficult using such narrowband signals.

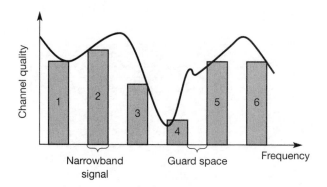

Figure 2.31
Narrowband interference without spread spectrum

How can spread spectrum help in such a situation? As already shown, spread spectrum can increase resistance to narrowband interference. The same technique is now applied to all narrowband signals. As shown in Figure 2.32, all narrowband signals are now spread into broadband signals using the same frequency range. No more frequency planning is needed (under these simplified assumptions), and all senders use the same frequency band. But how can receivers recover their signal?

To separate different channels, CDM is now used instead of FDM. This application shows the tight coupling of CDM and spread spectrum. Spreading of a narrowband signal is achieved using a special **code** as shown in sections 2.7.1 and 2.7.2. Each channel is allotted its own code, which the receivers have to apply to recover the signal. Without knowing the code the signal cannot be recovered and behaves like background noise. This is the security effect of spread spectrum if a secret code is used for spreading. Features that make spread spectrum and CDM very attractive for military applications are the co-existence of several signals without co-ordination (apart from the fact that the codes must have certain properties), robustness against narrowband interference, relative high security, and a characteristic like background noise.

Apart from military uses, the combination of spread spectrum and CDM is becoming more and more attractive for everyday applications. As mentioned before, frequencies are a scarce resource around the world. Spread spectrum now allows an overlay of new transmission technology at exactly the same frequency at which current narrowband systems are already operating. This is done with US mobile phone systems. While the frequency band around 850 MHz had already been in use for TDM and FDM systems (AMPS and IS-54), the introduction of a system using CDM (IS-95) was still possible.

Spread spectrum technologies also exhibit drawbacks. One disadvantage is the increased complexity of receivers that have to despread a signal. Today despreading can be performed up to high data rates thanks to digital signal processing. Another problem is the large frequency band that is needed due to the spreading of the signal. Although spread signals appear more like noise, they

Figure 2.32
Spread spectrum
to avoid
narrowband
interference

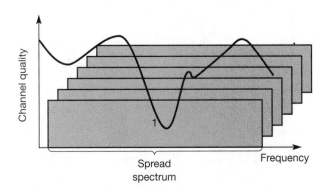

still raise the background noise level and may interfere with other transmissions if no special precautions are taken.

Spreading the spectrum can be achieved in two different ways.

2.7.1 Direct sequence spread spectrum

Direct sequence spread spectrum (DSSS) systems take a user bit stream and perform an XOR with a so-called **chipping sequence** as shown in Figure 2.33. The example shows that the result is either the sequence (0110101) or its complement. While each user bit has a duration t_b, the chipping sequence consists of smaller pulses, called **chips**, with a duration t_c. If the chipping sequence is generated properly it appears as random noise, thus this sequence is also sometimes called **pseudo-noise** sequence. The **spreading factor** $s = t_b/t_c$ determines the bandwidth of the resulting signal. If the original signal needs a bandwidth w, the resulting signal needs s·w after spreading. While the spreading factor of the very simple example is only 7 (and the chipping sequence 0110101 is not very random), civil applications use spreading factors between 10 and 100, military applications use factors of up to 10,000. Wireless LANs complying with the standard IEEE 802.11 (see section 7.3) use for example the sequence 10110111000, the so-called Barker code, if implemented using DSSS.

Up to now only the spreading has been explained. However, transmitters and receivers using DSSS need additional components as shown in the simplified block diagrams in Figure 2.34 and Figure 2.35. The first step in a DSSS transmitter, Figure 2.34, is the spreading of the user data with the chipping sequence (**digital modulation**). The spread signal is then modulated with a radio carrier as explained in section 2.6 (**radio modulation**). Assuming for example a user signal

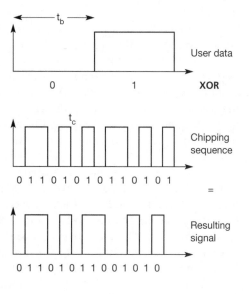

Figure 2.33
Spreading with DSSS

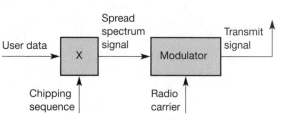

Figure 2.34
DSSS transmitter

Figure 2.35

DSSS receiver

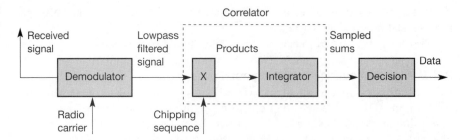

with a bandwidth of 1 MHz, spreading with the Barker code would result in a signal with 11 MHz bandwidth. The radio carrier then shifts this signal to the carrier frequency (e.g., 2.4 GHz in the ISM band). This signal is then transmitted.

The DSSS receiver is more complex than the transmitter. The receiver only has to perform the inverse functions of the two transmitter modulation steps. However, noise and multipath propagation require additional mechanisms to reconstruct the original data. The first step in the receiver involves demodulating the received signal. This is achieved using the same carrier as the transmitter reversing the modulation and results in a signal with approximately the same bandwidth as the original spread spectrum signal. Additional filtering can be applied to generate this signal.

While demodulation is well known from ordinary radio receivers, the next steps constitute a real challenge for DSSS receivers, contributing to the complexity of the system. The receiver has to know the original chipping sequence, i.e., the receiver basically generates the same pseudo random sequence as the transmitter. Sequences at the sender and receiver have to be precisely synchronized because the receiver calculates the product of a chip with the incoming signal. This comprises another XOR operation as explained in section 3.5, together with a medium access mechanism that relies on this scheme. During a bit period, which also has to be derived via synchronization, an **integrator** adds all these products. Calculating the products of chips and signal, and adding the products in an integrator is also called correlation, the device a **correlator**. Finally, in each bit period a **decision unit** samples the sums generated by the integrator and decides if this sum represents a binary 1 or a 0.

If transmitter and receiver are perfectly synchronized and the signal is not too distorted by noise or multipath propagation, DSSS works perfectly well according to the simple scheme shown. Sending the user data 01 and applying the Barker code results in the spread 'signal' 10110111000010011000111. On the receiver side, this 'signal' is XORed bit-wise after demodulation with the Barker code as chipping sequence. This results in the sum of products equal to 0 for the first bit and to 11 for the second bit. The decision unit can now map the first sum to a binary 0, the second sum to a binary 1 – which constitutes the original user data.

In real life, however, the situation is somewhat more complex. Assume that the demodulated signal shows some distortion, e.g., 101001010000110100111. The sum of products for the first bit would be 2, 10 for the second bit. Still, the decision unit can map, e.g., sums less than 4 to a binary 0 and sums larger than 7 to a binary 1. However, it is important to stay synchronized with the transmitter of a signal. But what happens in case of multipath propagation? Then several paths with different delays exist between a transmitter and a receiver. Additionally, the different paths may have different path losses. In this case, using so-called rake receivers provides a possible solution. A **rake receiver** uses n correlators for the n strongest paths. Each correlator is synchronized to the transmitter plus the delay on that specific path. As soon as the receiver detects a new path which is stronger, it assigns this path to the correlator with the currently weakest path. The output of the correlators are then combined and fed into the decision unit. Thus, rake receivers can even take advantage of the multipath propagation by combining the different paths in a constructive way (Viterbi, 1995).

2.7.2 Frequency hopping spread spectrum

For **frequency hopping spread spectrum (FHSS)** systems, the total available bandwidth is split into many channels of smaller bandwidth plus guard spaces between the channels. Transmitter and receiver stay on one of these channels for a certain time and then hop to another channel. This system thus implements FDM and TDM. The pattern of channel usage is called the **hopping sequence**, the time spend on a channel with a certain frequency is called the **dwell time**. FHSS comes in two variants, slow and fast hopping (see Figure 2.36).

In **slow hopping**, the transmitter uses one frequency for several bit periods. Figure 2.36 shows five user bits with a bit period t_b. Performing slow hopping,

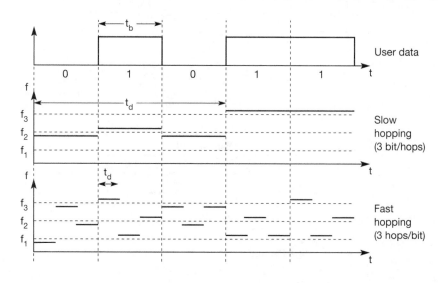

Figure 2.36
Slow and fast
frequency hopping

the transmitter uses the frequency f_2 for transmitting the first three bits during the dwell time t_d. Then, the transmitter hops to the next frequency f_3. Slow hopping systems are typically cheaper and have relaxed tolerances, but they are not as immune to narrowband interference as fast hopping systems. Slow frequency hopping is an option for GSM (see section 4.1).

For **fast hopping** systems, the transmitter changes the frequency several times during the transmission of a single bit. In the example, the transmitter hops three times during a bit period. Fast hopping systems are more complex to implement because the transmitter and receiver have to stay synchronized within smaller tolerances to perform hopping at more or less the same points in time. However, these systems are much better at overcoming the effects of narrowband interference and frequency selective fading for they only stick to one frequency for a very short moment. An example of an FHSS system is Bluetooth, which is presented in section 7.5. Bluetooth performs 1,600 hops per second and uses 79 hop carriers equally spaced with 1 MHz in the 2.4 GHz ISM band.

Figure 2.37 and Figure 2.38 show simplified block diagrams of FHSS transmitters and receivers respectively. The first step in an FHSS transmitter is the modulation of user data according to one of the digital-to-analog modulation schemes, e.g., FSK or BPSK, as discussed in section 2.6. This results in a narrowband signal, if FSK is used with a frequency f_0 for a binary 0 and f_1 for a binary 1. In the next step, frequency hopping is performed, based on a hopping sequence. The hopping sequence is fed into a frequency synthesizer generating the carrier frequencies f_i. A second modulation uses the modulated narrowband signal and the carrier frequency to generate a new spread signal with frequency

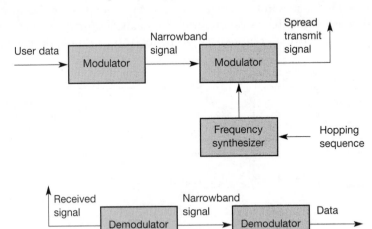

Figure 2.37
FHSS transmitter

Figure 2.38
FHSS receiver

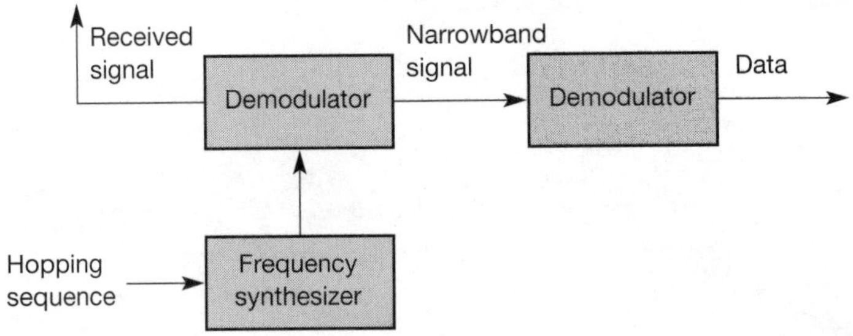

of f_i+f_0 for a 0 and f_i+f_1 for a 1 respectively. If different FHSS transmitters use hopping sequences that never overlap, i.e., if two transmitters never use the same frequency f_i at the same time, then these two transmissions do not interfere. This requires co-ordination of all transmitters and their hopping sequences. As for DSSS systems, pseudo-random hopping sequences can also be used without co-ordination. These sequences only have to fulfil certain properties to keep interference minimal.[10] Two or more transmitters may choose the same frequency for a hop, but dwell time is short for fast hopping systems and thus interference is minimal.

The receiver of an FHSS system has to know the hopping sequence and must stay synchronized. It then performs the inverse operations of the modulation to reconstruct user data. Additionally, several filters are needed (these are not shown in the simplified diagram in Figure 2.38).

Compared to DSSS, spreading is simpler using FHSS systems. FHSS systems only use a portion of the total band at any time while DSSS systems always use the total bandwidth available. DSSS systems on the other hand are more resistant to fading and multipath effects. Furthermore, DSSS signals are much harder to detect – without knowing the spreading code, detection is virtually impossible. If each sender has its own pseudo-random number sequence for spreading the signal (DSSS or FHSS), the system implements CDM. More details about spread spectrum applications and their theoretical background can be found in Viterbi (1995), Peterson (1995) and Dixon (1994).

2.8 Cellular systems

Cellular systems for mobile communications implement SDM. Each transmitter, typically called a **base station**, covers a certain area, a **cell**. Cell radii can vary from tens of metres in buildings, and hundreds of metres in cities, up to tens of kilometres in the countryside. The shape of cells are never perfect circles or hexagons (as shown in Figure 2.39), but depend on the environment (buildings, mountains, valleys etc.), on weather conditions, and sometimes even on system load. Typical systems using this approach are mobile telecommunication systems (see chapter 4), where a mobile station within the cell around a base station communicates with this base station and vice versa.

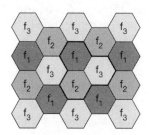 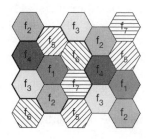

Figure 2.39
Cellular system
with three and
seven cell clusters

In this context, the question arises as to why mobile network providers install several thousands of base stations throughout a country, which is quite expensive, and do not use powerful transmitters with huge cells as, e.g., radio stations, use.

Advantages of cellular systems with small cells are the following:

- **Higher capacity:** Implementing SDM allows frequency reuse. If one transmitter is far away from another, i.e., outside the interference range, it can reuse the same frequencies. As most mobile phone systems assign frequencies to certain users (or certain hopping patterns), this frequency is blocked for other users. But frequencies are a scarce resource and, thus, the number of concurrent users per cell is very limited. Huge cells do not allow for more users. On the contrary, they are limited to less possible users per km². This is also the reason for using very small cells in cities – where many more people use mobile phones.
- **Less transmission power:** While power aspects are not a big problem for base stations, they are indeed problematic for mobile stations. A receiver far away from a base station would need much more transmit power than the current few Watts. But energy is a serious problem for mobile handheld devices.
- **Local interference only:** Having long distances between sender and receiver results in even more interference problems. With small cells, mobile stations and base stations only have to deal with 'local' interference.
- **Robustness:** Cellular systems are decentralized and, thus, more robust against failures of single components. If one antenna fails, this defect only influences communication within a small area.

Small cells also have some **disadvantages**:

- **Infrastructure needed:** Cellular systems need a complex infrastructure to connect all base stations. This infrastructure includes many antennas, switches for call forwarding, location registers to find a mobile station etc. This makes the whole system quite expensive.
- **Handover needed:** The mobile station has to perform a handover when changing from one cell to another. Depending on the cell size and the speed of movement, this can happen quite often.
- **Frequency planning:** To avoid interference between transmitters using the same frequencies, frequencies have to be distributed carefully. On the one hand interference should be avoided, on the other hand only a limited number of frequencies is available.

To avoid interference, different transmitters within each other's interference range use FDM. If FDM is combined with TDM (see Figure 2.19), the hopping pattern has to be co-ordinated. The general goal is never to use the same frequency at the same time within the interference range. Two possible models to create cell patterns with minimal interference are shown in Figure 2.39. Cells are combined in **clusters** – on the left side three cells form a cluster, on the right side seven cells form a cluster. All cells within a cluster use disjointed sets of frequencies. On the left side, one cell in the cluster uses set f_1, another cell f_2, and the third cell f_3. In real life transmission, the pattern will look somewhat different. The hexagonal pattern is chosen as a simple way of illustrating the model. This pattern also shows the repetition of the same frequency sets. The transmission power of a sender therefore has to be limited to avoid interference with the next cell using the same frequencies.

To reduce interference even further (and under certain traffic conditions, i.e., number of users per km^2) **sectorized antennas** can be used. Figure 2.40 shows the use of three sectors per cell in a cluster with three cells. Typically, it makes sense to use sectorized antennas instead of omnidirectional antennas for larger cell radii.

The fixed assignment of frequencies to cell clusters and cells respectively, is not very efficient if traffic load varies. In the case of a heavy load in one cell and a light load in a neighbouring cell, for instance, it could make sense to 'borrow' frequencies. Cells with more traffic are dynamically allotted more frequencies. This scheme is known as **borrowing channel allocation (BCA)**, while the first fixed scheme is called **fixed channel allocation (FCA)**. FCA is used, e.g., in the GSM system for it is much simpler to use, but requires careful traffic analysis before installation.

A **dynamic channel allocation (DCA)** scheme has been implemented in DECT (see section 4.2). In this scheme, frequencies can only be borrowed, but it is also possible to freely assign frequencies to cells. With dynamic assignment of frequencies to cells, the danger of interference with cells using the same frequency exists. Thus, the 'borrowed' frequency can be blocked in the surrounding cells.

Cellular systems using CDM instead of FDM do not need such elaborate channel allocation schemes. Here users are separated through the code they use, and not through the frequency. But here cell planning faces another problem – the cell size depends on the current load. Accordingly, **CDM cells** are commonly said to '**breathe**'. While a cell can cover a larger area under a light load, it shrinks if the load increases. The reason for this is the growing noise level if more users are in a cell. (Remember, if you do not know the code, other signals appear as noise, i.e., more and more people join the party.) The higher the noise, the higher the path loss and the higher the transmission errors will be. Finally, mobile stations further away from the base station drop out of the cell. (This is similar to the problem when trying to talk to someone far away at a crowded party.)

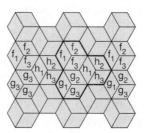

Figure 2.40

Cellular system with three cell clusters and three sectors per cell

2.9 Summary

This chapter introduced the basics of wireless communications, leaving out most formulae found in books dedicated to wireless transmission and the effects of radio propagation. However, the examples, mechanisms, and problems discussed will hopefully give the reader a good idea as to why wireless communication is fundamentally different from wired communication and why protocols and applications on higher layers have to follow different principles in order to take the missing wire into account.

A topic of worldwide importance is the regulation and harmonization of frequencies used for radio transmission. The chapter showed many different systems using either different or the same frequencies. In this respect, the future will hopefully bring frequencies which are available worldwide in order to avoid expensive multi-mode devices.

As electromagnetic waves are the basis for wireless communication, antennas are needed for the transmission and reception of waves. While base stations of mobile phone systems often use directed antennas, omnidirectional antennas are the choice for mobile devices. On the way from sender to receiver, many things can happen to electromagnetic waves. The standard effects, such as shadowing, fading, reflection, diffraction, and scattering have been presented. All these effects lead to one of the biggest problems in wireless communication: multipath propagation. Multipath propagation limits the bandwidth of a channel due to intersymbol interference, i.e., one symbol is 'smeared' into another symbol due to delay spread.

As we only have one 'medium' for wireless transmission, several multiplexing schemes can be applied to raise overall capacity. The standard schemes are SDM, FDM, TDM, and CDM. To achieve FDM, data has to be 'translated' into a signal with a certain carrier frequency. Therefore, two modulation steps can be applied. The digital modulation encodes data into a baseband signal, whereas analog modulation then shifts the centre frequency of the signal up to the radio carrier. Some advanced schemes have been presented that can code many bits into a single phase shift, thus raising the efficiency.

With the help of spread spectrum technology, several features can be implemented. One is (at least some) security – without knowing the spreading code, the signal appears as noise. Furthermore, as we will see in more detail in the next chapter, spread spectrum lays the basis for special medium access schemes using the code space. Spread spectrum also makes a transmission more robust against narrowband interference, as the signal is spread over a larger bandwidth and, thus, the narrowband interference only influences a small fraction of the signal.

Finally, this chapter has presented the concept of cellular systems. Cellular systems implement SDM to raise the overall capacity of mobile phone systems. While these systems requires detailed planning (i.e., matching the cell size with the traffic expected), it presents one of the basic solutions for using the scarce frequency resources efficiently.

2.10   Review exercises

1   Frequency regulations may differ between countries. Check out the regulations valid for your country (within Europe the European Radio Office may be able to help you, http:// www.ero.dk/, for the US try the FCC, http:// www.fcc.gov/).

2   Why can waves with a very low frequency follow the earth's surface? Why are they not used for data transmission in computer networks?

3   Why does the ITU-R only regulate 'lower' frequencies (up to some hundred GHz) and not higher frequencies (in the THz range)?

4   What are the two different approaches in regulation regarding mobile phone systems in Europe and the US? What are the consequences?

5   Why is the international availability of the same ISM bands important?

6   Is it possible to transmit a digital signal, e.g., coded as square wave as used inside a computer, using radio transmission without any loss? Why?

7   Is a directional antenna useful for mobile phones? Why? How can the gain of an antenna be improved?

8   What are the main problems of signal propagation? Why do radio waves not always follow a straight line? Why is reflection both useful and harmful?

9   Name several methods for ISI mitigation. How does ISI depend on the carrier frequency, symbol rate, and movement of sender/receiver? What are the influences of ISI on TDM schemes?

10   What are the means to mitigate narrowband interference? What is the complexity of the different solutions?

11   Why, typically, is digital modulation not enough for radio transmission? What are general goals for digital modulation? What are typical schemes?

12   Think of a phase diagram and the points representing bit patterns for a PSK scheme (see Figure 2.29). How can a receiver decide which bit pattern was originally sent when a received 'point' lies somewhere in between other points in the diagram? Why is it, thus, difficult to code more and more bits per phase shift?

13   What are the main benefits of a spread spectrum system? How can spreading be achieved? What replaces the guard space in Figure 2.31 when compared to Figure 2.32? How can DSSS systems benefit from multipath propagation?

14   What are the main reasons for using cellular systems? How is SDM typically realized and combined with FDM? How does DCA influence the frequencies available in other cells?

15   What limits the number of simultaneous users in a TDM/FDM system compared to a CDM system? What happens to the transmission quality of connections if the load gets higher in a cell, i.e., how does an additional user influence the other users in the cell?

2.11 References

Anderson, J.B.; Rappaport, T.S.; Yoshida, S. (1995) 'Propagation measurements and models for wireless communications channels', *IEEE Communications Magazine*, 33, (1).

Dixon, R. (1994) *Spread spectrum systems with commercial applications*. John Wiley.

ETSI (1997) *Digital Audio Broadcasting (DAB) to mobile, portable, and fixed receivers*, European Telecommunications Standards Institute, ETS 300 401.

Goodman, D. (1997) *Wireless personal communications systems*, Addison Wesley Longman.

Halsall, F. (1996) *Data communications, computer networks and open systems*, Addison Wesley Longman.

Peterson, R.; Ziemer, R.; Borth, D. (1995) *Introduction to spread spectrum communications*. Prentice Hall.

Stallings, W. (1997) *Data and computer communications*. Prentice Hall.

Viterbi, A. (1995) *CDMA: Principles of spread spectrum communication*. Addison Wesley Longman.

Wesel, E. (1997) *Wireless multimedia communications: networking video, voice, and data*. Addison Wesley Longman.

Medium access control

3

his chapter introduces several **medium access control (MAC)** algorithms which are specifically adapted to the wireless domain. Medium access control comprises all mechanisms that regulate user access to a medium using SDM, TDM, FDM, or CDM. MAC is thus similar to traffic regulations in the highway/multiplexing example introduced in chapter 2. The fact that several vehicles use the same street crossing in TDM, for example, requires rules; one mechanism to enforce these rules is traffic lights. While the previous chapter mainly introduced mechanisms of the physical layer, layer 1, of the ISO/OSI reference model, MAC belongs to layer 2, the **data link control layer (DLC)**. Layer 2 is subdivided into the **logical link control (LLC)**, layer 2b, and the MAC, layer 2a (Halsall, 1996). The task of DLC is to establish a reliable point to point or point to multipoint connection between different devices over a wired or wireless medium. The basic MAC mechanisms are introduced in the following sections, whereas LLC and higher layers, as well as specific relevant technologies will be presented in later chapters.

First of all, this chapter aims at explaining why special MACs are needed in the wireless domain and why standard MAC schemes known from wired networks often fail. (In contrast to wired networks, hidden and exposed terminals or near and far terminals present serious problems here.) Then, several MAC mechanisms will be presented for the multiplexing schemes introduced in chapter 2. While SDM and FDM are typically used in a rather fixed manner, i.e., a certain space or frequency (or frequency hopping pattern) is assigned for a longer period of time, the main focus of this chapter is on TDM mechanisms. TDM can be used in a very flexible way, as tuning in to a certain frequency does not present a problem, but time can be allocated on demand and in a distributed fashion. Well-known algorithms are Aloha (in several versions), different reservation schemes, or simple polling.

Finally, the use of CDM is discussed again, now showing how a MAC scheme using CDM has to assign certain codes to allow the separation of different users in code space. This chapter also shows that one typically does not use a single scheme in its pure form but mixes schemes to benefit from the specific advantages. A comparison of the four basic schemes concludes the chapter.

3.1 Motivation for a specialized MAC

The main question in connection with MAC in the wireless is whether it is possible to use elaborated MAC schemes from wired networks, for example, CSMA/CD as used in the original specification of IEEE 802.3 networks (a.k.a. Ethernet).

So let us consider **carrier sense multiple access with collision detection, (CSMA/CD)** which works as follows. A sender senses the medium (a wire or coaxial cable) to see if it is free. If the medium is busy, the sender waits until it is free. If the medium is free, the sender starts transmitting data and continues to listen into the medium. If the sender now detects a collision while sending, it stops at once and sends a jamming signal.

Why does this scheme fail in wireless networks? CSMA/CD is not really interested in collisions at the sender, but rather in those at the receiver. The signal should reach the receiver without collisions. But the sender is the one detecting collisions. This is not a problem using a wire, as more or less the same signal strength can be assumed all over the wire. If a collision occurs somewhere in the wire, everybody will notice it.

The situation is different in wireless networks. As shown in chapter 2, the strength of a signal decreases proportionally to the square of the distance to the sender. The sender may now apply carrier sense and detect an idle medium. Thus, the sender starts sending – but a collision happens at the receiver due to a second sender. Section 3.1.1 explains this hidden terminal problem. The same can happen to the collision detection. The sender detects no collision, assumes that the data has been transmitted without errors, but actually a collision might have destroyed the data at the receiver. Thus, this very common MAC scheme from wired network fails in a wireless scenario. The following sections show some more scenarios where schemes known from fixed networks fail.

3.1.1 Hidden and exposed terminals

Consider the scenario with three mobile phones as shown in Figure 3.1. The transmission range of A reaches B, but not C (the detection range does not

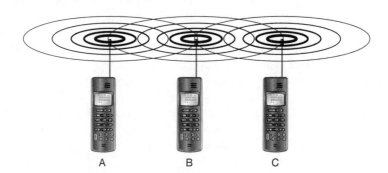

reach C either). The transmission range of C reaches B, but not A. Finally, the transmission range of B reaches A and C, i.e., A cannot detect C and vice versa.

A starts sending to B, C does not receive this transmission. C also wants to send something to B and senses the medium. The medium appears to be free, the carrier sense fails. Thus, C also starts sending causing a collision at B. But now A cannot detect this collision and continues with its transmission. A is **hidden** for C and vice versa.

While hidden terminals cause collision, the next effect only causes unnecessary delay. Now consider the situation that B sends something to A and C wants to transmit data to some other mobile phone outside the interference ranges of A and B. C senses the carrier and detects that the carrier is busy. Thus, C postpones its transmission. But as A is outside the interference range of C, waiting is not necessary. Causing a 'collision' at B does not matter because the collision is too weak to propagate to A. In this situation, C is **exposed** to B.

3.1.2 Near and far terminals

Consider the situation as shown in Figure 3.2. A and B are both sending with the same transmission power. As the signal strength decreases proportionally to the square of the distance, B's signal drowns out A's signal. As a result, C cannot receive A's transmission.

Now think of C as being an arbiter for sending rights. In this case, terminal B would already drown out terminal A on the physical layer. C in return would have no chance of applying a fair scheme for it would only hear B.

The **near/far effect** is a severe problem of wireless networks using CDM. All signals should arrive at the receiver with more or less the same strength. Otherwise, referring again to the party example of chapter 2, a person standing closer to somebody could always speak louder than a person further away. Even if the senders were separated by code, the closest one would simply drown out the others. Thus, precise power control is needed to receive all senders with the same strength at a receiver.

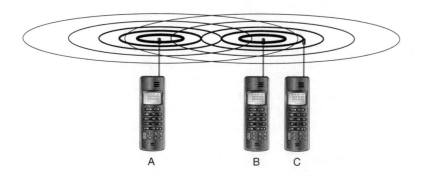

Figure 3.2
Near and far terminals

A   B   C

3.2 SDMA

Space Division Multiple Access (SDMA) is used for allocating a separated space to users in wireless networks. A typical application involves assigning an optimal base station to a mobile phone user. The mobile phone may receive several base stations with different quality. A MAC algorithm could now decide which base station is best, taking into account which frequencies (FDM), time slots (TDM) or code (CDM) are still available (depending on the technology). Typically, SDMA is never used in isolation but always in combination with one or more other schemes. The basis for the SDMA algorithm is formed by cells and sectorized antennas which constitute the infrastructure implementing **space division multiplexing (SDM)** (see section 2.5.1).

3.3 FDMA

Frequency division multiple access (FDMA) comprises all algorithms allocating frequencies to transmission channels according to the **frequency division multiplexing (FDM)** scheme as presented in section 2.5.2. Allocation can either be fixed (as for example used for radio stations or the general planning and regulation of frequencies) or dynamic (i.e., demand driven).

Channels can be assigned to the same frequency at all times, i.e., pure FDMA, or change frequencies according to a certain pattern, i.e., FDMA combined with TDMA. The latter example is the common practice for many wireless systems to circumvent narrowband interference at certain frequencies, known as frequency hopping. Sender and receiver have to agree on a hopping pattern, otherwise the receiver could not tune to the right frequency. Thus, hopping patterns are typically fixed, at least for a longer period. The fact that it is not possible to arbitrarily jump in the frequency space (i.e., the receiver must be able to tune to the right frequency) is one of the main differences between FDM schemes and TDM schemes.

Furthermore, FDM is often used for simultaneous access to the medium by base station and mobile station in cellular networks. Here the two partners typically establish a **duplex channel.** The two directions, mobile station to base station and vice versa are now separated using different frequencies. This scheme is then called **frequency division duplex (FDD).** Again, both partners have to know the frequencies in advance, they cannot just listen into the medium. The two frequencies are also known as **uplink**, i.e., from mobile station to base station or from ground control to satellite, and as **downlink**, i.e., from base station to mobile station or from satellite to ground control.

As example for FDM and FDD, Figure 3.3 shows the situation in a mobile phone network based on the GSM standard for 900 MHz. The basic frequency allocation scheme for GSM is fixed. All uplinks use the band between 890.2 and 915 MHz, all downlinks use 935.2 to 960 MHz. According to FDMA, the base station, shown on the right side, allocates a certain frequency for up- and downlink to establish a duplex channel with a mobile phone. Up- and downlink have a fixed relation. If the uplink frequency is f_u = 890 MHz + n·0.2 MHz, the downlink frequency is f_d = f_u + 45 MHz, i.e., f_d = 935 MHz + n·0.2 MHz for a certain channel n. This illustrates the use of FDM for multiple access and duplex according to a predetermined scheme. Similar FDM schemes for FDD are implemented in AMPS, IS-54, IS-95, IS-136, and PACS. Chapter 4 presents some more details regarding the combination of this scheme with TDM as implemented in GSM.

3.4 TDMA

Compared to FDMA, **time division multiple access (TDMA)** offers a much more flexible scheme, which comprises all technologies that allocate certain time slots for communication, i.e., controlling **TDM.** Now tuning in to a certain frequency is not necessary, i.e., the receiver can stay at the same frequency the whole time. Using only one frequency, and thus very simple receivers and transmitters, many different algorithms exist to control medium access. As already mentioned, listening to different frequencies at the same time is quite difficult, but listening to many channels separated in time at the same frequency is simple. Almost all MAC schemes for wired networks work according to this principle, e.g., Ethernet, Token Ring, ATM etc. (Halsall, 1996).

Now synchronization between sender and receiver has to be achieved in the time domain. Again this can be done by using a fixed pattern, i.e., allocating a certain time slot for a channel, or by using a dynamic allocation scheme. Dynamic allocation schemes require an identification for each transmission as this is the case for typical wired MAC schemes (e.g., sender address). Fixed schemes do not need an identification, but are not as flexible considering

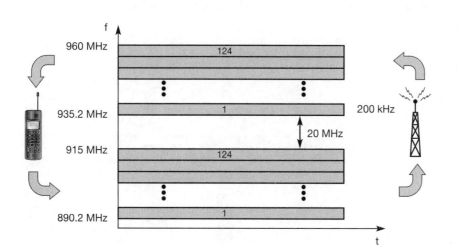

Figure 3.3
Frequency division multiplexing for multiple access and duplex

varying bandwidth requirements. The following sections present several examples for fixed and dynamic schemes as used for wireless transmission. Typically, those schemes can be combined with FDMA to achieve even greater flexibility.

3.4.1 Fixed TDM

The simplest algorithm for using TDM is allocating time slots for channels in a fixed pattern. This results in a fixed bandwidth and is the typical solution for wireless phone systems. MAC is quite simple, as the only crucial factor concerns accessing the reserved time slot at the right moment. If this is assured, each mobile station knows its turn and no interference will happen. The fixed pattern can be assigned by the base station, where competition between different mobile stations that want to access the medium is solved.

Fixed access patterns (at least fixed for some period in time) fit perfectly well for connections with a fixed bandwidth. Furthermore, these patterns guarantee a fixed delay – one can transmit, e.g., every 10 ms as this is the case for standard DECT systems. TDMA schemes with fixed access patterns are used for many digital mobile phone systems like IS-54, IS-136, GSM, DECT, PHS, and PACS.

Figure 3.4 shows how these fixed TDM patterns are used to implement multiple access and a duplex channel between a base station and mobile station. Assigning different slots for uplink and downlink using the same frequency is called **time division duplex (TDD).** As shown in the figure, the base station uses one out of 12 slots for the downlink, whereas the mobile station uses one out of 12 different slots for the uplink. Uplink and downlink are, thus, separated in time. Furthermore, up to 12 different mobile stations can use the same frequency without interference using this scheme. Each connection is allotted its own up- and downlink pair. In the example below, which is the standard case for the DECT cordless phone system, the pattern is repeated every 10 ms, i.e., each slot has a duration of 417 μs. This repetition guarantees access to the medium every 10 ms, independent of any other connections.

Figure 3.4
Time division
multiplexing for multiple
access and duplex

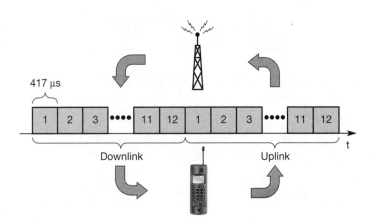

While the fixed access patterns, as shown for DECT, are perfectly apt for connections with a constant data rate, they are very inefficient for bursty data or asymmetric connections. i.e., if temporary bursts in data are sent from the base station to the mobile station often or vice versa (as, for example, in the case of web browsing, where no data transmission occurs while reading a page, whereas clicking on a hyperlink triggers a data transfer from the mobile station, often to the base station, often followed by huge amounts of data returned from the web server). While DECT can at least allocate asymmetric bandwidth (see section 4.2), this general scheme still wastes a lot of bandwidth, it is too static, too inflexible for data communication. In this case, connectionless, demand-oriented TDMA schemes can be used, as the following sections show.

3.4.2 Classical Aloha

As mentioned above, TDMA comprises all mechanisms controlling medium access according to TDM. But what happens if TDM is applied without controlling access? This is exactly what the classical **Aloha** scheme does, a scheme which was invented at the University of Hawaii and was used in the ALOHANET for wireless connection of several stations. Aloha neither co-ordinates medium access nor does it resolve contention on the MAC layer. Instead, each station can access the medium at any time as shown in Figure 3.5. This is a random access scheme, without a central arbiter controlling access and without co-ordination among the stations. If two or more stations access the medium at the same time, a **collision** occurs and the transmitted data is destroyed. Resolving this problem is left to higher layers (e.g., retransmission of data).

The simple Aloha works fine for a light load and does not require any complicated access mechanisms. Assuming Poisson arrival of the packets, maximum throughput is achieved for 18 per cent load (Abramson, 1977), (Halsall, 1996).

3.4.3 Slotted Aloha

The first refinement of the classical Aloha scheme is provided by the introduction of time slots (**slotted Aloha**). In this case, all senders have to be **synchronized**, transmission can only start at the begin of a **time slot** as shown in Figure 3.6. Still, access is not co-ordinated. Under the assumption stated above, the introduction of slots raises the throughput from 18 per cent to 36 per cent, i.e., slotting doubles the throughput.

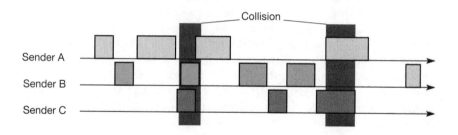

Figure 3.5
Classical Aloha multiple access

Figure 3.6
Slotted Aloha multiple
access

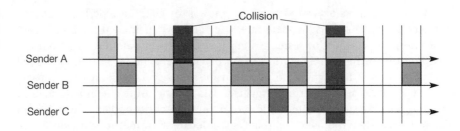

As we will see in the following sections, both basic Aloha principles occur in many systems that implement distributed access to a medium. Aloha systems work perfectly well under a light load (as most schemes do), but they cannot give any hard transmission guarantees, such as maximum delay before accessing the medium, or minimum throughput. Here one needs additional mechanisms, e.g., combining fixed schemes and Aloha schemes.

3.4.4 Carrier sense multiple access

One improvement to the basic Aloha is sensing the carrier before accessing the medium. This is what **carrier sense multiple access (CSMA)** schemes generally do (Kleinrock, 1975; Halsall, 1996). Sensing the carrier and accessing the medium only if the carrier is idle decreases the probability of a collision. But, as already mentioned in the introduction, hidden terminals cannot be detected. Thus, if a hidden terminal transmits at the same time as another sender, a collision might occur at the receiver. Still, this basic scheme is used in most wireless LANs (this aspect will be explained in more detail in chapter 7).

Several versions of CSMA exist. In **non-persistent CSMA**, stations sense the carrier and start sending immediately if the medium is idle. If the medium is busy, the station pauses a random amount of time before sensing the medium again and repeating this pattern. In **p-persistent CSMA** systems nodes also sense the medium, but only transmit with a probability of p, with the station deferring to the next slot with the probability 1-p, i.e., access is slotted in addition. In **1-persistent CSMA** systems, all stations wishing to transmit access the medium at the same time, as soon as it becomes idle. To create some fairness for stations waiting for a longer time, back-off algorithms can be introduced, which are sensitive to waiting time as this is done for standard Ethernet (Halsall, 1996).

CSMA with collision avoidance (**CSMA/CA**) is one of the access schemes used in wireless LANs following the standard IEEE 802.11. Here sensing the carrier is combined with a back-off scheme in case of a busy medium to achieve some fairness among competing stations. Another, very elaborate scheme is elimination yield – non-preemptive multiple access (**EY-NMPA**) used in the HIPERLAN 1 specification. Here several phases of sensing the medium and accessing the medium for contention resolution are interleaved before one 'winner' can finally access the medium for data transmission. Here, priority schemes can be included to assure preference of certain stations with more important data.

3.4.5 Demand assigned multiple access

A general improvement of Aloha access systems can also be achieved by **reservation** mechanisms and combinations with some (fixed) TDM patterns. These schemes typically have a reservation period followed by a transmission period. During the reservation period, stations can reserve future slots in the transmission period. While, depending on the scheme, collisions may occur during the reservation period, the transmission period can then be accessed without collision – or split into transmission periods with and without collision. In general, these schemes cause a higher delay under a light load, but allow higher throughput.

One basic scheme is **demand assigned multiple access (DAMA)** also called **reservation Aloha**, a scheme typical for satellite systems. DAMA, as shown in Figure 3.7 has two modes. During a contention phase following the slotted Aloha scheme, all stations can try to reserve future slots. For example, different stations on earth try to reserve access time for satellite transmission. Thus collisions during the reservation phase do not destroy data transmission, but only the short requests for data transmission. If successful, a time slot in the future is reserved, and no other station is allowed to transmit during this slot. Therefore, the satellite collects all successful requests (the others are destroyed) and sends back a reservation list indicating access rights for future slots. All ground stations have to obey this list. To maintain the fixed TDM pattern of reservation and transmission, the stations have to be synchronized from time to time. DAMA is an **explicit reservation** scheme. Each transmission slot has to be reserved explicitly.

3.4.6 PRMA packet reservation multiple access

An example for an **implicit reservation** scheme is **packet reservation multiple access (PRMA).** Here, slots can be reserved implicitly according to the following scheme. A certain number of slots forms a frame (Figure 3.8 shows eight slots in a frame). The frame is repeated in time (forming frames one to five in the example), i.e., a fixed TDM pattern is applied.

A base station now broadcasts the status of each slot (as shown on the left side of the figure) to all mobile stations. All stations receiving this vector will then know which slot is occupied and which slot is currently free. In the example, the base station broadcasts the reservation status 'ACDABA-F' to all stations, here A to F. This means that slots one to six and eight are occupied, but slot seven is free in the following transmission. All stations wishing to transmit can

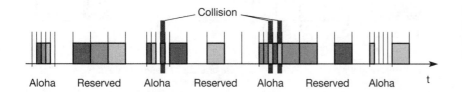

Figure 3.7
Demand assignment multiple access with explicit reservation

Figure 3.8
Demand assignment
multiple access with
implicit reservation

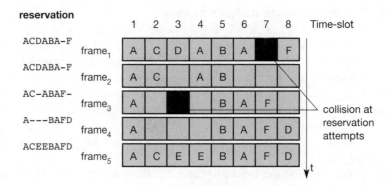

now compete for this free slot in Aloha fashion. In the example shown, more than one station wants to access this slot, thus a collision occurs. The base station returns the reservation status 'ACDABA-F', indicating that the reservation of slot seven failed (still indicated as free) and that nothing has changed for the other slots. Again, stations can compete for this slot. Additionally, station D has stopped sending in slot three and station F in slot eight. This is noticed by the base station after the second frame.

Before the third frame starts, the base station indicates that slots three and eight are now idle. Additionally, station F has succeeded in reserving slot seven as also indicated by the base station. PRMA constitutes yet another combination of fixed and random TDM schemes with reservation compared to the previous schemes. As soon as a station has succeeded with a reservation, all future slots are implicitly reserved for this station. This ensures transmission with a guaranteed data rate. The slotted aloha scheme is used for idle slots only, data transmission is not destroyed by collision.

3.4.7 Reservation TDMA

An even more fixed pattern that still allows some random access is exhibited by **reservation TDMA** (see Figure 3.9). In a fixed TDM scheme N mini-slots followed by N·k data-slots form a frame. Each station is allotted its own mini-slot and can use it to reserve up to k data-slots. This guarantees each station a cer-

Figure 3.9 Reservation
TDMA access scheme

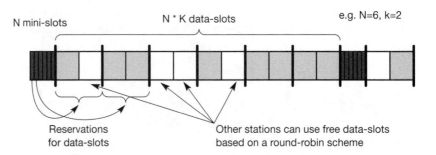

tain bandwidth and a fixed delay. Other stations can now send data in unused data-slots as shown. Using these free slots can be based on a simple round-robin scheme or can be uncoordinated using an Aloha scheme. This scheme allows for the combination of, e.g., isochronous traffic with fixed bit-rates and best-effort traffic without any guarantees.

3.4.8 Multiple access with collision avoidance

Let us go back to one of the initial problems: hidden terminals. How do the previous access schemes solve this? To all schemes with central base stations assigning TDM patterns, the problem of hidden terminals is unknown. If the terminal is hidden for the base station it cannot communicate anyway. But as mentioned above, more or less fixed access patterns are not as flexible as Aloha schemes. What happens when no base station exists at all, as is the case in so-called ad hoc networks, is presented in more detail in chapter 7.

Multiple access with collision avoidance (MACA) presents a simple scheme that solves the hidden terminal problem, does not need a base station, and is still a random access Aloha scheme – but with dynamic reservation. Figure 3.10 shows the same scenario as Figure 3.1 with the hidden terminals. Remember, A and C both want to send to B. A has already started the transmission, but is hidden for C, C also starts with its transmission, thereby causing a collision at B.

With MACA, A does not start its transmission at once, but sends a **request to send (RTS)** first. B receives the RTS that contains the name of sender and receiver, as well as the length of the future transmission. This RTS is not heard by C and triggers an acknowledgement from B, called **clear to send (CTS)**. The CTS again contains the names of sender and receiver, and the length of the future transmission. This CTS is now heard by C and the medium for future use by A is now reserved for the duration of the transmission. After receiving a CTS, C is not allowed to send anything for the duration indicated in the CTS toward B. Thus, a collision cannot occur at B during data transmission, and the hidden terminal problem is solved – provided that the transmission conditions remain the same.

Still, collisions can occur during the sending of an RTS. Both A and C could send an RTS. But RTS is very small compared to the data transmission, thus the probability for a collision is much lower. B resolves this contention and

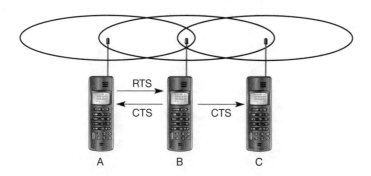

Figure 3.10
MACA can avoid hidden terminals

acknowledges only one station in the CTS (if it was able to recover the RTS at all). No transmission is allowed without an appropriate CTS. This is one of the medium access schemes that is optionally used in the standard IEEE 802.11 (more details can be found in section 7.3).

Can MACA also help to solve the 'exposed terminal' problem? Remember, B wants to send data to A, C to someone else. But C is polite enough to sense the medium before transmitting, thus sensing a busy medium caused by the transmission from B. C defers, although C could never cause a collision at A.

With MACA, B has to transmit an RTS first as shown in Figure 3.11, containing the name of the receiver (A) and the sender (B). C does not react to this message as it is not the receiver, but A acknowledges using a CTS which identifies B as the sender and A as the receiver of the following data transmission. C does not receive this CTS and concludes that A is outside the detection range. Thus, C can start its transmission assuming not to cause a collision at A. The problem with exposed terminals is solved without fixed access patterns or a base station. One problem of MACA is clearly the overhead associated with the RTS and CTS transmissions – for short data packets, this overhead is not negligible.

Figure 3.12 shows simplified state machines for a sender and receiver that could realize MACA. The sender is idle until a user requests the transmission of a data packet. The sender then issues an RTS and waits for the right to send. If the receiver gets an RTS and is in an idle state, it sends back a CTS and waits for data. The sender receives the CTS and sends the data. Otherwise, the sender would send an RTS again after a time-out (e.g., the RTS could be lost or collided). After transmission of the data, the sender waits for a positive acknowledgement to return into an idle state. The receiver sends back a positive acknowledgement if the received data was correct. Otherwise, or if the waiting time for data is too long, the receiver returns into idle state. If the sender does not receive any acknowledgement or a negative acknowledgement, it sends an RTS and again waits for the right to send. Additionally, a receiver could indicate that it is currently busy via a separate RxBusy. Real implementations have to add more states and transitions, e.g., in order to limit the number of retries.

Figure 3.11
MACA can avoid
exposed terminals

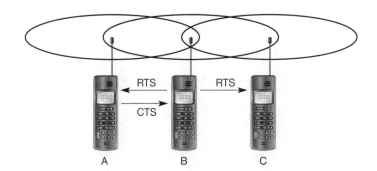

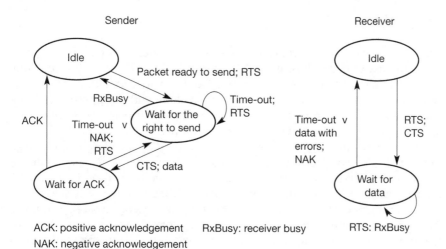

Sender

Receiver

Figure 3.12
Protocol machines for
multiple access with
collision avoidance

ACK: positive acknowledgement   RxBusy: receiver busy   RTS: RxBusy
NAK: negative acknowledgement

3.4.9 Polling

In the case where one station is to be heard by all others (e.g., the base station of a mobile phone network or any other dedicated station), **polling** schemes as known from the mainframe/terminal world can be applied. Polling is a strictly centralized scheme with one master station and several slave stations. The master can poll the slaves according to many schemes: round robin (only efficient if traffic patterns are similar over all stations), randomly, according to reservations (the classroom example with polite students) etc. The master could also establish a list of stations wishing to transmit during a contention phase. After this phase, the station polls each station on the list. Similar schemes are used, e.g., in the Bluetooth wireless LAN and as one possible access function in IEEE 802.11 systems as described in section 7.5.

3.4.10 Inhibit sense multiple access

Another combination of different schemes is represented by **inhibit sense multiple access (ISMA)**, a scheme which is used for the packet data transmission service Cellular Digital Packet Data (CDPD) in the AMPS mobile phone system, also known as **digital sense multiple access (DSMA)**. Here, the base station only signals a busy medium via a busy tone on the downlink (see Figure 3.13). After the busy tone stops, accessing the uplink is not co-ordinated any further. The base station acknowledges successful transmissions, a mobile station detects a collision only via the missing positive acknowledgement. In case of collisions, additional back-off and retransmission mechanisms are implemented.

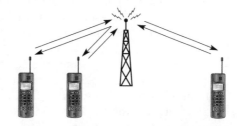

Figure 3.13
Inhibit sense multiple
access using a busy tone

3.5 CDMA

Finally, codes with certain characteristics can be applied to the transmission to enable the use of **code division multiplexing (CDM). Code division multiple access (CDMA)** systems use exactly these codes to separate different users in code space and to enable access to a shared medium without interference. The main problem is how to find 'good' codes and how to separate the signal from noise generated by other signals and the environment.

Chapter 2 already showed how to use the codes for spreading a signal (e.g., using DSSS). The code directly controlled the chipping sequence. But what is a good code for CDMA? A code for a certain user should have a good autocorrelation and should be **orthogonal** to other codes. Orthogonal in code space has the same meaning as in standard space (i.e., the three dimensional space). Think of a system of coordinates and vectors starting at the origin, i.e., in (0, 0, 0).[11] Two vectors are called orthogonal if their inner product is 0, as is the case for the two vectors (2, 5, 0)*(0, 0, 17) = 0 + 0 + 0 = 0. But also vectors like (3, –2, 4) and (–2, 3, 3) are orthogonal: (3, –2, 4)*(–2, 3, 3) = –6 – 6 + 12 = 0. In contrast, the vectors (1,2,3) and (4,2, –6) are not orthogonal (the inner product is –10), and (1, 2, 3) and (4, 2, –3) are 'almost' orthogonal, with their inner product being –1.

Now let us translate this into code space and explain what we mean by a good **autocorrelation.** The Barker code (+1, –1, +1, +1, –1, +1, +1, +1, –1, –1, –1), for example, has a good autocorrelation, i.e., the inner product with itself is large, the result is 11. But as soon as the Barker code is shifted 1 chip further (think of shifting the 11 chip Barker code over itself concatenated several times), the correlation drops to an absolute value of 1. It stays at this low value until the code matches itself again perfectly. This peak in the matching process helps the receiver to reconstruct the original data precisely.

The following (theoretical) example explains the basic function of CDMA:

- Two senders, A and B, want to send data. CDMA assigns the following key sequences: key A_k = 010011, key B_k = 110101. Sender A wants to send the bit A_d = 1, sender B sends B_d = 0. To illustrate this example, let us assume that we code a binary 0 as –1, a binary 1 as +1. We can then apply the standard addition and multiplication rules.
- Both senders spread their signal using their key as chipping sequence (the term 'spreading' here refers to the simple multiplication of the data bit with the whole chipping sequence). In reality, parts of a much longer chipping sequence are applied to single bits for spreading. Sender A then sends the signal A_s = A_d*A_k = +1*(–1, +1, –1, –1, +1, +1) = (–1, +1, –1, –1, +1, +1). Sender B does the same with its data to spread the signal with the code: B_s = B_d*B_k = –1*(+1, +1, –1, +1, –1, +1) = (–1, –1, +1, –1, +1, –1).
- Both signals are then transmitted at the same time using the same frequency, thus, the signals superimpose in space. Neglecting interference from other senders and environmental noise for this simple example, and assuming that the signals have the same strength at the receiver, the following signal C is received at a receiver: C = A_s+B_s = (–2, 0, 0, –2, +2, 0).

● The receiver now wants to receive data from sender A and, therefore, tunes
in to the code of A, i.e., applies A's code for despreading: $C*A_k = (-2, 0, 0, -2,$
$+2, 0)*(-1, +1, -1, -1, +1, +1) = 2 + 0 + 0 + 2 + 2 + 0 = 6$. As the result is much
larger than 0, the receiver detects a binary 1. Tuning in to sender B, i.e.,
applying B's code gives $C*B_k = (-2, 0, 0, -2, +2, 0)*(+1, +1, -1, +1, -1, +1) = -2$
$+ 0 + 0 - 2 - 2 + 0 = -6$. The result is negative, thus a 0 has been detected.

This example involved several simplifications. The codes were extremely simple,
but at least orthogonal. More importantly, noise was neglected. Noise would
add to the transmitted signal C, the results would not be as even with –6 and
+6, but would maybe be close to 0, making it harder to decide if this is still a
valid 0 or 1. Additionally, both signals are equally strong when they reach the
receiver. What would happen if, for example, B was much stronger? Let us for
instance assume that B's strength is five times A's strength. Then, $C' = A_s + 2*B_s =$
$(-1, +1, -1, -1, +1, +1) + (-5, -5, +5, -5, +5, -5) = (-6, -4, +4, -6, +6, -4)$. Again, a
receiver wants to receive B: $C'*B_k = -6 - 4 - 4 - 6 - 6 - 4 = -30$. It is easy to detect
the binary 0 sent by B. Now the receiver wants to receive A: $C'*A_k = 6 - 4 - 4 + 6$
$+ 6 - 4 = 6$. Clearly, the (absolute) value for the much stronger signal is higher
(30 compared to 6). While –30 might still be detected as 0, this is not so easy for
the 6 because compared to 30, 6 is quite close to zero and could be interpreted
as noise. Remember the party example. If one person speaks in one language
very loudly, it is of no more use to have another language as orthogonal code –
no one can understand you, your voice will only add to the noise. Although
extremely simplified, this example shows how essential power control is for
CDMA systems. This is one of the biggest problems CDMA systems face.

The following examples summarize the behaviour of CDMA together with
the DSSS spreading using orthogonal codes. The examples now use longer codes
or key sequences (i.e., longer as a single bit). Code sequences in IS-95, for example, (a mobile phone system that uses CDMA) are $2^{42} - 1$ chips long, the
chipping rate is 1228800 chips/s (i.e., the code repeats after 41.425 days). More
details about CDMA can be found in Viterbi (1995).

Figure 3.14 shows a sender A that wants to transmit the bits 101. The key of
A is shown as signal and binary key sequence A_k. After spreading, i.e., XORing
A_d and A_k, the resulting signal is A_s.

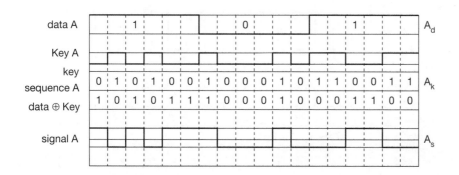

Figure 3.14
Coding and spreading of
data from sender A

Figure 3.15
Coding and spreading of
data from sender B

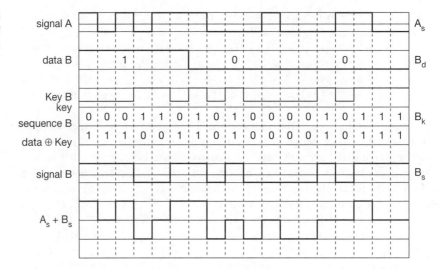

The same happens with data from sender B, here the bits are 100. The result of spreading with the code is the signal B_s. A_s and B_s now superimpose during transmission (again without noise and both signals having the same strength). Thus, the resulting signal is, simply the sum $A_s + B_s$ as shown in Figure 3.15.

A receiver now tries to reconstruct the original data from A, A_d. Therefore the receiver applies A's key, A_k, to the received signal and feeds the result into an integrator (see section 2.7.1). The integrator adds the products (i.e., calculates the inner product), a comparator then has to decide if the result is a 0 or a 1 (here simply inverted compared to the original data) as shown in Figure 3.16. As we can see, although the original signal form is distorted by B's signal, the result is still quite clear.

Figure 3.16
Reconstruction of A's
data

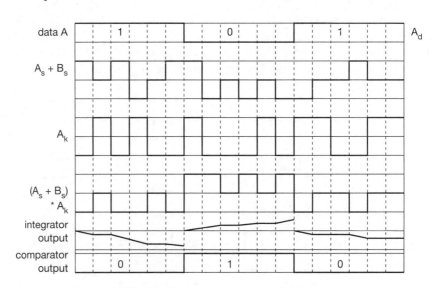

The same happens if a receiver wants to receive B's data (see Figure 3.17). The comparator can easily detect the original data. Looking at $(A_s+B_s)*B_k$ one can also imagine what could happen if A's signal was much stronger. The little peaks which are now caused by A's signal would be much higher, and thus the result of the integrator would be wrong.

Finally, Figure 3.18 shows what happens if a receiver has the wrong key or is not synchronized with the chipping sequence of the transmitter. The integrator still presents a value after each bit period, but now it is not always possible for the comparator to decide for a 1 or a 0, as the signal rather resembles noise. Even if the comparator could detect a clear 1, this could still not reconstruct the whole bit sequence transmitted by a sender.

3.5.1 Spread Aloha multiple access

As shown in the previous section, using different codes with certain properties for spreading data results in a nice multiple access scheme, namely CDMA. But CDMA senders and receivers are not really simple devices. Communicating with n devices requires programming of the receiver to be able to decode n different codes. While this scheme is valuable for connection-oriented services, like mobile phone services, it is too complicated for typical connectionless, bursty data traffic. Computers send data from time to time, maintaining codes might be too large an overhead. Aloha was a very simple, connection-less scheme, but could only provide a relatively low bandwidth due to collisions.

What happens if we combine the spreading of CDMA and the medium access of Aloha or, in other words, what if we use CDMA with only a single code, i.e., without CD? The resulting scheme is called **spread Aloha multiple access (SAMA)** and is a combination of CDMA and TDMA (Abramson, 1996).

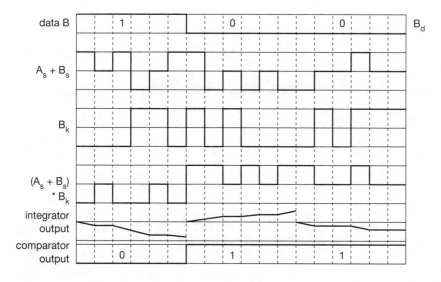

Figure 3.17
Reconstruction of B's data

Figure 3.18
Receiving a signal with
the wrong key

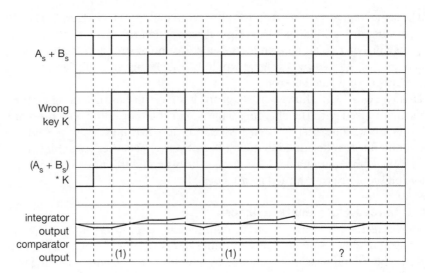

SAMA works as follow: each sender uses the same spreading code (in the example shown in Figure 3.19 this is the code 110101).[12] The standard case for Aloha access is shown in the upper part of the figure. Sender A and sender B access the medium at the same time in their narrowband spectrum, so that all three bits shown cause a collision.

The same data could also be transmitted sending with higher power for a shorter period as shown in the middle, but now spread spectrum is used to spread the shorter signals, i.e., to increase the bandwidth (spreading factor s = 6 in the example). Both signals are spread, but the chipping phase differs slightly. Thus, separation of the two signals is still possible if one receiver is synchronized to sender A and another one to sender B. The probability of a 'collision' is quite low if the number of simultaneous transmitters stays below 0.1–0.2s (Abramson, 1996)

Figure 3.19
Spread Aloha multiple
access

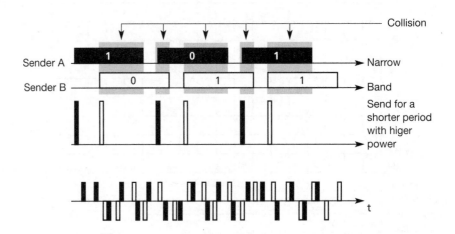

(also depending on the noise level of the environment). The main problem of this approach is finding good chipping sequences. Clearly, the code is not orthogonal to itself – it should have a good autocorrelation, but at the same time correlation should be low if the phase differs slightly. The maximum throughput is about 18 per cent, which is very similar to Aloha, but in addition the approach benefits from the advantages of spread spectrum techniques.

3.6 Comparison of S/T/F/CDMA

To conclude the chapter, a comparison of the four basic multiple access versions is given in Table 3.1. The table shows the MAC schemes without combination with other schemes. However, in real systems, the MAC schemes always occur in combinations. A very typical combination is constituted by SDMA/TDMA/FDMA as used in IS-54, GSM, DECT, PHS, and PACS phone systems, or the Iridium and ICO satellite systems. CDMA together with SDMA is used in the IS-95 mobile phone system and the Globalstar satellite system (see chapters 4 and 5).

Although many network providers and manufacturers have lowered their expectations regarding the performance of CDMA compared to the early 1980s due to experiences with the IS-95 mobile phone system, CDMA will be integrated into the future mobile phone system following the European UMTS proposal. CDMA can be used in combination with FDMA/TDMA access schemes to increase the capacity of a cell. In contrast to other schemes, CDMA has the advantage of a soft handover and soft capacity. Handover, explained in more detail in chapter 4, describes the switching from one cell to another, i.e., changing the base station that a mobile station is connected to. Soft handover means that a mobile station can smoothly switch cells, which is achieved by communicating with two base stations at the same time. With CDMA this is done using the same codes. TDMA/FDMA systems perform a hard handover, i.e., they switch base station and hopping sequences (time/frequency) precisely at the moment of handover. Handover decision is based on the signal strength, and oscillations between base stations are possible.

Soft capacity in CDMA systems describe the fact that CDMA systems can add more and more users to a cell, i.e., there is no hard limit. For TDMA/FDMA systems, a hard upper limit exists – if no more free time/frequency slots are available, the system rejects new users. If a new user is added to a CDMA cell, the noise level rises and the cell shrinks, but the user can still communicate. However, the shrinking of a cell can cause a problem, as other users could now drop out of the cell. Thus, cell planning is more difficult in CDMA systems compared to the more fixed TDMA/FDMA schemes.

While mobile phone systems using SDMA/TDMA/FDMA or SDMA/CDMA are centralized systems – a base station controls many mobile stations – arbitrary wireless communication systems need different MAC algorithms. As shown in the previous section, most distributed systems use some version of the basic

Approach	SDMA	TDMA	FDMA	CDMA
Idea	Segment space into cells/sectors	Segment sending time into disjoint time-slots, demand driven or fixed patterns	Segment the frequency band into disjoint sub-bands	Spread the spectrum using orthogonal codes
Terminals	Only one terminal can be active in one cell/one sector	All terminals are active for short periods of time on the same frequency	Every terminal has its own frequency, uninterrupted	All terminals can be active at the same place at the same moment, uninterrupted
Signal separation	Cell structure/ directed antennas	Synchroniz-ation in the time domain	Filtering in the frequency domain	Code plus special receivers
Advantages	Very simple, increases capacity per km^2	Established, fully digital, very flexible	Simple, established, robust	Flexible, less planning needed, soft handover
Disadvantages	Inflexible, antennas typically fixed	Guard space needed (multipath propagation), synchroni-zation difficult	Inflexible, frequencies are a scarce resource	Complex receivers, needs more complicated power control for senders
Comment	Only in combination with TDMA, FDMA or CDMA useful	Standard in fixed networks, together with FDMA/SDMA used in many mobile networks	Typically combined with TDMA (frequency hopping patterns) and SDMA (frequency reuse)	Still faces some problems, higher complexity, lowered expectations; will be integrated with TDMA/FDMA

Aloha. Typically, Aloha is slotted and some reservation mechanisms are applied to guarantee access delay and bandwidth. Each of the schemes exhibits both advantages and disadvantages. Simple CSMA is very efficient at low load, MACA can overcome the problem of hidden or exposed terminals, and polling guarantees bandwidth. There is no single scheme that combines all benefits. That is the reason why, for example, the wireless LAN standard IEEE 802.11 combines all three schemes (see section 7.3). Polling is used to set up a time structure via a base station. A CSMA version is used to access the medium during uncoordinated periods, and additionally, MACA can be used to avoid hidden terminals or in cases where no base station exists.

3.7 Review exercises

1 What is the main physical reason for the failure of many MAC schemes known from wired networks? What is done in wired networks to avoid this effect?

2 Recall the problem of hidden and exposed terminals. What happens in the case of such terminals if Aloha, slotted Aloha, reservation Aloha, or MACA is used?

3 How does the near/far effect influence TDMA systems? What happens in CDMA systems? What are countermeasures in TDMA systems, what about CDMA systems?

4 Who performs the MAC algorithm for SDMA? What could be possible roles of mobile stations, base stations, and planning from the network provider?

5 What is the basic prerequisite for applying FDMA? How does this factor increase complexity compared to TDMA systems? How is MAC distributed if we consider the whole frequency space as presented in chapter 1?

6 Considering duplex channels, what are alternatives for implementation in wireless networks? What about typical wired networks?

7 What are the advantages of a fixed TDM pattern compared to random, demand driven TDM? Compare the efficiency in the case of several connections with fixed data rates or in the case of varying data rates. Now explain why traditional mobile phone systems use fixed patterns, while computer networks generally use random patterns. In the future, the main data being transmitted will be computer-generated data. How will this fact change mobile phone systems?

8 Explain the term interference in the space, time, frequency, and code domain. What are countermeasures in SDMA, TDMA, FDMA, and CDMA systems?

9 Assume all stations can hear all other stations. One station wants to transmit and senses the carrier idle. Why can a collision still occur after the start of transmission?

10 What are benefits of reservation schemes? How are collisions avoided during data transmission, why is the probability of collisions lower compared to classical Aloha? What are disadvantages of reservation schemes?

11 How can MACA still fail in case of hidden/exposed terminals? Think of mobile stations and changing transmission characteristics.

12 Which of the MAC schemes can give hard guarantees related to bandwidth and access delay?

13 How are guard spaces realized between users in CDMA?

14 Redo the simple CDMA example of section 3.5, but now add random 'noise' to the transmitted signal (−2,0,0,−2,+2,0). Add, for example, (1,−1,0,1,0,−1). In this case, what can the receiver detect for sender A and B respectively? Now include the near/far problem. How does this complicate the situation? What would be possible countermeasures?

3.8 References

Abramson, N. (1996) 'Wideband random access for the last mile', *IEEE Personal Communications*, 3 (6).

Abramson, N. (1997) 'The throughput of packet broadcasting channels', *IEEE Transactions on Communication*, COM-25, (1).

Halsall, F. (1996) *Data communications, computer networks and open systems*, Addison Wesley Longman.

Kleinrock, L.; Tobagi, F. (1975) 'Packet switching in radio channels: part 1 – carrier sense multiple-access modes and their throughput-delay characteristics', *IEEE Transactions on Communications*, COM-23, (12).

Viterbi, A. (1995) *CDMA: principles of spread spectrum communication*, Addison Wesley Longman.

Telecommunication systems

4

Digital cellular networks are the segment of the market for mobile and wireless devices which are growing most rapidly. They are the wireless extensions of traditional PSTN or ISDN networks and allow for nationwide or even worldwide seamless roaming with the same mobile phone. Today, these systems are mainly used for voice traffic. However, data traffic is continuously growing and, therefore, this chapter presents several technologies for wireless data transmission using cellular systems.[13]

The systems presented fit into the traditional telephony architecture and do not originate from computer networks. Thus, the basic versions typically implement a circuit-switched service, focused on voice, and only offer data rates of up to, e.g., 9.6 kbit/s. However, service is provided up to a speed of 250 km/h (e.g., using GSM in a car) where most other wireless systems fail.

The **worldwide market** figures for cellular networks are as follows. The most popular digital system is GSM, with approximately 40 per cent market share. (This system will be presented in section 4.1.) The analog AMPS system still holds 30 per cent, whereas the Japanese PDC holds 15 per cent. The remainder is split between CDMA or TDMA-based systems and other technologies. In **Europe** most people use the digital GSM system (over 60 million) with some still using analog systems (less than 10 million). Almost all newly bought phones are digital. The situation is different in the **US** and **Canada**. Here, more than 80 per cent use the analog AMPS system with over 60 million users in 1998. The digital market is split into TDMA, CDMA, and GSM systems with 5 million TDMA, 3.3 million CDMA, and 2 million GSM users. While in Europe only one digital system exists, the market is divided into several systems in the US. This leads to severe problems regarding coverage and service availability, and is one of the examples where market forces did not ensure improved services (compared to a common standard in Europe).

Figure 4.1 shows the worldwide number of subscribers of different mobile phone technologies (GSMData, 1998). The figure combines different versions of the same technology (e.g., GSM working on 900, 1800, and 1900 MHz). Predictions for 1999–2001 should be treated cautiously.

This chapter uses GSM as the main example for a fully digital mobile phone system, not only because of market success, but also due to the system architecture

Figure 4.1
Worldwide subscribers
of different mobile
phone technologies

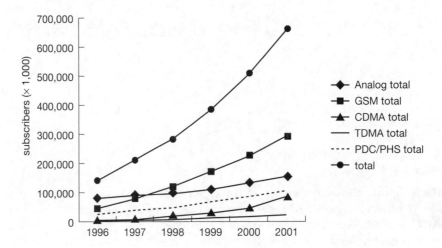

that served many other systems as an early example. Other systems adopted mobility management, mobile assisted handover and other basic ideas (Goodman, 1997). Furthermore, while the US systems typically focus on the air interface for their specification, a system like GSM has many open interfaces and network entities defined in the specification. While the first approach enables companies to have their own, proprietary solutions, the latter enables network providers to choose between many different products from different vendors.

After presenting GSM, the following sections will discuss DECT, the digital standard for cordless phones, and TETRA, the digital trunked radio. The main focus is always on data service, thus the evolution of GSM using higher data rates, packet-oriented transfer, and finally UMTS[14] are presented.

4.1 GSM

GSM represents today's most successful digital mobile telecommunication system – it is used by over 100 million people in more than 130 countries worldwide. Back in the early 1980s, Europe was facing the problem of many co-existing analog mobile phone systems, which were often based on similar standards (e.g., NMT 450), but running on slightly different carrier frequencies. To avoid this situation for a second generation fully digital system, the **groupe spéciale mobile (GSM)** was founded in 1982. Today, the system developed by this group is named **global system for mobile communications (GSM)**, with the specification process lying in the hands of ETSI (ETSI, 1999), (GSM MoU, 1999).

The primary goal of GSM was to provide a mobile phone system that allows roaming of users through Europe and provides voice services compatible to ISDN and other PSTN systems. The specification for the initial system already covers more than 5,000 pages; new services, in particular data services, now add even more specification details. Readers familiar with the ISDN reference model will recognize many similar acronyms, reference points, and interfaces. GSM standardization aims at adopting as much as possible.

GSM is a typical 2nd generation system, replacing the 1st generation analog systems, but not offering worldwide high data rates as the 3rd generation systems, such as UMTS, are promising. GSM has initially been deployed in Europe using 890-915 MHz for the uplinks and 935-960 MHz for downlinks – this system is now also sometimes called **GSM 900** to distinguish it from the later versions. These versions comprise GSM at 1800 MHz (1710–1785 MHz uplink, 1805–1880 MHz downlink), also called **DCS (digital cellular system) 1800**, and the GSM system mainly used in the US at 1900 MHz (1850–1910 MHz uplink, 1930–1990 MHz downlink), also called **PCS (personal communications service) 1900**.

The following section describes the architecture, services, and protocols of GSM that are common to all three solutions, **GSM 900**, **GSM 1800**, and **GSM 1900**. While GSM has mainly been designed for voice services and voice services still constitute the main use of GSM systems, one can foresee that many future applications for mobile communications will be data driven. Thus, the relation of data to voice traffic will shift more and more toward data.

4.1.1 Mobile services

GSM permits the integration of different voice and data services and the inter-working with existing networks. Services make a network interesting for customers. GSM has defined three different categories of services: bearer, tele, and supplementary services. These are described in the following subsections. Figure 4.2 shows a reference model for GSM services. A **mobile station MS** is connected to the **GSM public land mobile network (PLMN)** via the U$_m$ interface. (GSM-PLMN is the infrastructure needed for the GSM network.) This network is connected to transit networks, e.g., **integrated services digital network (ISDN)** or traditional **public switched telephone network (PSTN)**. There might be an additional network, the source/destination network, before another **terminal TE** is connected. **Bearer services** now comprise all services that enable the transparent transmission of data between the interfaces to the network, i.e., S in case of the mobile station, and a similar interface for the other terminal (e.g., S$_0$ for ISDN terminals). Interfaces like U, S, and R in case of ISDN have not been defined for all networks, thus it depends on the specific network which interface is used as a reference for the transparent transmission of data. In the classical GSM model, bearer services are connection-oriented and circuit- or packet-switched. These services only need the lower three layers of the ISO/OSI reference model.

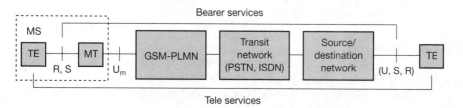

Bearer services

Tele services

Figure 4.2
Bearer and tele services reference model

Within the mobile station MS, the **mobile termination (MT)** performs all network specific tasks (TDMA, FDMA, coding etc.) and offers an interface for data transmission (S) to the terminal TE which can then be network independent. Depending on the capabilities of TE, further interfaces may be needed, such as R, according to the ISDN reference model (Halsall, 1996). **Tele services** are application specific and may thus need all seven layers of the ISO/OSI reference model. These services are specified end-to-end, i.e., from one terminal TE to another.

4.1.1.1 Bearer services

GSM specifies different mechanisms for data transmission, the original GSM allowing for data rates of up to 9600 bit/s for non-voice services. Bearer services permit transparent and non-transparent, synchronous or asynchronous data transmission. **Transparent bearer services** only use the functions of the physical layer (layer 1) to transmit data. Data transmission, thus, has a constant delay and throughput if no transmission errors occur. The only mechanism to increase transmission quality is the use of **forward error correction (FEC)**, which codes redundancy into the data stream and thus helps to reconstruct the original data in case of transmission errors. Depending on the FEC, data rates of 2.4, 4.8, or 9.6 kbit/s are possible. Transparent bearer services do not try to recover lost data in case of, for example, shadowing or interruptions due to handover.

Non-transparent bearer services use protocols of the layers two and three to implement error correction and flow control. These services use the transparent bearer services, adding a **radio link protocol (RLP)**. This protocol comprises mechanisms of **high-level data link control (HDLC)**, (Halsall, 1996) and special selective-reject mechanisms to trigger retransmission of erroneous data. The achieved bit error rate is less than 10^{-7}, but now throughput and delay may vary depending on transmission quality.

Using transparent and non-transparent services, GSM specifies several bearer services for interworking with PSTN, ISDN, and packet switched public data networks (PSPDN) like X.25, which is available worldwide. Data transmission can be full-duplex, synchronous with data rates of 1.2, 2.4, 4.8, and 9.6 kbit/s or full-duplex, asynchronous from 300 to 9,600 bit/s (ETSI, 1991a). Clearly, these relatively low data rates reflect the assumption that data services will only constitute some small percentage of the overall traffic. While this is still true in GSM networks today, the relation of data and voice services is changing, with data becoming more and more important. This development is also reflected in the new data services (see section 4.1.8).

4.1.1.2 Tele services

GSM mainly focuses on voice-oriented tele services. These comprise encrypted voice transmission, message services, and basic data communication with terminals as known from the PSTN or ISDN (e.g., fax). However, as the main service is

telephony, the primary goal of GSM was the provision of high-quality digital voice transmission, offering at least the typical bandwidth of 3.1 kHz of analog phone systems. Special codecs (coder/decoder) are used for voice transmission, while other codecs are used for the transmission of analog data for communication with traditional computer modems used in, e.g., fax machines.

Another service offered by GSM is the **emergency number**, the same number can be used throughout Europe. This service is mandatory for all providers and free of charge. This connection also has the highest priority, possibly pre-empting other connections, and will automatically be set up with the closest emergency centre.

A useful service for very simple message transfer is the **short message service (SMS)**, which offers transmission of messages of up to 160 characters. SMS messages do not use the standard data channels of GSM but exploit unused capacity in the signalling channels (see 4.1.3.1). Thus, sending and receiving of SMS is possible during data or voice transmission. SMS is typically used today for displaying road conditions, e-mail headers, stock quotes etc.

Another non-voice tele service is **group 3 fax**, which is available worldwide. In this service, fax data is transmitted as digital data over the analog telephone network according to the ITU-T standards T.4 and T.30 using modems. Typically, a transparent fax service is used, i.e., fax data and fax signalling is transmitted using a transparent bearer service. Lower transmission quality causes an automatic adaptation of the bearer service to lower data rates and higher redundancy for better FEC.

4.1.1.3 Supplementary services

In addition to tele and bearer services, GSM providers can offer **supplementary services**. Similar to ISDN networks, these services offer various enhancements for the standard telephony service. The services offered may vary from provider to provider. Typical services are user **identification**, call **redirection**, or **forwarding** of ongoing calls. Furthermore, standard ISDN features such as **closed user groups** and **multiparty** communication may be available. Closed user groups are of special interest for companies because they allow, for example, a company-specific GSM subnetwork, to which only members of the group have access.

4.1.2 System architecture

As with all systems in the telecommunication area, GSM comes with a hierarchical, complex system architecture comprising many entities, interfaces, and acronyms. Figure 4.3 gives a simplified overview of the GSM system as specified in ETSI (1991b). A GSM system consists of three subsystems, the **radio subsystem (RSS)**, the **network and switching subsystem (NSS)**, and the **operation subsystem (OSS)**. Each subsystem will be discussed in more detail in the following subsections. Generally, a GSM customer only notices a very small fraction of the whole network – the mobile stations (MS) and some antenna masts of the base transceiver stations (BTS).

Figure 4.3
Functional architecture
of a GSM system

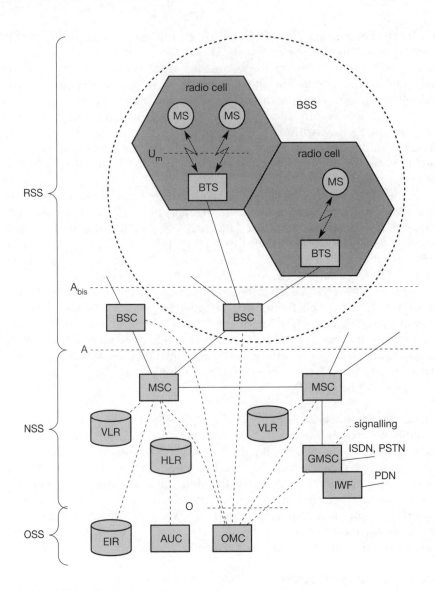

4.1.2.1 Radio subsystem

As the name implies, the **radio subsystem (RSS)** comprises all radio specific
entities, i.e., the **mobile stations (MS)** and the **base station subsystem (BSS)**.
Figure 4.3 shows the connection between the RSS and the NSS via the **A interface** (solid lines) and the connection to the OSS via the **O interface** (dashed
lines). The A interface is typically based on circuit-switched PCM-30 systems
(2.048 Mbit/s), carrying up to 30 64 kbit/s connections, whereas the O interface
uses the Signalling System No. 7 (SS7) based on X.25 carrying management data
to/from the RSS.

- **Base station subsystem (BSS):** A GSM network comprises many BSSs, each controlled by a base station controller (BSC). The BSS performs all functions necessary to maintain radio connections to an MS, coding/decoding of voice, and rate adaptation to/from the wireless network part. Besides a BSC, the BSS contains several BTSs.
- **Base transceiver station (BTS):** A BTS comprises all radio equipment, i.e., antennas, signal processing, amplifiers necessary for radio transmission. A BTS can form a radio cell or, using sectorized antennas, several cells (see section 2.8), and is connected to MS via the U_m **interface** (ISDN U interface for mobile use), and to the BSC via the A_{bis} **interface**. The U_m interface contains all mechanisms necessary for wireless transmission (TDMA, FDMA etc.) and will be discussed in more detail below. The A_{bis} interface consists of 16 or 64 kbit/s connections. A GSM cell can measure between some 100 m and 35 km depending on the environment (buildings, open space, mountains etc.) but also expected traffic.
- **Base station controller (BSC):** The BSC basically manages the BTSs. It reserves radio frequencies, handles the handover from one BTS to another within the BSS, and performs paging of the MS. The BSC also multiplexes the radio channels onto the fixed network connections at the A interface.

Table 4.1 gives an overview of the tasks assigned to the BSC and BTS or of tasks in which these entities support other entities in the network.

- **Mobile station (MS):** The MS comprises all user equipment and software needed for communication with a GSM network. An MS consists of user independent hard- and software and of the **subscriber identity module (SIM)**, which stores all user-specific data. While an MS can be identified via the **inter-**

Function	BTS	BSC
Management of radio channels		x
Frequency hopping	x	x
Management of terrestrial channels		x
Mapping of terrestrial onto radio channels		x
Channel coding and decoding	x	
Rate adaptation	x	
Encryption and decryption	x	x
Paging	x	x
Uplink signal measurement	x	
Traffic measurement		x
Authentication		x
Location registry, location update		x
Handover management		x

Table 4.1
Tasks of the BTS and BSC within a BSS

national mobile equipment identity (IMEI), a user can personalize any MS using his or her SIM, i.e., user-specific mechanisms like charging and authentication are based on the SIM, not on the device itself. Device specific mechanisms, e.g., theft protection, use the device specific EI. Without the SIM, only emergency calls are possible. Typical MSs for GSM 900 have a transmit power of up to 2 W, whereas for GSM 1800 1 W is enough due to the smaller cell size. Apart from the telephone interface, an MS can also offer other types of interfaces to users with display, loudspeaker, microphone, and programmable soft keys. Further interfaces comprise computer modems, IrDA, or Bluetooth. The SIM card contains many identifiers and tables, such as card-type, serial number, a list of subscribed services, a **personal identity number (PIN)**, a **PIN unblocking key (PUK)**, an **authentication key K_i**, and the **international mobile subscriber identity (IMSI)** (ETSI, 1991c). The PIN is used to unlock the MS, whereas using the wrong PIN three times will lock the SIM. In such cases, the PUK is needed for unlocking the SIM again. Furthermore, the MS stores dynamic information while logged into the GSM system, such as, e.g., the **cipher key Kc** and the location information consisting of a **temporary mobile subscriber identity (TMSI)** and the **location area identification (LAI)**. Typical MSs, e.g., mobile phones, comprise many more vendor-specific functions, such as using fingerprints as PIN, calendars, address functions, and even simple games.

4.1.2.2 Network and switching subsystem

The 'heart' of the GSM system is formed by the **network and switching subsystem (NSS)**. The NSS connects the wireless network with standard public networks, performs handovers between different BSSs, comprises functions for worldwide localization of users and supports charging, accounting, and roaming of users between different providers in different countries. The NSS consists of the following switches and databases:

- **Mobile services switching centre (MSC):** MSCs are high-performance digital ISDN switches. They set up connections to other MSCs and to the BSCs via the A interface. MSCs thus form the fixed backbone network of a GSM system. Typically, an MSC manages several BSCs of a geographical region. A **gateway MSC (GMSC)** has additional connections to other fixed networks, such as **PSTN** and **ISDN**. Using additional **interworking functions (IWF)**, an MSC can also connect to **public data networks (PDN)** such as X.25. An MSC handles all signalling needed for connection setup, connection release and handover of connections to other MSCs. For this purpose, the standard **signalling system No. 7 (SS7)** is used. An MSC also performs all functions needed for supplementary services such as call forwarding, multiparty calls, reverse charging etc.

- **Home location register (HLR):** The HLR is the most important database in a GSM system as it stores all user relevant information. This comprises static information, such as the **mobile subscriber ISDN number (MSISDN)**, sub-scribed services, and the authentication key K_i. Furthermore, dynamic information is needed, e.g., the current **location area (LA)** of the MS. As soon as an MS leaves its current LA, the information in the HLR is updated. This information is necessary to localize a user in the worldwide GSM networks. All these user-specific information elements only exist once for each user in a single HLR, which also supports charging and accounting.

● **Visitor location register (VLR):** The VLR associated to each MSC is a very dynamic database which stores all important information needed for the MS users currently in the LA that is associated to the MSC. If a new MS comes into an LA the VLR is responsible for, it copies all relevant information for this user from the HLR. This hierarchy of VLR and HLR avoids frequent HLR updates and long-distance signalling of user information. The typical use of HLR and VLR for user localization will be described in section 4.1.5.

4.1.2.3 Operation subsystem

The third part of a GSM system, the **operation subsystem (OSS)**, contains all functions necessary for network operation and maintenance. The OSS possesses network entities of its own and accesses other entities via SS7 signalling (see Figure 4.3). The following entities have been defined:

● **Operation and maintenance centre (OMC):** The OMC monitors and con-trols all other network entities via the O interface (SS7 with X.25). Typical OMC management functions are traffic monitoring, status reports of net-work entities, subscriber and security management, or accounting and billing. OMCs use the concept of **telecommunication management net-work (TMN)** as standardized by the ITU-T.

● **Authentication centre (AuC):** As the radio interface and mobile stations are particularly vulnerable, a separate AuC has been defined to protect user identity and data transmission. The AuC contains the algorithms for authentication as well as the keys for encryption and generates the values needed for user authentication in the HLR. The AuC may in fact be situated in a special protected part of the HLR.

● **Equipment identity register (EIR):** The EIR is a database for all IMEIs, i.e., it stores all device identifications registered for this network. As MSs are mobile, they can be easily stolen. With a valid SIM of their own, anyone could use the stolen MS. Thus, the EIR has a black list of stolen (or locked) devices. An MS is thus useless as soon as the owner has reported a theft. The EIR also contains a list of valid IMEIs, and a list of malfunctioning devices.

4.1.3 Radio interface

The most interesting interface in a GSM system is U_m, the radio interface, as it comprises many mechanisms presented in chapters 2 and 3 for multiplexing and media access. GSM implements SDMA using cells with BTS and assigns an

MS to a BTS. Furthermore, FDD is used to separate downlink and uplink as shown in Figure 4.4 and already in Figure 3.3. Media access combines TDMA and FDMA. In GSM 900, 124 channels, each 200 kHz wide, are used for FDMA, whereas in GSM 1800, 374 channels are used. The following example is based on the GSM 900 system, but GSM works similarly at 1800 and 1900 MHz.

While Figure 3.3 in chapter 3 has already shown the FDM in GSM, Figure 4.4 also shows the TDM used. Each of the 248 channels is additionally separated in time via a **GSM TDMA frame**, i.e., each 200 kHz carrier is subdivided into frames that are repeated continuously. The duration of a frame is 4.615 ms. A frame is again subdivided into 8 **GSM time-slots**, where each slot represents a physical TDM channel and lasts for 577 μs. Thus, each TDM channel occupies the 200 kHz carrier for 577 μs every 4.615 ms.

Data is transmitted in small portions, called **burst**. Figure 4.4 shows a so-called **normal burst** as used for data transmission inside a time-slot (user and signalling data). In the diagram, the burst is only 546.5 μs long and contains 148 bits. The remaining 30.5 μs are used as **guard space** to avoid overlapping with other bursts due to different path delays and to leave the transmitter time to turn on and off. Filling the whole slot with data allows for transmission of 156.25 bit within 577 μs. Thus, each physical TDM channel has a raw data rate of about 33.8 kbit/s, each radio carrier transmits approximately 270 kbit/s over the U_m interface.

Figure 4.4
GSM TDMA frame,
slots, and bursts

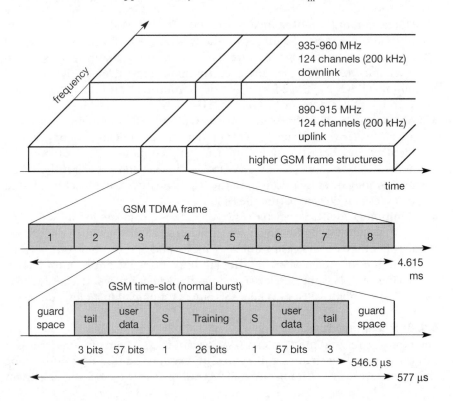

The first and last three bits of a normal burst (**tail**) are all set to 0 and can be used to enhance the receiver performance. The **training** sequence in the middle of a slot is used to adapt the parameters of the receiver to the current path propagation characteristics and to select the strongest signal in case of multipath propagation. A flag **S** indicates whether the **data** field contains user or network control data. Apart from the normal burst, ETSI (1993a) defines four more bursts for data transmission: a **frequency correction** burst allows the MS to correct the local oscillator to avoid interference with neighbouring channels, a **synchronization burst** with an extended training sequence synchronizes the MS with the BTS in time, an **access burst** is used for the initial connection setup between MS and BTS, and finally a **dummy burst** is used if no data is available for a slot.

Two factors allow for the use of simple transmitter hardware: on the one hand, the slots for uplink and downlink of a physical TDM channel are separated in frequency (45 MHz for GSM 900, 95 MHz for GSM 1800 using FDD). On the other hand, the TDMA frames are shifted in time for three slots, i.e., if the BTS sends data at time t_0 in slot one on the downlink, the MS accesses slot one on the uplink at time $t_0+3.577$ µs. An MS thus does not need a full-duplex transmitter, a simpler half-duplex transmitter switching between receiving and sending is enough.

In order to avoid frequency selective fading, GSM specifies an optional **slow frequency hopping** mechanism. MS and BTS may change the carrier frequency after each frame based on a common hopping sequence. An MS changes its frequency between up and downlink slots respectively.

4.1.3.1 Logical channels and frame hierarchy

While the previous section showed the physical separation of the medium into 8·124 duplex channels, this section presents logical channels and a hierarchy of frames based on the combination of these physical channels. A physical channel consists of a slot, repeated every 4.615 ms. Think of a logical channel C_1 that only takes up every fourth slot and another logical channel C_2 that uses every other slot. Both logical channels could use the same physical channel with the pattern $C_1C_2xC_2C_1C_2xC_2C_1$ etc. (The x indicates that the physical channel has still some capacity left.)

GSM specifies two basic groups of logical channels, i.e., traffic channels and control channels: [15]

- **Traffic channels (TCH):** GSM uses a TCH to transmit user data (e.g., voice, fax). Two basic categories of TCHs have been defined, i.e., **full-rate TCH (TCH/F)** and **half-rate TCH (TCH/H)**. A TCH/F has a data rate of 22.8 kbit/s, whereas TCH/H only has 11.4 kbit/s. With the voice codecs available at the beginning of the GSM standardization, 13 kbit/s were required, whereas the remaining capacity of the TCH/F was used for error correction **(TCH/FS)**.

Newer codes allow for better voice coding and can use a TCH/H. Using these TCH/Hs doubles the capacity of the GSM system for voice transmission. Data transmission is possible at many different data rates, e.g., **TCH/F4.8** for 4.8 kbit/s, **TCH/F9.6** for 9.6 kbit/s, and, as a newer specification, **TCH/F14.4** for 14.4 kbit/s. These logical channels differ in terms of their coding schemes and error correction capabilities.

- **Control channels (CCH):** Many different CCHs are used in a GSM system to control medium access, allocation of traffic channels or mobility management. Three groups of control channels have been defined, each again with subchannels (maybe you can imagine why the specification needs over 5,000 pages):

  - **Broadcast control channel (BCCH):** A BTS uses this channel to signal information to all MSs within a cell. Information transmitted in this channel is, e.g., the cell identifier, options available within this cell (frequency hopping), and frequencies available inside the cell and in neighbouring cells. Furthermore, the BTS sends information for frequency correction via the **frequency correction channel (FCCH)** and information about time synchronization via the **synchronization channel (SCH)**, where both channels are subchannels of the BCCH.

  - **Common control channel (CCCH):** Via the CCCH all information regarding connection setup between MS and BS is exchanged. For calls toward an MS, the BTS uses the **paging channel (PCH)** for paging the appropriate MS. If an MS wants to set up a call, it uses the **random access channel (RACH)** to send data to the BTS. The RACH implements multiple access (all MSs within a cell may access this channel) using slotted Aloha. This is a place where a collision may occur with other MSs in a GSM system. The BTS uses the **access grant channel (AGCH)** to signal an MS that it can use a TCH or SDCCH for further connection setup.

  - **Dedicated control channel (DCCH):** While the previous channels have all been unidirectional, the following channels are bidirectional. As long as an MS has not established a TCH with the BTS, it uses the **stand-alone dedicated control channel (SDCCH)** with a low data rate (782 bit/s) for signalling. This signalling can comprise authentication, registration or other data needed for setting up a TCH. Each TCH and SDCCH has a **slow associated dedicated control channel (SACCH)** associated with it. This channel is used to exchange system information, such as the channel quality and signal power level. Finally, if more signalling information needs to be transmitted and a TCH already exists, GSM uses a **fast associated dedicated control channel (FACCH)**. The FACCH uses the time slots which are otherwise used by the TCH and is necessary, e.g., in case of handovers where BTS and MS have to exchange larger amounts of data in less time.

However, these channels cannot use time slots arbitrarily – GSM specifies a very elaborate multiplexing scheme that integrates several hierarchies of frames. If we take a simple TCH/F for user data transmission, each TCH/F will have an associated SACCH for slow signalling, and if fast signalling is required, the FACCH uses the time slots for the TCH/F. A typical usage pattern of a physical channel for data transmission now looks like this (with T indicating the user traffic in the TCH/F and S indicating the signalling traffic in the SACCH):

TTTTTTTTTTTTSTTTTTTTTTTTTx
TTTTTTTTTTTTSTTTTTTTTTTTTx

Twelve slots with user data are followed by a signalling slot. Again 12 slots with user data follow, then an unused slot. This pattern of 26 slots is repeated over and over again. In this case, only 24 out of 26 physical slots are used for the TCH/F. Now recall that each normal burst used for data transmission carries 114 bit user data and is repeated every 4.615 ms. This results in a data rate of 24.7 kbit/s. As the TCH/F only uses 24/26 of the slots, the final data rate is 22.8 kbit/s as specified for the TCH/F. The SACCH thus has a capacity of 950 bit/s.

This periodic pattern of 26 slots occurs in all TDMA frames with a TCH. The combination of these frames is called **traffic multiframe**. Figure 4.5 shows the

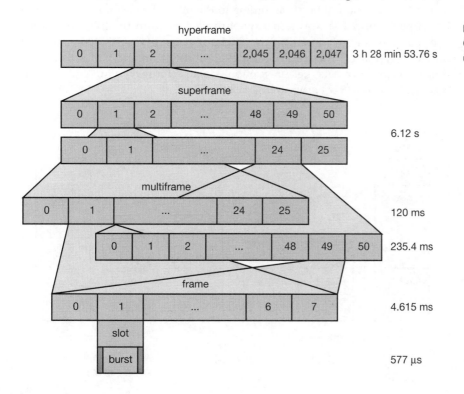

Figure 4.5
GSM structuring of time using a frame hierarchy

logical combination of 26 frames (TDMA frames with a duration of 4.615 ms) to a multiframe with a duration of 120 ms. This type of multiframe is used for TCHs, for SACCHs for TCHs, and for FACCHs. As these logical channels are all associated with user traffic, the multiframe is called traffic multiframe. TDMA frames containing (signalling) data for the other logical channels are combined to a **control multiframe**. Control multiframes consist of 51 TDMA frames and have a duration of 235.4 ms.

This logical frame hierarchy continues, combining 26 multiframes with 51 frames or 51 multiframes with 26 frames to form a **superframe**. 2,048 superframes build a **hyperframe** with a duration of almost 3.5 hours. Altogether, 2,715,648 TDMA frames form a hyperframe. This large logical structure is needed for encryption – GSM counts each TDMA frame, with the frame number forming input for the encryption algorithm. Furthermore, frame number plus slot number uniquely identifies each time slot in GSM.

4.1.4 Protocols

Figure 4.6 shows the protocol architecture of GSM with signalling protocols, interfaces, as well as the entities already shown in Figure 4.3. Again, the main interest lies in the U_m interface, as the other interfaces occur between entities in a fixed network. **Layer 1**, the physical layer, handles all **radio**-specific functions. This includes the creation of bursts according to the five different formats, **multiplexing** of bursts into a TDMA frame, **synchronization** with the BTS, detection of idle channels, and measurement of the **channel quality** on the downlink. The physical layer at U_m uses GMSK for digital **modulation** and performs **encryption/decryption** of data, i.e., encryption is not performed end-to-end, but only between MS and BTS over the air interface.

Figure 4.6
Protocol
architecture for
signalling

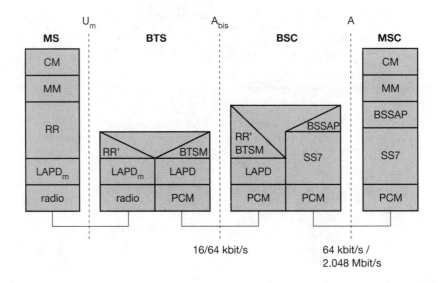

Synchronization also includes the correction of the individual path delay between an MS and the BTS. All MSs within a cell use the same BTS and thus must be synchronized to this BTS. The BTS generates the time-structure of frames, slots etc. A problematic aspect in this context are the different round trip times (RTT). An MS close to the BTS has a very short RTT, whereas an MS 35 km away already exhibits an RTT of around 0.23 ms. If the MS far away used the slot structure without correction, large guard spaces would be required, as 0.23 ms are already 40 per cent of the 0.577 ms available for each slot. Therefore, the BTS sends the current RTT to the MS, which then adjusts its access time so that all bursts reach the BTS within their limits. This mechanism reduces the guard space to only 30.5 µs or 5 per cent (see Figure 4.4). Adjusting the access is controlled via the variable **timing advance**, where a burst can be shifted up to 63 bit times earlier, with each bit having a duration of 3.69 µs (which results in the 0.23 ms needed).

The main tasks of the physical layer comprise **channel coding** and **error detection/correction**, which is directly combined with the coding mechanisms. Channel coding makes extensive use of different **forward error correction (FEC)** schemes. FEC adds redundancy to user data, thus allowing for the detection and correction of selected errors. The power of an FEC scheme depends on the amount of redundancy, coding algorithm, and further interleaving of data to minimize the effects of burst errors. The FEC is also the reason why error detection and correction occurs in layer one and not in layer two as in the ISO/OSI reference model. The GSM physical layer tries to correct errors, but it does not deliver erroneous data to the higher layer.

Different logical channels of GSM use different coding schemes with different correction capabilities. Speech channels need additional coding of voice data after analog to digital conversion, in order to achieve a data rate of 22.8 kbit/s (using the 13 kbit/s from the voice codec plus redundancy, CRC bits, and interleaving (Goodman, 1997). As voice was assumed to be the main service in GSM, the physical layer also contains special functions, such as **voice activity detection (VAD)**, which transmits voice data only when there is a voice signal. During periods of silence (e.g., if a user needs time to think before talking), the physical layer generates a **comfort noise** to fake a connection (complete silence would probably confuse a user), but no actual transmission takes place.

All this interleaving of data for a channel to minimize interference due to burst errors and the recurrence pattern of a logical channel generate a **delay** for transmission. The delay is about 60 ms for a TCH/FS and 100 ms for a TCH/F9.6. These times have to be added to the transmission delay if communicating with an MS instead of a standard fixed station (telephone, computer etc.) and may influence the performance of any higher layer protocols, e.g., for computer data transmission.

Signalling between entities in a GSM network requires higher layers (see Figure 4.6). For this purpose, the **LAPD$_\mathrm{m}$** protocol has been defined at the U$_\mathrm{m}$

interface for **layer two**. LAPD$_m$, as the name already implies, has been derived from link access procedure for the D-channel (**LAPD**) in ISDN systems, which is a version of HDLC (Goodman, 1997), (Halsall, 1996). LAPD$_m$ is a lightweight LAPD because it does not need synchronization flags or checksumming for error detection. (The GSM physical layer already performs these tasks.) LAPD$_m$ offers reliable data transfer over connections, re-sequencing of data frames, and flow control (ETSI, 1993b), (ETSI, 1993c). As there is no buffering between layer one and two, LAPD$_m$ has to obey the frame structures, recurrence patterns etc. defined for the U$_m$ interface. Further services provided by LAPD$_m$ include segmentation and reassembly of data and acknowledged/unacknowledged data transfer.

The network layer in GSM, **layer three**, comprises several sublayers as Figure 4.6 shows. The lowest sublayer is the **radio resource management (RR)**. Only a part of this layer, **RR'**, is implemented in the BTS, the remainder is situated in the BSC. The functions of RR' are supported by the BSC via the **BTS management (BTSM)**. The main tasks of RR are setup, maintenance, and release of radio channels. RR also directly accesses the physical layer for radio information and offers a reliable connection to the next higher layer.

Mobility management (MM) contains functions for registration, authentication, identification, location updating, and the provision of a **temporary mobile subscriber identity (TMSI)** that replaces the **international mobile subscriber identity (IMSI)** and is needed to hide the real identity of an MS user over the air interface. While the IMSI identifies a user, the TMSI is valid only in the current location area of a VLR. MM offers a reliable connection to the next higher layer.

Finally, the **call management (CM)** layer contains three entities: **call control (CC)**, **short message service (SMS)**, and **supplementary service (SS)**. SMS allows for message transfer using the control channels SDCCH and SACCH (if no signalling data is sent), while SS offers the services described in 4.1.1.3. CC provides a point-to-point connection between two terminals and is used by higher layers for call establishment, call clearing and change of call parameters. This layer also provides functions to send in-band tones, called **dual tone multiple frequency (DTMF)**, over the GSM network. These tones are used, e.g., for remote control of answering machines or entry of PINs for electronic banking, also for dialling in traditional analog telephone systems. These tones cannot be sent directly over the voice codec of a GSM MS, as the codec would distort the tones. Thus, these tones are transferred as signals and then converted into tones in the fixed network part of the GSM system.

Additional protocols are used at the A$_{bis}$ and A interfaces (and the internal interfaces of a GSM system not presented here). Data transmission at the physical layer is typically done using **pulse code modulation (PCM)** systems. While PCM systems offer transparent 64 kbit/s channels, GSM also allows for the sub-multiplexing of four 16 kbit/s channels into a single 64 kbit/s channel (16 kbit/s are enough for user data from an MS). The physical layer at the A interface typically includes leased lines with 2.048 Mbit/s capacity. LAPD is used for layer two at A$_{bis}$, BTSM for BTS management.

For signalling between an MSC and a BSC, the **signalling system No. 7 (SS7)** is used. This protocol also transfers all management information between MSCs, HLR, VLRs, AuC, EIR, and OMC. Additionally, an MSC can control a BSS via a **BSS application part (BSSAP)**.

4.1.5 Localization and calling

One fundamental feature of the GSM system is the automatic, worldwide local-ization of users. The system always knows where a user currently is, and the same phone number is valid worldwide. To provide this service, GSM performs periodic location updates even if a user does not use the mobile station (pro-vided that the MS is still logged into the GSM network and is not completely switched off). The HLR always contains information about the current location, and the VLR currently responsible for the MS informs the HLR about location changes. As soon as an MS moves into the range of a new VLR, the HLR sends all user data needed to the new VLR. Changing VLRs with uninterrupted avail-ability of all services is also called **roaming**. Roaming can take place within the network of one provider, between two providers in one country (national roam-ing, typically not supported), but also between different providers in different countries (international roaming).

To locate an MS and to address the MS, several numbers are needed:

- **Mobile station international ISDN number (MSISDN):**[16] The only impor-tant number for a user of GSM is the phone number. Remember that the phone number is not associated with a certain device but with the SIM, which is personalized for a user. The MSISDN follows the ITU-T standard E.164 for addresses as it is also used in fixed ISDN networks. This number consists of the **country code (CC)** (e.g., 49 for Germany; some countries need special prefixes, e.g., 009 or 00), the **national destination code (NDC)** (i.e., the address of the network provider and HLR), and the **subscriber number (SN)**.

- **International mobile subscriber identity (IMSI):** GSM uses the IMSI for internal unique identification of a subscriber. IMSI consists of a **mobile country code (MCC)** (e.g., 240 for Sweden, 208 for France), the **mobile network code (MNC)** (i.e., the code of the HLR), and finally the **mobile subscriber identification number (MSIN)**.

- **Temporary mobile subscriber identity (TMSI):** To hide the IMSI, which would give away the exact identity of the user which is signalling over the air interface, GSM uses the 4 byte TMSI for local subscriber identifica-tion. TMSI is selected by the current VLR and is only valid temporarily and within the location area of the VLR. Additionally, a VLR changes the TMSI periodically.

- **Mobile station**[17] **roaming number (MSRN):** Another temporary address that hides the identity and location of a subscriber is MSRN. The VLR gener-ates this address upon request from the MSC, and the address is also stored in the HLR. MSRN contains the current **visitor country code (VCC)**, the **visitor national destination code (VNDC)**, the identification of the current MSC together with the subscriber number. Thus, the MSRN helps the HLR to find a subscriber for an incoming call.

All these numbers are needed to find a subscriber and to maintain the connection with a mobile station. The interesting case is the **mobile terminated call (MTC)**, i.e., a situation in which a station calls a mobile station (the calling station could be outside the GSM network or another mobile station). Figure 4.7 shows the basic steps needed to connect the calling station with the mobile user. In step 1, a user dials the phone number of a GSM subscriber. The fixed network (PSTN) notices (looking at the destination code) that the number belongs to a user in the GSM network and forwards the call setup to the Gateway MSC (2). The GMSC identifies the HLR for the subscriber (which is coded in the phone number) and signals the call setup to the HLR (3). The HLR now checks whether the number exists and whether the user has subscribed to the requested services, and requests an MSRN from the current VLR (4). After receiving the MSRN (5), the HLR can determine the MSC responsible for the MS and forwards this information to the GMSC (6). The GMSC can now forward the call setup request to the MSC indicated (7).

From this point on, the MSC is responsible for all further steps. First, it requests the current status of the MS from the VLR (8). If the MS is available, the MSC initiates paging in all cells it is responsible for (10), as searching for the

Figure 4.7
Mobile terminated
call (MTC)

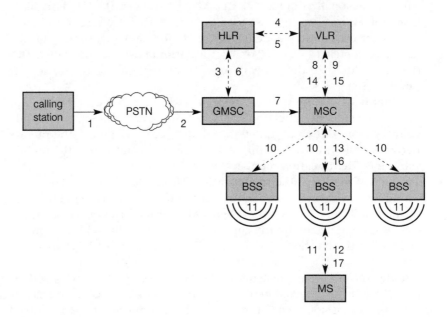

right cell would be too time consuming. The BTSs of all BSSs transmit this paging signal to the MS (11). If the MS answers (12 and 13), the VLR has to perform security checks (set up encryption etc.). The VLR then signals to the MSC to set up a connection to the MS (steps 15 to 17).

It is much simpler to perform a **mobile originated call (MOC)** compared to a MTC (see Figure 4.8). The MS transmits a request for a new connection (1), the BSS forwards this request to the MSC (2). The MSC then checks if this user is allowed to set up a call with the requested service (3 and 4) and checks the availability of resources through the GSM network and into the PSTN. If all resources are available, the MSC sets up a connection between the MS and the fixed network.

In addition to the steps mentioned above, some more messages are exchanged between an MS and BTS during connection setup (in either direction). Figure 4.9 shows the messages for an MTC and MOC. Paging is only necessary for an MTC, then similar message exchanges follow. The first step in this context is the channel access via the random access channel (RACH) with consecutive channel assignment; the channel assigned could be a traffic channel (TCH) or a slower signalling channel SDCCH.

The next steps, which are needed for communication security, comprise the authentication of the MS and the switching to encrypted communication. Now the system assigns a TCH (if this has not been done). Assigning a TCH at this point brings the advantage of only having to use an SDCCH during the first setup steps. If the setup fails, no TCH has been blocked. Using a TCH from the beginning, however, brings a speed advantage.

The following steps depend on the use of MTC or MOC. If someone is calling the MS, it answers now with 'alerting' that the MS is ringing and with 'connect' that the user has pressed the connect button. The same actions happen the other way round if the MS has initiated the call. After connection acknowledgement, both parties can exchange data.

Closing the connection comprises a user-initiated disconnect message (both sides can do this), followed by releasing the connection and the radio channel.

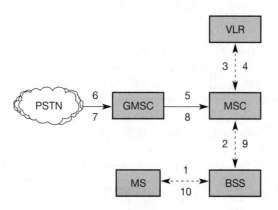

Figure 4.8
Mobile originated call (MOC)

Figure 4.9
Message flow for
MTC and MOC

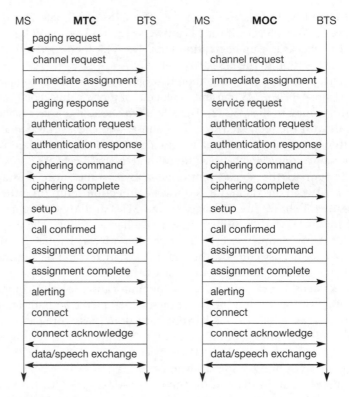

4.1.6 Handover

Cellular systems require **handover** procedures, as single cells do not cover the whole service area, but, e.g., only up to 35 km around each antenna (Tripathi, 1998). The smaller the cell size and the faster the movement of a mobile station through the cells (up to 250 km/h for GSM), the more handovers of ongoing calls are required. However, a handover should not cause a cut-off, also called **call drop**.

There are two basic reasons for a handover (about 40 have been identified in the standard):

- The mobile station **moves out of the range** of a BTS or a certain antenna of a BTS respectively. Thus, the received **signal level** becomes lower continuously until it falls underneath the minimal requirements for communication. Or the **error rate** may grow due to interference, the distance to the BTS may be too high (max. 35 km) etc. – all these effects may diminish the **quality of the radio link** and make radio transmission impossible in the near future.
- The wired infrastructure (MSC, BSC) may decide that the **traffic in one cell is too high** and shift some MS to other cells with a lower load (if possible). Thus, handover may be due to **load balancing**.

Figure 4.10 shows four possible handover scenarios in GSM:

- **Intra-cell handover:** Within a cell, narrow-band interference could make transmission at a certain frequency impossible. The BSC could then decide to change the carrier frequency (scenario 1).
- **Inter-cell, intra-BSC handover:** This is a typical handover scenario. The mobile station moves from one cell to another, but stays within the control of the same BSC. The BSC then performs a handover, assigns a new radio channel in the new cell and releases the old one (scenario 2).
- **Inter-BSC, intra-MSC handover:** As a BSC only controls a limited number of cells, GSM also has to perform handovers between cells controlled by different BSCs. This handover then has to be controlled by the MSC (scenario 3). This situation is also shown in Figure 4.12.
- **Inter MSC handover:** Finally, a handover could be required between two cells belonging to different MSCs. Now both MSCs perform the handover together (scenario 4).

In order to provide all information necessary for a handover due to a weak link, MS and BTS both perform periodic measurements of the downlink and uplink quality respectively. (Link quality comprises signal level and bit error rate.) Measurement reports are sent by the MS about every half-second and contain the quality of the current link used for transmission as well as the quality of certain channels in neighbouring cells (the BCCHs).

Figure 4.11 shows the typical behaviour of the received signal level while an MS moves away from one BTS (BTS_{old}) closer to another one (BTS_{new}). In this case, the handover decision does not depend on the actual value of the received signal level, but on the average value. Therefore, the BSC collects all values (bit

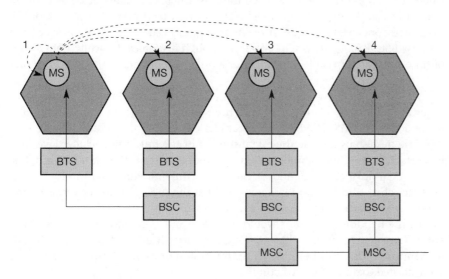

Figure 4.10
Types of handover
in GSM

Figure 4.11
Handover decision
depending on
receive level

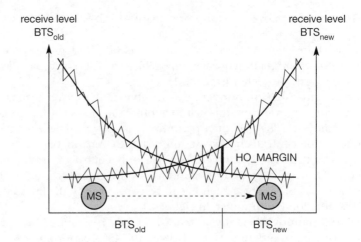

error rate and signal levels from uplink and downlink) from BTS and MS and calculates average values. These values are then compared to thresholds, i.e., the handover margin (HO_MARGIN), which includes some hysteresis to avoid a ping-pong effect (Wong, 1997). (Without hysteresis, even short-term interference, e.g., shadowing due to a building, could cause a handover.) Still, even with the HO_MARGIN, the ping-pong effect may occur in GSM – a value which is too high could cause a cut-off, and a value which is too low could cause too many handovers.

Figure 4.12 shows the typical signal flow during an inter-BSC, intra-MSC handover. The MS sends its periodic measurements reports, the BTS_{old} forwards these reports to the BSC_{old} together with its own measurements. Based on these values and, e.g., on current traffic conditions, the BSC_{old} may decide to perform a handover and sends the message HO_required to the MSC. The task of the MSC then comprises the request of the resources needed for the handover from the new BSC, BSC_{new}. This BSC checks if enough resources (typically frequencies or time slots) are available and activates a physical channel at the BTS_{new} to prepare for the arrival of the MS.

The BTS_{new} acknowledges the successful channel activation, BSC_{new} acknowledges the handover request. The MSC then issues a handover command that is forwarded to the MS. The MS now breaks its old radio link and accesses the new BTS. The next steps include the establishment of the link (this includes layer two link establishment and handover complete messages from the MS). Basically, the MS has then finished the handover, but it is furthermore important to release the resources at the old BSC and BTS and to signal the successful handover using the handover and clear complete messages as shown.

Future handover scenarios would include seamless handover between different systems, e.g., from GSM to DECT or satellite-based services without interruption. This can be done using multimode mobile stations and a more sophisticated roaming infrastructure.

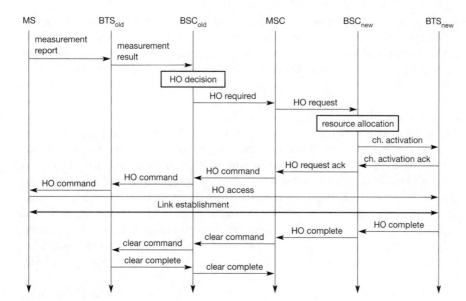

Figure 4.12
Intra-MSC handover

4.1.7 Security

GSM offers several security services using confidential information stored in the AuC and in the individual SIM (which is plugged into an arbitrary MS). As stated above, the SIM stores personal, secret data and is protected with a PIN against unauthorized use. (For example, the secret key K_i used for authentication and encryption procedures is stored in the SIM.) The security services offered by GSM are explained in the following:

- **Access control and authentication:** The first step includes the authentication of a valid user for the SIM. The user needs a secret PIN to access the SIM. The next step is the subscriber authentication (see Figure 4.9). This step is based on a challenge-response scheme as presented in 4.1.7.1.
- **Confidentiality:** All user-related data is encrypted. After authentication, BTS and MS apply encryption to voice, data, and signalling as shown in section 4.1.7.2. This confidentiality exists only between MS and BTS, but it does not exist end-to-end or within the whole fixed GSM/telephone network.
- **Anonymity:** To provide user anonymity, all data is encrypted before transmission, and user identifiers which would reveal an identity are not used over the air. Instead, GSM transmits a temporary identifier (TMSI), which is newly assigned by the VLR after each location update. Additionally, the VLR can change the TMSI at any time.

Three algorithms have been specified to provide security services in GSM. The **algorithm A3** is used for **authentication**, **A5** for **encryption**, and **A8** for the **generation of a cipher key**. In the GSM standard only the algorithm A5 was publicly available, whereas A3 and A8 were secret, but standardized with open interfaces.

Both A3 and A8 are not secret anymore but were published on the Internet in 1998. This is a good example that security by obscurity does not really work. As it turned out, the algorithms are not very strong. However, network providers can use stronger algorithms for authentication – or users can apply stronger end-to-end encryption.

4.1.7.1 Authentication

Before a subscriber can use any service from the GSM network, he or she must be authenticated. Authentication is based on the SIM, which stores the **individual authentication key K_i**, the **user identification IMSI**, and the algorithm used for authentication **A3**. Authentication uses a challenge-response method: the access control AC generates a random number **RAND** as challenge, and the SIM within the MS answers with **SRES** (signed response) as response (see Figure 4.13). The AuC performs the basic generation of random values RAND, signed responses SRES, and cipher keys K_c for each IMSI, and then forwards this information to the HLR. The current VLR requests the appropriate values for RAND, SRES, and K_c from the HLR.

For authentication, the VLR sends the random value RAND to the SIM. Both sides, network and subscriber module, perform the same operation with RAND and the key K_i, called A3. The MS sends back the SRES generated by the SIM, the VLR can now compare both values. If they are the same, the VLR accepts the subscriber, otherwise the subscriber is rejected.

Figure 4.13
Subscriber
authentication

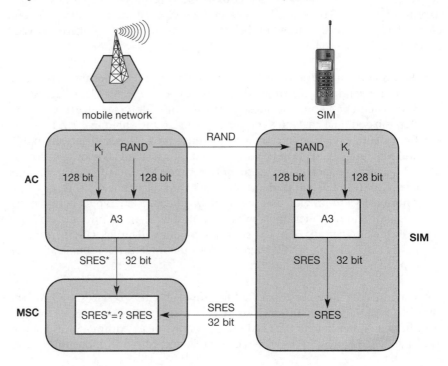

4.1.7.2 Encryption

To ensure privacy, all messages containing user-related information are encrypted in GSM. After authentication, MS and BTS can start using encryption by applying the cipher key K_c. K_c is generated using the individual key K_i and a random value by applying the algorithm A8. Note that the SIM in the MS and the network both calculate the same K_c based on the random value RAND. The key K_c itself is not transmitted over the air interface.

MS and BTS can now encrypt and decrypt data using the algorithm A5 and the cipher key K_c. As Figure 4.14 shows, K_c should be a 64 bit key – which is not very strong, but at least a good protection against simple eavesdropping. However, the publication of A3 and A8 on the Internet showed that in certain implementations 10 of the 64 bits are always set to 0, so that the real length of the key is thus only 54, and consequently the encryption is much weaker.

4.1.8 New data services

As mentioned above, the standard bandwidth of 9.6 kbit/s (14.4 kbit/s with some providers) available for data transmission is not much compared to the requirements of today's computers. When GSM was developed, not many people anticipated the tremendous growth of data communication compared to voice communication. At that time, 9.6 kbit/s was a lot, or at least enough for standard group 3 fax machines. But over the last years, people noticed that this

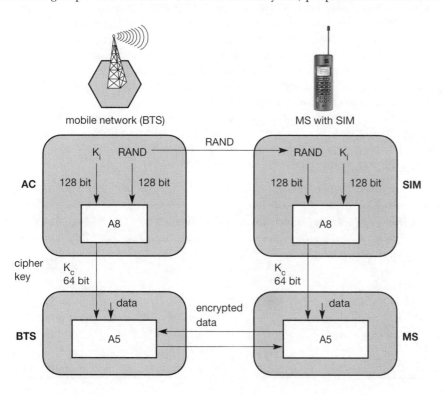

Figure 4.14
Data encryption

was not enough for the requirements of, e.g., web browsing, file download, or even intensive e-mail exchange with attachments.

In order to enhance the data transmission capabilities of GSM, two basic approaches are possible. As the basic GSM is based on connection-oriented traffic channels, e.g., with 9.6 kbit/s each, several channels could be combined to increase bandwidth. This system is called HSCSD and is presented in the following section. A somewhat more progressive step is the introduction of packet- oriented traffic in GSM, i.e., shifting the paradigm from connections/telephone thinking to packets/Internet thinking. The system, called GPRS, is presented in section 4.1.8.2.

4.1.8.1 HSCSD

A straightforward improvement of GSM's data transmission capabilities is **high speed circuit switched data (HSCSD)**, which is already available with some providers. In this system, higher data rates are achieved by bundling several TCHs. An MS requests one or more TCHs from the GSM network, i.e., it allocates several TDMA slots within a TDMA frame. This allocation can be asymmetrical, i.e., more slots can be allocated on the downlink than on the uplink, which fits the typical user behaviour of downloading more data compared to uploading. Basically, HSCSD only requires software upgrades in an MS and MSC (both have to be able to split a traffic stream into several streams, using a separate TCH each, and to combine these streams again).

In theory, an MS could use all eight slots within a TDMA frame to achieve an **air interface user rate (AIUR)** of, e.g., 8 TCH/F14.4 channels or 115.2 kbit/s (ETSI, 1998e). One problem of this configuration is that the MS is required to send and receive at the same time. Standard GSM does not require this capability – uplink and downlink slots are always shifted for three slots. ETSI (1997a) specifies the AIUR available at 57.6 kbit/s (duplex) using four slots in the uplink and downlink (Table 4.2 shows the permitted combinations of traffic channels and allocated slots for non-transparent services).

Although it appears attractive at first glance, HSCSD exhibits some major disadvantages. It still uses the connection-oriented mechanisms of GSM which are not at all efficient for computer data traffic, which is typically bursty. While downloading a larger file may require all channels reserved, typical web browsing would leave the

Table 4.2
Available data
rates for HSCSD in
GSM

AIUR	TCH/F4.8	TCH/F9.6	TCH/F14.4
4.8 kbit/s	1	–	–
9.6 kbit/s	2	1	–
14.4 kbit/s	3	–	1
19.2 kbit/s	4	2	–
28.8 kbit/s	–	3	2
38.4 kbit/s	–	4	–
43.2 kbit/s	–	–	3
57.6 kbit/s	–	–	4

channels idle most of the time. Allocating channels is reflected directly in the service costs, as, once the channels have been reserved, other users cannot use them, even though they may be idle.

Furthermore, for n channels HSCSD requires n times signalling during handover, connection setup and release. Each channel is treated separately. The probability of blocking or service degradation increases during handover, as in this case a BSC has to check resources for *n* channels, not only for one. All in all, HSCSD may be an attractive interim solution for higher bandwidth and rather constant traffic (e.g., file download). However, it does not make much sense for bursty Internet traffic as long as a user is charged for each channel allocated for communication.

4.1.8.2 GPRS

The next step toward more flexible and powerful data transmission avoids the problems of HSCSD by being fully packet-oriented. The **general packet radio service (GPRS)** provides packet mode transfer for applications that exhibit traffic patterns such as frequent transmission of small volumes (e.g., typical web requests) or infrequent transmissions of small or medium volumes (e.g., typical web responses) according to the requirement specification (ETSI, 1998a). Compared to existing data transfer services, GPRS should use the existing network resources more efficiently for packet mode applications, and should provide a selection of QoS parameters for the service requesters. Furthermore, GPRS should allow for broadcast, multicast, and unicast service. The overall goal in this context is the provision of a more efficient and, thus, cheaper packet transfer service for typical Internet applications that usually rely solely on packet transfer. Network providers could support this model by charging on volume and not connection time as is done today (for traditional GSM data services and for HSCSD). Clearly, GPRS was driven by the tremendous success of the packet-oriented Internet, and by the new traffic models and applications. However, GPRS, as shown in the following sections, needs additional network elements, i.e., software and hardware. Thus, unlike HSCSD, GPRS does not only represent a software update to allow for the bundling of channels.

The main concepts of GPRS are the following (ETSI, 1998b): For the new GPRS radio channels, the GSM system can allocate between one and eight time-slots within a TDMA frame. Time-slots are not allocated in a fixed, pre-determined manner but on demand. All time-slots can be shared by the active users, up- and downlink are allocated separately. Allocation of the slots is based on current load and operator preferences. Depending on the coding, a transfer rate of up to 150 kbit/s is possible, e.g., allocating all time-slots using the coding for 14.4 kbit/s traffic channels results in a 115.2 kbit/s channel. However, the GPRS concept is independent of channel characteristics and of the type of channel (traditional GSM traffic or control channel), and does not limit the maximum data rate (only the GSM transport system limits the rate). All GPRS services can be used parallel to conventional services.

In phase 1, GPRS offers a **point-to-point (PTP)** packet transfer service (ETSI, 1998c). One of the PTP versions offered is the **PTP connection oriented net-**

work service (PTP-CONS), which includes the ability of GPRS to maintain a virtual circuit upon change of the cell within the GSM network. This type of service corresponds to X.25, the typical circuit-switched packet-oriented transfer protocol available worldwide. The other PTP version offered is the **PTP connectionless network service (PTP-CLNS)**, which supports applications that are based on the Internet Protocol IP. Multicasting, called **point-to-multipoint (PTM)** service, is left for GPRS phase 2.

Users of GPRS can specify a **QoS-profile**. This profile determines the **service precedence** (high, normal, low), **reliability class** and **delay class** of the transmission, and **user data throughput**. GPRS should adaptively allocate radio resources to fulfil these user specifications. Table 4.3 shows the three reliability classes together with the maximum probabilities for a lost service data unit (SDU), a duplicated SDU, an SDU out of the original sequence, and the probability of delivering a corrupt SDU to the higher layer. Reliability class 1 could be used for very error-sensitive applications that cannot perform error corrections themselves. If applications exhibit greater error tolerance, class 2 could be appropriate. Finally, class 3 is the choice for error-insensitive applications or applications that can handle error corrections themselves.

Delay within a GPRS network is incurred by channel access delay and transfer delays in the fixed and wireless part of the GPRS network. The delay introduced by external fixed networks is out of scope. However, GPRS does not produce additional delay by buffering packets as store-and-forward networks do. If possible, GPRS tries to forward packets as fast as possible. Table 4.4 shows the specified maximum mean and 95 percentile delay values for packet sizes of 128 and 1024 byte. As we can clearly see, no matter which class, all delays are orders

Table 4.3
Reliability classes in GPRS according to ETSI (1998c)

Reliability class	Lost SDU probability	Duplicate SDU probability	Out of sequence SDU probability	Corrupt SDU probability
1	10^{-9}	10^{-9}	10^{-9}	10^{-9}
2	10^{-4}	10^{-5}	10^{-5}	10^{-6}
3	10^{-2}	10^{-5}	10^{-5}	10^{-2}

Table 4.4 Delay classes in GPRS according to ETSI (1998c)

Delay class	SDU size 128 byte		SDU size 1024 byte	
	mean	95 percentile	mean	95 percentile
1	<0.5s	<1.5s	<2s	<7s
2	<5s	<25s	<15s	<75s
3	<50s	<250s	<75s	<375s
4		Unspecified		

of magnitude higher than fixed network delays. This is a very important characteristic that has to be taken into account when implementing higher layer protocols such as TCP on top of GPRS networks (see chapter 10).

Finally, GPRS includes several **security services** such as authentication, access control, user identity confidentiality, and user information confidentiality. Even a completely **anonymous service** is possible, as, e.g., applied for road toll systems that only charge a user via the MS independent of the user's identity.

The **GPRS architecture** introduces two new network elements, which are called **GPRS support nodes (GSN)**. All GSNs are integrated into the standard GSM architecture, and many new interfaces have been defined (see Figure 4.15). The **gateway GPRS support node (GGSN)** is the interworking unit between the GPRS network and external **packet data networks (PDN)**. This node contains routing information for GPRS users, performs address conversion, and tunnels data to a user via encapsulation. The GGSN is connected to external networks (e.g., IP or X.25) via the G_i interface and transfers packets to the SGSN via an IP-based GPRS backbone network (G_n interface).

The other new element is the **serving GPRS support node (SGSN)** which supports the MS via the G_b interface. The SGSN, for example, requests user addresses from the **GPRS register (GR)**, keeps track of the individual MSs' location, is responsible for collecting billing information, and performs several security functions such as access control. The SGSN is connected to a BSC via frame relay and is basically on the same hierarchy level as an MSC. The GR, which is typically a part of the HLR, stores all GPRS-relevant data.

As shown in Figure 4.15, packet data is transmitted from a PDN, via the GGSN and SGSN directly to the BSS and finally to the MS. The MSC, which is responsible for data transport in the traditional circuit-switched GSM, is only

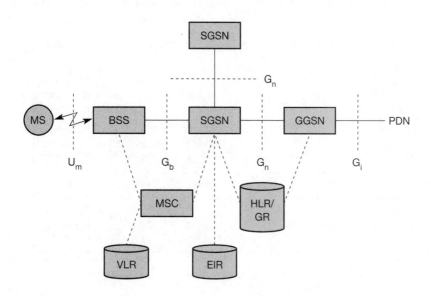

Figure 4.15
GPRS architecture
reference model

used for signalling in the GPRS scenario. Additional interfaces to further network elements and other PLMNs can be found in ETSI (1998b).

Before sending any data over the GPRS network, an MS must attach to it, following the procedures of the **mobility management**. The attachment procedure includes assigning a temporal identifier, called a **temporary logical link identity (TLLI)**, and a **ciphering key sequence number (CKSN)** for data encryption. For each MS, a **GPRS context** is set up and stored in the MS and in the corresponding SGSN. This context comprises the status of the MS (which can be ready, idle, or standby (ETSI, 1998b), the CKSN, a flag indicating if compression is used, and routing data (TLLI, the routing area RA, a cell identifier, and a packet data channel, PDCH, identifier). Besides attaching and detaching, mobility management also comprises functions for authentication, location management, and ciphering (here, the scope of ciphering lies between MS and SGSN, which is more than in standard GSM).

Figure 4.16 shows the protocol architecture of the transmission plane for GPRS. Architectures for the signalling planes can be found in ETSI (1998b). All data within the GPRS backbone, i.e., between the GSNs, is transferred using the **GPRS tunnelling protocol (GTP)**. GTP can use two different transport protocols, either the reliable **TCP** (needed for reliable transfer of X.25 packets) or the non-reliable **UDP** (used for IP packets). The network protocol for the GPRS backbone is **IP** (using any lower layers). In order to adapt to the different characteristics of the underlying networks, the **subnetwork dependent convergence protocol (SNDCP)** is used between an SGSN and the MS. On top of SNDCP and GTP, user packet data is tunnelled from the MS to the GGSN and vice versa. To achieve a high reliability of packet transfer between SGSN and MS, a special LLC is used, which comprises ARQ and FEC mechanisms for PTP (and later PTM) services.

A **base station subsystem GPRS protocol (BSSGP)** is used to convey routing and QoS-related information between the BSS and SGSN. BSSGP does not

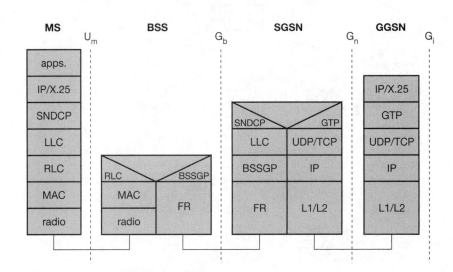

Figure 4.16
GPRS
transmission
plane protocol
reference model

perform error correction and works on top of a **frame relay (FR)** network. Finally, radio link dependent protocols are needed to transfer data over the U_m interface. The **radio link protocol (RLC)** provides a reliable link, while the **MAC** controls access with signalling procedures for the radio channel and the mapping of LLC frames onto the GSM physical channels. The **radio interface** at U_m needed for GPRS does not require fundamental changes compared to standard GSM (Brasche, 1997), (ETSI, 1998d). However, several new logical channels and their mapping onto physical resources have been defined. For example, one MS can allocate up to eight **packet data traffic channels (PDTCHs)**. Capacity can be allocated on demand and shared between circuit-switched channels and GPRS. This allocation can be done dynamically with load supervision or capacity can alternatively be pre-allocated.

A very important factor for any application working end-to-end is that it does not 'notice' any details from the GSM/GPRS related infrastructure. The application uses, e.g., TCP on top of IP, IP packets are tunnelled to the GGSN, which forwards them into the PDN. All PDNs forward their packets for a GPRS user to the GGSN, the GGSN asks the current SGSN for tunnel parameters, and forwards the packets via SGSN to the MS.

4.2 DECT

Another fully digital cellular network is the **digital enhanced cordless telecommunications (DECT)** system specified by ETSI (1999, 1998j, k), (DECT Forum, 1999). Formerly also called **digital European cordless telephone** and **digital European cordless telecommunications**, DECT replaces older analog cordless phone systems such as CT1 and CT1+. These analog systems only ensured security to a limited extent as they did not use encryption for data transmission and only offered a relatively low capacity. But DECT is also a more powerful alternative to the digital system CT2, which is mainly used in the UK (the DECT standard works throughout Europe). DECT is mainly used in offices, on campus, at trade shows, or at home. Furthermore, access points to the PSTN can be established within, e.g., railway stations, large government buildings and hospitals, offering a much cheaper telephone service compared to a GSM system. DECT could also be used to bridge the last few hundred metres between a new network operator and customers. Using this 'small range' local loop, new companies can offer their service without having their own lines installed in the streets. DECT systems offer many different interworking units, e.g., with GSM, ISDN, or data networks. Currently, more than 20 million DECT units are in use, so that the system holds more than 30 per cent of all wireless local loop (WLL) installations.

A big difference between DECT and GSM exists in terms of cell diameter and cell capacity. While GSM is designed for outdoor use with a cell diameter of up to 70 km, the range of DECT is limited to about 300 m from the base station (only around 50 m are feasible inside buildings depending on the walls). Due to this limited range and additional multiplexing techniques, DECT can offer its service to some 10,000 people within one km². This is a typical scenario within a big city, where thousands of offices are located in skyscrapers close together. DECT also uses base stations, but these base stations together with a mobile station are in a price range of some 100€ compared to several 10,000€ for a GSM base station. DECT can also handle handover, but it was not designed to work at a higher speed (e.g., up to 250 km/h like GSM systems).

DECT works at a frequency range of 1880–1990 MHz offering 120 full duplex channels. Time division duplex (TDD) is applied using 10 ms frames. The frequency range is subdivided into 10 carrier frequencies using FDMA, each frame being divided into 24 slots using TDMA. For the TDD mechanism, 12 slots are used as uplink, 12 slots as downlink. The digital modulation scheme is GMSK – each station has an average transmission power of only 10 mW with a maximum of 250 mW.

4.2.1 System architecture

Depending on the actual use of a DECT system, it can come in many different physical implementation variants. Different DECT entities can be integrated into one physical unit, entities can be distributed, replicated etc. However, all implementations are based on the same logical reference model of the system architecture as shown in Figure 4.17. A **global network** connects the local communication structure to the outside world and offers its services via the interface D_1. Global networks could be integrated services digital networks (ISDN), public switched telephone networks (PSTN), public land mobile networks (PLMN), e.g., GSM, or packet switched public data network (PSPDN). The services offered by these networks include transportation of data on the one hand and the translation of addresses and routing of data between the local networks on the other.

Figure 4.17
DECT system
architecture
reference model

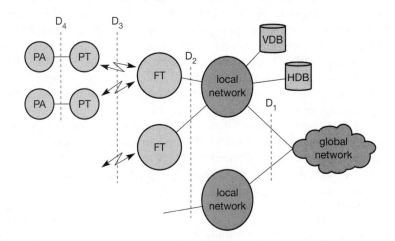

Local networks in the DECT context offer local telecommunication services that can include everything from simple switching to intelligent call forwarding, address translation etc. Examples for such networks are analog or digital private branch exchanges (PBXs) or LANs, e.g., those following the IEEE 802.x family of LANs. As the core of the DECT system itself is quite simple, all typical network functions have to be integrated in the local or global network, where the databases **home data base (HDB)** and **visitor data base (VDB)** are also located. Both databases support mobility with functions that are similar to those in the HLR and VLR in GSM systems. Incoming calls are automatically forwarded to the current subsystem responsible for the DECT user, and the current VDB informs the HDB about changes in location.

The DECT core network consists of the **fixed radio termination (FT)** and the **portable radio termination (PT)**, and basically only provides a multiplexing service. FT and PT cover the layers one to three at the fixed network side and mobile network side respectively.

4.2.2 Protocol architecture

The DECT protocol reference architecture follows the OSI reference model. Figure 4.18 shows the layers covered by the standard: the physical layer, medium access control, and data link control[18] for both the **control plane (C-Plane)** and the **user plane (U-Plane)**. Only for the C-Plane, an additional network layer has been specified, so that user data from layer two is directly forwarded to the U-Plane. A management plane covers all lower layers of a DECT system.

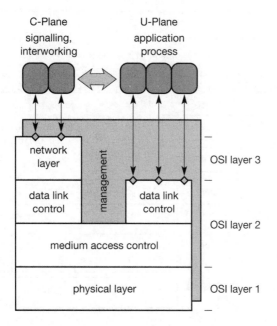

Figure 4.18
DECT protocol layers

4.2.2.1 Physical layer

As in all wireless networks, the **physical layer** comprises all functions for modulation/demodulation, incoming signal detection, sender/receiver synchronization, and collection of status information for the management plane. Furthermore, this layer generates the physical channel structure with a certain, guaranteed throughput. On request from the MAC layer, the physical layer assigns a channel for data transmission.

Figure 4.19 shows the standard TDMA frame structure used in DECT and some typical data packets. Each frame has a duration of 10 ms and contains 12 slots for the downlink and 12 slots for the uplink in the **basic connection** mode. If a mobile node receives data in slot s, it returns data in slot s+12. An **advanced connection** mode allows different allocation schemes. Each slot has a duration of 0.4167 ms and can contain several different physical packets. Typically, 420 bits are used for data, the remaining 52 µs are left as **guard space**. The 420 data bits are again divided into a 32 bit **synchronization pattern** followed by the **data** field D.

The fields for data transmission now use these remaining 388 bits for **network control** (A field), **user data** (B field), and the transfer of the **transmission quality** (X field). While network control is transmitted with a data rate of 6.4 kbit/s (64 bit each 10 ms), the user data rate depends on additional error correction mechanisms. The **simplex bearer** provides a data rate of 32 kbit/s in an **unprotected mode**, while using a 16 bit CRC **checksum** C for a data block of 64 bit in the **protected mode** reduces the data rate to 25.6 kbit/s. A **duplex bearer** service is

Figure 4.19
DECT multiplex and frame structure

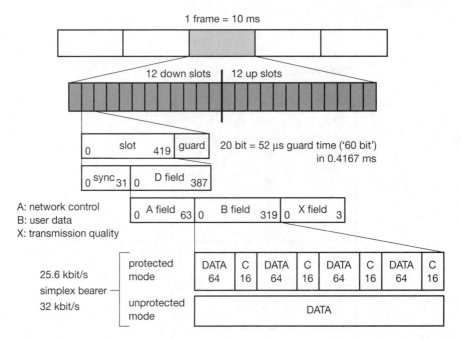

produced by combining two simplex bearers. DECT also defines bearer types with higher throughputs by combining slots, e.g., the **double duplex bearer** offers 80 kbit/s full-duplex.

4.2.2.2 Medium access control layer

The **medium access control (MAC)** layer establishes, maintains, and releases channels for higher layers by activating and deactivating physical channels. Furthermore, MAC multiplexes several logical channels onto physical channels. Logical channels exist for signalling network control, user data transmission, paging, or sending broadcast messages. Additional services offered include segmentation/reassembly of packets and error control/error correction.

4.2.2.3 Data link control layer

The purpose of the **data link control (DLC)** layer comprises creating and maintaining reliable connections between the mobile terminal and the base station. Two services have been defined for the **C-Plane**: a **connectionless broadcast** service for paging (called **Lb**) and a **point-to-point** protocol similar to LAPD in ISDN, but adapted to the underlying MAC (called **LAPC+Lc**).

Several services exist for the **U-Plane**, e.g., a transparent unprotected service (basically a null service), a forward error correction service, rate adaptation services, and services for future enhancements. If services are used, e.g., to transfer ISDN data at 64 kbit/s, then DECT also tries to transfer 64 kbit/s. However, in case of errors, DECT raises the transfer rate to 72 kbit/s, and includes FEC and a buffer for up to eight blocks to perform ARQ. This buffer then introduces an additional delay of up to 80 ms.

4.2.2.4 Network layer

The **network layer** of DECT is similar to those in ISDN and GSM and only exists for the **C-Plane**. This layer provides services to request, check, reserve, control, and release resources at the fixed station (connection to the fixed network, wireless connection) and the mobile terminal (wireless connection). The **mobility management (MM)** within the network layer is responsible for identity management, authentication, and the management of the location data bases. **Call control (CC)** handles connection setup, release, and negotiation. Two message services, the **connection oriented message service (COMS)** and the **connectionless message service (CLMS)** transfer data to and from the interworking unit that connects the DECT system with the outside world.

4.3 TETRA

Trunked radio systems constitute another method of wireless data transmission. These systems use many different radio carriers but only assign a specific carrier to a certain user for a short period of time according to demand. While, for example, taxi services, transport companies with fleet management systems and rescue teams all have their own unique carrier frequency in traditional systems, they can share a whole group of frequencies in trunked radio systems for better frequency reuse via FDM and TDM techniques. These types of radio systems typically offer interfaces to the fixed telephone network, i.e., voice and data services, but are not publicly accessible. Furthermore, these systems are not only simpler than most other networks, but they are also reliable and relatively cheap to set up and operate, as they do not have to cover whole countries, only in the regions local users operate, e.g., a city taxi service.

Again, to have a common system throughout Europe, ETSI standardized the **TETRA** system **(terrestrial trunked radio)**[19] in 1991 (ETSI, 1999), (TETRAMoU, 1999). This system should replace national systems, such as MODACOM, MOBI-TEX and COGNITO in Europe that typically connect to an X.25 packet network. (An example system from the US is ARDIS.) TETRA offers two standards: the **Voice+Data (V+D)** service (ETSI, 1998f) and the **packet data optimized (PDO)** service (ETSI, 1998m). While V+D offers circuit-switched voice and data transmission, PDO only offers packet data transmission, either connection-oriented to connect to X.25 or connectionless for the ISO CLNS (connectionless network service). The latter service can be point-to-point or point-to-multipoint, the typical delay for a short message (128 byte) being less than 100 ms. V+D connection modes comprise unicast and broadcast connections, group communication within a certain protected group, and a direct ad hoc mode without a base station. However, delays for short messages can be up to 500 ms or higher depending on the priority.

TETRA also offers bearer services of up to 28.8 kbit/s for unprotected data transmission and 9.6 kbit/s for protected transmission. Examples for end-to-end services are call forwarding, call barring, identification, call hold, call priorities, emergency calls and group joins. The system architecture of TETRA is very similar to GSM. Via the radio interface U_m, the **mobile station (MS)** connects to the **switching and management infrastructure (SwMI)**, which contains the user data bases (HDB, VDB), the base station, and interfaces to PSTN, ISDN, or PDN. The system itself, however, is much simpler in real implementation compared to GSM, as typically no handover is needed. Taxis mostly remain within a certain area which can be covered by one TETRA cell.

Several frequencies have been specified for TETRA which uses FDD (e.g., 380-390 MHz uplink/390-400 MHz downlink, 410-420 MHz uplink/420-430 MHz downlink). Each channel has a bandwidth of 25 kHz and can carry 36 kbit/s. Modulation is DQPSK. While V+D uses up to four TDMA voice or data channels per carrier, PDO performs statistical multiplexing. For accessing a channel, slotted Aloha is used.

Figure 4.20 shows the typical **TDMA frame structure** of TETRA. Each **frame** consists of four slots (thus four channels in the V+D service per carrier), with a frame duration of 56.67 ms. Each **slot** carries 510 bits within 14.17 ms, i.e., 36 kbit/s. 16 frames together with one **control frame** (CF) form a **multiframe**, and

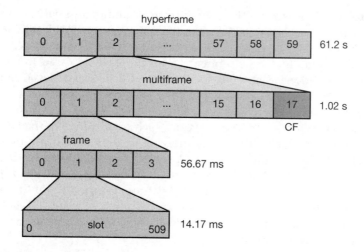

Figure 4.20
TETRA frame
structure

finally, a **hyperframe** contains 60 multiframes. In order to avoid sending and receiving at the same time, TETRA shifts the uplink for a period of two slots compared to the downlink.

Similar to GSM, TETRA offers **traffic channels (TCH)** and **control channels (CCH)**. Typical TCHs are TCH/S for voice transmission, and TCH/7.2, TCH/4.8, TCH/ 2.4 for data transmission (depending on the FEC mechanisms required).

However, in contrast to GSM, TETRA offers additional services like group call, acknowledged group call, broadcast call, and discreet listening. Emergency services need a sub-second group-call setup in harsh environments which possibly lack all infrastructure. These features are currently not available in GSM or other typical mobile telephone networks.

4.4 UMTS and IMT-2000

The International Telecommunication Union (ITU) made a request for proposals for Radio Transmission Technologies (RTT) for the International Mobile Telecommunications (IMT) 2000 program (ITU, 1999), (Callendar, 1997), (Shafi, 1998). IMT-2000, formerly called future public land mobile telecommunication system (FPLMTS) tries to establish a worldwide communication system that allows for terminal and user mobility supporting the idea of universal personal telecommunication (UPT). Within this context, ITU has created several recommendations for FPLMTS systems, e.g., network architectures for FPLMTS (M.817), Requirements for the Radio Interface(s) for FPLMTS (M.1034), or Framework for Services Supported by FPLMTS (M.816). The number 2000 in IMT-2000 should indicate the start of the system (year 2000+x) and the spectrum used (around 2000 MHz). IMT-2000 includes different environments such as indoor use, vehicles, satellites and pedestrians. The WRC 1992 identified

1885–2025 and 2110–2200 MHz as the frequency bands that should be available worldwide for the new IMT-2000 systems (Recommendation ITU-R M.1036).

For the RTT, several proposals were received in 1998 for indoor, pedestrian, vehicular, and satellite environments. These proposals came from many different organizations, e.g., **UWC-136** from the Universal Wireless Communications Consortium (US) that extends the IS-136 standard into the third generation systems, **cdma2000** that is based on the IS-95 system (US), and wideband packet CDMA, US **(WP-CDMA)**, which tries to align to the European UTRA proposal. Basically, there are three big regions submitting proposals to the ITU: ETSI for Europe, ARIB (Association of Radio Industries and Broadcasting) and TTC (Telecommunications Technology Council) for Japan, and ANSI (American National Standards Institute) for the US. Up to now, no final decision about the RTT candidates has been made by the ITU, but there are continuing discussions of a rather political than technical nature about the most appropriate candidates.

The European proposal for IMT-2000 prepared by ETSI is called **universal mobile telecommunications system (UMTS)** (Dasilva, 1997), (Ojanperä, 1998), the specific proposal for the radio interface RTT is **UMTS terrestrial radio access (UTRA)** (ETSI, 1998n), (UMTS Forum, 1999). UMTS as proposed by ETSI rather represents an evolution from the second generation GSM system to the third generation than a completely new system. In this way, many solutions have been proposed for a smooth transition from GSM to UMTS, in order to be able to save money by extending the current system rather than introducing a new one (GSMMoU, 1998), (Nilsson, 1998). One enhancement of GSM toward UMTS is **enhanced data rates for GSM evolution (EDGE)**, which uses enhanced modulation schemes and other techniques for data rates of up to 384 kbit/s using the same 200 kHz wide carrier and the same frequencies as GSM (i.e., a data rate of 48 kbit/s per time slot is available). EDGE can be introduced incrementally offering some channels with EDGE enhancement that can switch between EDGE and GSM/GPRS. Besides enhancing data rates, new additions to GSM, like **customized application for mobile enhanced logic (CAMEL)** introduce intelligent network support. This system supports, for example, the creation of a **virtual home environment (VHE)** for visiting subscribers. GSMMoU (1999) provides many proposals covering QoS aspects, roaming, services, billing, accounting, radio aspects, core networks, access networks, terminal requirements, security, application domains, operation and maintenance, and several migration aspects.

UMTS fits into a bigger framework developed by ETSI, called **global multimedia mobility (GMM)**. GMM provides an architecture to integrate mobile and fixed **terminals**, many different **access networks** (GSM BSS, DECT, ISDN, UMTS, LAN, WAN, CATV, MBS), and several **core transport networks** (GSM NSS+IN, ISDN+IN, B-ISDN+TINA, TCP/IP) (ETSI, 1999). Within this framework, ETSI developed **basic requirements** for UMTS and for UTRA, the radio interface (ETSI, 1998h). Key requirements are minimum data rates of 144 kbit/s for rural outdoor access (with the goal of 384 kbit/s) at a maximum speed of 500 km/h.[20] For suburban outdoor use a minimum of 384 kbit/s should be achieved with the goal of 512 kbit/s at 120 km/h. For indoor or city use with relatively short ranges, up to 2 Mbit/s are required at 10 km/h (walking).

Furthermore, UMTS should provide several bearer services, real-time and non real-time services, circuit and packet switched transmission, and many different data rates. Handover should be possible between UMTS cells, but also between UMTS and GSM or satellite networks. The system should be compatible with GSM, ATM, IP, and ISDN-based networks. In order to reflect the asymmetric bandwidth needs of typical users, UMTS should provide a variable division of uplink and downlink data rates. Finally, UMTS has to fit into the IMT-2000 framework (this factor is probably decisive for its success). As the global UMTS approach is rather ambitious, a more realistic alternative for the initial stages would be UMTS cells in cities providing a subset of services.

Several companies and interest groups have handed in proposals for UTRA (ETSI, 1998i), of which ETSI selected two for UMTS in January 1998. For the **paired band** (using FDD as duplex mechanism), ETSI adopts the **W-CDMA** (Wideband CDMA) proposal, for the **unpaired band** (using TDD as duplex mechanism) the **TD-CDMA** (Time Division CDMA) proposal is used (Adachi, 1998), (Dahlman, 1998), (ETSI, 1998n). The paired band is typically used for public mobile network providers (wide area, see GSM), while the unpaired band is often used for local and indoor communication (see DECT). The following sections will present key properties of the two components of UMTS. However, due to unsolved patent problems related to the use of certain CDMA technologies, it is uncertain whether the final system will in fact use these systems.

4.4.1 UMTS basic architecture

Figure 4.21 shows a simplified UMTS architecture which applies to both UTRA solutions. The **UTRA network (UTRAN)** handles cell level mobility and comprises several **radio network subsystems (RNS)**. The functions of the RNS include radio channel ciphering and deciphering, handover control, radio resource management etc. The UTRAN is connected to the **user equipment (UE)** via the radio interface U_u (which is comparable to the U_m interface in GSM). Via the I_u interface (which is similar to the A interface in GSM), UTRAN communicates with the **core network (CN)**. The CN contains functions for inter-system handover, gateways to other networks (fixed or wireless) etc. While the basic concepts for I_u are already defined, the interface has not been standardized yet.

As it is typical for this type of telecommunications standards, signalling data and user data is separated. For this purpose, UMTS introduces a C-Plane (control) and U-Plane (user data). The architecture includes the three lower layers: layer one at the radio interface comprises functions for FEC, signal level measurements,

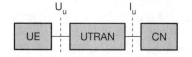

Figure 4.21
Simplified UMTS architecture

multiplexing and demultiplexing, modulation, spreading, synchronization, and power control. Layer two is responsible for MAC connections, medium access control, priority handling, contention resolution, and the scheduling of data packets. Finally, all control functions for connection setup etc. are situated in layer three.

4.4.2 UTRA FDD mode

The FDD mode for UTRA uses **wideband CDMA (W-CDMA)** with direct sequence spreading. As implied by FDD, uplink and downlink use different frequencies. A mobile station sends via the uplink using a carrier between 1920 and 1980 MHz, the base station uses 2110 to 2170 MHz for the downlink. This mode roughly provides 250 channels for user traffic, e.g., voice channels. Each physical channel corresponds to a carrier frequency, a certain spreading code (DS), and a relative phase (uplink only), and carries up to 2 Mbit/s data.

Similar to GSM, several physical and logical channels have been defined. On the **uplink**, user data (from layer two and higher) is transported over the **uplink dedicated physical data channel (uplink DPDCH)**, layer one control data (e.g. for power control) is transported via the **uplink dedicated physical control channel (uplink DPCCH)**. Both channels are transmitted in parallel, DPCCH on the Q branch of the signal (see chapter 2), DPDCH on the I branch. For both channels, different spreading factors are possible. The **physical random access channel (PRACH)** carries control data from a mobile station for random access. It uses slotted Aloha with 1.25 ms slots, whereas a common broadcast channel signals which slots are available for random access within a cell.

On the **downlink**, the **downlink dedicated physical channel (downlink DPCH)** carries user data and control data from layer one in a time multiplexed fashion. UTRA defines additional common physical channels for radio control. Figure 4.22 shows the frame structure of UTRA in FDD mode and selected channels. A **superframe** with a duration of 720 ms consists of 72 frames. A **frame** contains 16 slots and has a duration of 10 ms. The example shows three different channels that can use a slot. The uplink DPCCH contains a **pilot** to support channel estimation, the **transmit power control (TPC)**, and the optional **transport format identifier (TFI)**. The uplink DPDCH, which is transmitted at the same time as the uplink DPCCH, contains user **data**. The downlink DPCH contains the same fields (i.e., pilot, TPC, TFI, and data), but in a time-multiplexed version in one slot.

The chip rate used in this scheme is 4.096 Mchip/s and can be extended to 8.192 and 16.384 Mchip/s for future applications. For modulation of data bits, QPSK is used. Due to the use of CDMA, soft handover is possible between different base stations (Wong, 1997), and an even 'softer handover' is defined within one base station (i.e., between different sectors). Furthermore, the CDMA scheme allows for the localization of mobile stations with a maximum accuracy of approximately 18 m. However, CDMA needs a more complex power control

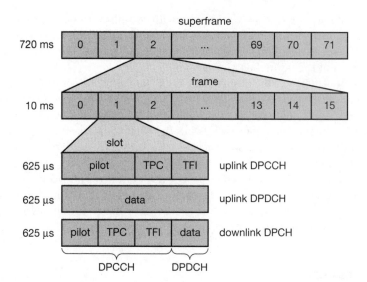

Figure 4.22
UMTS FDD mode
frame structures

scheme with 1,600 power control cycles per second. Sender and receiver operate continuously during a call.

4.4.3 UTRA TDD mode

The TDD mode of UTRA uses **wideband TDMA/CDMA** for medium access, and in this mode uplink and downlink use the same frequency. This mode also offers 2 Mbit/s for approximately 120 orthogonal channels for user traffic, which is roughly half the capacity of the FDD mode, but this TDD scheme only requires half the bandwidth. Physical channels are now represented by a slot and spreading code (direct sequence). Typically, the system can transmit eight bursts from different channels within a single slot. Figure 4.23 shows a typical burst structure (a **traffic burst**) within a slot. This burst contains user **data**, a **midample** for channel estimation, and a **guard period (GP)** to avoid interference between different slots (23.4 µs). Each **slot** has a duration of 625 µs and contains 2,560 chips. 16 slots make a **frame** with a duration of 10 ms.

To reflect different user needs in terms of data rates, the TDD frame can be **symmetrical** or **asymmetrical**, i.e., the frame can contain the same number of uplink and downlink slots or any arbitrary combination. Furthermore, the

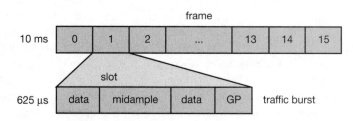

Figure 4.23
UMTS TDD mode
frame structures

frame can have only one **switching point** from uplink to downlink or several switching points. However, at least one slot must be allocated for the uplink and downlink respectively. Furthermore, the system can change the spreading factor as a function of the desired data rate.

The modulation scheme of this mode is QPSK. The power control can be slower compared to FDD (only 100 to 800 power control cycles per second are needed). Sender and receiver only operate in allocated slots, i.e., they do not operate continuously. Due to the time multiplexing scheme, tight synchronization is required within a small area (several cells) to ensure successful handover. This scheme only allows for hard handover like GSM.

Both schemes, FDD and TDD, can coexist. Handover between the schemes is feasible due to the similar frame structure and the frame duration of 10 ms. Furthermore, the multiframe structure specified for the UTRA modes allows for a seamless handover to GSM systems.

4.5 Summary

This chapter mainly presented GSM as the most successful digital cellular network. Although GSM was primarily designed for voice transmission, the chapter showed the evolution toward a more data-oriented transfer via HSCSD and GPRS. This evolution also includes the transition from a circuit-switched network to a packet-switched system that comes closer to the Internet model. Other systems presented include DECT, the digital standard for cordless phones, and TETRA, a trunked radio system. DECT can be used for wireless data transmission on a campus or indoors, but also for wireless local loops (WLL). Finally, for special scenarios, e.g., emergencies, trunked radio systems such as TETRA can be the best choice. They offer a fast connection setup (even within communication groups) and can work in an ad hoc network, i.e., without a base station.

The situation in the US is different from Europe. Based on the analog AMPS system, the US industry developed the TDMA system IS-54 that adds digital traffic channels. IS-54 uses dual mode mobile phones and incorporates several GSM ideas, such as, associated control channels, authentication procedures using encryption, and mobile assisted handover (called handoff). The Japanese PDC system was designed following many ideas in IS-54.

The next step, IS-136, includes digital control channels (IS-54 uses analog AMPS control channels) and is more efficient. Now fully digital phones can be used, several additional services are offered, e.g., voice mail, call waiting, identification, group calling, or SMS. IS-136 is also called North American TDMA (NA-TDMA) or Digital AMPS (D-AMPS) and operates at 800 and 1,900 MHz. Enhancements of D-AMPS/IS-136 toward IMT-2000 include advanced modulation techniques for the 30 kHz radio carrier, shifting data rates up to 64 kbit/s (first phase, called 136+). The second phase, called 136HS (High Speed) comprises a new air interface specification based on the EDGE technology.

IS-95 is based on CDMA, which is a completely different medium access method. Before deployment, the system was proclaimed as having many advantages over TDMA systems, such as its much higher capacity of users per cell, e.g., 20 times the capacity of AMPS. Today, CDMA providers are making more realistic estimates of around five times as many users. IS-95 offers soft handover, thus avoiding the GSM ping-pong effect (Wong, 1997). However, IS-95 needs precise synchronization of all base stations (using GPS satellites which are military satellites and are thus not under control of the network provider), frequent power control, and typically dual mode mobile phones due to the limited coverage. Up to now, the big advantages compared to TDMA systems have not been proven. However, the basic ideas of CDMA will be integrated in many future systems as the UMTS example shows.

It is still an open question which system(s) will be used for the third generation of mobile phone networks. UMTS, as presented in this chapter, is one of the proposals, currently supported by Europe and Japan. However, it is rather a political than a technical question, what the systems(s) of the future will look like that allow worldwide communication with seamless handover between different systems. One possible system combines the different approaches and uses the Internet as common base (Nilsson, 1998). Mobile devices are dual or triple mode devices supporting, e.g., GSM and IS-136, or UMTS and CDMA2000. Each mobile network has MSCs and a packet switching core (e.g., GSM with UMTS, D-AMPS with an IMT-2000 solution). Communication is performed via the Internet and existing telephone networks. The location registers have to cooperate via an interworking location register (ILR).

4.6 Review exercises

1 Name some key features of the GSM, DECT, and TETRA systems. Which features do the systems have in common? Why have three different systems been specified? In what scenarios could one system replace another? What are the specific advantages of each system?

2 What are the main problems when transmitting data using wireless systems that were made for voice transmission? What are the possible steps to mitigate the problems and to raise efficiency? How can this be supported by billing?

3 Which types of different services does GSM offer? Name some examples and give reasons why these services have been separated.

4 Compared to the TCHs offered, standard GSM could provide a much higher data rate (33.8 kbit/s) when looking at the air interface. What lowers the data rates available to a user?

5 Name the main elements of the GSM system architecture and describe their functions. What are the advantages of specifying not only the radio interface but also all internal interfaces of the GSM system?

6   Describe the functions of the MS and SIM. Why does GSM separate the MS and SIM? How and where is user-related data represented/stored in the GSM system? How is user data protected from unauthorized access, especially over the air interface? How could the position of an MS (not only the current BTS) be localized? Think of the MS reports regarding signal quality.

7   Looking at the HLR/VLR database approach used in GSM – how does this architecture limit the scalability in terms of users, especially moving users?

8   Why is a new infrastructure needed for GPRS, but not for HSCSD? Which components are new and what is their purpose?

9   What are the limitations of a GSM cell in terms of diameter and capacity (voice, data) for the traditional GSM, HSCSD, GPRS? How can the capacity be increased?

10 What multiplexing schemes are used in GSM for what purposes? Think also of other layers apart from the physical layer.

11 How is synchronization achieved in GSM? Who is responsible for synchronization and why is synchronization very important?

12 What are the reasons for the delays in a GSM system for packet data traffic? Distinguish between circuit-switched and packet-oriented transmission.

13 Where and when can collisions occur while accessing the GSM system? Compare possible collisions caused by data transmission in standard GSM, HSCSD, and GPRS.

14 Why and when are different signalling channels needed? What are the differences?

15 How is localization, location update, roaming, etc. done in GSM and reflected in the data bases? What are typical roaming scenarios?

16 Why are so many different identifiers/addresses (e.g., MSISDN, TMSI, IMSI) needed in GSM? Give reasons and distinguish between user related and system related identifiers.

17 Give reasons for a handover in GSM and the problems associated with it. Which are the typical steps for handover, what types of handover can occur? Which resources need to be allocated during handover for data transmission using HSCSD or GPRS respectively? What about QoS guarantees?

18 What are the functions of authentication and encryption in GSM? How is system security maintained?

19 How can higher data rates be achieved in standard GSM, how is this possible with the additional schemes HSCSD, GPRS, EDGE? What are the main differences of the approaches, also in terms of complexity? What problems remain even if the data rate is increased?

20 What limits the data rates that can be achieved with GPRS and HSCSD using real devices (compared to the theoretical limit in a GSM system)?

21 Using the best delay class in GPRS and a data rate of 115.2 kbit/s – how many bytes are in transit before a first acknowledgement from the receiver could reach the sender (neglect further delays in the fixed network and receiver system)? Now think of typical web transfer with 10 kbyte average transmission size – how would a standard TCP behave on top of GPRS (see chapter 10 and chapter 11)? Think of slow start and its relation to the round-trip time. What changes are needed?

22 How much of the original GSM network does GPRS need? Which elements of the network perform the data transfer?

23 What are typical data rates in DECT? How are they achieved considering the TDMA frames? What multiplexing schemes are applied in DECT for what purposes? Compare the complexity of DECT with that of GSM.

24 Who would be the typical users of a trunked radio system? What makes trunked radio systems particularly attractive for these user groups? What are the main differences to existing systems for that purpose? Why are trunked radio systems cheaper compared to, e.g., GSM systems for their main purposes?

25 Summarize the main features of 3rd generation mobile phone systems. How do they achieve higher capacities and higher data rates? How does UMTS implement asymmetrical communication and different data rates?

26 Compare the current situation of mobile phone networks in Europe, Japan, and North America. What are the main differences, what are efforts to find a common system or at least interoperable systems?

4.7 References

Adachi, F.; Sawahashi, M.; Suda, H. (1998) 'Wideband DS-CDMA for next-generation mobile communications systems', *IEEE Communications Magazine*, 36, (9).

Brasche, G.; Walke, B. (1997) 'Concepts, services, and protocols of the new GSM phase 2+ General Packet Radio Service', *IEEE Communications Magazine*, 35, (8).

Callendar, M. (1997) 'International Mobile Telecommunications-2000 standards efforts of the ITU', collection of articles in *IEEE Personal Communications*, 4, (4).

Dahlman, E.; Gudmundson, B.; Nilsson, M.; Sköld, J. (1998) 'UMTS/IMT-2000 based on wideband CDMA', *IEEE Communications Magazine*, 36, (9).

Dasilva, J.; Ikonomou, D.; Erben, H. (1997) 'European R&D programs on third-generation mobile communication systems', *IEEE Personal Communications*, 4, (1).

DECT Forum (1999), http://www.dect.ch/.

ETSI (1991a) *Bearer services supported by a GSM PLMN*, European Telecommunications Standards Institute, GSM recommendations 02.02.

ETSI (1991b) *General description of a GSM PLMN*, European Telecommunications Standards Institute, GSM recommendations 01.02.

ETSI (1991c) *Subscriber Identity Modules, Functional Characteristics*, European Telecommunications Standards Institute, GSM recommendations 02.17.

ETSI (1993a) *Multiplexing and multiple access on the radio path*, European Telecommunications Standards Institute, GSM recommendations 05.02.

ETSI (1993b) *MS-BSS data link layer – general aspects*, European Telecommunications Standards Institute, GSM recommendations 04.05.

ETSI (1993c) *MS-BSS data link layer specification*, European Telecommunications Standards Institute, GSM recommendations 04.06.

ETSI (1997a) *High Speed Circuit Switched Data (HSCSD)*, Stage 1, European Telecommunications Standards Institute, GSM 02.34, V5.2.1.

ETSI (1998a) *General Packet Radio Service (GPRS); Requirements specification of GPRS*, European Telecommunications Standards Institute, TR 101 186, V6.0.0 (1998–04).

ETSI (1998b) *General Packet Radio Service (GPRS); Service description; Stage 2*, European Telecommunications Standards Institute, EN 301 344, V6.1.1 (1998–08).

ETSI (1998c) *General Packet Radio Service (GPRS); Service description; Stage 1*, European Telecommunications Standards Institute, EN 301 113, V6.1.1 (1998–11).

ETSI (1998d) *General Packet Radio Service (GPRS); Overall description of the GPRS radio interface; Stage 2*, European Telecommunications Standards Institute, TS 101 350, V6.0.1 (1998–08).

ETSI (1998e) *High Speed Circuit Switched Data (HSCSD); Stage 2*, European Telecommunications Standards Institute, TS 101 038, V5.1.0 (1998–07).

ETSI (1998f) *Universal Mobile Telecommunications System (UMTS); Concept groups for the definition of the UMTS Terrestrial Radio Access (UTRA)*, European Telecommunications Standards Institute, TR 101 397, V3.0.1 (1998–10).

ETSI (1998g) *Universal Mobile Telecommunications System (UMTS); High level requirements relevant for the definition of the UMTS Terrestrial Radio Access (UTRA) concept*, European Telecommunications Standards Institute, TR 101 398, V3.0.1 (1998–10).

ETSI (1998h) *High level requirements relevant for the definition of the UMTS Terrestrial Radio Access (UTRA) concept*, European Telecommunications Standards Institute, TR 101 398, V3.0.1 (1998–10).

ETSI (1998i) *Concept groups for the definition of the UMTS Terrestrial Radio Access (UTRA)*, European Telecommunications Standards Institute, TR 101 397, V3.0.1 (1998–10).

ETSI (1998j) *Digital Enhanced Cordless Telecommunications (DECT), Generic Access Profile (GAP)*, European Telecommunications Standards Institute, EN 300 444, V1.3.2 (1998–03).

ETSI (1998k) *Digital Enhanced Cordless Telecommunications (DECT), Common Interface (CI)*, European Telecommunications Standards Institute, EN 300 175, V1.4.1 (1998–02).

ETSI (1998l) *Terrestrial Trunked Radio (TETRA), Voice plus Data (V+D)*, European Telecommunications Standards Institute, ETS 300 392 series of standards.

ETSI (1998m) *Terrestrial Trunked Radio (TETRA), Packet Data Optimized (PDO)*, European Telecommunications Standards Institute, ETS 300 393 series of standards.

ETSI (1998n) *The ETSI UMTS Terrestrial Radio Access (UTRA) ITU-R Radio Transmission Technologies (RTT) Candidate Submission*, European Telecommunications Standards Institute.

European Telecommunications Standards Institute (1999), http://www.etsi.org/.

Goodman, D. (1997) *Wireless Personal Communications Systems*. Addison Wesley Longman.

GSM Data, Intel Corporation (1998), http://www.gsmdata.com/.

GSM MoU (1998) *Vision for the evolution from GSM to UMTS*, GSM MoU Association, Permanent Reference Document, V 3.0.0.

GSM Memorandum of Understanding Association (1999) http://www.gsmworld.com/.

Halsall, F. (1996) *Data communications, computer networks and open systems*. Addison Wesley Longman.

International Telecommunication Union, International Mobile Telecommunications (1999), http://www.itu.int/ imt/.

Nilsson, T. (1998) 'Toward third-generation wireless communication', *Ericsson Review No. 2*, http://www.ericsson.com/.

Ojanperä, T.; Prasad, R. (1998) 'An overview of third-generation wireless personal communications: A European perspective,' *IEEE Personal Communications*, 5, (6).

Shafi, M.; Sasaki, A.; Jeong, D. (1998) 'IMT-2000 developments in the Asia Pacific region', collection of articles, *IEEE Communications Magazine*, 36, (9).

TETRA Memorandum of Understanding (1999), http://www.tetramou.com/.

Tripathi, N.D.; Reed, J.H.; VanLandingham, H.F. (1998) 'Handoffs in cellular systems', *IEEE Personal Communications*, 5, (6).

UMTS Forum (1999) http://www.umts-forum.org/.

Wong, D.; Lim, T. (1997) 'Soft handoffs in CDMA mobile systems', *IEEE Personal Communications*, 4, (6).

Satellite systems 5

This chapter on satellite communication introduces another system supporting mobile communications. Satellites offer global coverage without wiring costs for base stations and are almost independent of varying population densities. After a short history of satellite development and presentation of different areas of application, this chapter introduces the basics of satellite systems. Orbit, visibility, transmission quality, and other system characteristics are all closely linked. Several restrictions and application requirements result in three major classes of satellites, GEO, MEO, and LEO, as discussed further on. The high speed of satellites with a low altitude raises new problems for routing, localization of mobile users, and handover of communication links. Several aspects of these topics are therefore presented in separate sections. Finally, the chapter deals with four examples of currently planned or already installed systems for global satellite communication.

5.1 History

Satellite communication began after the second world war. Scientists knew that it was possible to build rockets carrying radio transmitters into space. In 1945, Arthur C. Clarke published his essay on 'Extra Terrestrial Relays'. But it was not until 1957, in the middle of the cold war, when the sudden launching of the first satellite SPUTNIK by the Soviet Union shocked the Western world. SPUTNIK is not at all comparable to a satellite today, it was basically a small sender transmitting a periodic 'beep'. But this was enough for the US to put all its effort into the development of its first satellite, and only three years later, in 1960, the first reflecting communication satellite ECHO was in space. ECHO was basically a mirror in the sky enabling communication by reflecting signals. Three years further on, the first geostationary (or geosynchronous) satellite SYNCOM followed. Even today, geostationary satellites are the backbones of news broadcasting in the sky. Their great advantage, as explained in more detail in section 5.3.1, is the fixed position in the sky. Their rotation is synchronous to the rotation of the earth, thus they appear to be pinned to a certain location.

Finally, in 1965, the first commercial geostationary communication satellite INTELSAT 1, also known as 'Early Bird', went into operation. It was in service for 1.5 years, weighing 68 kg and offering 240 duplex telephone channels or alternatively a single TV channel. INTELSAT 2 followed in 1967, INTELSAT 3 in 1969 already offering 1,200 telephone channels. While communication on land always provides the alternative of using wires, this is not the case for ships at sea. Therefore, three MARISAT satellites went into operation in 1976 which offered worldwide maritime communication. Still, sender and receiver had to be installed on the ships with large antennas (1.2 m antenna, 40 W transmit power). The first mobile satellite telephone system, INMARSAT-A, was introduced in 1982. Six years later, INMARSAT-C followed as the first satellite system offering mobile phone and data services. (Data rates are about 600 bit/s, interfaces to the X.25 packet data network exist.) In 1993, satellite telephone systems finally became fully digital. The actual mobility, however, was relative from a user's point of view, as the devices needed for communication via geostationary satellites are heavy (several kilograms) and need a lot of transmit power to achieve decent data rates. Nineteen ninety-eight marked the beginning of a new age of satellite data communication with the introduction of global satellite systems for small mobile phones, such as, e.g., Iridium and Globalstar (see section 5.7). The current number of almost 200 geostationary satellites for commercial use shows the impressive growth of satellite communication over the last 30 years (Miller, 1998), (Maral, 1998), (Pascall, 1997).

5.2 Applications

Traditionally, satellites have been used in the following areas:

- **Weather forecasting:** Several satellites deliver pictures of the earth using, e.g., infrared or visible light. Without the help of satellites forecasting of hurricanes would be impossible.
- **Radio and TV broadcast satellites:** Hundreds of radio and TV programmes are available via satellite. This technology competes with cable in many places, for it is cheaper to install and in most cases no extra fees have to be paid for this service. Today's satellite dishes have diameters of 30–40 cm in central Europe, whereas the diameters in northern countries are slightly larger.
- **Military satellites:** One of the earliest applications of satellites was their use for carrying out espionage. In addition to that, many communication links are managed via satellites for they are much safer from attack by enemies.
- **Satellites for navigation:** Even though it was only used for military purposes in the beginning, the global positioning system (GPS) is nowadays well-known and available for everyone. The system allows for precise localization worldwide, and with some additional techniques, the precision is in the range of some metres. Almost all ships and aircraft rely on GPS as an

addition to traditional navigation systems. Furthermore, many trucks and cars come with installed GPS receivers. This system is also used, e.g., for fleet management of trucks or for vehicle localization in case of theft.

In the context of mobile communication, the capabilities of satellites to transmit data are of particular interest.

- **Global telephone backbones**: As mentioned above, one of the first applications of satellites for communication was the establishment of international telephone backbones. Instead of using cables it was sometimes faster to launch a new satellite. However, while still in use for some applications, satellites functioning as backbones for telecommunication networks are increasingly being replaced by fibre optical cables crossing the oceans. The main reasons for this are the tremendous capacity of fibre optical links (some 10 Gbit/s using wavelength division multiplexing) and in particular the much lower delay compared to satellites. While the signal to a geostationary satellite has to travel about 72,000 km from a sender via the satellite to the receiver, the distance is typically less than 10,000 km if a fibre optical link crossing the Pacific or Atlantic Ocean is used. Unfortunately the speed of light is limited, resulting in a one-way, single-hop time delay of 0.25 s for geostationary satellites. Using satellites for telephone conversation is therefore sometimes annoying and requires particular discipline in discussions.
- **Connections for remote places or developing areas**: Many places all over the world do not have direct wired connection to the telephone network or Internet due to their geographical location (e.g., researchers on Antarctica) or to the current state of the infrastructure of a country. Satellites now offer a simple and quick connection to global networks (Schwartz, 1996).
- **Global mobile communication**: The latest trend for satellites is the support of global mobile data communication. Due to the high latency, geostationary satellites are not ideal for this task, therefore, satellites using lower orbits are needed (see section 5.3). The basic purpose of satellites for mobile communication is not the replacement of existing mobile phone networks, but their extension into areas without coverage. Cellular phone systems, such as AMPS (and its successors) and GSM frequently do not cover all parts of a country. Exceptions in coverage are usually places with low population where it is too expensive to install a base station. With the integration of satellite communication, however, the mobile phone can switch to satellites offering worldwide connectivity to a customer (Jamalipour, 1998).

While in the beginning satellites were simple transponders, today's satellites rather resemble flying routers. Transponders basically receive a signal on one frequency, amplify the signal and transmit it on another frequency. While in the beginning only analog amplification was possible, the use of digital signals also allows for a signal regeneration. The satellite decodes the signal into a bit-stream, and codes it again into a signal. The advantage of digital regeneration compared to pure analog amplification is the higher quality of the received signal on the earth. As explained in the following sections, today's communication satellites provide many functions of higher communication layers, e.g., inter-satellite routing, error correction etc.

Figure 5.1 shows a typical scenario for satellite systems supporting global mobile communication (Lutz, 1998). Depending on the type of the satellite, each can cover a certain area on the earth with its beam, the so-called footprint (see section 5.3). Within the footprint, communication with the satellite is possible for mobile users via a **mobile user link (MUL)** and for the base station controlling the satellite and acting as gateway to other networks via the **gateway link (GWL)**. Additionally, satellites might have the capabilities to communicate directly with each other via **inter-satellite links (ISL)**. This facilitates direct communication between users within different footprints without using base stations or other networks on earth. Saving extra links from satellite to earth can reduce latency for data packets and voice data. Some satellites might have special antennas to create smaller cells using spot beams (e.g., 163 spot beams per satellite in the ICO system (ICO, 1998)).

Satellite systems are and will be a valuable addition to the many networks already existing on earth. Users might communicate using ISDN or other PSTN, even cellular networks such as GSM. Many gateways provide seamless communication between these different networks. A real challenge for example is the smooth, seamless handover between a cellular network and a satellite system.

Figure 5.1

Typical satellite system for global mobile telecommunication

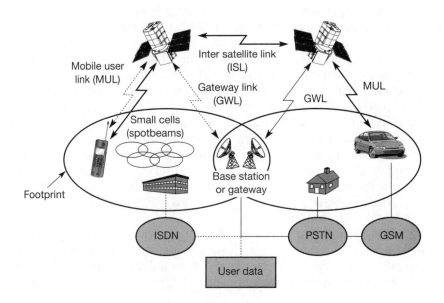

5.3 Basics

Satellites circulate in orbits around the earth. Depending on the application, these orbits can be circular or elliptical. Satellites in circular orbits always keep the same distance to earth surface following a simple law:

- The attractive force F_g of the earth due to gravity equals $m \cdot g \cdot (R/r)^2$.
- The centrifugal force F_c trying to pull the satellite away equals $m \cdot r \cdot \omega^2$.

The variables have the following meaning:

- m is the mass of the satellite,
- R is the radius of earth with $R = 6{,}370$ km,
- r is the distance of the satellite to the centre of the earth,
- g is the acceleration of gravity with $g = 9.81$ m/s^2,
- and ω is the angular velocity with $\omega = 2 \cdot \pi \cdot f$, f is the frequency of the rotation.

To keep the satellite in a stable circular orbit, the following equation must hold:

- $F_g = F_c$, i.e., both forces must be equal. Looking at this equation the first thing to be noticed is that the mass m of a satellite is irrelevant (it appears on both sides of the equation).
- Solving the equation for the distance r of the satellite to the centre of the earth results in the following equation:

   The distance $r = (g \cdot R^2 / (2 \cdot \pi \cdot f)^2)^{1/3}$

From the last equation it can be concluded that the distance of a satellite to the earth's surface depends on its rotation frequency. Figure 5.2 shows this dependency in addition to the relative velocity of a satellite. The interesting point of the diagram is when the satellite period equals 24 hours. This is exactly the case for a distance of 35,786 km. Having an orbiting time of 24 hours implies a geostationary satellite if it is additionally placed above the equator. (Satellites of this type will be discussed in a later section.)

   Important parameters in satellite communication are the inclination and elevation angles. The **inclination angle** δ (see Figure 5.3) is defined as the angle between the equatorial plane and the plane described by the satellite orbit. An inclination angle of 0 degrees means that the satellite is exactly above the equator. If the satellite does not have a circular orbit, the closest point to the earth is called the perigee.

   The **elevation angle** ε (see Figure 5.4) is defined as the angle between the centre of the satellite beam and the plane tangential to the earth's surface. Furthermore, a so-called **footprint** can be defined as the area on earth where the signals of the satellite can be received.

Figure 5.2
Dependency of satellite
period and distance to
earth

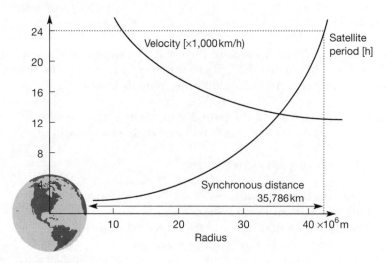

Figure 5.2
Dependency of satellite
period and distance to
earth

Figure 5.3
Inclination angle of a
satellite

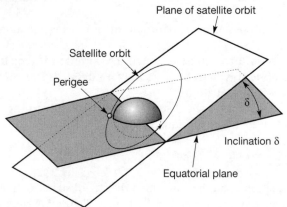

Figure 5.4
Elevation angle of a
satellite

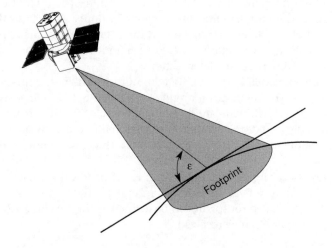

Another effect of satellite communication is the propagation loss of the signals. This attenuation of the signal power depends on the distance between a receiver on earth and the satellite, and, additionally, on satellite elevation and atmospheric conditions. The loss L depending on the distance r between sender and receiver can be calculated as:

$$L = (4 \cdot \pi \cdot r \cdot f \, / \, c)^2,$$

with f being the carrier frequency and c the speed of light.

This means that the power of the received signal decreases with the square of the distance. This also directly influences the maximum data rates achievable under certain assumptions (transmit power, antenna diameter, operating frequency etc.) as shown in Comparetto (1997). While with antennas used for mobile phones a data rate of 10 kbit/s is achievable with a 2 GHz carrier for satellites in some 100 km distance as discussed in section 5.3.2, only some 10 bit/s are possible with geostationary satellites in a distance of 36,000 km.

The attenuation of the signal due to certain atmospheric conditions is more complex (see Figure 5.5). Depending on the elevation, the signal has to penetrate a smaller or larger percentage of the atmosphere. Generally, an elevation less than 10 degrees is considered useless for communication. Especially rain absorption can be quite strong in tropical areas (here, the error rates increase dramatically during the afternoon rainfalls).

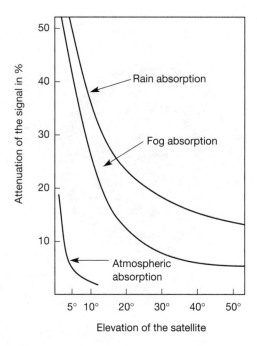

Figure 5.5
Signal attenuation due to atmospheric absorption

Four different types of orbits can be identified as shown in Figure 5.6:

- **Geostationary (or geosynchronous) earth orbit (GEO):** GEO satellites have a distance of almost 36,000 km to the earth. Examples are almost all TV and radio broadcast satellites, many weather satellites and satellites operating as backbones for the telephone network (see section 5.3.1).
- **Medium earth orbit (MEO):** MEOs operate at a distance of about 5,000 – 12,000 km. Up to now there have not been many satellites in this class, but some upcoming systems (e.g., ICO) use this class for various reasons (see section 5.3.3).
- **Low earth orbit (LEO):** While some time ago LEO satellites were mainly used for espionage, several of the new satellite systems now rely on this class using altitudes of 500-1,500 km (see section 5.3.2).
- **Highly elliptical orbit (HEO):** This class comprises all satellites with non-circular orbits. Currently, only a few commercial communication systems using satellites with elliptical orbits are planned. These systems have their perigee over large cities to improve communication quality.

The Van Allen radiation belts, belts consisting of ionized particles, at heights of about 2,000–6,000 km (inner Van Allen belt) and about 15,000–30,000 km (outer Van Allen belt) respectively make satellite communication very difficult in these orbits.

Figure 5.6
Different types of
satellite orbits

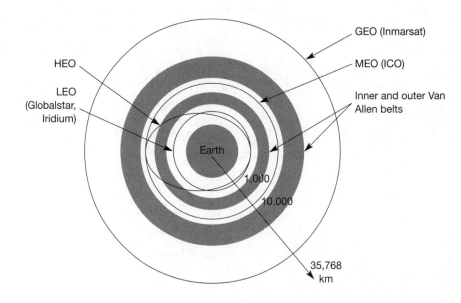

5.3.1 GEO

If a satellite should appear fixed in the sky, it requires a period of 24 hours. Using the equation for the distance between earth and satellite $r = (g \cdot R^2/(2 \cdot \pi \cdot f)^2)^{1/3}$ and the period of 24 hours $f = 1/24h$, the resulting distance is 35,786 km. Furthermore, the orbit must have an inclination of 0 degrees.

- **Advantages**: Three GEO satellites are enough for a complete coverage of almost any spot on earth. Senders and receivers can use fixed antenna positions, no adjusting is needed. Therefore, GEOs are ideal for TV and radio broadcasting. Lifetime expectations for GEOs are rather high, at about 15 years. GEOs typically do not need a handover due to the large footprint. Furthermore, GEOs do not exhibit any Doppler shift because the relative movement is zero.
- **Disadvantages**: Northern or southern regions of the earth have more problems receiving these satellites due to the low elevation above a latitude of 60°, i.e., larger antennas are needed in this case. The transmit power needed is relatively high (some 10 W) which causes problems for battery powered devices. Therefore, these satellites cannot be used for small mobile phones. The biggest problem for voice and also data communication is the high latency of over 0.25 s one-way. Thus, many retransmission schemes which are known from fixed networks fail. Furthermore, due to the large footprint, either frequencies cannot be reused or the GEO satellite needs special antennas focusing on a smaller footprint. Transferring a GEO into orbit is very expensive.

5.3.2 LEO

As LEOs circulate on a lower orbit, it is obvious that they discover a much shorter period (the typical duration of LEO periods are 95 to 120 minutes). Additionally, LEO systems try to ensure a high elevation for every spot on earth to provide a high quality communication link. Each LEO satellite will only be visible from the earth for around 10 minutes. A further classification of LEOs into little LEOs with low bandwidth services (some 100 bit/s), big LEOs (some 1,000 bit/s) and broadband LEOs with plans reaching into the Mbit/s range can be found in Comparetto (1997).

- **Advantages**: Using advanced compression schemes, transmission rates of about 2,400 bit/s can be enough for voice communication. LEOs even provide this bandwidth for mobile terminals with omni-directional antennas using low transmit power in the range of 1 W. Furthermore, the delay for packets delivered via a LEO is relatively low (approx. 10 ms). Thus, the delay is comparable to long-distance wired connections (about 5–10 ms). Smaller footprints of LEOs allow for a better frequency reuse, similar to the concepts used for cellular networks (Gavish, 1998). LEOs can provide a much higher elevation in polar regions and, thus, a better global coverage.

● **Disadvantages**: The biggest problem of the LEO concept is the need for many satellites if global coverage is to be reached. Several concepts involve 50–200 or even more satellites in orbit. The short time of visibility with a high elevation requires additional mechanisms for connection handover between different satellites. (Different cases for handover are explained in section 5.4.) The high number of satellites combined with the fast movements results in a high complexity of the whole satellite system. One general problem of LEOs is the short lifetime of about 5–8 years due to atmospheric drag and radiation from the inner Van Allen belt. Thus, assuming 48 satellites and a lifetime of eight years (as expected for the system Globalstar), a new satellite would be needed every two months. The low latency via a single LEO is only half of the story. Other factors are the need for routing of data packets from satellite to satellite (or several times from base stations to satellites and back) if a user wants to set up communication around the world. Due to the large footprint, a GEO typically does not need this type of routing, as senders and receivers are most likely in the same footprint.

5.3.3 MEO

MEOs can be positioned somewhere between LEOs and GEOs, both in terms of their orbit and due to their advantages and disadvantages.

● **Advantages**: Using orbits around 10,000 km, the system only requires a dozen satellites which is more than a GEO system, but much less than a LEO system. Furthermore, these satellites move slower relative to the earth's rotation allowing a simpler system design (satellite periods are about six hours). Depending on the inclination, a MEO can cover larger populations, thus requiring less handovers.

● **Disadvantages**: Again, due to the larger distance to the earth, delay increases to about 70–80 ms. The satellites need higher transmit power and special antennas for smaller footprints.

5.4 Routing

A satellite system together with gateways and fixed terrestrial networks as shown in Figure 5.1 has to route data transmissions from one user to another as any other network does. Routing in the fixed segment (on earth) is achieved as usual, while two different solutions exist for the satellite network in space. If satellites offer ISLs, traffic can be routed between the satellites. If not, all traffic is relayed to earth, routed there, and relayed back to a satellite.

Assume two users of a satellite network exchange data. If the satellite system supports ISLs, one user sends data up to a satellite and the satellite forwards it to the one responsible for the receiver via other satellites. This last satellite now sends the data down to the earth. This means that only one uplink and one downlink per direction is needed. The ability of routing within the satellite network reduces the number of gateways needed on earth.

If a satellite system does not offer ISLs, the user also sends data up to a satellite, but now this satellite forwards the data to a gateway on earth. Routing takes place in fixed networks as usual until another gateway is reached which is responsible for the satellite above the receiver. Again data is sent up to the satellite which forwards it down to the receiver. This solution requires two uplinks and two downlinks. Depending on the orbit and the speed of routing in the satellite network compared to the terrestrial network, the solution with ISLs might offer lower latency. The drawbacks of ISLs are a higher system complexity due to additional antennas and routing hard- and software for the satellites.

5.5 Localization

Localization of users in satellite networks is done similarly to that of terrestrial cellular networks. One additional problem arises from the fact that now the 'base stations', i.e., the satellites, move as well. The gateways of a satellite network maintain several registers. **A home location register (HLR)** stores all static information about a user as well as his or her current location. The last known location of a mobile user is stored in the **visitor location register (VLR)**. Functions of the VLR and HLR are similar to those of the registers in, e.g., GSM (see chapter 4). A particularly important register in satellite networks is the **satellite user mapping register (SUMR)**. This register stores the current position of satellites and a mapping of each user to the current satellite through which communication with a user is possible.

Registration of a mobile station is achieved as follows. The mobile station initially sends a signal which one or several satellites can receive. Satellites receiving such a signal report this event to a gateway. The gateway can now determine the location of the user via the location of the satellites. User data is requested from the user's HLR, VLR and SUMR are updated.

Calling a mobile station is again similar to GSM. The call is forwarded to a gateway which localizes the mobile station using HLR and VLR. With the help of the SUMR, the appropriate satellite for communication can be found and the connection can be set up.

5.6 Handover

An important topic in satellite systems using MEOs and in particular LEOs is handover. Imagine a cellular mobile phone network with fast moving base stations. This is exactly what such satellite systems are – each satellite represents a base station for a mobile phone. Thus, compared to terrestrial mobile phone networks, additional instances of handover can be necessary due to the movement of the satellites.

- **Intra-satellite handover:** A user might move from one spot beam of a satellite to another spot beam of the same satellite. Using special antennas, a satellite can create several spot beams within its footprint. The same effect might be caused by the movement of the satellite.
- **Inter-satellite handover:** If a user leaves the footprint of a satellite or if the satellite moves away, a handover of the user to the next satellite takes place. This might be a hard handover switching at one moment or a soft handover using both satellites (or even more) at the same time as this is possible with CDMA systems. Inter-satellite handover can also take place between satellites if they support ISLs. The satellite system can trade high transmission quality for handover frequency. The higher the transmission quality should be, the higher the elevation angles that are needed. But high elevation angles imply frequent handovers which in turn make the system more complex.
- **Gateway handover:** While the mobile user and satellite might still have good contact, the satellite might move away from the current gateway. Therefore, the satellite has to connect to another gateway.
- **Inter-system handover:** While the three types of handover mentioned above take place within the satellite-based communication system, this type of handover concerns different systems. Typically, satellite systems are used in remote areas if no other network is available. As soon as traditional cellular networks are available, users might switch to this type for it is typically cheaper and offers lower latency. Current systems allow for the use of dual-mode (or even more modes) mobile phones, but unfortunately, seamless handover between satellite systems and terrestrial systems or vice versa has not been possible up to now.

5.7 Examples

Table 5.1 shows four examples of new satellite networks (see also Miller, 1998 and Lutz, 1998). A system which is already in operation is the **Iridium** system, which was originally targeted for 77 satellites (hence the name Iridium with its 77 electrons), now running with 66 satellites plus six spare satellites (Iridium, 1998). It is the first commercial LEO system covering the whole world. Satellites orbit at an altitude of 780 km, the weight of a single satellite is about 700 kg. The fact that the satellites are heavier than, e.g., the competitor Globalstar results from their capability of routing data between Iridium satellites by using ISLs, thus a satellite needs more memory, processing power etc. Mobile stations (MS in Table 5.1) operate at 1.6138-1.6265 GHz according to an FDMA/TDMA scheme with TDD, feeder links to the satellites at 29.1-29.3 GHz for the uplink and 19.4-19.6 GHz for the downlink. ISLs use 23.18-23.38 GHz.

A direct competitor of Iridium is **Globalstar**. This system uses a lower number of satellites with fewer capabilities per satellite. This makes the satellites

	Iridium	Globalstar	ICO	Teledesic
No. of satellites	66 + 6	48 + 4	10 + 2	288
Altitude [km] coverage	780 global	1,414 ±70° latitude	10,390 global	Approx. 700 global
Minimum elevation	8°	20°	20°	40°
Frequencies [GHz (circa)]	1.6 MS 29.2 ↑ 19.5 ↓ 23.3 ISL	1.6 MS ↑ 2.5 MS ↓ 5.1 ↑ 6.9 ↓	2 MS ↑ 2.2 MS ↓ 5.2 ↑ 7 ↓	19 ↓ 28.8 ↑ 62 ISL
Access method	FDMA/TDMA	CDMA	FDMA/TDMA	FDMA/TDMA
ISL	Yes	No	No	Yes
Bit rate	2.4 kbit/s	9.6 kbit/s	4.8 kbit/s	64 Mbit/s ↓ 2/64 Mbit/s ↑
No. of channels	4,000	2,700	4,500	2,500
Lifetime [years]	5-8	7.5	12	10
Cost estimate	$4.4 bn	$2.9 bn	$4.5 bn	$9 bn

Table 5.1
Example MEO and LEO systems

lighter (about 450 kg weight) and the overall system cheaper. Globalstar does not provide ISLs and global coverage, but higher bandwidth is granted to the customers. Using CDMA and utilizing path diversity, Globalstar can provide soft handovers between different satellites by receiving signals from several satellites simultaneously. Globalstar uses 1.61-1.6265 GHz for uplinks from mobile stations to the satellites and 2.4835-2.5 GHz for the downlink. Feeder links for the satellites are at 5.091-5.250 GHz gateway to satellite and 6.875-7.055 GHz satellite to gateway.

While the other three systems presented in Table 5.1 are LEOs, Intermediate Circular Orbit, (ICO) (ICO, 1998) represents a MEO system as the name indicates. Thus ICO needs less satellites, 10 plus 2 spare, to reach global coverage. Each satellite covers about 30 per cent of earth's surface, but the system works with an average elevation of 40°. Due to the higher complexity within the satellites (i.e., larger antennas and larger solar paddles to generate enough power for transmission), these satellites weigh about 2,600 kg. While launching ICO satellites is more expensive due to weight and higher orbit, their expected lifetime is higher with 12 years compared to Globalstar and Iridium with eight years and less. Thus, ICO satellites need less replacements making the whole system cheaper in return.

A very ambitious LEO project is **Teledesic** which plans to provide high bandwidth satellite connections worldwide with high quality of service (Teledesic, 1998). In contrast to the other systems, this satellite network is not primarily planned for access using mobile phones, but to enable worldwide access to the Internet via satellite. Primary customers are businesses, schools etc. in remote places. Teledesic wants to offer 64 Mbit/s downlinks and 2 Mbit/s uplinks. With special terminals even 64 Mbit/s uplinks should be possible. Receivers will be, e.g., roof-mounted laptop-sized terminals that connect to local networks in the building. Service start is targeted for 2003. The initial plans of 840 satellites plus 84 spares were dropped, now 288 plus spares are planned, divided into 12 planes with 24 satellites each. Considering an expected lifetime of 10 years per satellite, this still means a new satellite will have to be launched at least every other week. Due to the high bandwidth, higher frequencies are needed, thus Teledesic operates in the Ka-band with 28.6–29.1 GHz for the uplink and 18.8–19.3 GHz for the downlink. At these high frequencies, communication links can easily be blocked by rain or other obstacles. Therefore, a high elevation of at least 40° is needed. Teledesic uses ISL for routing between the satellites and implements fast packet switching on the satellites.

Only Globalstar uses CDMA as access method, while the other systems rely on different TDMA/FDMA schemes. The cost estimates in Table 5.1 are just rough figures to compare the systems. They directly reflect system complexity. ICO satellites for example are more complicated compared to Iridium, thus the ICO system has similar initial costs. Smaller and simpler Globalstar satellites make the system cheaper than Iridium.

5.8 Summary

Satellite systems evolved quickly from the early stages of GEOs in the late 1960s to many systems in different orbits of today. The trend for communication satellites is moving away from big GEOs, toward the smaller MEOs and LEOs mainly for the reason of lower delay which is essential for voice communication. Different systems will offer global coverage with services ranging from simple voice and low bit rate data up to high bandwidth communications with quality of service. However, satellite systems are not aimed at replacing terrestrial mobile communication systems but at complementing them. Up to now it has not been clear how high the costs for operation and maintenance of satellite systems are and how much data transmission via satellites really costs for a customer. Special problems for LEOs in this context are the high system complexity and the relatively short lifetime of the satellites. Initial system costs thus only constitute part of the overall costs.

Yet another market for new systems might appear between the low orbiting LEOs and terrestrial antennas. Several companies are planning to use high-altitude aircraft or Zeppelins for carrying antennas. These antennas could be placed high above large cities offering high-quality transmission at lower costs compared to satellite systems.

5.9 Review exercises

1   Name basic applications for satellite communication and describe the trends.

2   Why are GEO systems for telecommunications currently being replaced by fibre optics?

3   How do inclination and elevation determine the use of a satellite?

4   What characteristics do the different orbits have? What are their pros and cons?

5   What are the general problems of satellite signals travelling from a satellite to a receiver?

6   Considered as an interworking unit in a communication network, what function can a satellite have?

7   What special problems do customers of a satellite system with mobile phones face if they are using it in big cities? Think of in-building use and skyscrapers.

8   Why is there hardly any space in space for GEOs?

5.10 References

Comparetto, G.; Ramirez, R. (1997) 'Trends in mobile satellite technology', *IEEE Computer*, 30, (2), February.

Gavish, B.; Kalvenes, J.(1998) 'The impact of satellite altitude on the performance of LEOS based communication systems', *Wireless Networks*, J.C. Baltzer, 4,(2),

Globalstar L.P. (1998) San Jose, CA, USA, http://www.globalstar.com/

ICO Global Communications (1998), London, UK, http://www.ico.com/

Iridium LLC, (1998) Washington, DC, USA, http://www.iridium.com/.

Jamalipour, A. (1998) *Low earth orbital satellites for personal communication networks*, Artech House.

Lutz, E.: 'Issues in satellite personal communication systems', *Wireless Networks*, J.C. Baltzer, 4, (2).

Maral, G.; Bousquet, M. (1998) *Satellite communications systems: Systems, techniques and technology,* 3rd edition, John Wiley & Sons.

Miller, B. (1998) 'Satellites free the mobile phone', *IEEE Spectrum*, March.

Pascall, S. C.; Withers, D. J. (1997) *Commercial satellite communication*, Focal Press, 1997

Schwartz, R. (1996) *Wireless communications in developing countries: cellular and satellite systems*, Artech House.
Teledesic Corporation (1998) Kirkland, WA, USA, http://www.teledesic.com/.

Broadcast systems

6

Although this book mostly deals with different communication technologies allowing individual two-way communication, it is important to understand the role of unidirectional broadcast systems within future mobile communication scenarios. Typical broadcast systems, such as radio and television, distribute information regardless of the needs of individual users. As an addition to two-way communication technologies, broadcasting information can be very cost effective.

Future television and radio transmissions will be fully digital. Already several radio stations produce and transmit their programmes digitally via the Internet or digital radio (see later sections in this chapter). Digital television is on its way. Besides transmitting video and audio, digital transmission allows for the distribution of arbitrary digital data, i.e., multimedia information can accompany radio and TV programmes at very low cost compared to individual wireless connections.

The following sections give a general introduction into asymmetric communication up to the extreme case of unidirectional broadcasting. One important issue is the cyclic repetition of data (as discussed in the sections about broadcast disks). A broadcasting system which will be explained in detail is digital audio broadcasting (DAB), which is already standardized and in use. One interesting feature with respect to data communication is the ability of DAB to carry multimedia information. Finally, one possible successor to today's analog TV system is presented: digital video broadcasting (DVB). In combination with satellite transmission and the use of the Internet, this system is able to deliver high bandwidth to individual customers at low cost (ETSI, 1999).

6.1 Overview

Unidirectional distribution systems or broadcast systems are an extreme version of asymmetric communication systems. Quite often, bandwidth limitations, differences in transmission power, or cost factors prevent a communication system from being symmetrical. **Symmetrical communication systems** offer the same transmission capabilities in all communication directions, i.e., the channel characteristics from A to B are the same as from B to A (e.g., bandwidth, delay, costs).

Examples of symmetrical communication services are the plain old tele-phone service (POTS) or GSM, if end-to-end communication is considered. In this case, it does not matter if one mobile station calls the other or the other way round, bandwidth and delay are the same in both scenarios.

This symmetry is necessary for a telephone service, but many other applica-tions do not require the same characteristics for both directions of information transfer. Consider a typical client/server environment. Typically, the client needs much more data from the server than the server needs from the client. Today's most prominent example of this is the World Wide Web. Millions of users download data using their browsers (clients) from web servers. Only from time to time does a user return information to the server. Single requests for new pages with a typical size of several hundred bytes result in responses of up to some 10 kbytes on average.

A television with a set-top box represents a more extreme scenario. While a high-resolution video stream requires several Mbit/s, a typical user returns some bytes from time to time to switch between channels or return some information for TV shopping.

Finally, today's pagers and radios work completely one-way. These devices can only receive information, and a user needs additional communication tech-nology to send any information back to, e.g., the radio station. Typically, the telephone system is used for this purpose.

A special case of **asymmetrical communication systems** are **unidirec-tional broadcast systems** where typically a high bandwidth data stream exists from one sender to many receivers. The problem arising from this is that the sender can only optimize transmitted data for the whole group of receivers and not for an individual user. Figure 6.1 shows a simple broadcast scenario. A

Figure 6.1
Broadcast transmission

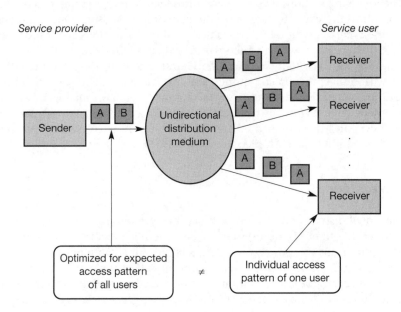

sender tries to optimize the transmitted packet stream for the access patterns of all receivers without knowing their exact requirements. All packets are then transmitted via a broadcast to all receivers. Each receiver now picks up the packets needed and drops the others.

These additional functions are needed to personalize distributed data depending on individual requirements and applications. A very simple example of this process could be a user-defined filter function that filters out all information which is not of interest to the user. A radio in a car, for example, could only present traffic information for the local environment, a set-top box could only store the starting times of movies and drop all information about sports.

However, the problem concerning which information to send at what time still remains for a sender. The following section shows several solutions to this.

6.2 Cyclical repetition of data

A broadcast sender of data does not know when a receiver starts to listen to the transmission. While for radio or television this is no problem (if you do not listen you will not get the message), transmission of other important information, such as traffic or weather conditions, has to be repeated to give receivers a chance to receive this information after having listened for a certain amount of time (like the news every full hour).

The cyclical repetition of data blocks sent via broadcast is often called a **broadcast disk** according to the project in Acharya (1995). Different patterns are possible (Figure 6.2 shows three examples). The sender repeats the three data blocks A, B, and C in a cycle. Using a **flat disk**, all blocks are repeated one after another. Every block is transmitted for an equal amount of time, the average waiting time for receiving a block is the same for A, B, and C. **Skewed disks** favour one or more data blocks by repeating them once or several times. This raises the probability of receiving a repeated block (here A) if the block was corrupted the first time. Finally, **multi-disks** distribute blocks that are repeated more often than others evenly over the cyclic pattern. This minimizes the delay if a user wants to access, e.g., block A.

It is only possible to optimize these patterns if the sender knows something about the content of the data blocks and the access patterns of all users. Let us assume that the broadcast sender is a radio station transmitting information about road conditions (block A), the weather report (block B), the latest events in town (block C) and a menu to access these and other topics (block D) in addition to music. The sender can now assume, knowing something about the importance of the data blocks, that block D is the most important to enable access to the

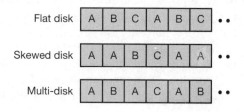

Figure 6.2
Different broadcast patterns

other information. The second important block is A, then B and finally C. A possible broadcast disk for this scenario could now look as follows:

DADBDADCDADBDADC ...

It is now the receiver's task to cache data blocks to minimize access delay as soon as a user needs a specific type of information. Again, the receiver can only optimize caching if it knows something about the content of the data blocks. Furthermore, the receiver can store typical access patterns of a user to be able to guess which blocks the user will access with a higher probability. **Caching** generally follows a cost-based strategy: what are the costs for a user (caused by the waiting time) if a data block has been requested but is currently not available in the cache?

Considering the above example, the radio of the future might remember that a user always checks the latest events in town in the evening, but the road conditions in the morning. Therefore, the radio will cache block A in the morning and block C in the evening. This procedure will generally reduce the waiting time for a user if he or she stays with this access pattern.

6.3 Digital audio broadcasting

Today's analog radio system still follows the basic principle of frequency modulation invented back in 1933. In addition to audio transmission, very limited information such as the station identification can accompany the programme. Transmission quality varies greatly depending on multipath effects and interference. The fully digital **DAB** system does not only offer sound in a CD-like quality, it is also practically immune to interference and multipath propagation effects (ETSI, 1997a), (WorldDAB, 1999).

DAB systems can use **single frequency networks (SFN)**, i.e., all senders transmitting the same radio programme operate at the same frequency. Today, different senders have to use different frequencies to avoid interference although they are transmitting the same radio program. Using an SFN is very frequency efficient, as a single radio station only needs one frequency throughout the whole country. DAB uses VHF and UHF frequency bands (depending on national regulations), e.g., the terrestrial TV channels 5 to 12 (174–230 MHz) or the L-band (1452–1492 MHz). The modulation scheme used is **DQPSK**. DAB is one of the systems using **COFDM** (see chapter 2) with 192 to 1536 carriers (the so-called **ensemble**) within a DAB channel of 1.5 MHz. Additionally, DAB uses **FEC** to reduce the error rate and introduces **guard spaces** between single symbols during transmission. COFDM and the use of guard spaces reduce ISI to a minimum. DAB can even benefit from multipath propagation by recombining the signals from different paths.

Within every frequency block of 1.5 MHz, DAB can transmit up to six stereo audio programmes with a data rate of 192 kbit/s each. Depending on the redundancy coding, a data service with rates up to 1.5 Mbit/s is available as an alternative. For the DAB transmission system, audio is just another type of data (besides different coding schemes). DAB uses two basic transport mechanisms:

- **Main service channel (MSC):** The MSC carries all user data, e.g. audio, multimedia data. The MSC consists of **common interleaved frames (CIF)**, i.e., data fields of 55,296 bits that are sent every 24 ms (this interval depends on the transmission mode (ETSI, 1997a)). This results in a data rate of 2.304 Mbit/s. A CIF consists of **capacity units (CU)** with a size of 64 bits, which form the smallest addressable unit within a DAB system.
- **Fast information channel (FIC):** The FIC contains **fast information blocks (FIB)** with 256 bits each (16 bit checksum). An FIC carries all control information which is required for interpreting the configuration and content of the MSC.

Two transport modes have been defined for the MSC. The **stream mode** offers a transparent data transmission from the source to the destination with a fixed bit rate in a sub-channel. A **sub-channel** is a part of the MSC and comprises several CUs within a CIF. The fixed data rate can be multiples of 8 kbit/s. The **packet mode** transfers data in addressable blocks (packets). These blocks are used to convey MSC data within a sub-channel.

DAB defines many service information structures accompanying an audio stream. This **programme associated data (PAD)** can contain programme information, control information, still pictures for display on a small LCD, title display etc. Audio coding uses PCM with a sampling rate of 48 kHz and MPEG audio compression. The compressed audio stream can have bit rates ranging from 8 kbit/s to 384 kbit/s. Audio data is interleaved for better burst tolerance.[21]

Figure 6.3 shows the general frame structure of DAB. Each frame has a duration T_F of 24, 48, or 96 ms depending on the transmission mode. DAB defines

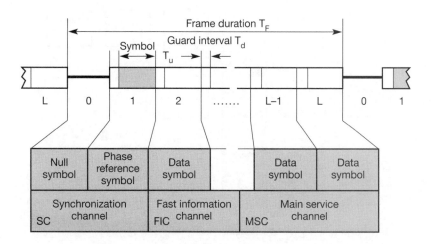

Figure 6.3
DAB frame structure

four different transmission modes, each of which has certain strengths that make it more efficient for either cable, terrestrial, or satellite transmission (ETSI, 1997a). Within each frame, 76 or 153 symbols are transmitted using 192, 384, 768, or 1,536 different carriers for COFDM. The guard intervals T_d protecting each symbol can be 31, 62, 123, or 246 µs.

Each frame consists of three parts. The **synchronization channel (SC)** marks the start of a frame. It consists of a null symbol and a phase reference symbol to synchronize the receiver. The **fast information channel (FIC)** follows, containing control data in the FIBs. Finally, the **main service channel (MSC)** carries audio and data service components.

Figure 6.4 gives a simplified overview of a DAB sender. Audio services are encoded (MPEG compression) and coded for transmission (FEC). All data services are multiplexed and also coded with redundancy. The MSC multiplexer combines all user data streams and forwards them to the transmission multiplexer. This unit creates the frame structure by interleaving the FIC. Finally, OFDM coding is applied and the DAB signal is transmitted.

DAB does not require a fixed, pre-determined allocation of channels with certain properties to services. Figure 6.5 shows the possibilities of dynamic reconfiguration during transmission. Initially, DAB transmits six audio pro-

Figure 6.4
Components of a DAB sender (simplified)

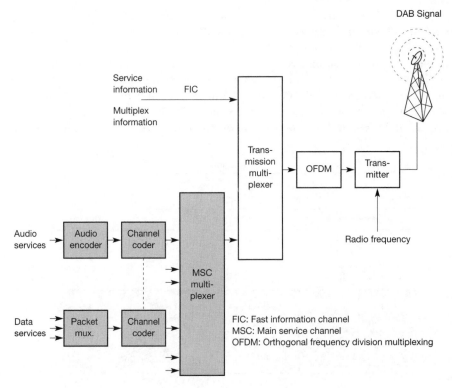

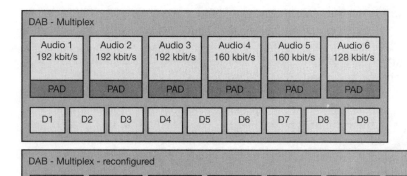

Figure 6.5
Dynamic reconfiguration
of the DAB multiplexer

grammes of different quality together with nine data services. Each audio programme has its PAD. In the example, audio 1, 2, and 3 have a high quality, 4
and 5 a lower quality, while 6 has the lowest quality. Programmes 1 to 3 could,
e.g., be higher quality classic transmissions, while programme 6 could be voice
transmissions (news etc.). The radio station could now decide that for audio 3
128 kbit/s are enough when, for example, the news programme starts. News
may be in mono or stereo with lower quality but additional data (here D10 and
D11 – headlines, pictures etc.). The DAB multiplexer dynamically interleaves
data from all different sources. To inform the receiver about the current configuration of the MSC carrying the different data streams, the FIC sends **multiplex
configuration information (MCI)**.

6.3.1   Multimedia object transfer protocol

A problem which technologies like DAB are facing is the broad range of different receiver capabilities. Receivers could be simple audio-only devices with
single-line text displays or more advanced radios with extra colour graphics displays. DAB receivers can also be adapters in multimedia PCs. However, all
different types of receivers should at least be able to recognize all programme-
associated and programme-independent data, and process some of the data.

   In order to solve this problem, DAB defines a common standard for data
transmission, the **multimedia object transfer (MOT)** protocol (ETSI, 1998a).
The primary goal of MOT is the support of data formats used in other multimedia systems (e.g., online services, Internet, CD-ROM). Example formats
are multimedia and hypermedia information coding experts group (MHEG),
Java, joint photographic experts group (JPEG), American standard code for

information interchange (ASCII), moving pictures expert group (MPEG), hypertext markup language (HTML), hypertext transfer protocol (HTTP), bitmap (BMP), graphics interchange format (GIF).

MOT data is transferred in MOT objects consisting of a header core, a header extension, and a body (Figure 6.6).

- **Header core:** This seven byte field contains the sizes of the header and the body, and the content type of the object. Depending on this header information, the receiver may decide if it has enough resources (memory, CPU power, display etc.) available to decode and further process the object.
- **Header extension:** The extension field of variable size contains additional handling data for the object, such as, e.g., the repetition distance to support advanced caching strategies (see section 6.2), the segmentation information, and the priority of the data. With the help of the priority information a receiver can decide which data to cache and which to replace. For example, the index HTML page may have a higher priority than an arbitrary page.
- **Body:** Arbitrary data can be transferred in the variable body as described in the header fields.

Larger MOT objects will be segmented into smaller segments. DAB can apply different interleaving and repetition schemes to objects and segments:

- **Object repetition:** DAB can repeat objects several times. If an object A consists of four segments (A_1, A_2, A_3, and A_4), a simple repetition pattern would be $A_1A_2A_3A_4A_1A_2A_3A_4A_1$ $A_2A_3A_4$...
- **Interleaved objects:** To mitigate burst error problems, DAB can also interleave segments from different objects. Interleaving the objects A, B, and C could result in the pattern $A_1B_1C_1A_2B_2C_2A_3B_3C_3$...
- **Segment repetition:** If some segments are more important than others, DAB can repeat these segments more often (e.g. $A_1A_1A_2A_2$ $A_2A_3A_4A_4$...).
- **Header repetition:** If a receiver cannot receive the header of an MOT, it will not be able to decode the object. Thus, it can be useful to retransmit the header several times. Then, the receiver can synchronize with the data stream as soon as it receives the header and can start decoding. A pattern could be $HA_1A_2HA_3A_4HA_5A_6H$... with H being the header of the MOT object A.

Obviously, DAB can also apply all interleaving and repetition schemes at the same time.

Figure 6.6
MOT object structure

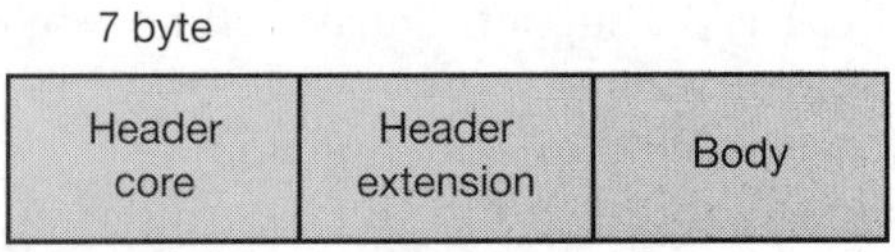

7 byte

Header core	Header extension	Body

6.4 Digital video broadcasting

The logical consequence of applying digital technology to radio broadcasting is doing the same for the traditional television system. The analog system used today has basically remained unchanged for decades. The only invention worth mentioning was the introduction of colour TV for the mass market back in the 1960s. Therefore, television still uses the low resolution of 768×576 for the European PAL system or 720×460 for the US NTSC respectively. The display is interlaced with 25 or 30 frames per second respectively. So, compared with today's computer displays with resolutions of 1,280×1,024 and more than 75 Hz frame rate, non-interlaced, TV performance is not very impressive.

There have been many attempts to change this and to introduce digital TV with higher resolution, better sound and additional features, but no approach has yet been truly successful. One reason for this failure is the huge base of installed old systems that will not be replaced as fast as is done with computers (we can watch the latest movie on an old TV, but it is impossible to run new software on older computers!). Furthermore, varying political and economic interests are counterproductive to a common standard for digital TV. One approach toward such a standard is presented in the following sections.

After some national failures in introducing digital TV, the so-called European Launching Group was founded in 1991 with the aim of developing a common digital television system for Europe. In 1993 these common efforts were named **digital video broadcasting (DVB)** (Reimers, 1998), (DVB, 1999). Although the name shows a certain affinity to DAB, there are some fundamental differences regarding the transmission technology, frequencies, modulation etc. The goal of DVB is to introduce digital television broadcasting using satellite transmission (DVB-S, (ETSI, 1997c)), cable technology (DVB-C, (ETSI, 1998b)), and at a later stage also terrestrial transmission (DVB-T, (ETSI, 1997b)).

Figure 6.7 shows components that should be integrated into the DVB architecture. The centre point is an integrated receiver-decoder (set-top box) connected to a high-resolution monitor. This set-top box can receive DVB signals via satellites, terrestrial local/regional senders (multipoint distribution systems, terrestrial receiver), cable, B-ISDN, ADSL, or other possible future technologies. Cable, ADSL, and B-ISDN connections also offer a return channel, i.e., a user can send data such as channel selection, authentication information, or a shopping list. Additionally, audio/video streams can be recorded, processed, and replayed using **digital versatile disk (DVD)**, **digital video tape recorder (DVTR)** or multimedia PCs. Different levels of quality are envisaged: **standard definition TV (SDTV)**, **enhanced definition TV (EDTV)**, and **high definition TV (HDTV)** with a resolution of up to 1,920×1,080 pixels.

Similar to DAB, DVB also transmits data using flexible containers. These containers are basically MPEG-2 frames that do not restrict the type of information. DVB sends service information contained in its data stream, which specifies the content of a container. The following contents have been defined:

Figure 6.7
Digital video
broadcasting scenario

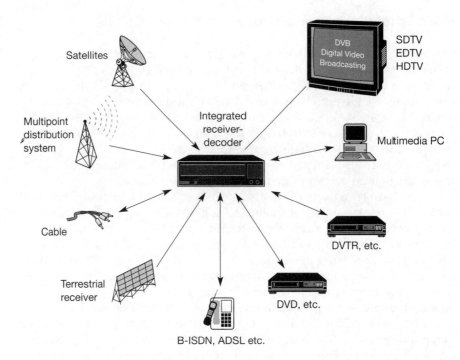

- **Network information table (NIT):** NIT lists the services of a provider and contains additional information for set-top boxes.
- **Service description table (SDT):** SDT lists names and parameters for each service within an MPEG multiplex channel.
- **Event information table (EIT):** EIT contains status information about the current transmission and some additional information for set-top boxes.
- **Time and date table (TDT):** Finally, TDT contains update information for set-top boxes.

As shown in Figure 6.8, an MPEG-2/DVB container can store different types of data. It either contains a single channel for HDTV, multiple channels for EDTV or SDTV, or arbitrary multimedia data (data broadcasting).

Apart from this multimedia broadcasting, DVB could be also used for high-bandwidth, asymmetrical Internet access. A typical scenario could be the following (see Figure 6.9): An information provider, e.g., video store, offers its data to potential customers with the help of a service provider. If a customer wants to download high-volume information, the information provider transmits this information to a satellite provider via a service provider. In fixed networks this is typically done using leased lines due to the fact that high bandwidth and QoS guarantees are needed. The satellite provider now multiplexes this data stream together with other digital TV channels and transmits it to the

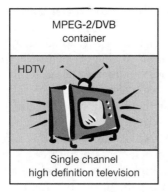

MPEG-2/DVB
container

HDTV

Single channel
high definition television

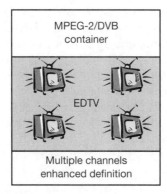

MPEG-2/DVB
container

EDTV

Multiple channels
enhanced definition

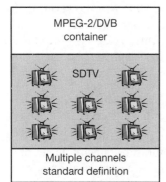

MPEG-2/DVB
container

SDTV

Multiple channels
standard definition

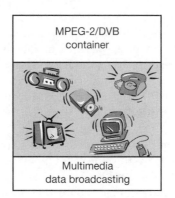

MPEG-2/DVB
container

Multimedia
data broadcasting

Figure 6.8
Different contents of
MPEG-2/DVB containers

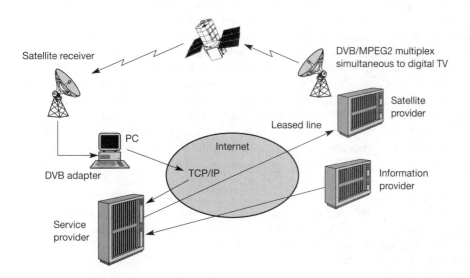

Satellite receiver

DVB/MPEG2 multiplex
simultaneous to digital TV

Satellite
provider

Leased line

PC

Internet

DVB adapter

TCP/IP

Information
provider

Service
provider

Figure 6.9
High-bandwidth Internet
access using DVB

customer via satellite and a satellite receiver. The customer can now receive the requested information with the help of a DVB adapter inside a multimedia PC. Typically, the information for the customer will be encrypted to ensure that only paying customers can use the information. The return channel for requests etc. can be a standard TCP/IP connection via the Internet because this channel only requires a low bandwidth.

Typical data rates planned per user are 6-38 Mbit/s for the downlink via satellite and a return channel with 33 kbit/s using a standard modem, 64 kbit/s with ISDN, or several 100 kbit/s using ADSL. One advantage of this approach is that it is transmitted along with the TV programmes using free space in the transmitted data stream. Therefore, this approach does not require additional lines or hardware per customer. This factor is particularly important for remote areas or developing countries where high bandwidth wired access such as ADSL is not available. A clear disadvantage of the approach, however, is the shared medium 'satellite'. If many users request data streams via DVB, they have to share the satellite's bandwidth. Therefore, this system cannot give hard QoS guarantees to all users without being very expensive.

6.5 Summary

This chapter has presented two examples of broadcast technologies that somehow stand out from the other mobile communication technologies presented in this book. DAB and DVB are most likely the successors of the traditional radio and television in many countries (probably not everywhere due to varying political and economic interests). In addition to the transmission of audio or video streams, these systems allow for the broadcasting of multimedia data streams. Although both technologies only support unidirectional communication, both will be an integral part of tomorrow's mobile communication scenarios. DAB and DVB will be used to distribute mass data in a cost-effective manner and rely on other low bandwidth wireless technologies for the return channel if required. These technologies support the ongoing merger of computer, communication, and entertainment industries by merging TV/radio data streams with personalized multimedia streams. We can imagine a scenario in which a movie is distributed to everyone, but for example with individual commercials depending on the user's interest. The set-top box will merge both data streams and the user will, e.g., watch a soccer game with fully individualized billboards. Another feature, which makes DAB particularly attractive for mobile communication, is the fact that DAB is the only commercial radio system suitable for high speeds and high data rates: up to 1.5 Mbit/s at 900 km/h! This makes it possible to install, for example, TV sets in trains and in other vehicles that would suffer from multipath propagation using other technologies. The fact that DVB was not designed for fast moving receivers, however, is countered by the ability of DAB to carry video data.

6.6 Review exercises

1 GSM and the next generation GSM can both transfer data. Compare these approaches with DAB and list reasons for and against the use of DAB.

2 Which web pages would be appropriate for distribution via DAB or DVB?

3 How could the global positioning system (GPS) and DAB work together?

6.7 References

Acharya, S.; Franklin, M.; Zdonik, S. (1995) 'Dissemination-based data delivery using broadcast disks', *IEEE Personal Communications*, 2, (6).

DVB Project Office (1999), http://www.dvb.org/.

ETSI (1997a) *Digital Audio Broadcasting (DAB) to mobile, portable, and fixed receivers,* European Telecommunications Standards Institute, ETS 300 401.

ETSI (1997b) *Framing structure, channel coding and modulation for digital terrestrial television,* European Telecommunications Standards Institute, ETS 300 744.

ETSI (1997c) *Framing structure, channel coding and modulation for 11/12 GHz satellite services,* European Telecommunications Standards Institute, ETS 300 421.

ETSI (1998a) *DAB Multimedia Object Transfer (MOT) protocol,* European Telecommunications Standards Institute, ETS 301 234.

ETSI (1998b) *Framing structure, channel coding and modulation for cable systems,* European Telecommunications Standards Institute, ETS 300 429.

ETSI (1999) *Digital Audio and Video Broadcasting,* European Telecommunications Standards Institute, http://www. etsi.org/.

Reimers, U. (1998) 'Digital Video Broadcasting', *IEEE Communications Magazine,* 36, (6).

World DAB Forum (1999) http://www. worlddab.org/.

Wireless LAN 7

This chapter presents several wireless local area network (WLAN) technologies, which constitute a fast-growing market introducing the flexibility of wireless access into office, home, or production environments. In contrast to the technologies described in chapters 4 through 6, WLANs are typically restricted in their diameter to buildings, a campus, single rooms etc. and are operated by individuals, not by large-scale network providers. The global goal of WLANs is to replace office cabling and, additionally, to introduce a higher flexibility for ad hoc communication in, e.g., group meetings. The following points illustrate some general advantages and disadvantages of WLANs compared to their wired counterparts.

Some **advantages** of WLANs are:

- **Flexibility**: Within radio coverage, nodes can communicate without further restriction. Radio waves can penetrate walls, senders and receivers can be placed anywhere (also non-visible, e.g., within devices, in walls etc.). Furthermore, sometimes wiring is difficult if firewalls separate buildings (real firewalls made out of, e.g., bricks, not routers set up as a firewall). Penetration of a firewall is only permitted at certain points to prevent fire from spreading too fast.
- **Planning**: Only wireless ad hoc networks allow for communication without previous planning, any wired network needs wiring plans. As long as devices follow the same standard, they can communicate. For wired networks, additional cabling with the right plugs and probably interworking units (such as switches) have to be provided.
- **Design**: Only wireless networks allow for the design of small, independent devices which can for example be put into a pocket. Cables not only restrict users but also designers of small PDAs, notepads etc. Furthermore, wireless senders and receivers can be hidden in historic buildings, i.e., current networking technology can be introduced without being visible.
- **Robustness**: Wireless networks can survive disasters, e.g., earthquakes or users pulling a plug. If the wireless devices survive, people can still communicate. Networks requiring a wired infrastructure will typically break down completely.

But WLANs also exhibit several **disadvantages**:

- **Quality of service**: WLANs typically offer lower quality than their wired counterparts. The main reasons for this drawback are the lower bandwidth due to limitations in radio transmission (e.g., only 1–10 Mbit/s), higher error rates due to interference (e.g., 10^{-4} instead of 10^{-10} for fibre optics), and higher delay/delay variation.
- **Cost**: While, e.g., high-speed Ethernet adapters are in the range of some 10 €, wireless LAN adapters, e.g., as PC-Card, still cost some 100 €.
- **Proprietary solutions**: Due to slow standardization procedures, many companies have come up with proprietary solutions offering standardized functionality plus many enhanced features (typically a higher bit rate using a patented coding technology). However, these additional features only work in a homogeneous environment, i.e., when adapters from the same vendors are used for all wireless nodes.
- **Restrictions**: All wireless products have to comply with national regulations. Several government and non-government institutions worldwide regulate the operation and restrict frequencies to minimize interference. Consequently, it takes a very long time to establish global solutions like, e.g., IMT-2000. WLANs are limited to low-power senders and certain licence-free frequency bands.
- **Safety and security**: Using radio waves for data transmission might interfere with other high-tech equipment in, e.g., hospitals. Here special precautions have to be taken. Additionally, the open radio interface makes eavesdropping much easier in WLANs than, e.g., in the case of fibre optics.

Many different and sometimes competing design goals have to be taken into account for WLANs to ensure their commercial success.

- **Global operation**: WLAN products should sell in all countries, therefore, many national and international frequency regulations have to be considered. In contrast to wireless WANs, LAN equipment may be carried from one country into another – the operation should still be legal in this case.
- **Low power**: Devices communicating via a WLAN are typically also wireless devices running on battery power. The LAN design should take this into account and implement special power-saving modes and power management functions. Wireless communication with devices plugged into a power outlet is only useful in some cases (e.g., no additional cabling should be necessary for the network in historic buildings). However, the future clearly lies in small handheld devices without any restricting wire.
- **Licence-free operation**: LAN operators do not want to apply for a special licence in order to be able to use the product. Thus, the equipment must operate in a licence-free band, such as the 2.4 GHz ISM band.

- **Robust transmission technology**: Compared to their wired counterparts, WLANs operate under difficult conditions. If they use radio transmission, many other electrical devices may interfere. Additionally, WLAN transceivers cannot be adjusted for perfect transmission in a standard office or production environment. Antennas are typically omnidirectional, not directed.
- **Simplified spontaneous co-operation**: To be useful in practice, WLANs should not require complicated setup routines but should operate spontaneously after power-up. Otherwise these LANs would not be useful for supporting, e.g., ad hoc meetings.
- **Easy to use**: In contrast to huge and complex wireless WANs, wireless LANs are made for simple users. Consequently, these LANs should not require complex management but rather work on a plug-and-play basis.
- **Protection of investment**: A lot of money has already been invested into wired LANs. The new WLANs should protect this investment by being interoperable with the existing networks. This means that simple bridging between the different LANs should be enough to interoperate, i.e., the wireless LANs should support the same data types and services that standard LANs support.
- **Safety and security**: Wireless LANs should be safe to operate, especially regarding low radiation if used, e.g., in hospitals. Furthermore, no users should be able to read personal data during transmission, i.e., encryption mechanisms should be integrated. The networks should also take into account user privacy, i.e., it should not be possible to collect roaming profiles for tracking persons if they do not agree.
- **Transparency for applications**: Existing applications should continue to run over WLANs, the only difference being higher delay and lower bandwidth. The fact of wireless access and mobility should be hidden if not relevant, but the network should also support location aware applications, e.g., by providing location information.

The following sections first introduce basic transmission technologies used for WLANs, infrared and radio, then the two basic settings for WLANs, infrastructure-based and ad hoc, are presented. The three main sections of this chapter present the IEEE standard for WLANs, IEEE 802.11, the European ETSI standard for a high-speed WLAN, HIPERLAN 1, and finally an industry approach toward wireless personal area networks, i.e., WLANs at an even smaller range, called Bluetooth.

7.1 Infrared vs. radio transmission

Today, two different basic transmission technologies are used to set up WLANs. One technology is based on the transmission of infrared light (e.g, at 900 nm wavelength), the other one uses radio transmission in the GHz range (e.g., 2.4 GHz in the licence-free ISM band). Both technologies can be used to set up ad hoc connections for work groups, to connect, e.g, a desktop with a printer without a wire, or to support mobility within a small area.

Infrared technology uses diffuse light reflected at walls, furniture etc. or directed light if a line-of-sight (LOS) exists between sender and receiver. Senders can be simple light emitting diodes (LEDs) or laser diodes, whereas photodiodes act as receivers. Details about infrared technology, such as modulation, channel impairments etc. can be found in Wesel (1998) and Santamaría (1994).

- The main **advantages** of infrared technology are its simple and extremely cheap senders and receivers which are integrated in almost all mobile devices available today. PDAs, laptops, notebooks, mobile phones etc. have an infrared data association (IrDA) interface. Version 1.0 of this industry standard implements data rates of up to 115 kbit/s, while IrDA 1.1 defines higher data rates of 1.152 and 4 Mbit/s. No licences are needed for infrared technology and shielding is very simple. Furthermore, electrical devices do not interfere with infrared transmission.
- **Disadvantages** of infrared transmission are its low bandwidth compared to other LAN technologies. Typically, IrDA devices are internally connected to a serial port limiting transfer rates to 115 kbit/s. Even 4 Mbit/s are not a particularly high data rate. However, their main disadvantage is that infrared is quite easily shielded. Infrared transmission cannot penetrate walls or other obstacles, for good transmission quality and high data rates typically a LOS, i.e., direct connection, is needed.

Almost all networks described in this book use **radio** waves for data transmission, e.g., GSM at 900, 1,800, and 1,900 MHz, DECT at 1,880 MHz etc.

- **Advantages** of radio transmission include the long-term experiences made with radio transmission for wide area networks (e.g., microwave links) and mobile cellular phones. Radio transmission can cover larger areas and can penetrate (thinner) walls, furniture, plants etc. Thus, radio typically does not need a LOS if the frequencies are not too high (then radio waves behave more and more like light). Furthermore, current radio-based products offer higher transmission rates (e.g., 10 Mbit/s) than infrared.
- Again, the main advantage is also a big **disadvantage** of radio transmission. Shielding is not so simple and, thus, radio transmission can interfere with other senders or electrical devices can destroy data transmitted via radio. Additionally, radio transmission is only permitted in certain frequency bands. Very limited ranges of licence-free bands are available worldwide and those available are typically not the same in all countries.

Of the three WLAN technologies presented in this chapter, only one (IEEE 802.11) offers infrared transmission in addition to radio transmission. The other two (HIPERLAN and Bluetooth) rely on radio. The main reason for this are the shielding problems of infrared. WLANs should, e.g., cover a whole floor of a building and not only one room where LOSs exist. Furthermore, future mobile devices may have to communicate while still in a pocket or a suitcase and, thus, cannot rely on infrared.

7.2 Infrastructure and ad hoc networks

Many WLANs of today need an **infrastructure** network. Infrastructure networks not only provide access to other networks, but also include forwarding functions, medium access control etc. In these infrastructure-based wireless networks, communication typically takes place only between the wireless nodes and the access point (see Figure 7.1), but not directly between the wireless nodes.

The access point additionally acts as a bridge to other wireless or wired networks. Figure 7.1 shows three access points with their three wireless networks and a wired network. Several wireless networks may form one logical wireless network, thus, the access points together with the fixed network in between can connect several wireless networks to form a larger network beyond actual radio coverage.

Typically, the design of infrastructure-based wireless networks is simpler because most of the network functionality lies within the access point, whereas the wireless clients can remain quite simple. This structure is reminiscent of switched Ethernet or other star-based networks, where a central element (e.g., a switch) controls network flow. This type of network can use different access schemes with or without collision. Collisions may occur if medium access of the wireless nodes and the access point is not co-ordinated. However, if only the access point controls medium access, no collisions are possible. This setting may be useful for quality of service guarantees such as minimum bandwidth for certain nodes. Then, the access point may poll the single wireless nodes to ensure the data rate.

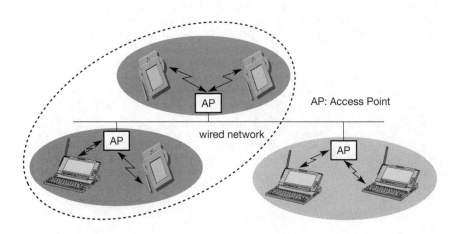

Figure 7.1
Example of three infrastructure-based wireless networks

Infrastructure-based networks lose some of the flexibility wireless networks can offer, e.g., they cannot be used for disaster relief in cases where no infrastructure is left. Typical cellular phone networks are infrastructure-based networks for a wide area. Also satellite-based cellular phones have an infrastructure – the satellites. Thus, infrastructure does not necessarily imply a wired fixed network.

Ad hoc wireless networks, however, do not need any infrastructure to work. Each node can communicate with another node, no access point controlling medium access is necessary. Figure 7.2 shows two ad hoc networks with three nodes each. Nodes within an ad hoc network can only communicate if they can reach each other physically, i.e., if they are within each other's radio range or if other nodes can forward the message. Nodes from the two networks shown in Figure 7.2 cannot, therefore, communicate with each other if they are not within the same radio range.

In ad hoc networks, the complexity of each node is higher because every node has to implement medium access mechanisms, mechanisms to handle hidden or exposed terminal problems, and perhaps priority mechanisms to provide a certain quality of service. This type of wireless network exhibits the greatest possible flexibility as it is, for example, needed for unexpected meetings, quick replacements of infrastructure or communication scenarios far away from any infrastructure.

Clearly, the two basic variants of wireless networks (here especially WLANs), infrastructure-based and ad hoc, do not always come in their pure form. There are networks that rely on access points and infrastructure for basic services (e.g., authentication of access, control of medium access for data with associated quality of service, management functions), but also allow for direct communication between the wireless nodes.

However, ad hoc networks might only have selected nodes with the capabilities of forwarding data. Most of the nodes have to connect to such a special node first in order to transmit data if the receiver is out of their range.

From the three WLANs presented, IEEE 802.11 (see 7.3) and HIPERLAN 1 (see 7.4) are typically infrastructure-based networks, which additionally support ad hoc networking (although HIPERLAN does not explicitly mention an

Figure 7.2

Example of two ad hoc wireless networks

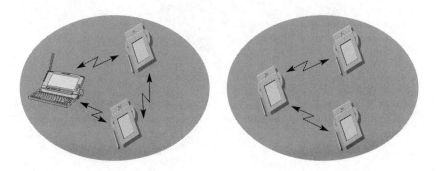

infrastructure, this will be the typical scenario). However, many implementations only offer the basic infrastructure-based version. The third WLAN, Bluetooth (see 7.5), is a typical wireless ad hoc network. Bluetooth focuses precisely on spontaneous ad hoc meetings or on the simple connection of two or more devices without the setup of an infrastructure.

7.3 IEEE 802.11

The IEEE standard 802.11 (IEEE, 1997) specifies the most famous family of WLANs in which many products are already available. As the standards number indicates, this standard belongs to the group of 802.x LAN standards, e.g., 802.3 Ethernet or 802.5 Token Ring. This means that the standard specifies the physical and medium access layer adapted to the special requirements of wireless LANs, but offers the same interface as the others to higher layers to maintain interoperability.

The primary goal of the standard was the specification of a simple and robust WLAN which offers time-bounded and asynchronous services. Furthermore, the MAC layer should be able to operate with multiple physical layers, each of which exhibits a different medium sense and transmission characteristic. Candidates for physical layers were infrared and spread spectrum radio transmission techniques.

Additional features of the WLAN should include the support of power management to save battery power, the handling of hidden nodes, and the ability to operate worldwide. Therefore, the 2.4 GHz ISM band, which is available in most countries around the world, was chosen for the standard. Data rates envisaged for the standard were 1 Mbit/s mandatory and 2 Mbit/s optional.

The following sections will introduce the system and protocol architecture of IEEE 802.11 and then discuss each layer, i.e., physical layer and medium access. Finally, the complex and very important management functions of the standard are presented.

7.3.1 System architecture

Wireless networks can exhibit two different basic system architectures as shown in section 7.2, infrastructure-based or ad hoc. Figure 7.3 shows the components of an infrastructure and a wireless part as specified for IEEE 802.11. Several nodes, called **stations (STA$_i$)**, are connected to **access points (AP)**. Stations are terminals with access mechanisms to the wireless medium and radio contact to the AP. The stations and the AP which are within the same radio coverage form a **basic service set (BSS$_i$)**. The example shows two BSSs – BSS$_1$ and BSS$_2$ – which are connected via a **distribution system**. A distribution system connects several BSSs via the AP to form a single network and thereby extends the wireless coverage area. This network is now called an **extended service set (ESS)**. Furthermore, the distribution system connects the wireless networks via the APs with a **portal**, which forms the interworking unit to other LANs.

The architecture of the distribution system is not specified further in IEEE 802.11. It could consist of bridged IEEE LANs, wireless links, or any other networks. However, **distribution system services** are defined in the standard.

Stations can select an AP and associate with it. The APs support roaming (i.e., changing access points), the distribution system then handles data transfer between the different APs. Furthermore, APs provide synchronization within a BSS, support power management, and can control medium access to support time-bounded service. These and further functions are explained in the following sections.

In addition to infrastructure-based networks, IEEE 802.11 allows the building of ad hoc networks between stations, thus forming one or more BSSs as shown in Figure 7.4. In this case, a BSS comprises a group of stations using the same radio frequency. Stations STA_1, STA_2, and STA_3 are in BSS_1, STA_4 and STA_5 in BSS_2. This means for example that STA_3 can communicate directly with STA_2 but not with STA_5. Several BSSs can either be formed via the distance between the BSSs (Figure 7.4) or by using different carrier frequencies (then the BSSs could overlap physically). IEEE 802.11 does not specify any special nodes that support routing, forwarding of data or exchange of topology information as, e.g., HIPERLAN 1 (see section 7.4).

7.3.2 Protocol architecture

As indicated by the standard number, IEEE 802.11 fits seamlessly into the other 802.x standards for wired LANs (see Halsall, 1996). Figure 7.5 shows the most common scenario: an IEEE 802.11 wireless LAN connected to an IEEE 802.3 Ethernet via a bridge. Applications should not notice any difference apart from the lower bandwidth and perhaps higher access time from the wireless LAN. Consequently, the higher layers (application, TCP, IP) look the same for the wireless node as for the wired node. The upper part of the data link control layer, the logical link control (LLC), covers the differences of the medium access control layers needed for the different media. In many of today's networks, no explicit LLC layer is visible. Further details like Ethertype or sub-network access protocol (SNAP) and bridging technology are explained in, e.g., Perlman (1992).

The IEEE 802.11 standard only covers the physical layer **PHY** and medium access layer **MAC** like the other 802.x LANs do. The physical layer is subdivided into a **physical layer convergence protocol (PLCP)** and the **physical medium dependent** sublayer **PMD** (see Figure 7.6). The basic tasks of the MAC layer comprise medium access, fragmentation of user data, and encryption. The PLCP sublayer provides a carrier sense signal, called clear channel assessment (CCA), and provides a common PHY service access point (SAP) independent of the transmission technology. Finally, the PMD sublayer handles modulation and encoding/decoding of signals. The PHY layer (comprising PMD and PLCP) and MAC layer will be explained in more detail in the following sections.

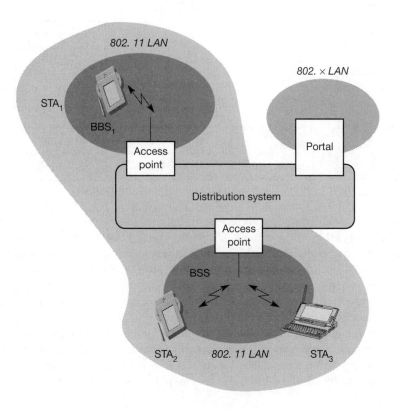

Figure 7.3
Architecture of an
infrastructure-based
IEEE 802.11

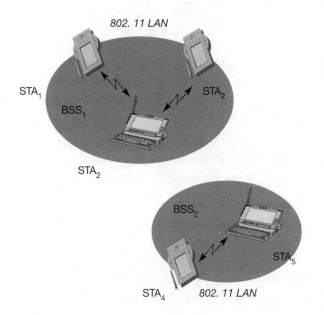

Figure 7.4
Architecture of IEEE
802.11 ad hoc wireless
LANs

Figure 7.5
IEEE 802.11 protocol
architecture and bridging

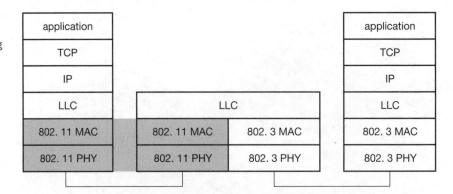

Figure 7.5
IEEE 802.11 protocol
architecture and bridging

Apart from the protocol sublayers, the standard specifies management layers and the station management. The **MAC management** supports the association and re-association of a station to an access point and roaming between different access points. Furthermore, it controls authentication mechanisms, encryption, synchronization of a station with regard to an access point, and power management to save battery power. MAC management also maintains the MAC management information base (MIB).

The main tasks of the **PHY management** include channel tuning and PHY MIB maintenance. Finally, **station management** interacts with both management layers and is responsible for additional higher layer functions (e.g., control of bridging and interaction with the distribution system in the case of an access point).

7.3.3 Physical layer

IEEE 802.11 supports three different physical layers: one layer based on infrared and two layers on the basis of radio transmission (primarily in the ISM band at 2.4 GHz, which is available worldwide). All PHY variants include the provision of the **clear channel assessment** signal **(CCA)**. This signal is needed for the MAC mechanisms controlling medium access and indicates if the medium is currently idle. The transmission technology (which will be discussed later) determines exactly how this signal is obtained.

Furthermore, the PHY layer offers a service access point (SAP) with 1 or 2 Mbit/s transfer rate to the MAC layer. The remainder of this section presents the three versions of a PHY layer defined in the standard.

Figure 7.6
Detailed IEEE 802.11
protocol architecture and
management

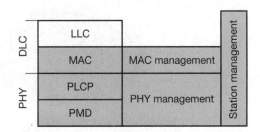

7.3.3.1 Frequency hopping spread spectrum

Frequency hopping spread spectrum (FHSS) is a spread spectrum technique which allows for the coexistence of multiple networks in the same area by separating different networks using different hopping sequences. The standard defines 79 hopping channels for North America and Europe, and 23 hopping channels for Japan (each with a bandwidth of 1 MHz in the 2.4 GHz ISM band). The selection of a particular channel is achieved by using a pseudo random hopping pattern. National restrictions also determine further parameters, e.g., maximum transmit power is 1 W EIRP (equivalent isotropically radiated power) in the US, 100 mW EIRP in Europe.

The standard specifies Gaussian shaped FSK (frequency shift keying), GFSK, as modulation for the FHSS PHY. For 1 Mbit/s a 2 level GFSK is used (i.e., 1 bit is mapped to one frequency, see chapter 2), a 4 level GFSK for 2 Mbit/s (i.e., 2 bits are mapped to one frequency). While sending and receiving at 1 Mbit/s is mandatory for all devices, operation at 2 Mbit/s is optional. This facilitates the production of low-cost devices for the lower rate only and more powerful devices for both transmission rates.

Figure 7.7 shows a frame of the physical layer used with FHSS. The frame consists of two basic parts, the PLCP part (preamble and header) and the payload part. While the PLCP part is always transmitted at 1 Mbit/s, payload, i.e. MAC data, can use 1 or 2 Mbit/s. Additionally, MAC data is scrambled using the polynomial $s(z) = z^7+z^4+1$ for DC blocking and whitening of the spectrum. The fields of the frame fulfil the following functions:

- **Synchronization**: The PLCP preamble starts with 80 bit synchronization, which is a 010101... bit pattern. This pattern is used for synchronization of potential receivers and signal detection by the CCA.
- **Start frame delimiter (SFD)**: The following 16 bits indicate the start of the frame and thus provide frame synchronization. The SFD pattern is 0000110010111101.
- **PLCP_PDU length word (PLW)**: This first field of the PLCP header indicates the length of the payload in bytes including the 32 bit CRC at the end of the payload. PLW can range between 0 and 4,095.
- **PLCP signalling field (PSF)**: Only one bit is currently specified in this 4 bit field indicating the data rate of the payload following (1 or 2 Mbit/s).
- **Header error check (HEC)**: Finally, the PLCP header is protected by a 16 bit checksum with the standard ITU-T generator polynomial $G(x) = x^{16}+x^{12}+x^5+1$.

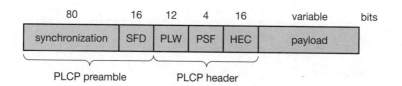

Figure 7.7
Format of an IEEE 802.11 PHY frame using FHSS

7.3.3.2 Direct sequence spread spectrum

Direct sequence spread spectrum (DSSS) is the alternative spread spectrum method separating by code and not by frequency. In the case of IEEE 802.11 DSSS, spreading is achieved using the 11-chip sequence (+1, –1, +1, +1, –1, +1, +1, +1, –1, –1, –1), also called Barker Code. The key characteristics of this method are its robustness against interference and its insensitivity to multipath propagation (time delay spread).

IEEE 802.11 DSSS PHY also uses the 2.4 GHz ISM band and offers both 1 or 2 Mbit/s data rates. The system uses differential binary phase shift keying (DBPSK) for 1 Mbit/s transmission and differential quadrature phase shift keying (DQPSK) for 2 Mbit/s as modulation schemes. Again, the maximum transmit power is 1 W EIRP (equivalent isotropically radiated power) in the US, 100 mW EIRP in Europe. The symbol rate is 1 MHz, resulting in a chipping rate of 11 MHz. All bits transmitted by the DSSS PHY are scrambled with the polynomial $s(z) = z^7 + z^4 + 1$ for DC blocking and whitening of the spectrum.

Figure 7.8 shows a frame of the physical layer using DSSS. The frame consists of two basic parts, the PLCP part (preamble and header) and the payload part. While the PLCP part is always transmitted at 1 Mbit/s, payload, i.e., MAC data, can use 1 or 2 Mbit/s. The fields of the frame have the following functions:

- **Synchronization**: The first 128 bits are not only used for synchronization, but also gain setting, energy detection (for the CCA), and frequency offset compensation. The synchronization field only consists of scrambled 1 bits.
- **Start frame delimiter (SFD)**: This 16 bit field is used for synchronization at the beginning of a frame and consists of the pattern 1111001110100000.
- **Signal**: Up to now, only two values have been defined for this field to indicate the data rate of the payload. The value 0x0A indicates 1 Mbit/s (and thus DBPSK), 0x14 indicates 2 Mbit/s (and thus DQPSK). Other values have been reserved for future use, i.e., higher bit rates.
- **Service**: This field is reserved for future use, however, 0x00 indicates an IEEE 802.11 compliant frame.
- **Length**: As for the other system, 16 bits are used in this case for length indication of the payload.
- **Header error check (HEC)**: Signal, service, and length fields are protected by this checksum using the ITU-T CRC-16 standard polynomial.

Figure 7.8
Format of an
IEEE 802.11 PHY frame
using DSSS

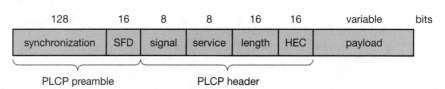

128	16	8	8	16	16	variable	bits
synchronization	SFD	signal	service	length	HEC	payload	

PLCP preamble   PLCP header

7.3.3.3 Infrared

The PHY layer, which is based on infrared (IR) transmission, uses near visible light at 850–950 nm, which is not regulated apart from safety restrictions (using lasers instead of LEDs). The standard does not require a line-of-sight between sender and receiver, but should also work with diffuse light. This allows for point-to-multipoint communication. The maximum range is about 10 m if no sunlight or heat sources interfere with the transmission. Typically, such a network will only work in buildings, e.g., classrooms, meeting rooms etc. Frequency reuse is very simple – a wall is more than enough to shield one IR based IEEE 802.11 network from another. (See also section 7.1 for a comparison between IR and radio transmission and Wesel, 1998 for more details.)

7.3.4 Medium access control layer

The MAC layer has to fulfil several tasks. First of all, it has to control medium access, but it can also offer support for roaming, authentication, and power conservation. The basic services provided by the MAC layer are the mandatory **asynchronous data service** and an optional **time-bounded service**. While 802.11 only offers the asynchronous service in ad hoc network mode, both service types can be offered using an infrastructure-based network together with the access point coordinating medium access. The asynchronous service supports broadcast and multicast packets, and packet exchange is based on a 'best effort' model, i.e., no delay bounds can be given for transmission.

The following three basic access mechanisms have been defined for IEEE 802.11: the mandatory basic method based on a version of CSMA/CA, an optional method avoiding the hidden terminal problem, and finally a contention-free polling method for time-bounded service. The first two methods are also summarized as **distributed coordination function (DCF)**, the third method is called **point coordination function (PCF)**. DCF only offers asynchronous service, while PCF offers both asynchronous and time-bounded service but needs an access point to control medium access and to avoid contention. The MAC mechanisms are also called **distributed foundation wireless medium access control (DFWMAC)**.

For all access methods, several parameters for controlling the waiting time before medium access are important. Figure 7.9 shows three different parameters defining the priorities of medium access. The medium, as shown, can be busy or idle (which is detected by the CCA). If the medium is busy this can be due to data frames or other control frames. During a contention phase several nodes try to access the medium.

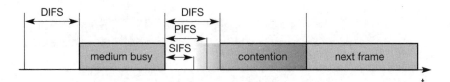

Figure 7.9

Medium access and inter-frame spacing

- **DCF inter-frame spacing (DIFS):** This parameter denotes the longest waiting time and thus the lowest priority for medium access. This waiting time is used for asynchronous data service within a contention period (this parameter and the basic access method will be explained in section 7.3.4.1).
- **PCF inter-frame spacing (PIFS):** A waiting time between DIFS and SIFS (and thus a medium priority) is used for a time-bounded service. That is, an access point polling other nodes only has to wait PIFS for medium access (see section 7.3.4.3 for further details).
- **Short inter-frame spacing (SIFS):** The shortest waiting time for medium access (and thus the highest priority) is defined for short control messages, such as acknowledgements for data packets or polling responses. The use of this parameter will be explained in sections 7.3.4.1 through 7.3.4.3.

7.3.4.1 Basic DFWMAC-DCF using CSMA/CA

The mandatory access mechanism of IEEE 802.11 is based on **carrier sense multiple access with collision avoidance** (CSMA/CA), which is a random access scheme with carrier sense and collision avoidance through random backoff. The basic CSMA/CA mechanism is shown in Figure 7.10. If the medium is sensed idle for at least the duration of DIFS (with the help of the CCA signal of the physical layer), a node can access the medium at once. This allows for short access delay under light load. But as soon as more and more nodes try to access the medium, additional mechanisms are needed.

If the medium is busy, nodes have to wait for the duration of DIFS, entering a contention phase afterwards. Each node now chooses a **random backoff time** within a **contention window** and additionally delays medium access for this random amount of time. As soon as a node senses the channel is busy, it has lost this cycle and has to wait for the next chance, i.e., until the medium is idle again for at least DIFS. But if the randomized additional waiting time for a node is over and the medium is still idle, the node can access the medium immediately. The additional waiting time is measured in multiples of **slots**. Slot time is derived from the medium propagation delay, transmitter delay, and other PHY dependent parameters.

Obviously, the basic CSMA/CA mechanism is not fair. Independent of the overall waiting time for transmission, each node has the same chances for transmitting data in the next cycle. To provide fairness, IEEE 802.11 adds a **backoff**

Figure 7.10
Contention window and
waiting time

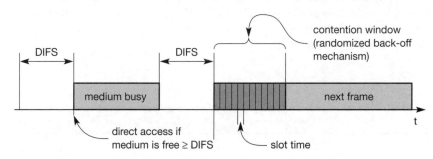

timer. Again, each node selects a random waiting time within the range of the contention window. If a certain station does not get access to the medium in the first cycle, it stops its backoff timer, waits for the channel to be idle again for DIFS and starts the counter again. As soon as the counter expires, the node accesses the medium. This means that deferred stations do not choose a randomized backoff time again but continue to count down. Thus, longer waiting stations have the advantage over newly entering stations, in that they only have to wait for the remainder of their backoff timer from the previous cycle(s).

Figure 7.11 explains the basic access mechanism of IEEE 802.11 for five stations trying to send a packet at the marked points in time. Station$_3$ has the first request from a higher layer to send a packet, waits for DIFS and accesses the medium, i.e., sends the packet. Station$_1$, station$_2$, and station$_5$ have to wait at least until the medium is idle for DIFS again after station$_3$ has stopped sending. Now all three stations choose a backoff time within the contention window and start counting down their backoff timers.

Figure 7.11 shows the random backoff time of station$_1$ as sum of bo$_e$ (the elapsed backoff time) and bo$_r$ (the residual backoff time). The same is shown for station$_5$. Station$_2$ has a total backoff time of only bo$_e$ and thus gets access to the medium first. Therefore, no residual backoff time for station$_2$ is shown. The backoff timers of station$_1$ and station$_5$ stop, and the stations store their residual backoff times. While a new station has to choose its backoff time from the whole contention window, the two old stations have statistically smaller backoff values using their old values.

Now station$_4$ wants to send a packet as well and thus after DIFS waiting time, three stations try to get access. It can now happen, as shown in the figure, that two stations accidentally have the same backoff time, no matter whether

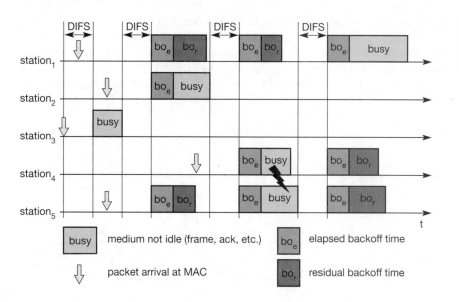

Figure 7.11
Basic DFWMAC-DCF with several competing senders

remaining or newly chosen. This results in a collision on the medium as shown, i.e., the transmitted frames are destroyed. Station$_1$ stores its residual backoff time again. In the last cycle shown station$_1$ finally gets access to the medium, while station$_4$ and station$_5$ have to wait. A collision triggers a retransmission with a new random selection of the backoff time.

Still, the access scheme has problems under heavy or light load. Depending on the size of the contention window (CW), the random values can either be too close together, causing too many collisions, or the values are too high, causing unnecessary delay. Therefore, the system tries to adapt to the current number of stations trying to send.

The contention window starts with a size of, e.g., CW$_{min}$ = 7. Each time a collision occurs, indicating a higher load on the medium, the contention window doubles up to a maximum of, e.g., CW$_{max}$ = 255 (the window can take on the values 7, 15, 31, 63, 127, and 255). The larger the contention window is, the greater is the resolution power of the randomized scheme. It is less likely to choose the same random backoff time using a large CW. However, under a light load, a small CW ensures shorter access delays. This algorithm is also called **exponential backoff** and is already familiar from IEEE 802.3 CSMA/CD in a similar version.

While this process describes the complete access mechanism for broadcast frames, an additional feature is provided by the standard for unicast data transfer. Figure 7.12 shows a sender accessing the medium and sending its data. But now the receiver answers directly with an **acknowledgement (ACK)**. The receiver accesses the medium after waiting for a duration of SIFS and, thus, no other station can access the medium in the meantime and cause a collision. The other stations have to wait for DIFS plus their backoff time. This acknowledgement ensures the correct reception (correct checksum CRC at the receiver) of a frame on the MAC layer, which is especially important in error-prone environments such as wireless connections. If no ACK is returned, the sender automatically retransmits the frame. But now the sender has to wait again and compete for the access right. The are no special rights for retransmissions. The number of retransmissions is limited, and final failure is reported to the higher layer.

Figure 7.12
IEEE 802.11 unicast
data transfer

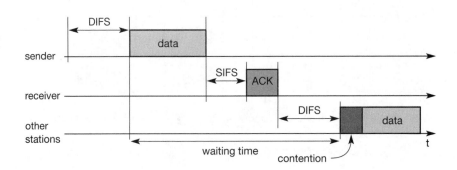

7.3.4.2 DFWMAC-DCF with RTS/CTS extension

Section 3.1 discussed the problem of hidden terminals, a situation that can also occur in IEEE 802.11 networks. The problem occurs if one station can receive two others, but those stations cannot receive each other. Then those two stations may sense the channel idle, send a frame, and cause a collision at the receiver in the middle. To deal with this problem, the standard defines an additional mechanism using two control packets, RTS and CTS. The use of the mechanism is optional, however, every 802.11 node has to implement the functions to react properly upon reception of RTS/CTS control packets.

Figure 7.13 illustrates the use of RTS and CTS. After waiting for DIFS (plus a random backoff time if the medium was busy), the sender can issue a **request to send (RTS)** control packet. The RTS packet thus is not given any higher priority compared to other data packets. The RTS packet includes the receiver of the data transmission to come and the duration of the whole data transmission. This duration specifies the time interval necessary to transmit the whole data frame and the acknowledgement related to it. Every node receiving this RTS now has to set its **net allocation vector (NAV)** in accordance with the duration field. The NAV specifies then the earliest point in time at which the station can try to access the medium again.

If the receiver of the data transmission receives the RTS, it answers with a **clear to send (CTS)** message after waiting for SIFS. This CTS packet contains the duration field again and all stations receiving this packet from the receiver of the intended data transmission have to adjust their NAV. The latter set of receivers need not be the same as the first set receiving the RTS packet. Now all nodes within receiving distance around sender and receiver are informed that they have to wait more time before accessing the medium. Basically, this mechanism reserves the medium for one sender exclusively (this is why it is sometimes called a virtual reservation scheme).

Finally, the sender can send the data after SIFS. The receiver waits for SIFS after receiving the data packet and then acknowledges whether the transfer was correct. Now the transmission has been completed and thus the NAV in each node marks the medium as free and the standard cycle can start again.

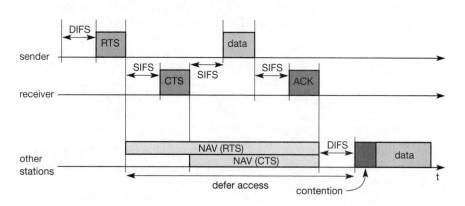

Figure 7.13
IEEE 802.11 hidden
node provisions for
contention-free access

Within this scenario (i.e., using RTS and CTS to avoid the hidden terminal problem), collisions can only occur at the beginning while the RTS is sent. Two or more stations may start sending at the same time (RTS or other data packets). Using RTS/CTS can result in a non-negligible overhead causing a waste of bandwidth and higher delay. Therefore, an RTS threshold can determine when to use the additional mechanism (basically at larger frame sizes) and when to disable it (short frames). Chhaya (1996) and Chhaya (1997) give an overview of the asynchronous services in 802.11 and discuss performance under different load scenarios in particular.

Wireless LANs have bit error rates in transmission that are typically several orders of magnitude higher than, e.g., fibre optics. Thus, the probability of an erroneous frame is much higher for wireless links assuming the same frame length. One way to decrease the error probability of frames is to use shorter frames. In this case, bit error rate is the same, but now only short frames are destroyed and, thus, the frame error rate decreases.

However, the mechanism of fragmenting a user data packet into several smaller parts should be transparent for a user. Furthermore, the MAC layer should have the possibility of adjusting the transmission frame size to the current error rate on the medium. Therefore, the IEEE 802.11 standard specifies a **fragmentation** mode (see Figure 7.14). Again, a sender can send an RTS control packet to reserve the medium after a waiting time of DIFS. This RTS packet now includes the duration for the transmission of the first fragment and the corresponding acknowledgement. A certain set of nodes may receive this RTS and set their NAV according to the duration field. The receiver answers with a CTS, again including the duration of the transmission up to the acknowledgement. A (possibly different) set of receivers gets this CTS message and sets the NAV.

As shown in Figure 7.13, the sender can now send the first data frame, $frag_1$, after waiting only for SIFS. The new aspect of this fragmentation mode is that it includes another duration value in the frame $frag_1$. This duration field reserves the medium for the duration of the transmission following, comprising the second fragment and its acknowledgement. Again, several nodes may receive this reservation and adjust their NAV. If all nodes are static and transmission conditions have not changed, then the set of nodes receiving the duration field in $frag_1$ should be the same as the set that has received the initial reservation in

Figure 7.14
IEEE 802.11
fragmentation of user
data

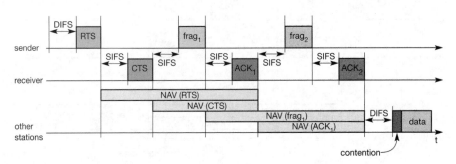

the RTS control packet. However, due to the mobility of nodes and changes in the environment, this could also be a different set of nodes.

The receiver of $frag_1$ answers directly after SIFS with the acknowledgement packet ACK_1 including the reservation for the next transmission as shown. Again, a fourth set of nodes may receive this reservation and adjust their NAV (which again could be the same as the second set of nodes that has received the reservation in the CTS frame).

If $frag_2$ was not the last frame of this transmission, it would also include a new duration for the third consecutive transmission. (In the example shown, $frag_2$ is the last fragment of this transmission and, therefore, the sender does not reserve the medium any longer.) The receiver acknowledges this second fragment, not reserving the medium again. After ACK_2, all nodes can compete for the medium again after having waited for DIFS.

7.3.4.3 DFWMAC-PCF with polling

The two access mechanisms presented so far cannot guarantee a maximum access delay or minimum transmission bandwidth. To provide a time-bounded service, the standard specifies a **point co-ordination function (PCF)** on top of the standard DCF mechanisms. Using PCF requires an access point that controls medium access and polls the single nodes. Ad hoc networks cannot use this function and, thus, provide no QoS but 'best effort' in IEEE 802.11 WLANs.

The **point co-ordinator** in the access point splits the access time into super frame periods as shown in Figure 7.15. A **super frame** comprises a **contention-free period** and a **contention period**. The contention period can be used for the two access mechanisms presented above. The figure also shows several wireless stations (all on the same line) and the stations' NAV (again on one line).

At time t_0 the contention-free period of the super frame should theoretically start, but another station is still transmitting data (i.e., the medium is busy). This means that PCF also defers to DCF, and thus, the start of the super frame may be postponed. The only possibility of avoiding variations is not to have any contention period at all. After the medium has been idle until t_1, the point coordinator has to wait for PIFS before accessing the medium. Since PIFS is smaller than DIFS, no other station can start sending earlier.

The point coordinator now sends data D_1 downstream to the first wireless station. This station can answer at once after SIFS (see Figure 7.15). After waiting for SIFS again, the point coordinator can poll the second station by sending D_2. This station may answer upstream to the coordinator with data U_2. Polling continues with the third node. This time the node has nothing to answer and, thus, the point coordinator will not receive a packet after SIFS.

After waiting for PIFS, the coordinator can resume polling the stations. Finally, the point coordinator can issue an end marker (CF_{end}), indicating that the contention period may start again. Using PCF automatically sets the NAV, preventing other stations from sending. In the example, the contention free period planned initially would have been from t_0 to t_3. However, the point coor-

Figure 7.15
Contention-free access
using polling
mechanisms (PCF)

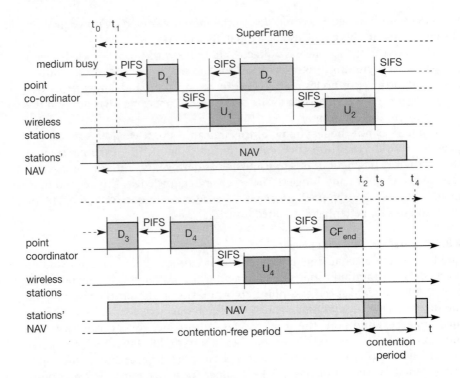

dinator finished polling earlier thus shifting the end of the contention free period to t_2. At t_4, the cycle starts again with the next super frame.

The transmission properties of the whole wireless network are now determined by the polling behaviour of the access point. If only PCF is used and polling is distributed evenly, the bandwidth is also distributed evenly among all polled nodes. This would resemble a static, centrally controlled time division multiple access (TDMA) system with time division duplex (TDD) transmission. This method comes with an overhead if nodes have nothing to send, but the access point polls them permanently. Anastasi (1998) elaborates the example of voice transmission using 48 byte packets as payload. In this case, PCF introduces an overhead of 75 byte.

7.3.4.4 MAC frames

Figure 7.16 shows the basic structure of an IEEE 802.11 MAC data frame. The fields in the figure refer to the following:

- **Frame control**: The first 2 bytes serve several purposes and, thus, contain several sub-fields. These fields indicate the protocol version, the type of frame (management, control, data), whether the frame has been fragmented, privacy information, and the 2 **DS bits** (distribution system bits), indicating the meaning of the four address fields in the frame.

bytes	2	2	6	6	6	2	6	0–2312	4
	Frame control	Duration ID	Address 1	Address 2	Address 3	Sequence control	Address 4	Data	CRC

Figure 7.16
IEEE 802.11 packet structure

- **Duration ID**: For the virtual reservation mechanism using RTS/CTS and during fragmentation, the duration field contains a value indicating the period of time in which the medium is occupied.
- **Address 1 to 4**: The four address fields contain standard IEEE 802 MAC addresses (48 bit each), as they are known from other 802.x LANs. The meaning of each address depends on the DS bits in the frame control field and is explained in more detail in a separate paragraph.
- **Sequence control**: Due to the acknowledgement mechanism it may happen that frames are duplicated. Therefore a sequence number is used to filter duplicates.
- **Data**: The MAC frame may contain arbitrary data (max. 2312 byte), which is transferred transparently from a sender to the receiver(s).
- **Checksum (CRC)**: Finally, a 32 bit checksum is used to protect the frame as this is common procedure in all 802.x networks.

MAC frames can be transmitted between mobile stations, between mobile stations and an access point, and between access points over a DS (see Figure 7.3). Two bits within the Frame Control field, 'to DS' and 'from DS', differentiate these cases and thus control the meaning of the four addresses used. Table 7.1 gives an overview of the four possible bit values of the DS bits and the associated interpretation of the four address fields.

Every station, access point or wireless node, filters on **address 1**. This address identifies the physical receiver(s) of the frame. Based on this address, a station can decide whether the frame is relevant or not. The second address, **address 2**, represents the physical transmitter of a frame. This information is important because this particular sender is also the recipient of the MAC layer acknowledgement. The remaining two addresses, **address 3** and **address 4**, are mainly necessary for the logical assignment of frames (logical sender, BSS identifier, logical receiver).

For addressing, the following four scenarios are possible (see Table 7.1):

to DS	from DS	Address 1	Address 2	Address 3	Address 4
0	0	DA	SA	BSSID	–
0	1	DA	BSSID	SA	–
1	0	BSSID	SA	DA	–
1	1	RA	TA	DA	SA

Table 7.1
Interpretation of the MAC addresses in a 802.11 MAC frame

- **Ad hoc network:** If both DS bits are zero, the MAC frame constitutes a packet which is exchanged between two wireless nodes without a distribution system involved. **DA** indicates the **destination address**, **SA** the **source address** of the frame, which are identical to the physical receiver and sender addresses respectively. The third address identifies the **basic service set (BSSID)** (see Figure 7.4), the fourth address is unused.
- **Infrastructure network, from AP:** If only the 'from DS' bit is set, the frame physically originates from an access point. DA is the logical and physical receiver, the second address identifies the BSS, the third address specifies the logical sender, the source address of the MAC frame. This case is an example for a packet sent to the receiver via the access point.
- **Infrastructure network, to AP:** If a station sends a packet to another station via the access point, only the 'to DS' bit is set. Now the first address represents the physical receiver of the frame, the access point, via the BSS identifier. The second address is the logical and physical sender of the frame, while the third address indicates the logical receiver.
- **Infrastructure network, within DS:** Finally, for packets transmitted between two access points over the distribution system, both bits are set. The first **receiver address (RA)**, represents the MAC address of the receiving access point. Similarly, the second address **transmitter address (TA)**, identifies the sending access point within the distribution system. Now two more addresses are needed to identify the original destination DA of the frame and the original source of the frame SA. Without these additional addresses, some encapsulation mechanism would be necessary to transmit MAC frames over the distribution system transparently.

7.3.5 MAC management

MAC management plays a central role in an IEEE 802.11 station as it more or less controls all functions related to system integration, i.e., integration of a wireless station into a BSS, formation of an ESS, synchronization of stations etc. The following functional groups have been identified and will be discussed in more detail in the following sections:

- **Synchronization:** Functions to support finding a wireless LAN, synchronization of internal clocks, generation of beacon signals.
- **Power management:** Functions to control transmitter activity for power conservation, e.g., periodic sleep, buffering, without missing a frame.
- **Roaming:** Functions for joining a network (association), changing access points, scanning for access points.
- **Management information base (MIB):** All parameters representing the current state of a wireless station and an access point are stored within a MIB for internal and external access. A MIB can be accessed via standardized protocols such as the simple network management protocol (SNMP).

7.3.5.1 Synchronization

Each node of an 802.11 network maintains an internal clock. To synchronize the clocks of all nodes, IEEE 802.11 specifies a **timing synchronization function (TSF)**. As we will see in the following section, synchronized clocks are needed for power management, but also for coordination of the PCF and for synchronization of the hopping sequence in an FHSS system. Using PCF, the local timer of a node can predict the start of a super frame, i.e. the contention free and contention period. FHSS physical layers need the same hopping sequences for all nodes to be able to communicate within a BSS.

Within a BSS, timing is conveyed by the (quasi)periodic transmissions of a beacon frame. A **beacon** contains a timestamp and other management information used for power management and roaming (e.g., identification of the BSS). The timestamp is used by a node to adjust its local clock. The node is not required to hear every beacon to stay synchronized; however, from time to time internal clocks should be adjusted. The transmission of a beacon frame is not always periodic for the beacon frame is also deferred if the medium is busy.

Within **infrastructure-based** networks, the access point performs synchronization by transmitting the (quasi)periodic beacon signal, whereas all other wireless nodes adjust their local timer to the time stamp. This represents the simple case as shown in Figure 7.17. The access point is not always able to send its beacon B periodically if the medium is busy. However, the access point always tries to schedule transmissions according to the expected beacon interval **(target beacon transmission time)**, i.e., beacon intervals are not shifted if one beacon is delayed. The timestamp of a beacon always reflects the real transmit time, not the scheduled time.

For ad hoc networks, the situation is slightly more complicated as they do not have an access point for beacon transmission. In this case, each node maintains its own synchronization timer and starts the transmission of a beacon frame after the beacon interval. Figure 7.18 shows an example where multiple stations try to send their beacon. However, the standard random backoff algorithm is also applied to the beacon frames and, thus, typically only one beacon wins. Now all other stations adjust their internal clocks according to the received beacon and suppress their beacons for this cycle. If collision occurs, the

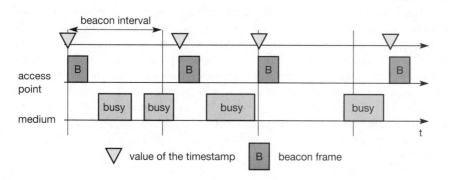

Figure 7.17
Beacon transmission in a busy 802.11 infrastructure network

Figure 7.18

Beacon transmission in a
busy 802.11 ad hoc
network

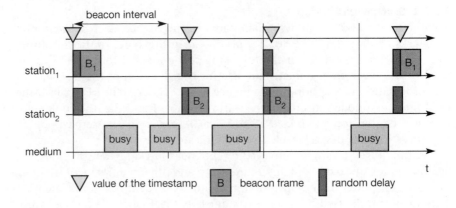

beacon is lost. In this scenario, the beacon intervals can be shifted slightly in
time because all clocks may vary and, thus, also the start of a beacon interval
from a node's point of view. However, after synchronization all nodes again
have the same consistent view.

7.3.5.2 Power management

Wireless devices are battery powered (unless a solar panel is used). Therefore,
power-saving mechanisms are crucial for the success of such devices. Standard
LAN protocols assume that stations are always ready to receive data, although
receivers are idle most of the time in lightly loaded networks. However, this permanent readiness of the receiving module is critical for battery lifetime as the
receiver current may be up to 100 mA (Woesner, 1998).

The basic idea of IEEE 802.11 power management is to switch off the
transceiver whenever it is not needed. Since the power management cannot
know in advance when the transceiver has to be active for a specific packet, it
has to 'wake up' the transceiver periodically. Switching off the transceiver
should be transparent to existing protocols and should be flexible enough to
support different applications. However, throughput can be traded-off for battery life. Longer off-periods save battery life but reduce average throughput
and vice versa.

The basic idea of power saving includes two states for a station, **sleep** and
awake, and buffering of data in senders. If a sender intends to communicate
with a power-saving station it has to buffer data if the station is asleep. The
sleeping station on the other hand has to wake up periodically and stay awake
for a certain time. During this time, all senders can announce the destinations
of their buffered data frames. If a station detects that it is a destination of a
buffered packet it has to stay awake until the transmission takes place. Waking
up at the right moment requires the **timing synchronization function (TSF)**
introduced in section 7.3.5.1. All stations have to wake up or be awake at the
same time.

Power management in **infrastructure**-based networks is much simpler compared to ad hoc networks. The access point buffers all frames destined for stations operating in power-save mode. With every beacon sent by the access point, a **traffic indication map (TIM)** is transmitted. The TIM contains a list of stations for which unicast data frames are buffered in the access point.

The TSF assures that the sleeping stations will wake up periodically and listen to the beacon and TIM. If the TIM indicates a unicast frame buffered for the station, the station stays awake for transmission. For multicast/broadcast transmission, stations will always stay awake. Another reason for waking up is a frame which has to be transmitted from the station to the access point. A sleeping station still has the TSF timer running.

Figure 7.19 shows an example with an access point and one station. The state of the medium is indicated. Again, the access point transmits a beacon frame each beacon interval. This interval is now the same as the TIM interval. Additionally, the access point maintains a **delivery traffic indication map (DTIM)** interval for sending broadcast/multicast frames. The DTIM interval is always a multiple of the TIM interval.

All stations (in the example, only one is shown) wake up prior to an expected TIM or DTIM. In the first case, the access point has to transmit a broadcast frame and the station thus stays awake to receive this broadcast frame. After receiving the broadcast frame, the stations return to the sleeping mode. The station wakes up again just before the next TIM transmission. This time the TIM is delayed due to a busy medium and, thus, the station stays awake. The access point has nothing to send and the station goes back to sleep.

At the next TIM interval, the access point indicates that the station is the destination for a buffered frame. Now the station answers with a **PS** (power saving) **poll** and stays awake to receive data. The access point then transmits the data for the station, the station acknowledges the receipt and may also send

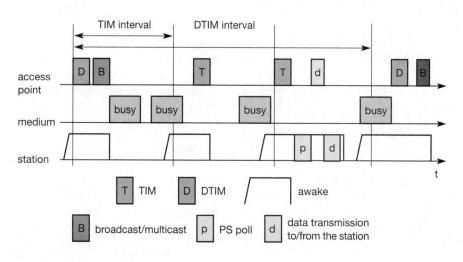

Figure 7.19
Power management in IEEE 802.11 infrastructure networks

some data (as shown in the example), this time acknowledged by the access point (acknowledgments are not shown in the figure). Afterwards, the station switches to the sleeping mode again.

Finally, the access point has more broadcast data to send at the next DTIM interval, which is again deferred by a busy medium. Depending on internal thresholds, a station may stay awake if the sleeping period would be too short. This mechanism clearly shows the tradeoff between short delays in station access and saving battery power. The shorter the TIM interval, the shorter the delay, but also the lower the power-saving effect.

In ad hoc networks, power management is much more complicated than in infrastructure networks. In this case, there is no access point to buffer data in one location but each station needs the ability to buffer data if it wants to communicate with a power-saving station. All stations now announce a list of buffered frames during a period when they are all awake. Destinations are announced using **ad hoc traffic indication map (ATIMs)** – the announcement period is called the **ATIM window**.

Figure 7.20 shows a simple ad hoc network with two stations. Again, the beacon interval is determined by a distributed function (different stations may send the beacon). However, due to this synchronization, all stations within the ad hoc network wake up at the same time. All stations stay awake for the ATIM interval as shown in the first two steps and go to sleep again if no frame is buffered for them. In the third step, station$_1$ has data buffered for station$_2$. This is indicated in an ATIM transmitted by station$_1$. Station$_2$ acknowledges this ATIM and stays awake for the transmission. After the ATIM window, station$_1$ can transmit the data frame, and station$_2$ acknowledges its receipt. In this case, the stations stay awake for the next beacon.

One problem of this approach is scalability. If many stations within an ad hoc network operate in power-save mode, many stations may also want to transmit their ATIM within the ATIM window. The more ATIM transmissions take place, the more collisions happen and the more stations are deferred.

Figure 7.20
Power management in IEEE 802.11 ad hoc networks

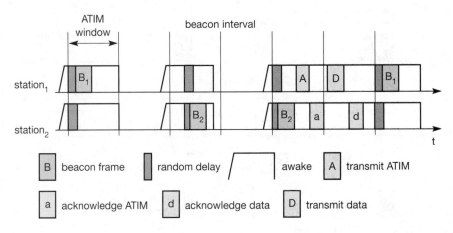

7.3.5.3 Roaming

Typical wireless networks within buildings require more than just one access point to cover all rooms. Depending on the solidity and material of the walls, one access point has a transmission range of 10–20 m if transmission is to have a decent quality. If a user walks around with a wireless station, the station has to move from one access point to another to provide uninterrupted service. Moving between access points is called **roaming.**

The steps for roaming between access points are the following:

- A station decides that the current link quality to its access point AP_1 is too poor. The station then starts **scanning** for another access point.
- Scanning involves the active search for another BSS and can also be used for setting up a new BSS in case of ad hoc networks. IEEE 802.11 specifies scanning on single or multiple channels (if available at the physical layer) and differentiates between passive scanning and active scanning. **Passive scanning** simply means listening into the medium to find other networks, i.e. receiving the beacon of another network issued by the synchronization function within an access point. **Active scanning** comprises sending a **probe** on each channel and waiting for response. Beacon and probe response contain the information necessary to join the new BSS.
- The station then selects the best access point for roaming based on, e.g., signal strength, and sends an **association request** to the selected access point AP_2.
- The new access point AP_2 answers with an **association response**. If the response is successful, the station has roamed to the new access point AP_2. Otherwise, the station has to continue scanning for new access points.
- The access point accepting an association request indicates the new station in its BSS to the distribution system (DS). The DS then updates its database, which contains the current location of the wireless stations. This database is needed for forwarding frames between different BSSs, i.e. between the different access points controlling the BSSs, which combine to form an ESS (see Figure 7.3). Additionally, the DS can inform the old access point AP_1 that the station is no longer within its BSS.

7.3.6 Future development

While more and more products following the IEEE 802.11 standard are available, several new groups have been formed within the IEEE to discuss enhancements of the standard and new applications.

One of these projects (running under **802.11a**) is a wireless LAN following the 802.11 standard – i.e., the MAC layers are compatible – but using the 5 GHz band. This higher carrier frequency allows for transmission rates of 20 Mbit/s. This group works in close co-operation with the broadband radio access networks (BRAN) group of the European Telecommunications Standards Institute (ETSI) to reach the goal of a common physical layer. ETSI BRAN has already specified a WLAN with 23.5 Mbit/s in the 5 GHz range (see section 7.4).

Another project, **802.11b**, deals with the provision of higher data rates at 2.4 GHz. As discussed above, the structure of the PLCP headers already supports different rates with a special field indicating the rate of the following payload. The study group within this project discusses fully compatible packets with headers at the familiar 1 Mbit/s rate, but payloads at higher rates of about 3 Mbit/s for FHSS and 11 Mbit/s for DSSS physical layers. It should be noted that single proprietary products already offer 10 Mbit/s at 2.4 GHz using special coding techniques together with high-performance signal processors.

Finally, the **wireless personal area networks (WPAN)** study group under 802.11 discusses wireless networks under the following five criteria:

- **Market potential**: How many applications, devices, vendors, customers are available for a certain technology?
- **Compatibility**: One requirement is compatibility to IEEE 802.
- **Distinct identity**: The study group does not want to establish a second 802.11 standard. However, many topics, such as low cost, low power, or small form factor are not addressed in the 802.11 standard.
- **Technical feasibility**: Prototypes are necessary for further discussion, so the study group will not rely on paper work.
- **Economic feasibility**: Finally, everything developed within this group should be cheaper than other solutions and allow for high-volume production.

Section 7.5 shows a technology that fits into the above description: Bluetooth. Consequently, there is co-operation between the WPAN study group and the Bluetooth consortium.

7.4 HIPERLAN

In 1996, the ETSI standardized HIPERLAN 1 as a WLAN allowing for node mobility and supporting ad hoc and infrastructure-based topologies (ETSI, 1996). (HIPERLAN stands for **high performance local area network**.) HIPER-LAN 1 was originally one out of four HIPERLANs envisaged, as ETSI decided to have different types of networks for different purposes. The key feature of all four networks is their integration of time-sensitive data transfer services. Table 7.2 gives an overview of the standardization plans for all four HIPERLANs. Today, the names have changed and the former HIPERLANs 2, 3, and 4 are now called HIPERLAN 2, HIPERACCESS, and HIPERLINK. These three types of networks are discussed together with the wireless ATM technology and broadband radio access networks (BRAN) in chapter 8.

For the rest of this chapter, the name HIPERLAN is used for HIPERLAN type 1. The current version of the standard (ETSI, 1998) describes a wireless LAN supporting priorities and packet life time for data transfer at 23.5 Mbit/s, including forwarding mechanisms, topology discovery, user data encryption, network

	HIPERLAN type 1	HIPERLAN type 2	HIPERLAN type 3	HIPERLAN type 4
Application	Wireless LAN	Access to ATM fixed networks	Wireless local loop	Point-to-point wireless ATM connections
Frequency	5.1-5.3 GHz			17.2-17.3 GHz
Topology	Decentralized ad hoc/infra-structure	Cellular, centralized	Point-to-multipoint	Point-to-point
Antenna	Omni-directional		Directional	
Range	50 m	50-100 m	5000 m	150 m
QoS	Statistical	ATM traffic classes (VBR, CBR, ABR, UBR)		
Mobility	<10 m/s	<10 m/s	Stationary	Stationary
Interface	Conventional LAN	ATM networks		
Data rate	23.5 Mbit/s	>20 Mbit/s		155 Mbit/s
Power conservation		Yes	Yes	Not necessary

Table 7.2
Original specifications for the HIPERLAN family of wireless networks

identification and power conservation mechanisms. HIPERLANs operate at 5.1-5.3 GHz with a range of 50 m in buildings at 1 W transmit power.

The service offered by a HIPERLAN is compatible with the standard MAC services known from IEEE 802.x LANs. Thus, addressing is based on standard 48 bit MAC addresses. A special HIPERLAN identification scheme allows for the concurrent operation of two or more physically overlapping HIPERLANs without mingling their communication. Communication confidentiality is ensured by an encryption/decryption algorithm that requires the identical keys and initialization vectors for successful decryption of a data stream encrypted by a sender.

An innovative feature of HIPERLAN which other wireless networks do not offer is its ability to forward data packets using several relays. Relays can extend the communication on the MAC layer beyond the radio range. For power conservation, a node may set up a specific wake-up pattern. This pattern determines at what time the node is ready to receive, so that in the remaining time the node can turn off its receiver and save energy. These nodes are called p-savers and need so-called p-supporters that contain information about the wake-up patterns of all p-savers they are responsible for. A p-supporter only forwards data to a p-saver at the moment the p-saver is awake. This action also requires buffering mechanisms for packets on p-supporting forwarders.

The following sections describe the protocol architecture of HIPERLAN as well as naming conventions, the three sublayers and, finally, the information bases needed in HIPERLAN nodes to support routing in a dynamic topology.

7.4.1 Protocol architecture

Figure 7.21 shows the comparison between the HIPERLAN reference model and the OSI and IEEE 802.x layers known from most LANs. The standards of the IEEE 802.x family cover the logical link control (LLC), the medium access control (MAC), and the physical layer (PHY). LLC plus MAC form the data link layer of the OSI reference model.

The HIPERLAN standard only covers a part of the data link layer and the physical layer with respect to the OSI reference model. The service provided at the HIPERLAN MAC layer is compatible with the ISO MAC service definition in ISO 15802-1 (ISO, 1995) and the IEEE 802.1a architecture (IEEE, 1990). The LLC layer is not part of the HIPERLAN standardization. However, HIPERLAN subdivides the MAC layer known from IEEE into a sublayer called the **medium access control (MAC)** layer on the one hand and the **channel access control (CAC)** layer on the other. The meaning of the **physical layer (PHY)** is the same for all reference models.

The following explains the tasks, data units, protocols, and services of all three layers specified in the HIPERLAN standard with the help of Figure 7.22. The HIPERLAN MAC layer offers its service to the next higher layer at the MAC service access point (MSAP). This is typically the LLC layer. This MAC service includes a communication service over a single HIPERLAN, the transport of an MAC service data unit (MSDU), and the exploration of currently available HIPERLANs for dynamic HIPERLAN access. The HIPERLAN MAC entities (HM-entity) use the MAC protocol to exchange an HMPDU (HIPERLAN MAC PDU) and offer the MAC service. The MAC layer is further explained in section 7.4.4.

The HIPERLAN CAC layer was specifically designed to provide channel access with priorities and to free the higher layers from special wireless channel characteristics. The CAC service accepts HIPERLAN CAC SDUs (HCSDU) at the HCSAP and the HC-entities exchange HCPDUs using the CAC protocol (this process is explained in further detail in section 7.4.3). This layer contains the access scheme EY-NPMA, which is unique for HIPERLAN and will therefore be explained in greater detail.

Figure 7.21
HIPERLAN standard compared with OSI and IEEE

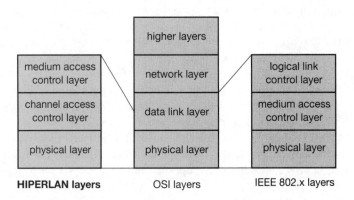

| HIPERLAN layers | OSI layers | IEEE 802.x layers |

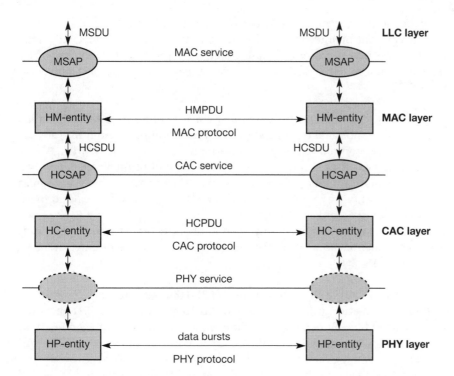

Figure 7.22
HIPERLAN protocols,
services, and data units

Finally, the physical layer PHY offers mechanisms to transfer bitstreams and specifies radio channels, modulation techniques, transmit power etc. The HIPERLAN standard does not specify an explicit SAP for the PHY layer. Data is sent in the form of bursts of different bit rates (see section 7.4.2).

7.4.2 Physical layer

The lowest layer of the HIPERLAN specification, the physical layer, is responsible for modulation/demodulation of a radio carrier with a bit stream, for synchronization between transmitters and receivers, as well as for forward error correction mechanisms, measuring the signal strength, and channel sensing.

The standard specifies three carriers as mandatory and two as optional. The **mandatory carriers** have nominal centre frequencies:

- $F(0) = 5.1764680$ GHz,
- $F(1) = 5.1999974$ GHz, and
- $F(2) = 5.2235268$ GHz.

The **optional carriers** which are not available in all countries are:

- $F(3) = 5.2470562$ GHz and
- $F(4) = 5.2705856$ GHz.

The bandwidth of a channel using these carriers is 23 MHz.

The constant maintenance of the high bitrate of 23.5294 Mbit/s (±235 bit/s) for all devices is very power consuming and, thus, problematical for mobile terminals. Therefore, HIPERLAN specifies two types of so-called data bursts (see Figure 7.23):

- **LBR-HBR data burst**: This data burst consists of a **low bit-rate** stream, a synchronization and training sequence, and a number of **high bit-rate** data blocks. A minimum of one and a maximum of 47 data blocks with 496 bits each are permitted. However, for higher velocities of the wireless terminal, the maximum number of data blocks has to be reduced. The synchronization and training sequence consists of a 450 bit pattern specified in the HIPERLAN standard.
- **LBR data burst**: This burst only consists of a **low bit-rate** part comprising a receiver identification. The LBR part works at a data rate of only 1.4705875 Mbit/s (±15 bit/s).

The data blocks within the HBR part of an LBR-HBR burst are encoded with forward error correction using Bose-Chaudhuri-Hocquenghem (BCH) encoding, interleaving of bits, bit toggling, and differential precoding (ETSI, 1998).

The LBR part is modulated using simple frequency shift keying (FSK) with F(i)–368 kHz for a logical 0 and F(i)+368 kHz for a logical 1. F(i) is the centre frequency as specified. For the HBR part, Gaussian minimum shift keying (GMSK) is used. The transmit power of a HIPERLAN device can be either 1 W, 100 mW, or 10 mW.

7.4.3 Channel access control sublayer

The channel access control (CAC) sublayer offers a connectionless data transfer service to the higher MAC layer. The data unit transferred is called the **HIPERLAN CAC service data unit (HCSDU)**. Transfer starts at the source **HIPERLAN CAC service access point (HCSAP)** and ends at one destination HCSAP or multiple destination HCSAPs. Transfer of data is transparent with a maximum size of 2,422 bytes. Additionally, the MAC layer using this service may specify a priority, the **HIPERLAN CAC quality of service (HCQoS)**, determining the channel access priority as used in the EY-NPMA mechanism, which will be described later.

The HCSAP address can be an individual address identifying a single HCSAP or a group address identifying a group of HCSAPs. The individual HCSAP address can be used for source and destination address (unicast), whereas the

Figure 7.23
LBR-HBR data burst

group address can only be used for the destination address (multicast). These addresses comply with the 48 bit IEEE 802.x LAN MAC addresses.

The two service primitives for data transfer in the CAC sublayer are the following:

- **HC-UNITDATA.req** (source HCSAP, destination HCSAP, HCSDU, HIPERLAN identifier, channel access priority): This service primitive is used for sending data.
- **HC-UNITDATA.ind** (source HCSAP, destination HCSAP, HCSDU, HIPERLAN identifier): This service primitive indicates incoming data.

The HIPERLAN identifier is used to separate different HIPERLANs from each other. This value can be 0 (specifying any HIPERLAN) and is determined by the MAC layer.

Elimination-yield non-preemptive priority multiple access (EY-NPMA) is not only a complex acronym, but also the heart of the channel access providing priorities and different access schemes. EY-NPMA divides the medium access of different competing nodes into three phases:

- **Prioritization**: Determine the highest priority of a data packet ready to be sent on competing nodes.
- **Contention**: Eliminate all but one of the contenders, if more than one sender has the highest current priority.
- **Transmission**: Finally, transmit the packet of the remaining node.

In a case where several nodes compete for the medium, all three phases are necessary (called 'channel access in **synchronized channel condition**'). If the channel is free for at least 2,000 high rate bit-periods plus a dynamic extension, only the third phase, i.e. transmission, is needed (called 'channel access in **channel-free condition**'). The dynamic extension is randomly chosen between 0 and 3 times 200 high rate bit-periods with equal likelihood. This extension further minimizes the probability of collisions accessing a free channel if stations are synchronized on higher layers and thus try to access the free channel at the same time. In addition to those two conditions, HIPERLAN supports 'channel access in the **hidden elimination condition**' to handle the problem of hidden terminals as described in ETSI (1998).

The contention phase is further subdivided into an **elimination phase** and a **yield phase**. The purpose of the elimination phase is to eliminate as many contending nodes as possible (but surely not all). The result of the elimination phase is a more or less constant number of remaining nodes, almost independent of the initial number of competing nodes. Finally, the yield phase completes the work of the elimination phase with the goal of only one remaining node.

Figure 7.24 gives an overview of the three main phases and some more details which will be explained in the following sections. For every node ready to send data, the access cycle starts with synchronization to the current sender. The first phase, prioritization, follows. After that, the elimination and yield part of the contention phase follow. Finally, the remaining node can transmit its data. Every phase has a certain duration which is measured in numbers of slots and is determined by the variables I_{PS}, I_{PA}, I_{ES}, I_{ESV}, and I_{YS}.

7.4.3.1 Prioritization phase

HIPERLAN offers five different priorities for data packets ready to be sent. After one node has finished sending, many other nodes could compete for the right to send. The first objective of the prioritization phase is to make sure that no node with a lower priority gains access to the medium while packets with higher priority are waiting at other nodes. This mechanism always grants nodes with higher priority access to the medium, no matter how high the load on lower priorities.

In the first step of the prioritization phase, the priority detection, time is divided into five slots, slot 0 (highest priority) to slot 4 (lowest priority). Each slot has a duration of I_{PS} = 168 high rate bit-periods. If a node has the access priority p, it has to listen into the medium for p slots (priority detection). If the node senses the medium idle for the whole period of p slots, the node asserts the priority by immediately transmitting a burst for the duration I_{PA} = 168 high rate bit-periods (priority assertion). The burst consists of the following high rate bit sequence, which is repeated as many times as necessary for the duration of the burst:

111110101000100111000001100010110

If the node senses activity in the medium, it stops its attempt to send data in this transmission cycle and waits for the next one. The whole prioritization phase ends as soon as one node asserts the access priority with a burst. This means that the prioritization phase is not limited by a fixed length, but depends on the current highest priority.

Figure 7.24
Phases of the EY-NPMA
access scheme

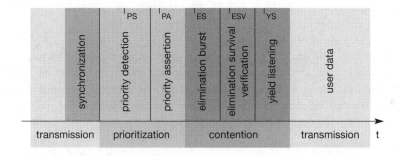

Let us assume, for example, that there are three nodes with data ready to be sent, the packets of node 1 and node 2 having the priority 2, the packet of node 3 having the priority 4. Then nodes 1, 2 and 3 listen into the medium and sense slots 0 and 1 idle. Nodes 1 and 2 both send a burst in slot 2 as priority assertion. Node 3 stops its attempt to transmit its packet. In this example the prioritization phase has taken three slots.

After this first phase at least one of the contending nodes will survive, the surviving nodes being all nodes with the highest priority of this cycle.

7.4.3.2 Elimination phase

Several nodes may now enter the elimination phase. Again, time is divided into slots, using the elimination slot interval I_{ES} = 212 high rate bitperiods. The length of an individual elimination burst is 0 to 12 slot intervals long, the probability of bursting within a slot is 0.5. The probability $P_E(n)$ of an elimination burst to be n elimination slot intervals long is given by:

- $P_E(n) = 0.5^{n+1}$ for $0 \leq n < 12$
- $P_E(n) = 0.5^{12}$ for $n = 12$

The elimination phase now resolves contention by means of elimination bursting and elimination survival verification. Each contending node sends an elimination burst with length n as determined via the probabilities and then listens to the channel during the survival verification interval I_{ESV} = 256 high rate bitperiods. The burst sent is the same as for the priority assertion. A contending node survives this elimination phase if and only if it senses the channel idle during its survival verification period. Otherwise, the node is eliminated and stops its attempt to send data during this transmission cycle.

The whole elimination phase will last for the duration of the longest elimination burst among the contending nodes plus the survival verification time. Finally, one or more nodes will survive this elimination phase, which can then continue with the next phase.

7.4.3.3 Yield phase

During the yield phase, the remaining nodes only listen into the medium without sending any additional bursts. Again, time is divided into slots, this time called yield slots with a duration of I_{YS} = 168 high rate bit-periods. The length of an individual yield listening period can be 0 to 9 slots with equal likelihood. Thus, the probability $P_Y(n)$ for a yield listening period to be n slots long is 0.1 for all n, $0 \leq n \leq 9$.

Each node now listens for its yield listening period. If it senses the channel idle during the whole period, it has survived the yield listening. Otherwise, a node withdraws for the rest of the current transmission cycle. This time, the length of the yield phase is determined by the shortest yield listening period among all contending nodes. At least one node will survive this phase and can start to transmit data. This sending of data is exactly what the other nodes with longer yield listening period can sense. It is important to note that at this point there can still be more than one surviving node and thus, a collision is still possible.

7.4.3.4 Transmission phase

A node that has survived the prioritization and contention phase can now send its data, called a low bit-rate high bit-rate HIPERLAN CAC protocol data unit (LBR-HBR HCPDU). This PDU can either be multicast or unicast. In case of a unicast transmission, the sender expects to receive an immediate acknowledgement from the destination, called an acknowledgement HCPDU (AK-HCPDU), which is an LBR HCPDU containing only an LBR part.

7.4.3.5 Format of an HCPDU

As shown in section 7.4.2, a frame transmitted in HIPERLAN can consist of a **low bit-rate (LBR)** part, a synchronization period, and a **high bit-rate (HBR)** part. This structure is reflected in an LBR-HBR HCPDU. The following section presents the structure of a data PDU of the CAC sublayer, called a DT-HCPDU (Figure 7.25).

All HCPDUs start with the **LBR** part. The LBR part exhibits a fixed bit pattern in the first 10 bits (1010101001). The next field, the **HBR-part indicator HI**, shows whether an HBR part is present in this transmission. For a DT-HCPDU, an HBR part is present and, thus, HI = 1. The following 9 bits represent the hashed address of the service access point of the destination CAC sublayer and are called the **hashed destination HCSAP address** field **HDA**. The HDA is

Figure 7.25

Data PDU of the CAC sublayer (DT-HCPDU)

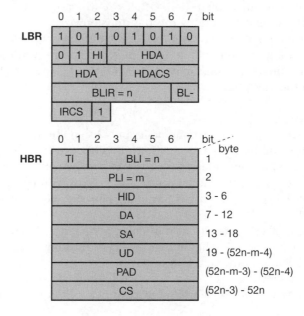

protected by a simple 4 bit checksum using the polynomial $G(x) = x^4+x+1$, the **HDA checksum HDACS**. The next 6 bits **block length indicator replica** field, **(BLIR)** contain the number of blocks in the HBR part and are replicated from the BLI field there. A block in the HBR part consists of 52 bytes, and between 1 and 47 blocks are permitted. Again, the BLIR field is protected by the **BLIR checksum (BLIRCS)**, using $G(x)$. The final bit of the LBR part is always 1.

Between the LBR and HBR part, the physical layer inserts the synchronization bit sequence (see section 7.4.2). The **HBR** part starts with the **type indicator (TI)**, a 2 bit field which equals 1 for a data PDU. As mentioned above, the HBR part contains a **block length indicator** field **(BLI)**, indicating the number of blocks in the HBR part. The following byte is the **padding length indicator (PLI)**, which contains the number of padding bytes used in the padding field PAD.

The next three fields identify sender, receiver, and HIPERLAN. The first 4 byte field, the **HIPERLAN identifier (HID)**, identifies a specific HIPERLAN (there could be several HIPERLANs running within the same area). The **destination HCSAP-address** field **(DA)** is a 48 bit LAN MAC address as known from IEEE 802.x LANs identifying the destination SAP. Similarly, the **source HCSAP-address** field **(SA)** represents the source SAP.

The **user data** field **(UD)** contains 1 to 2,422 bytes of user data, the HCSDU (HIPERLAN CAC SDU). If necessary, the **padding field (PAD)** can pad the PDU with 0 to 51 bytes. Finally, a strong **checksum CS** protects the HBR part. This checksum is generated using the polynomial $H(x) = x^{32} + x^{26} + x^{23} + x^{22} + x^{16} + x^{12} + x^{11} + x^{10} + x^8 + x^7 + x^5 + x^4 + x^2 + x + 1$.

The acknowledgement PDU, AK-HCPDU, only consists of an LBR part (a so-called LBR HCPDU) as illustrated in Figure 7.26. Thus, after starting with the fixed sequence (1010101001), the HBR-part indicator field HI is 0. The following **acknowledgement identifier** field **AID** contains the identifier for the acknowledgement. This field is also protected using $G(x)$ via the **AID CheckSum AIDCS**.

7.4.4 Medium access control sublayer

The MAC sublayer offers a connectionless service to transport an MSDU from a source MSAP to a single destination MSAP or a group of destination MSAPs. The MSDU is transferred transparently without any restrictions to its content. Additionally, this transfer can be time-bounded, or it can have a special priority or lifetime as determined by the user of this service. The addresses used for the MSAPs are identical with those for the HCSAPs, i.e., they are the standard 48 bit LAN MAC addresses.

The quality of service offered by the MAC layer is based on three parameters (**HMQoS-parameters**). The user can set a **priority** for data, priority = 0 denotes a high priority, priority = 1 a low priority. Furthermore, the

Figure 7.26
Acknowledgement PDU of the CAC sublayer (AK-HCPDU)

user can determine the lifetime of an MSDU to specify time-bounded delivery. The **MSDU lifetime** specifies the maximum time which may elapse between sending and receiving an MSDU. Beyond this lifetime, delivery of the MSDU becomes unnecessary. The MSDU lifetime has a range of 0–16,000 ms. Finally, the **residual MSDU lifetime** shows the remaining lifetime of a packet.

For data transfer, the MAC layer offers two service primitives:

- **HM-UNITDATA.req** (source address, destination address, MSDU, user priority, MSDU lifetime): This primitive can be used to send the MSDU with a certain priority and lifetime to one or more destination(s).
- **HM-UNITDATA.ind** (source address, destination address, MSDU, user priority, MSDU lifetime, residual MSDU lifetime): This primitive indicates an MSDU received and also includes the residual lifetime.

Besides data transfer, the MAC layer offers functions for looking up other HIPERLANs within radio range as well as special power conserving functions. **Power conservation** is achieved by setting up certain recurring patterns when a node can receive data instead of constantly being ready to receive. Special group-attendance patterns can be defined to enable multicasting. All nodes participating in a multicast group must be ready to receive at the same time when a sender transmits data for this group.

HIPERLAN MAC also offers user data **encryption** and **decryption** using a simple XOR-scheme together with random numbers. A key is chosen from a set of keys using a key identifier (KID) and is used together with an initialization vector IV to initialize the pseudo random number generator. This random sequence is XORed with the user data (UD) to generate the encrypted data. Decryption of the encrypted UD works the same way, using the same random number sequence. This is not a strong encryption scheme and, thus, strong encryption is left to higher layers.

It is interesting to see how the HIPERLAN MAC layer selects the next PDU for transmission if several PDUs are ready and how the waiting time of a PDU before transmission is reflected in its channel access priority. The selection has to reflect the user priority (0 or 1) and the residual lifetime in order to guarantee a time-bounded service. The MAC layer then has to map this information onto a channel access priority used by the CAC, thus competing with other nodes for the transmit rights.

First of all, the MAC layer determines the **normalized residual HMPDU lifetime (NRL).** This is the residual lifetime divided by the estimated number of hops the PDU has to travel. The computation reflects both the waiting time of a PDU in the node and the distance, and thus the additional waiting times in other nodes. Then the MAC layer computes the channel access priority for each PDU following the mapping shown in Table 7.3.

The final selection of the most important HMPDU is performed in the following order:

NRL	MSDU priority = 0	MSDU priority = 1
NRL < 10 ms	0	1
10 ms ≤ NRL < 20 ms	1	2
20 ms ≤ NRL < 40 ms	2	3
40 ms ≤ NRL < 80 ms	3	4
80 ms ≤ NRL	4	4

Table 7.3
Mapping of the normalized residual lifetime to the CAC priority

- First HMPDUs with the highest priority are selected,
- from these, all HMPDUs with the shortest NRL are selected,
- from which finally any one without further preferences is selected from the remaining HMPDUs.

Figure 7.27 shows the structure of a data PDU, DT-HMPDU as an example for HMPDUs. The first two bytes, the **length indicator (LI)**, represents the length of the whole HMPDU in bytes. The **type indicator (TI)** contains the HMPDU type (e.g., 1 for a DT-HMPDU). Other PDU types are reserved for topology control, address lookups, wake-up patterns etc. (ETSI, 1998). The following 2 byte field contains the **residual lifetime (RL)** used for priority calculation.

The **PDU sequence number** field **PSN** is used to differentiate and to specify the relative order of PDUs generated by the same HM-entity. Sequence numbers are assigned per PDU and do not count bytes. The sequence number of the next PDU is thus calculated by (the previous sequence number + 1) modulo 65536. If two PDUs A and B have the sequence numbers a and b respectively, A is a successor of B if ((65536 + (a-b)) modulo 65536) < 32768. Otherwise B is a successor of A.

The next two fields, **DA** and **SA**, represent the **destination MSAP-address** and the **source MSAP-address** respectively. Both fields follow the standards for 48 bit LAN MAC addresses. The following two fields also contain addresses: the **alias destination MSAP-address ADA** and the **alias source MSAP-address ASA**. Again, both addresses are encoded as 48 bit LAN MAC addresses. Alias addresses are used for MSAPs outside the HIPER-LAN as described in 7.4.5.

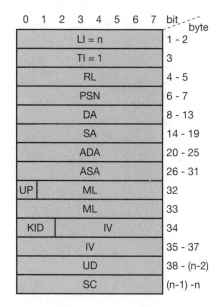

Figure 7.27
Data PDU of the MAC sublayer (DT-HMPDU)

The **user priority** of an MSDU is coded in the **UP** field. The next field contains the **MSDU lifetime (ML)**. The default value of this field is 500, representing 500 ms, the maximum 16000 (up to 32767 would be possible). The **key identifier (KID)** and the **initialization vector (IV)** are used for decryption of user data in the manner described above. From byte 38 onwards, **user data (UD)** follows. Since the CAC service limits the HCSDU size to 2,422 bytes, the MAC service restricts the user data to a maximum size of 2,383 bytes (additionally, further restrictions can hold). Finally, a **sanity check** field **(SC)** ends the DT-HMPDU. Sanity check is not a strong checksum, but a special sum over the unencrypted octets of the HMPDU.

7.4.5 Information bases and networking

Besides transferring data from a sender to a receiver within the same radio coverage, HIPERLAN offers functions to forward traffic via several other wireless nodes – a feature which is especially important in wireless ad hoc networks without an infrastructure. This forwarding mechanism can also be used if a node can only reach an access point via other HIPERLAN nodes.

Figure 7.28 depicts an ad hoc HIPERLAN with six nodes. Nodes can function as packet relays, in this case they are called **forwarders**. For routing of their own packets and forwarding of other packets, nodes maintain a **route information base (RIB)**. The entries in this RIB consist of the triple (R_{dest}, R_{next}, R_{dist}), where R_{dest} is the destination MSAP address, R_{next} is the HCSAP address of the next node toward the destination MSAP, and R_{dist} represents the estimation of hops to the destination node.

Figure 7.28

Example with two ad hoc HIPERLANs

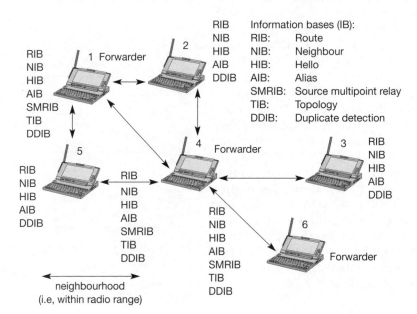

HIPERLAN nodes also include a **neighbour information base (NIB)**, which records information about each communication link of the node with its neighbours. In intervals of 10 s (or less), a HIPERLAN node declares its NIB to all neighbours using an HO-HMPDU (HellO-HMPDU). The entries (N_{nbor}, N_{status}) describe the current link status N_{status} with respect to the neighbour N_{nbor} (which is represented by an HCSAP address). Each entry has a holding time (20 s) associated with it after which the entry is deleted. The value of N_{status} can be:

- **N_Asym**, indicating that the node has an asymmetric link with the neighbour,
- **N_Sym**, indicating that the node has a symmetric link with the neighbour, and
- **N_MultiRelay**, indicating that the node has a symmetric link with the neighbour and has selected the neighbour as its multipoint relay.

The **hello information base (HIB)** records additional information about the neighbours of a HIPERLAN node. The entries are the triples (H_{dest}, H_{status}, H_{next}), specifying the status H_{status} of the HM-entity at the HCSAP address H_{dest}. This HM-entity can be reached via the neighbour with the HCSAP address H_{next}. H_{status} can take on the following values:

- **H_NeigborNF**: This status indicates that H_{dest} is a neighbouring nonforwarder and thus $H_{next} = H_{dest}$.
- **H_NeigborF**: This status indicates that H_{dest} is a neighbouring forwarder and thus $H_{next} = H_{dest}$.
- **H_TwoHop**: This status indicates that H_{dest} is 2 hops away and that H_{next} is the HCSAP address of a neighbouring forwarder.

HIPERLAN nodes can communicate with nodes outside the HIPERLAN on the MAC layer, i.e., an MSDU has to be delivered to a destination MSAP outside the set of HIPERLAN MSAPs. Therefore, a HIPERLAN node can store a mapping from outside MSAPs to a so-called alias MSAP which is a member of the HIPERLAN. This allows for the application of HIPERLAN routing mechanisms and RIBs. Aliases for outside nodes are stored as pairs (A_{ori}, A_{alias}) in the **alias information base (AIB)**. A_{ori} specifies the original MSAP address of an entity outside the HIPERLAN, whereas A_{alias} contains its associated alias MSAP address. This mechanism allows for independent MSAP address allocation within and outside a HIPERLAN and provides a simple mapping mechanism. All entries have their specific associated holding time – upon expiry an entry is removed.

HIPERLAN nodes having the role of a forwarder require two additional data bases, the source multipoint relay information base and the topology information base (nodes 1, 4, and 6 in Figure 7.28). If one node selects a neighbouring forwarder as its multipoint relay, it becomes a so-called source multipoint relay of this forwarder (e.g., node 5 may select node 1 as its forwarder). The forwarder now records all its source multipoint relays in its **source multipoint relay information base (SMRIB)**. The entries are the pairs (S_{SMR}, S_{seq}), with S_{SMR} specifying that the node with HCSAP address S_{SMR} has selected the local forwarder with the SMRIB as its multipoint relay within its **multipoint relay set** with the sequence number S_{seq}. At least every 20 s, a forwarder transmits its SMRIB to all other forwarders in the HIPERLAN using a TC-HMPDU (Topology Control-HMPDU); the holding time for SMRIB entries is 40 s.

Nodes in the multipoint relay set are used for forwarding HMPDUs from a local node to all other nodes within the HIPERLAN. By selecting an appropriate set of multipoint relays, forwarding can be optimized. Each node selects its multipoint relay set based on information stored in the NIB and in the HIB. A neighbour can be a member of this set if it is a forwarder and N_{status} is either N_Sym or N_MultiRelay. Additionally, a node has to check for each HM-entity identified by H_{dest} with the H_{status} = H_TwoHop in the HIB (i.e., H_{dest} is two hops away), that the multipoint relay set contains at least one of the forwarders identified by H_{next}. In other words, nodes in the multipoint relay set must be forwarders, the local node must have a symmetrical link to the nodes, and the local node can reach the nodes stored in the HIB via these forwarders. The multipoint relay set changes over time and, thus, a sequence number is associated to each set.

Additionally, the forwarders maintain a **topology information base (TIB)**, which reflects the current topology of the HIPERLAN based on information about forwarders and their source multipoint relays. Each entry in the TIB is a triple $(T_{dest}, T_{last}, T_{seq})$ specifying that the node with the HCSAP address T_{dest} has selected the forwarder with the HCSAP address T_{last} as its multipoint relay in the multipoint relay set with the sequence number T_{seq}. This entry shows how to reach the node T_{dest} in the last hop – i.e., via the forwarder T_{last}.

The **duplicate detection information base (DDIB)** is independent of all routing, relaying, and topology information. In wireless networks there are many possibilities for packets to get duplicated. For example, sometimes the only way to send a unicast packet is to multicast or broadcast the packet via several nodes if the exact route to the destination is currently unknown. Thus, one or several duplicates of a packet may reach a node. To avoid redundant processing, each node stores information about received packets in the form (D_{src}, D_{seq}) in its DDIB. D_{src} identifies the sender's HCSAP address, D_{seq} represents the sequence number of the HMPDU. This information also has an associated holding time.

HIPERLAN nodes maintain additional data bases needed for power conservation mechanisms. These data bases store, e.g., individual wake up patterns of other nodes a forwarder has to forward data to (ETSI, 1998).

The following example shows the sample databases for nodes 1 and 5 of Figure 7.28. Let us assume that node 5 and node 2 have chosen node 1 as their forwarder and, thus, node 1 has those two nodes in its source multipoint relay information base. The node numbers should also serve as addresses here (MSAP and HCSAP).

The databases relevant for routing of **node 5** have the following content:

- **RIB:** The RIB is always a snapshot of parts of the current topology, and destinations to other nodes may change over time. The current topology could be represented with the entries $\{(R_{dest}, R_{next}, R_{dist})\} = \{(1, 1, 1), (2, 1, 2), (3, 1, 3), (4, 1, 2), (6, 1, 3)\}$.
- **NIB:** The NIB may be specified by $\{(N_{nbor}, N_{status})\} = \{(4, N\_Asym), (1, N\_MultiRelay)\}$.
- **HIB:** The neighbouring information in the HIB could be $\{(H_{dest}, H_{status}, H_{next})\} = \{(1, H\_NeighborF, 1), (4, H\_NeighborF, 4), (2, H\_TwoHop, 1), (4, H\_TwoHop, 1), (1, H\_TwoHop, 4), (2, H\_TwoHop, 4), (6, H\_TwoHop, 4), (3, H\_TwoHop, 4)\}$.

The forwarder **node 1** maintains the following databases:

- **RIB:** $\{(R_{dest}, R_{next}, R_{dist})\} = \{(5, 5, 1), (2, 2, 1), (4, 4, 1), (3, 4, 2), (6, 4, 2)\}$
- **NIB:** $\{(N_{nbor}, N_{status})\} = \{(5, N\_Sym), (2, N\_Sym), (4, N\_MultiRelay)\}$
- **HIB:** $\{H_{dest}, H_{status}, H_{next})\} = \{(5, H\_NeigborNF, 5), (2, H\_NeighborNF, 2), (4, H\_NeighborF, 4), (3, H\_TwoHop, 4), (6, H\_Two\_Hop, 4)\}$
- **SMRIB:** The sequence numbers shown for the source multipoint relays have been chosen by the S_{SMR} self. This database could be: $\{(S_{SMR}, S_{seq})\} = \{(5, 4711), (2, 1234), (4, 30967)\}$.
- **TIB:** Topology information could be $\{(T_{dest}, T_{last}, T_{seq})\} = \{(2, 1, 1234), (5, 1, 4711), (4, 1, 30967), (3, 4, 6415), (6, 4, 22058)\}$.

7.5 Bluetooth

Compared to the WLAN technologies presented in 7.3 and 7.4, the Bluetooth technology discussed here aims at so-called ad hoc piconets, which are local area networks with a very limited coverage and without the need for an infrastructure. This different type of network is needed in order to connect different small devices in close proximity without expensive wiring or the need for a wireless infrastructure (Bisdikian, 1998). Many of today's devices already offer an infrared data association (IrDA) interface with transmission rates of, e.g., 115 kbit/s. Problems of IrDA involve its very limited range (typically 2 m for built-in interfaces), the need for a line-of-sight between the interfaces, and, typically, a limitation of only two participants, i.e., only point-to-point connections are supported. IrDA has no abilities of internet working, media access, or other enhanced communication mechanisms. The big advantage of IrDA is its low cost, and therefore it can be found in almost any mobile device (laptops, PDAs, cellular phones).

After some studies initiated by Ericsson in 1994 (Haartsen, 1998) around a so-called multi-communicator link, five companies (Ericsson, Intel, IBM, Nokia, Toshiba) founded the Bluetooth[22] consortium in spring 1998. Bluetooth represents a single-chip, low-cost, radio-based wireless network technology. Many other companies and research institutions joined the special interest group around Bluetooth (1998), whose goal is the development of mobile phones, laptops, notebooks, headsets etc. including Bluetooth technology by the end of 1999. This means that up to now Bluetooth is not a standard like IEEE 802.11 or HIPERLAN 1, but it soon should become a de facto standard – a fact which is established by the industry and promoted by the Bluetooth consortium.

7.5.1 User scenarios

Many different user scenarios can be imagined for wireless piconets:

- **Connection of peripheral devices**: Today, most devices are connected to a desktop computer via wires (e.g., keyboard, mouse, joystick, headset, speakers). This type of connection involves various disadvantages: Each device has its own type of cable, different plugs are needed, wires block office space. Using a wireless network, no wires are needed for data transmission. However, batteries now have to replace the power supply, for the wires not only transfer data but also supply the peripheral devices with power.
- **Support of ad hoc networking**: Imagine several people coming together, discussing issues, exchanging data (schedules, sales figures etc.). For instance, students might join a lecture, with the teacher distributing data to their personal digital assistants (PDAs). Wireless networks can support this type of interaction; however, small devices might not have WLAN adapters following the IEEE 802.11 standard, but cheaper Bluetooth chips built in.
- **Bridging of networks**: Using wireless piconets, a mobile phone can be connected to a PDA or laptop in a simple way. Mobile phones will not have full WLAN adapters built in, but could have a Bluetooth chip. Then the mobile phone can act as a bridge between the local piconet and, e.g., the global GSM network (see Figure 7.29). For instance, on arrival at an airport, a person's mobile phone could already receive e-mail via GSM and forward it to the laptop which is still in the suitcase. Or via a piconet, a fileserver could update local information stored on a laptop or PDA while the person is walking into the office.

Figure 7.29
Example configuration with a Bluetooth-based piconet

When comparing Bluetooth with other WLAN technology we have to keep in mind that one of the goals of Bluetooth was to provide local wireless access at very low costs. From a technical point of view, WLAN technologies like those presented above could also be used, however, WLAN adapters, e.g., for IEEE 802.11, have been designed for higher bandwidth and larger range and are, thus, more expensive.

7.5.2 Physical layer

For the design of Bluetooth's physical layer, several limitations had to be taken into account. Bluetooth devices will be integrated into typical mobile devices and, thus, must rely on battery power. This requires small, low power chips which can be built into handheld devices. Worldwide operation also requires the use of a frequency available worldwide. Finally, the combined use for data and voice transmission has to be reflected in the design, i.e., Bluetooth has to support multimedia data.

Bluetooth uses the licence-free frequency band at 2.4 GHz allowing for worldwide operation with some minor adaptations to national restrictions. A frequency-hopping/time-division duplex scheme is used for transmission with a fast hopping rate of 1,600 hops per second. The time between two hops is called a slot, which is an interval of 625 µs, thus, each slot uses a different frequency. In countries where the available bandwidth is at least 80 MHz (US, most parts of Europe) Bluetooth uses 79 hop carriers equally spaced with 1 MHz. In Japan, France, and Spain, national restrictions only permit 23 hop carriers. On average, the frequency-hopping sequence 'visits' each hop carrier with an equal probability. All devices using the same hopping sequence with the same phase form a Bluetooth **piconet**.

With transmitting power of up to 100 mW, Bluetooth devices have a range of up to 10 m (or even up to 100 m with special transceivers). Having this power and relying on battery power, a Bluetooth device cannot be in an active transmit mode all the time. Therefore, Bluetooth defines several low-power states for the device. Figure 7.30 shows the states of a Bluetooth device and possible transitions. Every device which is currently not participating in a piconet (and not switched off) is in **STANDBY** mode. In this mode, a device listens for paging messages periodically (every 2,048 slots or 1.28 s). The devices listen to a subset of hop carriers, the so-called wake-up carriers. This subset of 32 (or 16 in the regions mentioned above) wake-up carriers is chosen pseudo-randomly, based on the device's identity. As determined by a wake-up sequence, a device visits every hop carrier of the wake-up carriers, forwarding one hop in the wake-up sequence every 1.28 s. (Visiting a hop carrier means listening into this carrier for 18 slots or 11.25 ms respectively.) Listening into a single wake-up hop carrier enables the device to correlate the incoming signal (if any) with the access code for the piconet derived from its own identity. If the correlator triggers, the device activates itself.

Connections (and thus piconets) can be initiated by any device which then becomes the master. This is done via sending **page** messages if the device

Figure 7.30
States of a Bluetooth
device

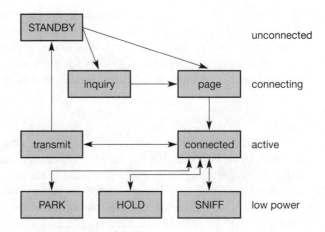

already knows the address of the receiver, or **inquiry** messages followed by a page message if the receiver's address is unknown. The master unit sends 16 identical page messages on 16 different hop frequencies defined for the device to be paged, which is now by definition the slave. If this slave does not respond, the master sends page messages on the remaining 16 wake-up hop carriers. This method assures a maximum delay before reaching any slave of 2.56 s and an average delay of 0.64 s.

To save battery power, a Bluetooth device can go into one of three low power states if no data is ready to be sent:

- **PARK state:** In this state the device has the lowest duty cycle and, thus, the lowest power consumption. The device releases its MAC address, but remains synchronized with the piconet. Therefore, the device occasionally listens to the traffic of the master device to resynchronize and check for broadcast messages.
- **HOLD state:** The power consumption of this state is a little higher; in this mode, the device does not release its MAC address and can resume sending at once after transition out of the HOLD state.
- **SNIFF state:** The sniff state has the highest power consumption of the low-power states. Here, the device listens to the piconet at a reduced rate. The interval for listening into the medium can be programmed and is application dependent.

7.5.3 MAC layer

Several mechanisms control medium access in a Bluetooth system. First of all, one device within a piconet acts as master, all other devices (up to seven) act as slaves. The master determines the hopping sequence using its unique device identifier as well as the phase of the sequence using its internal hardware clock. This unique setting of master parameters prevents two different piconets from having the same hopping sequence and thus separates them via CDMA. Within a piconet, the master controls medium access using a polling and a reservation scheme.

All Bluetooth devices have the same networking capabilities, i.e., they can be master or slave. There is no distinction between terminals and base stations, any two or more devices can form a piconet. The unit establishing the piconet automatically becomes the master, all other devices will be slaves. Within a piconet only one master can exist at any time.

7.5.3.1 Services

Bluetooth offers two different types of services, a synchronous connection-oriented link and an asynchronous connectionless link:

- **Synchronous connection-oriented link (SCO):** Standard telephone (voice) connections require symmetrical, circuit-switched, point-to-point connections. For this type of link, the master reserves two consecutive slots (forward and return slots) at fixed intervals.
- **Asynchronous connectionless link (ACL):** Typical data applications require symmetrical or asymmetrical (e.g., web traffic), packet-switched, point-to-multipoint transfer scenarios (including broadcast). Here the master uses a polling scheme.

Bluetooth can either support a single ACL, three SCOs, or an ACL and an SCO at the same time. SCOs always support 64 kbit/s synchronous connections. ACLs can be symmetric or asymmetric, supporting different bit rates depending on the packet types as explained in the next section. Data rates are up to 432.6 kbit/s on a symmetric link using five consecutive slots and unprotected data. Asymmetric links can carry up to 721.0 kbit/s in one direction and 57.6 kbit/s in the other direction, also using five consecutive slots in one direction and no data protection.

7.5.3.2 Packet format

The general packet format transmitted in one slot is illustrated in Figure 7.31. Each packet uses this fixed format starting with a 72 bit access code derived from the master device's identity, which is unique for the channel.

Each packet exchanged on the channel possesses this access code. Each receiver on the piconet now compares the code of an incoming packet with the stored access code; if they do not match, the rest of the packet is ignored. Furthermore, the access code is the means for synchronization. Then a packet header follows (see Figure 7.32) and finally 0-2,745 bit payload is sent.

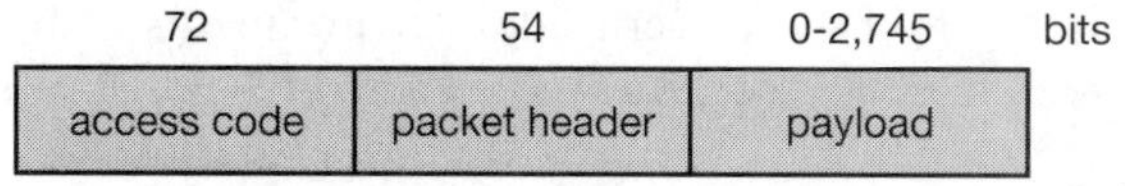

72	54	0-2,745	bits
access code	packet header	payload	

Figure 7.31
Format of a Bluetooth packet sent within one slot

Figure 7.32
Format of a Bluetooth
packet header

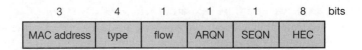

3	4	1	1	1	8	bits
MAC address	type	flow	ARQN	SEQN	HEC	

The packet header starts with 3 bits MAC address, so a piconet can contain a maximum of one master and seven slaves. Sixteen link types can be defined. If acknowledgement of packets is required, Bluetooth sends this acknowledgement in the slot following the data (using its time division duplex scheme). Thus, it is sufficient to use a simple alternating bit protocol with a single bit sequence number SEQN and acknowledgement number ARQN. An 8 bit header error check HEC secures the header. Additionally, the packet header is protected by a one-third rate forward error correction (FEC) code because it contains valuable link information and should survive bit errors. Therefore, the 18 bit header requires 54 bits in the packet.

Typically, each packet fills exactly one slot. If higher data rates are required, Bluetooth can send **multi-slot packets**, covering three or five consecutive slots. Multi-slot packets are always sent on the same hop frequency, i.e., no hopping takes place during the transmission of a three or five slot packet. After sending this type of packet, hopping does not continue with the next frequency in the sequence, but with the next frequency that would have been chosen if only single slot packets had been sent, i.e., the sequence is not interrupted. This behaviour is important for all other devices to remain synchronized, because the piconet is uniquely defined by having the same hopping sequence with the same phase. Shifting the phase in one device would destroy the piconet.

Using an **SCO** link, three different types of single-slot packets can be used. Each SCO link carries voice at 64 kbit/s, additionally no forward error correction (FEC), 2/3 FEC, or 1/3 FEC can be selected. The 1/3 FEC is as strong as the FEC for the packet header and triples the amount of data. Depending on the error rate of the channel, different FEC schemes can be applied. FEC always causes an overhead, but avoids retransmission of data with a higher probability. However, voice data over an SCO is never retransmitted – a very robust voice-encoding scheme, **continuous variable slope delta (CVSD)**, is applied (Haartsen, 1998).

For **ACLs** carrying data, 1-slot, 3-slot or 5-slot packets can be used. Additionally, data can be protected using a 2/3 FEC scheme. This FEC protection helps in noisy environments with a high link error rate. However, the overhead introduced by FEC might be too high. Bluetooth therefore offers a fast automatic repeat reqeust (ARQ) scheme for reliable transmission. Each packet is acknowledged in the slot following the packet. If a packet is lost, a sender can retransmit it immediately in the next slot after the negative acknowledgement. This scheme hardly exhibits any overhead in environments with low error rates, as only packets which are lost or destroyed have to be retransmitted.

7.5.4 Networking

All users within one piconet have the same hopping sequence and, thus, share the same 1 MHz channel. As more users join the piconet, the throughput per user drops quickly. Having only one piconet available within the 80 MHz in total is thus not very efficient. This led to the idea of forming groups of piconets called **scatternet** (see Figure 7.33). Only those units that really have to exchange data share the same piconet, so that many piconets with overlapping coverage can exist simultaneously.

In the example, the scatternet consists of three piconets, in which two devices participate in two different piconets. All three piconets now use a different hopping sequence, always determined by the master of the piconet. Now in an average sense all piconets can share the total of 80 MHz bandwidth available. Adding more piconets leads to a graceful performance degradation of a single piconet because more and more collisions may occur. A collision occurs if two or more piconets use the same carrier frequency for a slot.

If a device wants to participate in more than just one piconet, it has to synchronize to the hopping sequence of the piconet it wants to take part in. If a device acts as slave in one piconet, it simply starts to synchronize with the hopping sequence of the piconet it wants to join. After synchronization, it acts as a slave in this piconet and does not participate in its former piconet any longer. To enable synchronization, a slave has to know the identity of the master determining the hopping sequence of a piconet. Before leaving one piconet, a slave informs the current master that it will be unavailable for a certain amount of time. The remaining devices in the piconet continue communication as usual.

Figure 7.33
Scatternet as a group of piconets

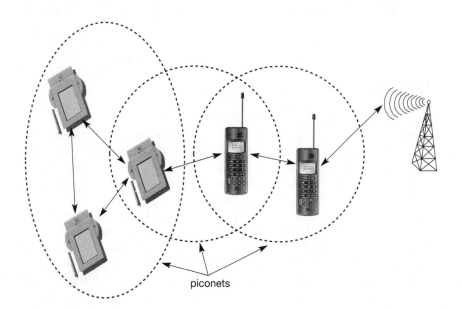

piconets

A master can also leave its piconet and act as a slave in another piconet. It is clearly not possible for a master of one piconet to act as the master of another piconet for this would lead to the identical behaviour of those two piconets (both would have the same hopping sequence, which is determined by the master per definition). As soon as a master leaves a piconet, all traffic within this piconet is suspended until the master returns.

Communication between different piconets thus takes place through devices jumping back and forth between theses nets. If this is done periodically, for instance, isochronous data streams can be forwarded from one piconet to another.

7.5.5 Security

A radio interface is by nature very easy to access. Especially Bluetooth devices may transmit private data, e.g., schedules between a PDA and a mobile phone. A user clearly does not want another person to eavesdrop the data transfer. Just imagine a scenario where two Bluetooth enabled PDAs in suitcases 'meet' on the conveyor belt of an airport exchanging personal information! Thus, Bluetooth offers mechanisms for authentication and encryption on the MAC layer, which must be implemented in the same way within each device.

The main security features offered by Bluetooth include a challenge-response routine for authentication, a stream cipher for encryption, and a session key generation. Each connection may require a one-way, two-way, or no authentication using the challenge-response routine. Key lengths of 0, 40, or 64 bits can be used for encryption, resulting in a relatively weak security. However, all these schemes have to be implemented in silicon, and higher layers should offer stronger encryption if needed. The security features included in Bluetooth only help to set up a local domain of trust between devices.

The security algorithms use the public identity of a device, a secret private user key, and an internally generated random key as input parameters. For each transaction, a new random number is generated on the Bluetooth chip. Key management is left to higher layer software.

7.5.6 Link management

A Bluetooth system is managed by a **link manager** (LM). An LM handles the authentication procedure, negotiates authentication parameters, carries out link setup and release, configures links etc. LMs on different devices communicate using the **link manager protocol** (LMP), and all LMs use the services provided by the **link controller** (LC).

An LC provides the basic service of sending and receiving data and requesting names of other devices. Furthermore, it sets up connections, triggers authentication and negotiates link modes, which could be data or voice. The LC can also put a device into sniff mode where it only listens every n slots; the LM negotiates the value of n. Similarly, LC can set a device on hold or in park mode as described in 7.5.2.

7.6 Summary

This chapter has introduced three different technologies designed for WLANs. The basic goals of all three LAN types are the provision of a much higher flexibility for nodes within a network. All WLANs suffer from limitations of the air interface and higher complexity compared to their wired counterparts, but allow for a new degree of freedom for their users within rooms, buildings or production halls. WLANs are already in use in, e.g., warehouses, class rooms, meeting rooms, hospitals and many other places.

However, the three technologies also differ in some respects. Whereas in the early beginning of WLANs several proprietary products existed, nowadays they mostly offer basic support for IEEE 802.11. Compared to the technical development of certain products, this standard appeared rather late. Thus, one can buy much more powerful WLAN devices than the standard specifies.

For HIPERLAN, the situation is different. Here, a standardization body (ETSI) developed a completely new standard, but no products are available yet. HIPERLAN comprises many interesting features, is much more powerful than IEEE 802.11, has a higher data rate (23.5 Mbit/s instead of 2 Mbit/s), but it is questionable if it will ever be a commercial success. Furthermore, the 5 GHz band required for HIPERLAN is not available worldwide compared to the 2.4 GHz used for IEEE 802.11. Anastasi (1998) gives a good overview of the capabilities of the two MAC schemes used in IEEE 802.11 and HIPERLAN respectively, and investigates whether those access schemes can be used for QoS provision as it is required for, e.g., wireless ATM (see chapter 8).

For Bluetooth, the situation is completely different. Here several companies founded a consortium and tried to set up a de facto industry standard. Up to now, no standardization body has set up any specification regarding Bluetooth; however, the first products with this solution integrated should come out towards the end of 1999. The primary goal of Bluetooth is not a complex standard covering many aspects of wireless networking, but a quick and very cheap solution enabling ad hoc personal communication within a short range in the licence-free 2.4 GHz band.

The typical mobile device of tomorrow will comprise several technologies with the ability of connecting to different networks, e.g., a GSM follow-on (such as UMTS) for wide area communication, a satellite antenna (e.g., for Iridium), and different WLAN devices (e.g., IEEE 802.11 and Bluetooth). Depending on cost, application, and location, the device will automatically choose the optimal communication device and network. Roaming between those different networks is still an open topic (in particular with regard to ensuring a certain quality of service) and has to be solved on higher layers.

7.7 Review exercises

1 How is mobility restricted using WLANs? What additional elements are needed for roaming between networks, how and where can WLANs support roaming? In your answer, think of the capabilities of layer 2 where WLANs reside.

2 What are the basic differences between wireless WANs and WLANs, and what are the common features? Consider mode of operation, administration, frequencies, capabilities of nodes, services, national/international regulations.

3 With a focus on security, what are the problems of WLANs. What level of security can WLANs provide, what is needed additionally and how far do the standards go?

4 Compare IEEE 802.11, HIPERLAN, and Bluetooth with regard to their ad hoc capabilities. Where is the focus of these technologies?

5 If Bluetooth is a commercial success, what are remaining reasons for the use of infrared transmission for WLANs?

6 Why is the PHY layer in IEEE 802.11 subdivided? What about HIPERLAN?

7 Compare the power saving mechanisms in all three LANs introduced in this chapter. What are the negative effects of the power saving mechanisms, what are the trade-offs between power consumption and transmission QoS?

8 Compare the offered QoS in all three LANs in ad hoc mode. What advantages does an additional infrastructure offer? How is QoS provided in Bluetooth? Can one of the LAN technologies offer hard QoS (i.e., not only statistical guarantees regarding a QoS parameter)?

9 How do IEEE 802.11 and Bluetooth, respectively, solve the hidden terminal problem? Check out ETSI (1998) for HIPERLAN.

10 How are fairness problems regarding channel access solved in IEEE 802.11 and HIPERLAN respectively? How is the waiting time of a packet ready to transmit reflected?

11 What different solutions do all three networks offer regarding an increased reliability of data transfer?

12 In what situations can collisions occur in all three networks? Distinguish between collisions on PHY and MAC layer. How do the three wireless networks try to solve the collisions or minimize the probability of collisions?

13 Compare the overhead introduced by the three medium access schemes and the resulting performance at zero load, light load, high load of the medium. How does the number of collisions increase with the number of stations trying to access the medium, and how do the three networks try to solve the problems? What is the overall scalability of the schemes in number of nodes?

14 How is roaming on layer 2 achieved, and how are changes in topology reflected? What are the differences between infrastructurebased and ad hoc networks regarding roaming?

15 What are advantages and problems of forwarding mechanisms in ad hoc networks regarding security, power saving, and network stability? Compare Bluetooth and HIPERLAN.

7.8 References

Anastasi, G.; Lenzini, L.; Mingozzi, E.; Hettich, A.; Krämling, A. *(1998)* 'MAC protocols for wideband wireless local access: evolution toward wireless ATM', *IEEE Personal Communications*, 5, (5), October.

Bisdikian, C.; Bhagwat, P.; Gaucher, B.P.; Janniello, F.J.; Naghshineh, M.; Pandoh, P.; Korpeoglu, I. (1998): 'WiSAP A wireless personal access network for handheld computing devices', *IEEE Personal Communications*, 5, (6).

The Bluetooth Consortium, (1998) http://www.bluetooth.com.

Chhaya, H. S.; Gupta, S.(1996) 'Performance of asynchronous data transfer methods of IEEE 802.11 MAC protocol', *IEEE Personal Communications*, 3, (5).

Chhaya, H. S.; Gupta, S.(1997) 'Performance modeling of asynchronous data transfer methods of IEEE 802.11 MAC protocol', *Wireless Networks* 3(1997), Baltzer Science Publishers.

ETSI (1996) *Radio Equipment and Systems (RES); High Performance Radio Local Area Network (HIPERLAN) Type 1; Functional specification,* European Telecommunication Standard, ETS 300 652, European Telecommunications Standards Institute.

ETSI (1998) *Broadband Radio Access Networks (BRAN); High Performance Radio Local Area Network (HIPERLAN) Type 1; Functional specification,* EN 300 652 v1.2.1, European Telecommunications Standards Institute.

Haartsen, J. (1998) 'Bluetooth – the universal radio interface for ad hoc, wireless connectivity', *Ericsson Review* No. 3, http:// www.ericsson.com.

Halsall, F. (1996) *Data communications, computer networks and open systems.* Addison Wesley Longman.

IEEE (1990) *Local Area Network and Metropolitan Area Network – Overview and Architecture*, The Institute of Electrical and Electronics Engineers, IEEE 802.1a.

IEEE (1997) *Wireless LAN Medium Access Control (MAC) and Physical Layer (PHY) specifications*, The Institute of Electrical and Electronics Engineers, IEEE 802.11.

ISO (1995) *Information technology – Telecommunications and information exchange between systems – Local and metropolitan area networks – Common specifications – Part 1: Medium Access Control (MAC) service definition*, International Organization for Standardization, ISO 15802-1.

Perlman, R. (1992) *Interconnections*: *bridges and routers*. Addison Wesley Longman.

Santamaría, A.; López-Hernández, F. (1994) *Wireless LAN systems*, Artech House.

Wesel, E. K. (1998) *Wireless multimedia communications*. AddisonWesley Longman.

Woesner, H.; Ebert, J.–P.; Schläger, M.; Wolisz, A. (1998) 'Power-saving mechanisms in emerging standards for wireless LANs', *IEEE Personal Communications*, 5, (3).

Wireless ATM

8

This chapter gives an overview of **wireless ATM (WATM)** technology. Similar to the ATM technology for fixed networks (Händel, 1994), WATM does not only describe a transmission technology but tries to specify a complete communication system. While many aspects of the systems presented in chapters 7, 9, 10, and 11 originate from the data communication community, many WATM aspects come from the telecommunication industry. This specific situation can be compared to the case of competition and merging with regard to the concepts TCP/IP and ATM.

The following sections describe several aspects of WATM and mobility extensions required in the fixed ATM network. First, the reference model shows several entities familiar from ATM and highlights the extensions needed. Many new functions have to be implemented in mobile terminals – these will be described in a separate section. The WATM working group of the ATM Forum discusses several new mechanisms. Handover, routing, location management etc. are fundamental for a wireless network supporting user mobility. A factor of special interest in this context is 'mobile QoS', as this should be the key difference between WATM and other technologies which merely support best effort.

It is very important to note that up to now, WATM is not a standard determining all the aspects discussed here. Specification in the field of WATM consists of many proposals (e.g., AMES: ATM mobility extension service (Bhat, 1998a)), discussions (see Rauhala, (1998b)), field trials (here, Ayanoglu (1996) offers an overview). Since there is no standard covering all these aspects, the following sections can only reflect some proposals put forward by researchers and companies contributing to the WATM working group of the ATM Forum, and the current state-of-the-art with respect to discussions and drafts. These proposals give a good impression of current problems and offer some solutions, but they should not be seen as the only solutions, as these suggestions only represent a snapshot of ongoing work. This may lead to some confusion comparing several documents from different sources as the names for entities and protocol messages of WATM have not been standardized yet. For the sake of a clearer presentation, not all details of ongoing discussions are included in this chapter.

8.1 Motivation for WATM

Several reasons led to the development of WATM:

- The main reason for WATM is the need for seamless integration of wireless terminals into an ATM network. This integration is a basic requirement for supporting the same integrated services and different types of traffic streams as ATM does in fixed networks.
- ATM networks scale well from LANs to WANs – and mobility is needed in local and wide area applications. Thus, strategies are needed to extend ATM for wireless access in local and global environments.
- For ATM to be successful, it must offer a wireless extension. Otherwise it cannot participate in the rapidly growing field of mobile communications.
- WATM could offer QoS for adequate support of multimedia data streams. Many other wireless technologies (e.g., IEEE 802.11) typically only offer best effort services or to some extend time-bounded services. However, these services do not provide as many QoS parameters as ATM networks do.
- For telecommunication service providers, it appears natural that merging of mobile wireless communication and ATM technology leads to wireless ATM. One goal in this context is the seamless integration of mobility into B-ISDN which already uses ATM as its transfer technology.

Considering all these aspects of WATM, it is clear that this system will be more complex than most of the other wireless systems. While, for example, IEEE 802.11 only covers local area access methods, Bluetooth only builds up piconets, or Mobile IP only works on the network layer, WATM tries to build up a comprehensive system covering physical layer, media access, routing, integration into the fixed ATM network, service integration into B-ISDN etc.

8.2 Wireless ATM working group

In order to develop this rather complex system, the ATM Forum formed the **Wireless ATM Working Group** in 1996. This group aims to develop a set of specifications that extends the use of ATM technology to wireless networks. These wireless networks should cover many different networking scenarios, such as private and public, local and global, mobility and wireless access (Raychaudhuri, 1996).

   The main goal of this working group involves ensuring the compatibility of all new proposals with existing ATM Forum standards. Thus, it should be possible to upgrade existing ATM networks, i.e., ATM switches and ATM end-systems, with certain functions to support mobility and radio access if required. Two main groups of open issues have been identified in this context: on the one hand the extensions needed for the 'fixed' ATM to support mobility, on the other hand all protocols and mechanisms related to the radio access.

The following more general extensions of the ATM system need to be considered for a **mobile ATM**:

● **Location management**: Similar to other cellular networks, WATM networks must be able to locate a wireless terminal or a mobile user, i.e., to find the current access point of the terminal to the network.
● **Mobile routing**: Even if the location of a terminal is known to the system, it still has to route the traffic through the network to the access point currently responsible for the wireless terminal. Each time a user moves to a new access point, the system must reroute traffic.
● **Handover signalling**: The network must provide mechanisms which search for new access points, set up new connections between intermediate systems and signal the actual change of the access point.
● **QoS and traffic control**: In contrast to wireless networks offering only best effort traffic, and to cellular networks offering only a few different types of traffic, WATM should be able to offer many QoS parameters. To maintain these parameters, all actions such as rerouting, handover etc. have to be controlled. Furthermore, the network must pay attention to the incoming traffic (and check if it conforms to some traffic contract) in a similar way to today's ATM (policing).
● **Network management**: Finally, all extensions of protocols or other mechanisms also require an extension of the management functions to control the network

To ensure wireless access, the working group is currently discussing the following topics belonging to a **radio access layer** (RAL):

● **Radio resource control**: As for any wireless network, radio frequencies, modulation schemes, antennas, channel coding etc. have to be determined.
● **Wireless media access**: Different media access schemes are possible, each with specific strengths and weaknesses for, e.g., multimedia or voice applications. Different centralized or distributed access schemes working on ATM cells can be imagined.
● **Wireless data link control**: The data link control layer might offer header compression for an ATM cell that carries almost 10 per cent overhead using a 5 byte header in a 53 byte cell. Furthermore, this layer can apply ARQ or FEC schemes to improve reliability.
● **Handover issues**: During handover cells cannot only be lost but can also be out of sequence (depending on the handover mechanisms). Thus, cells must be re-sequenced and lost cells must be retransmitted if required.

8.3 WATM services

The following section includes several example scenarios in which WATM can be used from a user's perspective. These examples show that the idea behind WATM goes beyond the mere provision of wireless access or the construction of a wireless LAN. The services offered cover many aspects of today's wireless and mobile communications.

WATM systems will be designed for transferring voice, classical data, video (from low quality to professional quality), multimedia data, short messages etc. Several **service scenarios** can be identified (Rauhala, 1998a), (Barton, 1998), such as for example:

- **Office environments**: This includes all kinds of extensions for existing fixed networks offering a broad range of Internet/Intranet access, multimedia conferencing, online multimedia database access, and telecommuting. Using WATM technology, the office can be virtually expanded to the actual location of an employee.
- **Universities, schools, training centres**: The main focus in this scenario is distance learning, wireless and mobile access to databases, Internet access, or teaching in the area of mobile multimedia computing.
- **Industry**: WATM may offer an extension of the Intranet supporting database connection, information retrieval, surveillance, but also real-time data transmission and factory management.
- **Hospitals**: Due to the quality of service offered for data transmission, WATM is the prime candidate for reliable, high-bandwidth mobile and wireless networks. Applications could include the transfer of medical images, remote access to patient records, remote monitoring of patients, remote diagnosis of patients at home or in an ambulance, as well as tele-medicine. The latter needs highly reliable networks with guaranteed quality of service to enable, e.g., remote surgery.
- **Home**: Many electronic devices at home (e.g., TV, radio equipment, CD-player, PC with Internet access) could be connected using WATM technology. Here, WATM would permit various wireless connections, e.g., a PDA with TV access.
- **Networked vehicles**: All vehicles used for the transportation of people or goods will have a local network and network access in the future. While currently vehicles such as trucks, aircraft, buses, or cars only have very limited communication capabilities (e.g., via GSM), WATM could provide them with a high-quality access to the Internet, company databases, multimedia conferencing etc. On another level, local networks among the vehicles within a certain area are of increasing importance, e.g., to prevent accidents or increase road capacity by platooning (i.e., forming a train of cars or trucks on the road with very low safety distance between single vehicles).

Mobility within an ATM network will be provided by the **ATM mobility extension service (AMES)**. AMES will facilitate the use of these ATM networks by different equipment and applications requiring mobility. Wireless equipment should obtain equivalent services from the network as wired terminals from a user's perspective. AMES comprises the extensions needed to support terminal portability for home and business use. Users can rearrange devices without losing access to the ATM network and with a guaranteed service quality.

Furthermore, WATM will offer a personal cellular system (PCS) **access service**. PCSs like GSM, IS-95, UMTS etc. may use the mobility supporting capabilities of the fixed ATM network to route traffic to the proper base station controller. Public services for users could be a multimedia telephony service, a symmetric service offering speech and low bit rate video with medium mobility, as well as the asymmetrical service of real-time online data transfer, e.g., web browsing, e-mail and downloading of files. Private services could include a multimedia cordless telephone with higher quality compared to the public version. Furthermore, special private data transfer services, e.g., carrying production data, could be deployed on a campus.

Another field of services is provided by **satellite ATM services (SATM)**. Future satellites will offer a large variety of TV, interactive video, multimedia, Internet, telephony and other services (see chapter 5). The main advantage in this context is the ubiquitous wide area coverage in remote, rural, and even urban areas. Satellites can be used directly (direct user access service), e.g., via a mobile phone or a terminal with antenna, which enables the user to access the ATM network directly. Furthermore, a whole network can be connected to a satellite using a mobile switch (fixed access service). For example, all computers in a remote school could be connected to a switch, which connects to a satellite. Even ships can carry ATM networks and can then use the seamless integration of their onboard ATM network to a global ATM network (mobile platform service).

8.4 Reference model

Compared to fixed ATM, wireless ATM provides several additional functions. The following sections present examples for reference models which illustrate the integration of wireless components, access points, and extensions for mobility support into the ATM architecture.

8.4.1 Example configurations

WATM supports different types of wireless access such as wireless local loops or wireless mobile end users. As this book concentrates on mobile communications, only protocols and architectures supporting mobility and wireless access will be highlighted here.

Figure 8.1 shows a simplified reference model for an ATM network supporting mobility and wireless access (Bhat, 1998a). **Wireless mobile ATM terminals (WMT)**[23] have radio links to **radio transceivers (RT)**.[24] These RTs are connected to an **access point (AP)** via wires. One AP can control several RTs. An AP implements all radio access functions and, thus, handles radio resource management, radio medium access control, and other radio-specific functions. Signalling of radio-relevant information takes place between the AP and a WMT. Several APs are connected to an **end-user mobility-supporting ATM switch – entry (EMAS-E)**. EMAS-Es exchange signalling messages on the ATM layer with the WMT and offer additional mobility functions as described in the following sections. In the WATM architecture, radio-related signalling between AP and WMT and ATM related signalling between EMAS-E and WMT is separated. To coordinate these two levels of signalling, EMAS-E and AP use the **access point control protocol (APCP)**. APCP is integrated in addition to the UNI protocol with mobility extension (UNI+M). EMAS-Es communicate with other **end-user mobility-supporting ATM switch – network (EMAS-N)** via a mobility enhanced version of the NNI protocol, NNI+M.

The reference model shown in Figure 8.1 is only one possible outcome. AP functionality may also be integrated into the EMAS-E. It is interesting to note that in a wireless access scenario, the AP acts as a virtual multiplexer for ATM data streams. The AP receives ATM cells (probably modified for radio transmission) and multiplexes them over an output link (cell multiplexing in the ATM).

The reference model shown here is similar to the one used in a GSM network (see section 4.1). RTs are similar to a base transceiver station (BTS), APs implement functions like base station controllers (BSC), and finally an EMAS-E acts like a mobile switch controller (MSC).

WATM is not limited to the basic scenario illustrated in Figure 8.1. Other scenarios include wireless ad hoc networks, mobile switches (e.g., on board of an aircraft), or fixed wireless access for the local loop (see Figure 8.20 and Rauhala (1998a).

Figure 8.1

Example reference model for wireless access (Bhat, 1998a)

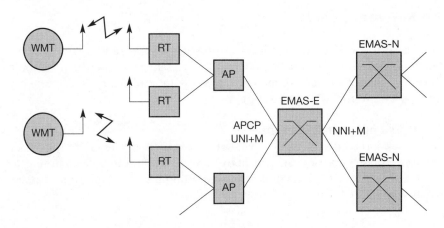

8.4.2 Generic reference model

The changes needed for the fixed ATM network to make it mobility aware and to support wireless access are illustrated following a proposal for the start-up of the WATM working group (Raychaudhuri, 1996a), (Raychaudhuri, 1996b) and the current drafts for wireless ATM protocol stacks (Bhat, 1998a).

Several reference models exist for wireless access, mobile access, and, as shown in Figure 8.2, for wireless mobile access to an ATM network. A mobile ATM (MATM) terminal uses a WATM terminal adapter to gain wireless access to an WATM access point. MATM terminals could be represented by, e.g., laptops using an ATM adapter for wired access plus software for mobility. The WATM terminal adapter enables wireless access, i.e., it includes the transceiver etc., but it does not support mobility. The access point with the radio transceivers is connected to a mobility enhanced ATM switch (EMAS-E), which in turn connects to the ATM network with mobility aware switches (EMAS-N) and other standard ATM switches. Finally, a wired, non-mobility aware ATM end system may be the communication partner in this example.

The radio segment spans from the terminal and the terminal adapter to the access point, whereas the fixed network segment spans from the access point to the fixed end system. Furthermore, the fixed mobility support network, comprising all mobility aware switches EMAS-E and EMAS-N, can be distinguished from the standard ATM network with its non-mobility aware switches and end systems.

ATM separates the user from the control plane, a separation which is also reflected in the protocol layers reference models (see Figure 8.3 and Figure 8.4). Mobility and wireless access do not affect the user plane to a great extent. As user processes should not notice the wireless access, higher protocol layers remain the same for wireless or wired transmission. Data transfer over the radio link, however, might be completely different from data transfer over wires. The **radio access layer (RAL)** can perform header compression to increase efficiency, apply FEC for a higher reliability, or insert new control information in an ATM cell header. The RAL includes LLC, MAC, and PHY layers (see section 8.6). However, on the user side of the terminal adapter and the network side of the access point, there appears to be no difference to the usual ATM cell stream.

While on the user plane not too many new features are required, the control plane integrates many new functions on different entities in the network as shown in Figure 8.4. The MATM needs additional signalling functions for the

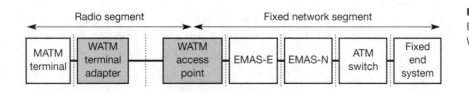

Figure 8.2

Example for a generic WATM reference model

Figure 8.3
User plane protocol layers in a WATM reference model

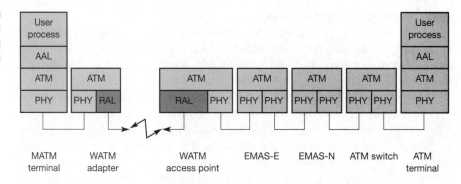

Figure 8.4
Control plane protocol layers in a WATM reference model

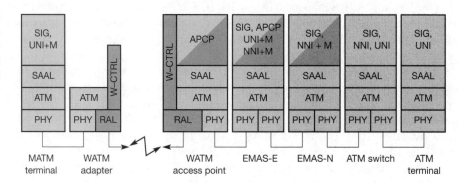

UNI (user-to-network interface), **UNI+M**, to support mobility. UNI+M offers all traditional functions of the UNI. To control the radio transceivers, additional functions are necessary on the terminal adapter and the access point (**W-CTRL**). These functions may control signal strength or other radio-specific issues.

Between the access point and the EMAS-E, **APCP** implementations are needed to exchange control information. APCP is used for access point related information only, not for any other ATM-related topics. The access point does not perform any switching. The control plane of the EMAS-E implements the counterpart for the terminal's UNI+M and the access point's APCP. Furthermore, it contains an NNI (network-to-network interface) with mobility support functions, **NNI+M**. The next switch, EMAS-N, supports mobility with an NNI+M, but has no connection to access points. These switches can also connect to standard ATM switches.

It should be noted that it is not yet clear how much about mobility needs to be known to fixed-end systems. However, there will be functions in the network to enable communication between legacy ATM-end systems and mobile terminals.

8.5 Functions

Many additional functions are needed both on the user side as well as on the network side to support mobility, wireless access, security etc. In the following sections, some examples for these functions are enumerated. It should be noted, however, that some of the examples presented are still under discussion (Bhat, 1998a) and that the list is not complete. Figure 8.5 gives an overview of the functions and their logical interconnection. A user identification module (UIM) is part of the wireless mobile terminal (WMT). Via a radio link the WMT connects to the AP, which is connected to an end-user mobility-supporting ATM switch at the edge of the fixed network (EMAS-E).

8.5.1 Wireless mobile terminal side

To support administration, data transmission service, authentication etc., the following functions have been identified (index T indicates terminal side):

- **Mobility management function (MMF$_T$):** This function is used for network analysis and monitoring, location update initiation, and paging response.
- **Call control and connection control function (CCF$_T$):** Similar to fixed networks, this function handles call setup and release. Thus, it also comprises access control, connection control, and QoS-related requests. CCF$_T$ also maintains and modifies ATM connections in the ATMC$_T$.
- **Identity management function (IMF$_T$):** Similar to the subscriber and equipment identity functions of GSM mobile terminals, the user of an ATM mobile terminal needs functions to store identification and security related information.
- **Mobile terminal security agent (MTSA):** The terminal itself might need additional functions for security, independent of any user and the information stored on the UIM. This function can help to authenticate the terminal as hardware, which is not necessarily associated to a special user.

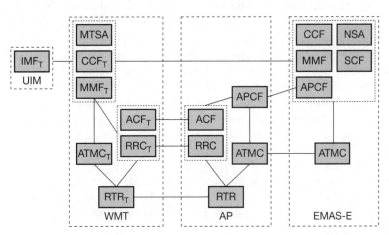

Figure 8.5
Functions and interactions needed to support mobility

More functions are needed for radio and wireless access control:

- **Radio transmission and reception (RTR$_T$):** This is the basic function enabling sending and receiving of data. RTR$_T$ comprises the logical link control (LLC), medium access control (MAC), and physical (PHY) layers. Mechanisms included are error control to improve transmission quality (retransmission and/or forward error correction), multiplexing and demultiplexing, ciphering and deciphering. The PHY layer handles modulation, scrambling, power setting, and more radio channel related functions.
- **Radio resource control function (RRC$_T$):** Radio resources need to be controlled, i.e., selected, released, reserved, as determined by the control plane. Furthermore, RRC$_T$ can trigger handovers, and monitor and analyze radio access.
- **Association control function (ACF$_T$):** This function handles the association of a wireless terminal to its access point. It includes setup and release of an association and support for intra-AP handover, power saving, and radio handover.
- **ATM connection function (ATMC$_T$):** This function is responsible for ATM connections, i.e., connection setup, release and modification, and provides the bearer service for the control and user plane. This function controls the ATM connection elements providing ATM standard services, i.e., constant bitrate (CBR), real-time variable bitrate (rt-VBR), non real-time variable bitrate (nrt-VBR), available bitrate (ABR), and unspecified bitrate (UBR) (Händel, 1994), (ATMForum, 1996).

8.5.2 Mobility supporting network side

The network side implements the counterparts of the terminal's functions and some additional mechanisms for network integration and administration purpose. The following functions support service and connection control:

- **Access point control function (APCF):** Implemented on the access point as well as on the EMAS-E, this function is used for paging, handover, AP management, and reporting of radio conditions and link load.
- **Call control and connection control function (CCF):** To set up a connection with any other system, CCF establishes, maintains, and releases connections. It furthermore performs connection admission control as needed for ATM networks and requests network and radio resources.
- **Network security agent (NSA):** It is important for networks with wireless access to control the wireless terminals. Thus, this function performs identity management, authenticates subscribers, controls confidentiality, and encrypts data.
- **Service control function (SCF):** This high-level function supports storage of and access to service profiles and provides consistency checks on these profiles. It is the highest function for an overall service control.

- **Mobility management function (MMF):** Finally, MMF is the function that comprises mobility support on the network side, such as location management, handover, storage of location data and subscriber identity. Furthermore, it controls paging, routing, and location updates.

Similar to the wireless terminal, the network side also requires functions to control radio and access to the medium:

- **Associated control function (ACF):** This function handles association setup and release between the mobile terminal and the access point. This includes paging, handover decision and execution, and monitoring and analysis of the link. Furthermore, it broadcasts system information and supports power saving.
- **Radio resource control function (RRC):** RRC implements the main control for all radio resources shared by many wireless terminals. It manages the radio channels, analyzes the mobile radio environment, and is able to initiate handover if transmission conditions change.
- **Radio transmission and reception function (RTR):** The RTR function on the network side also contains LLC, MAC, and PHY layers like the terminal does. The main additional mechanism for the network side is the multiplexing of ATM cells according to the traffic contract and QoS parameters of the connections. This is also one of the main differences between WATM networks and many other wireless networks. WATM tries to support as many traffic parameters as ATM does.
- **ATM connection function (ATMC):** This function controls ATM connections for the terminal. Additionally, it includes multiplexing functions for ATM traffic streams.

8.6 Radio access layer

Figure 8.3 and Figure 8.4 show the location of the radio access layer (RAL) in the WATM reference model. The following sections list the requirements for an RAL and gives one example for an RAL, the ETSI BRAN (broadband radio access networks) standard.

8.6.1 Requirements

Wireless access to WATM will be provided by adding a radio-specific layer RAL under the ATM specific layers. RAL should operate in the 5 GHz frequency range and fulfil the following requirements.

8.6.1.1 Physical layer

The physical layer must specify frequencies, efficient reuse of frequencies, antennas, transmit power, the maximum range, cell characteristics, carrier frequencies, symbol rate, modulation scheme, channel coding, training sequences etc. Furthermore, interfaces for data and control flow to and from the radio unit have to be defined.

The requirements specified for the physical layer in the RAL are:

- **Bit error rate (BER)**: This rate should be less than 10^{-4} with an availability of 99.5 per cent measured at the PHY SAP.
- **Packet size**: The physical layer should support single cell PDUs efficiently. However, the more common case of several cells per PDU should be more efficient and, thus, also be possible.
- **Data rate**: 25 Mbit/s should be available for the ATM layer on top of the RAL (i.e., more than 50,000 cells/s)
- **Maximum range**: Depending on local regulations and the environment, coverage of 30-50 m indoors and 200-300 m outdoors should be possible.
- **Error correction**: Due to the high risk of bit errors, the physical layer should include some error-correcting mechanisms.
- **Transmit power**: Typically, transmit power is limited by local regulations. The physical layer requirements assume at least 100 mW EIRP.

8.6.1.2 Medium access control layer

The MAC layer has to control the simultaneous access of several wireless mobile terminals to the medium. This includes the definition of a MAC protocol, a PDU format, and a MAC control algorithm. Furthermore, the MAC layer must support user mobility and provide interfaces to the physical and logical link control layers. The following general goals have been defined:

- **Logical channels**: As shown in Figure 8.3, the MAC layer within the RAL connects the ATM layers of the access point and the wireless mobile terminal. Thus, the MAC layer must also support logical channels for ATM virtual connections, each associated with a set of ATM QoS and traffic parameters.
- **QoS/traffic parameters**: The MAC layer should support QoS and traffic parameters in accordance with the ATM specification TM 4.0 (ATMForum, 1996). MAC should not compromise end-to-end QoS, which is one of the advantages of ATM over other best effort technologies such as Mobile IP (see section 9.1) in combination with a WLAN (e.g., IEEE 802.11, see section 7.3).
- **Architecture**: The typical WATM architecture uses an infrastructure network (see Figure 8.1). Support of this architecture is mandatory for the MAC layer. It is an optional requirement to support ad hoc configurations.
- **Service provision**: The services offered by the MAC layer must include the ATM service classes CBR, VBR-rt, VBR-nrt, ABR, and UBR including QoS control. The efficiency of the MAC layer must be higher than 60-75 per cent (recent research shows that an efficiency of more than 90 per cent is possible (Anastasi, 1998), (Petras, 1997), (Sanchez, 1997)). The peak data rate supported is at least 25 Mbit/s with a sustained data rate of 6 Mbit/s.

MAC must also support low data rates per connection, such as 32 kbit/s CBR for telephony.

8.6.1.3   Logical link control layer

The logical link control (LLC) layer, which is located between the ATM and MAC layers, has to solve specific problems in the field of wireless transmission and combines with the MAC layer to form the data link control (DLC) layer. Again, LLC PDUs and the LLC protocol have to be defined, which includes special wireless headers for data packets, control messages, and possibly special functions for the ATM service classes. The main focus of the LLC layer comprises error control, error detection and correction, using the mechanisms of selective retransmission and forward error correction. The main requirements for the LLC layer are:

- **Automatic repeat request (ARQ)**: It is mandatory for the LLC layer to support ARQ. However, it is optional to use different ARQ schemes for different service classes. Furthermore, it is optional to support a small cell delay variation (CDV) using a special ARQ scheme.
- **Optional miscellaneous features**: LLC can provide special forward error correction (FEC) mechanisms to support real-time service classes. Furthermore, the level of redundancy and the FEC scheme can be adapted to the QoS requirements of a connection. LLC can also provide means to support handover and to restore cell sequence during handover. In addition, authentication, encryption, and further security mechanisms can be implemented in the LLC.

8.6.2 BRAN

The broadband radio access networks (BRAN), which have been standardized by the European Telecommunications Standards Institute (ETSI), are a possible choice for an RAL for WATM. Although BRAN has been standardized independently from WATM, there is co-operation between the two to concentrate the common efforts on one goal.

The main motivation behind BRAN is the deregulation and privatization of the telecommunication sector in Europe. Many new providers experience problems getting access to customers because the telephone infrastructure belongs to a few big companies. One possible technology to provide network access for customers is radio. Advantages of radio access are the high flexibility and quick installation. Different types of traffic are supported, one can multiplex traffic for higher efficiency, and the connection can be asymmetrical (as, e.g., in the typical WWW scenario where many customers pull a lot of data from servers but only put very small amounts of data on the servers). Furthermore, radio access allows for an economical growth of access bandwidth. If more bandwidth is needed, additional transceiver systems can be installed easily, while for wired transmission this would involve the installation of additional wires. The primary market for BRAN includes private customers and small to medium size companies with Internet applications, multimedia conferencing, and virtual private networks.

BRAN standardization has a rather large scope including indoor and campus mobility, transfer rates of 25-155 Mbit/s, and a transmission range of 50 m - 5 km. Standardization efforts are co-ordinated with the ATM Forum, the IETF, other groups from ETSI, the IEEE etc. BRAN has specified four different network types (ETSI, 1998a):

● **HIPERLAN 1**: This high-speed WLAN supports mobility at data rates above 20 Mbit/s. Range is 50 m, connections are multi-point-to-multi-point using ad hoc or infrastructure networks (ETSI, 1998b). HIPERLAN 1 is discussed in detail in section 7.4.
● **HIPERLAN 2**: This technology can be used for wireless access to ATM or IP networks and supports up to 25 Mbit/s in a point-to-multi-point configuration. Transmission range is 50 m with support of slow (< 10 m/s) mobility (ETSI, 1997).
● **HIPERACCESS**: This technology can be used to cover the 'last mile' to a customer via a fixed radio link. Thus, this is an alternative to cable modems or xDSL technologies (ETSI, 1998c). Transmission range is up to 5 km, data rates of up to 25 Mbit/s are supported.
● **HIPERLINK**: To connect different HIPERLAN access points or HIPERACCESS nodes with a high-speed link, HIPERLINK technology can be chosen. HIPER-LINK provides a fixed point-to-point connection with up to 155 Mbit/s.

Common characteristics of HIPERLAN 2, HIPERACCESS, and HIPERLINK include their support of the ATM service classes CBR, VBR-rt, VBR-nrt, UBR, and ABR. Thus it is clear that only HIPERLAN 2 can be a candidate for the RAL of WATM. This technology fulfils the requirements of ATM QoS support, mobility, wireless access, and high bandwidth.

As access networks, BRAN technology is independent from the protocols of the fixed network. Thus, BRAN can be used for ATM and TCP/IP networks as

Figure 8.6
Layered model of BRAN
access networks

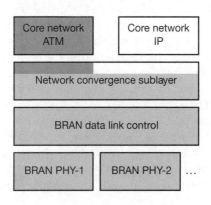

illustrated in Figure 8.6. Based on possibly different physical layers, the DLC layer of BRAN offers a common interface to higher layers. To cover special characteristics of wireless links and to adapt directly to different higher layer network technologies, BRAN provides a network convergence sublayer. This is the layer which can be used by a wireless ATM network or an IP network. In the case of BRAN as the RAL for

WATM, the core ATM network would use services of the BRAN network convergence sublayer.

Looking at the reference model of HIPERLAN 2 (Figure 8.7) (ETSI, 1997), many similarities can be found to the generic reference model of WATM (Figure 8.2). Again, the external network is connected to a mobility enhanced switch. This switch has a wireless access point AP which can be subdivided into an AP controller part and an AP transceiver part. The next component after the air interface H2.1.1 is the wireless terminal adapter. AP and wireless terminal adapter together form the wireless sub-system. Finally, a user module is connected to the wireless terminal adapter. This user now has to handle mobility, but not the problems of wireless access.

8.7 Handover

One of the most important topics in a WATM environment is handover. Connectionless, best-effort protocols supporting handover, such as mobile IP, do not have to take too much care about handover quality. These protocols do not guarantee certain traffic parameters as WATM does. The main problem for WATM during the handover is rerouting of all connections and maintaining connection quality. While in connectionless, best-effort environments handover mainly involves rerouting of a packet stream without reliable transport, an end-system in WATM networks could maintain many connections, each with different quality of service requirements (e.g., limited delay, bounded jitter, minimum bandwidth etc.). Thus, handover does not only involve rerouting of connections but also reserving resources in switches, testing of availability of radio bandwidth, tracking of terminals to perform look-ahead reservations etc.

8.7.1 Handover reference model

A simple reference model for handover in WATM systems is shown in Figure 8.8. An ATM end-to-end connection is separated into different segments. A **fixed segment** is a part of the connection that is not affected by the handover,

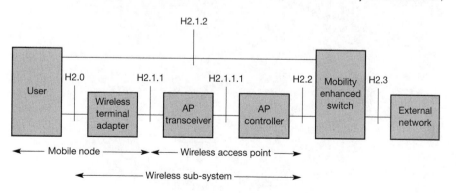

Figure 8.7
HIPERLAN 2
reference model

while the **handover segment** is affected by the handover and is located completely within a **handover domain**. The handover domain can comprise several switches, access points, and is most likely situated within one administrative domain. The **anchor point** is the boundary between a handover segment and a fixed segment.

If both end-systems are wireless mobile ATM terminals, there might be no fixed segment at all. The anchor point then connects the two handover segments which might be in different handover domains.

8.7.2 Handover requirements

Many different requirements have been set up for handover, the following list presents some of the requirements according to Toh (1997), Bhat (1998b):

●   **Handover of multiple connections**: As ATM is a connection-oriented technology where end-systems can support many connections at the same time, handover in WATM must support more than only one connection. This results in the rerouting of every connection after handover. However, it might be the case that resource availability does not allow rerouting of all connections or forces QoS degradation. Then the terminal may decide to accept a lower quality or to drop single connections.

●   **Handover of point-to-multipoint connections**: Seamless support of point-to-multipoint connections is one of the major advantages of the ATM technology. Therefore, WATM handover should also support these types of connection. However, due to the complexity of the scheme, some restrictions might be necessary. One example could be the requirement of not

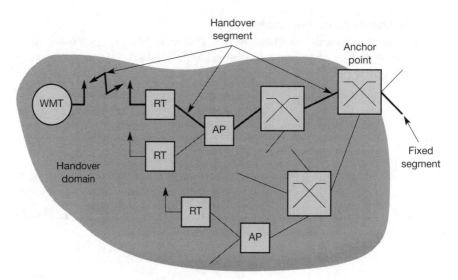

Figure 8.8
Simple handover
reference model

having a splitting point[25] within the handover segment. This restriction avoids having to move splitting points during handover.

- **QoS support**: Handover should aim to preserve the QoS of all connections during handover. However, due to the limited resources, this is not always possible. Therefore, functions for QoS re-negotiation and dropping of connections on a priority basis may be required. Candidate access points should advertise their resources to the terminal, and this information could then be used by a handover algorithm to optimize handover and to balance the load between different access points.
- **Data integrity and security**: WATM handover should minimize cell loss and avoid all cell duplication or re-ordering. Furthermore, security associations between the terminal and the network should not be compromised by handover.
- **Signalling and routing support**: WATM must provide the means to identify mobility-enabled switches in the network, to determine radio adjacent switches by another switch, and to reroute partial connections in the handover domain.
- **Performance and complexity**: The fact that WATM systems are complex by nature is mainly due to their support of connections with QoS. Thus, the simplicity of the handover functionality should be the central goal of the handover design. Modifications to the mobility-enabled switches should be extremely limited, but the functions required could have rather stringent processing time requirements. Due to performance reasons, ATM switches are very much hardware based and, therefore, it is more difficult to integrate updates and new features. The handover code needed for the terminals should be rather simple due to the fact that increasing code size also requires more processing power, i.e., more battery power, which is typically a serious limit in the design of mobile terminals.

8.7.3 Types of handover

WATM will support the following types of handover:

- **Hard handover**: WATM does not support soft handover, i.e., it does not permit a wireless mobile terminal having more than one radio connection at the same time. Typically, soft handover is supported by CDMA-based systems where several access points can receive the same signal at the same time. WATM only supports a single connection to one access point at a certain point in time. Therefore, it is particularly important to avoid interruptions during handover.
- **Terminal initiated**: The WATM terminal could decide to initiate a handover based on, e.g., the current signal quality.
- **Network initiated**: The network, too, could decide that a handover is necessary due to signal strength or current network load etc.

- **Network initiated, terminal assisted**: The wireless terminal could provide the network with information about the current radio conditions and other parameters. Based on this information the network can decide to initiate a handover.
- **Network controlled**: The network is the last instance to decide about a handover, as this is the place where information about the current load situation, free resources etc. resides.
- **Backward handover**: The standard type of handover is called 'backward'. Here, the wireless mobile terminal WMT notices, e.g., a fading signal and initializes the handover to a new AP. The terminal continues to maintain the radio connection while the handover is in process and switches over to a new AP after radio resources have been reserved and all entities involved are prepared for the handover.
- **Forward handover**: A handover is called 'forward' if the WMT suddenly arrives at a new AP which has to initiate and control the handover from then on. This could be the case if the wireless terminal suddenly loses its connection to the old AP. In this case, there is no time to perform a backward handover for the WATM system. Loss of connection could be due to interference or a fast-moving terminal.

8.7.4 Handover scenarios

Figure 8.9 shows three basic handover scenarios for WATM:

- **Intra-EMAS-E/Intra-AP**: This type of handover occurs when the terminal WMT moves from RT_1 to RT_2. The handover remains in the domain of the current AP_1 and the current $EMAS-E_1$. The main task for the AP is to switch between the RTs.

Figure 8.9
Three basic handover scenarios for WATM

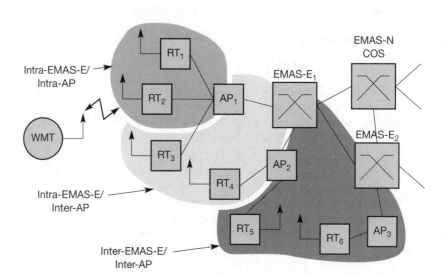

- **Intra-EMAS-E/Inter-AP**: In the second scenario, the WMT moves from RT_3 to RT_4. The handover remains in the domain of EMAS-E_1, but now the switch has to hand over the connection from AP_1 to AP_2. Accordingly, the respective APs have to tear down or to set up the connection.
- **Inter-EMAS-E/Inter-AP**: Finally, the handover could involve different EMAS-Es as illustrated in the third scenario. The WMT moves from RT_5 to RT_6. Now another intermediate switch, known as the **cross over switch (COS)**, has to manage the handover between the switches EMAS-E_1 and EMAS-E_2. The COS does not necessarily have to be the next switch (see Figure 8.9), but can be anywhere between the anchor point (see Figure 8.8) and the two EMAS-Es involved, including the possibility that one of the EMAS-Es or the anchor point itself is the COS. (Akyol, 1996) presents several rerouting schemes to support inter-EMAS-E/inter-AP handover and compares them in terms of signalling bandwidth needed for handover, number of signalling messages, switches involved, handover execution time, robustness to instabilities in handover etc.

8.7.5 Backward handover

In the case of backward handover, the WATM system can select the best AP in terms of terminal and network requirements (see Figure 8.10). Initially, the WMT is connected to RT_2 (see Figure 8.9). As soon as the WMT notices that a handover is required, it sends a BW_HO_REQUEST to the switch EMAS-E_1. This message includes a list of target radio transceivers, e.g., RT_1, RT_4, and RT_6. EMAS-E_1 now looks up the APs controlling the RTs in the list. (These are AP_1 for RT_1, AP_2 for RT_4, and AP_3 for RT_6.)

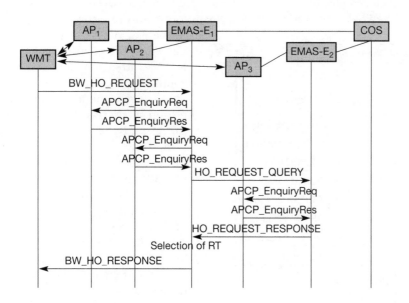

Figure 8.10
Backward handover
with multiple
possible access
points

The next step involves checking the availability of radio resources. Thus, EMAS-E$_1$ sends an APCP_EnquiryReq message to AP$_1$ and another one to AP$_2$. EMAS-E$_1$ cannot send an APCP_EnquiryReq message directly to AP$_3$, so it sends an HO_REQUEST_QUERY to EMAS-E$_2$, which in turn sends an APCP_EnquiryReq message to AP$_3$. All three messages sent by EMAS-E$_1$ are timer-bound. After receiving APCP_EnquiryRes messages or a time-out for a request, EMAS-E$_1$ selects one of the RTs as the new target for the WMT. This selection can be based on traffic patterns, current resources etc. or can be in accordance to proprietary algorithms. After selecting an RT, EMAS-E$_1$ returns a BW_HO_ RESPONSE message to the WMT, indicating that the RT has been chosen and that the connections can now be handed over as explained in the following sections.

8.7.5.1 Intra-EMAS-E/Intra-AP backward handover
In case of an Intra-EMAS-E/Intra-AP backward handover, the WMT also indicates a handover by sending a BW_HO_REQUEST message to its EMAS-E (see Figure 8.11). EMAS-E now checks the availability of radio resources at the AP the WMT is already connected to. Apart from the list of RTs received from the WMT, the APCP_EnquiryRes message contains all identifiers of connections that have to be handed over. Additionally, each connection is associated with ATM traffic and QoS parameters.

As soon as the AP receives the APCP_ EnquiryReq message, it checks the available radio resources and reserves the resources required for the handover. If the AP can choose between several RTs, it selects the one that can support a maximum number of connections with their QoS requirements. The AP returns the selected RT to the EMAS-E in the APCP_EnquiryRes message. This message also includes a list of connections which can be handed over.

The EMAS-E can now forward this information from the AP to the WMT in the BW_HO_RESPONSE message. The WMT then cuts off the connection to the old RT and starts communicating with the new RT. This triggers the allocation of the resources reserved by the AP. After the loss of the old radio connection, the AP may send an APCP_DisassocReq message to the EMAS-E, which in turn responds with an APCP_DisassocCnf. After reconnecting the WMT, the messages APCP_AssocReq and APCP_ AssocCnf may follow. These four messages indicate the release of an old and the setup of a new radio connection to the EMAS-E.

Figure 8.11
Intra-EMAS-E/Intra-AP
backward handover

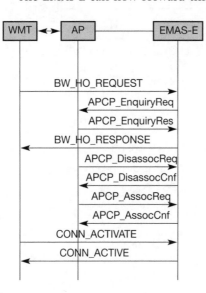

Finally, the WMT signals the EMAS-E that it is ready to resume sending and receiving user data via the CONN_ACTIVATE message. The EMAS-E responds with the CONN_ ACTIVE message, which includes references of connections that have finally been handed over.

8.7.5.2 Intra-EMAS-E/Inter-AP backward handover

A handover needs some more messages between WMT, AP, and EMAS-E if it takes place between different APs connected to the same EMAS-E (see Figure 8.12). Again, the WMT sends a BW_HO_REQUEST message to the switch EMAS-E including a list of connections that should be handed over and a list of possible new RTs. The EMAS-E now identifies the appropriate AP(s) (in our example only AP_2), and sends an APCP_EnquiryReq to this AP.

On receiving this message, the AP checks the available resources to support the connections in the list involved in the handover. It then selects the RT and sends back an APCP_EnquiryRes message to specify the selection and the list of connections that the AP can support. At this stage, the AP has not reserved resources for the handover. The EMAS-E now selects the AP which can support the maximum number of connections for the handover or the one which, e.g., ensures the highest quality. The BW_HO_RESPONSE message transfers this information to the WMT.

Furthermore, the EMAS-E requests the reservation of resources at the chosen AP with another APCP_Enquiry_Req message, and the AP answers with information about the actual reservation in an APCP_EnquiryRes message. After receiving the BW_HO_RESPONSE message, the WMT can release the radio

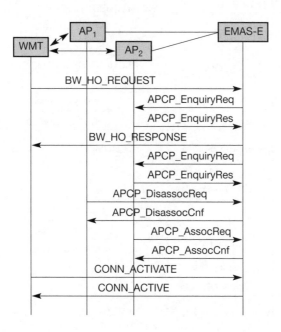

Figure 8.12
Intra-EMAS-E/Inter-AP backward handover

connection, which is signalled via an APCP_ DisassocReq message from the old AP (here AP_1) and answered by an APCP_DisassocCnf. The new AP, AP_2, informs the EMAS-E about the arrival of the WMT with an APCP_ AssocReq message, which is answered by means of an APCP_AssocCnf message.

Now the WMT is ready to send and receive data again, which is indicated by a CONN_ACTIVATE message. EMAS-E answers with a CONN_ACTIVE message containing information about the connections that have been handed over.

8.7.5.3 Inter-EMAS-E/Inter-AP backward handover

The most complex case is the handover from one AP to another where the APs belong to different EMAS-Es (see Figure 8.13). Now the cross over switch (COS) is needed to hand over connections from one switch to the other. Again, the WMT starts with sending a BW_HO_REQUEST to its $EMAS-E_1$, which detects that it is not responsible for the RTs listed by the WMT in the message. Thus, it sends an HO_REQUEST_QUERY to the EMAS-E responsible for the appropriate AP the RT is attached to. The procedure of finding the appropriate EMAS-E depends on the addressing scheme of the RTs.

As explained above, this $EMAS-E_2$ checks the resources available at AP_2 with an APCP_EnquiryRes and receives an APCP_ EnquiryRes in return. Depending

Figure 8.13
Inter-EMAS-E/
Inter-AP backward
handover

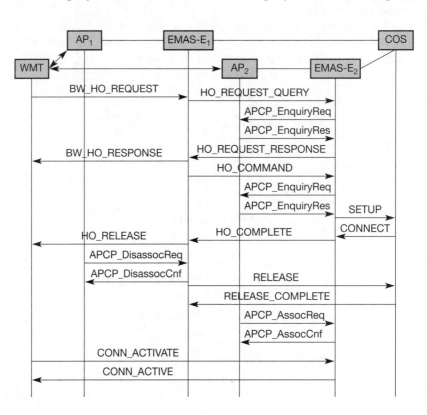

on the information in the return message, the EMAS-E_2 selects the best AP and returns this information to the old EMAS-E_1 using an HO_REQUEST_RESPONSE message. The EMAS-E_1 can now inform the WMT via a BW_HO_RESPONSE message about the right RT to choose. Furthermore, EMAS-E_1 issues an HO_COMMAND message to EMAS-E_2 containing a list of the connections involved in the handover and their QoS requirements, and, if known, the COS responsible for rerouting the user connections. There are several possible locations for the COS. It could be the old EMAS-E1 itself, in which case the handover is called a **VC extension**, because the handover extends the current connections from the old EMAS-E to the new one. Alternatively, the EMAS acting as COS may be known to the old EMAS-E either by pre-configuration or by dynamic configuration at connection setup – this case is called **anchor-based rerouting**. A third alternative is the **dynamic COS discovery**, where EMAS-E_1 includes a possible COS candidate address in the HO_COMMAND message.

EMAS-E_2 now reserves the resources at AP$_2$ using APCP_EnquiryReq and receives APCP_ EnquiryRes. If EMAS-E_2 has received the address of a COS, it issues a SETUP message to this COS. Otherwise it has to apply further mechanisms to send a SETUP message to the COS (ATMForum, 1998a), (ATMForum, 1998b). If a connection between EMAS-E_2 and COS could be set up, EMAS-E_2 sends an HO_COMPLETE message to EMAS-E_1 to indicate that the handover of this connection has been successful. Setting up new connections between EMAS-E_2 and COS is required for every connection indicated in the HO_COMMAND message. A WMT could have many connections active simultaneously, and thus every single connection requires a handover, which is achieved by means of issuing SETUP/CONNECT messages and indicated with an HO_COMPLETE to the old EMAS-E.

After the old EMAS-E has received the HO_COMPLETE message for the last connection it sends an HO_RELEASE to the WMT. This message signals the WMT that it can release the radio connection to the old RT associated to AP$_1$. AP$_1$ signals this event using APCP_DisassocReq, EMAS-E_1 answers with APCP_DisassocCnf. This releases all radio resources at AP$_1$. EMAS-E_1 can now release all connections it still holds to the COS and which have been part of the connections to the WMT. This is done for each connection using the RELEASE message, to which the COS answers with a RELEASE_ COMPLETE message. At the same moment as the COS releases a connection to the old EMAS-E, it switches over to the new EMAS-E using the connections which have been set up before.

The association of the WMT with the new AP triggers the APCP_AssocReq message, answered by an APCP_AssocCnf message by the new EMAS-E. By sending the CONN_ ACTIVATE message, the WMT signals that it is ready to receive data. The new EMAS-E responds with a CONN_ACTIVE message, and the handover is completed.

While Figure 8.13 assumes that there are no failures during handover, several instances may occur that prevent a perfect handover of all connections. If for example the new EMAS-E cannot set up a connection to the COS, it issues an HO_FAILURE message to the old EMAS-E, which then informs the WMT about the failure. The WMT can then decide to drop the connection or try to initiate a forward handover. Additionally, all operations are controlled by timers, thus, if any operation takes too long, the switches may change to other EMAS-Es or signal a failure to the WMT.

It can also happen that the message exchange cannot be completed by one of the entities due to a fast-moving WMT. Then time-outs reset the state of a switch. The example only showed one AP involved per EMAS-E. However, many APs could be involved in the handover process, making the whole handover even more complex. This handover example clearly shows that it is much more complicated to hand over connections which guarantee certain QoS parameters compared to other technologies which do not guarantee any quality (such as, e.g., the Internet Protocol IP, see section 9.1).

It has to be mentioned again, that the handover examples shown here only represent the current state of the discussion, and that there is no finalized standard specifying all identifiers and procedures yet.

8.7.6 Forward handover

The advantage of a backward handover is the possibility to choose the best AP and RT for the WMT to connect to. In case of a forward handover, the WMT suddenly interrupts the old connection and tries to connect to a new AP. This new AP cannot reserve resources in advance and may be a bad choice from a system point of view. However, if radio interference interrupts the current connection, this is the only possibility to reconnect fast enough. The WMT has to optimize its AP choice locally. The following sections describe the same situations that have previously been illustrated for backward handover for the forward handover mode. The messages shown for forward handover carry the same parameters, e.g., list of connections, resources like RTs etc. as they do for the backward handover.

8.7.6.1 Intra-EMAS-E/Intra-AP forward handover

If a WMT disconnects from the AP due to interference, the AP signals this event with the APCP_DisassocReq message, and the EMAS-E responds with APCP_DisassocCnf. In the scenario shown in Figure 8.14, the WMT moves to another RT of the same AP indicated by the messages APCP_AssocReq, APCP_AssocCnf. Now the WMT can send an FW_HO_REQUEST message to the EMAS-E, including a list of currently active connections and their QoS parameters.

The EMAS-E can then try to reserve the necessary resources at the AP with APCP_EnquiryReq, which the AP answers with APCP_EnquiryRes, a message containing a list of connections the AP can hand over. The number of connections might be less due to resource limitations. The EMAS-E switch now forwards this list to the WMT in an FW_HO_RESPONSE message, so that the WMT can then resume communication immediately on all connections indicated in the message.

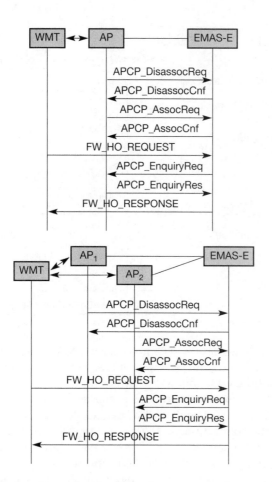

Figure 8.14
Intra-EMAS-E/Intra-AP
forward handover

Figure 8.15
Intra-EMAS-E/Inter-AP
forward handover

8.7.6.2 Intra-EMAS-E/Inter-AP forward handover

For a handover between two APs at the same EMAS-E (see Figure 8.15), the situation is comparable to the previous scenario. The only difference is that the EMAS-E exchanges the message pairs (APCP_DisassocReq, APCP_DisassocCnf) with the old AP (i.e., AP_1) and the message pairs (APCP_AssocReq, APCP_AssocCnf) and (APCP_EnquiryReq, APCP_EnquiryRes) with the new AP (i.e., AP_2). Again, after having received the message FW_HO_RESPONSE, the WMT can resume communication on all connections indicated in this message.

8.7.6.3 Inter-EMAS-E/Inter-AP forward handover

The third handover situation, inter-EMAS-E/inter-AP, is again most complex (see Figure 8.16). Up to the FO_HO_REQUEST message from the WMT to the new EMAS-E, the situation is similar to the intra-EMAS-E/inter-AP handover. $EMAS-E_2$ does not know anything about the old EMAS-E responsible for the WMT. Thus, the FW_HO_REQUEST message contains the old RT identifier and a list of currently active connections, their QoS parameters, and a candidate

Figure 8.16
Inter-EMAS-
E/Inter-AP forward
handover

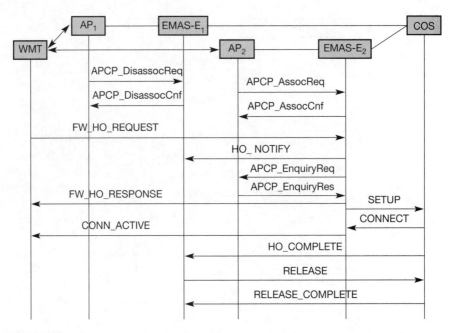

COS information. Based on the RT information, EMAS-E$_2$ can look-up the old EMAS-E of the WMT and can then issue an HO_NOTIFY message to inform the old EMAS-E about the initiation of the handover.

After checking resources with the exchange of APCP_EnquiryReq and APCP_EnquiryRes, EMAS-E$_2$ sends an FW_HO_RESPONSE message to the WMT, indicating that the connection can now be handed over. For each connection listed by the WMT, the following steps have to be performed: EMAS-E$_2$ sets up a connection to the COS (SETUP, CONNECT) and sends a CONN_ACTIVE message to the WMT. The COS informs the old EMAS about the completion of the handover using HO_COMPLETE. EMAS-E$_1$ now releases the connection to the COS (RELEASE), which confirms the release with RELEASE_COMPLETE.

Again, timers control every operation, and HO_FAILURE messages indicate the failure of the handover. However, forward handover does not include the possibility to connect to several APs or EMAS-E. The WMT decides which RT to use and, thus, specifies the new AP and EMAS-E.

8.8 Location management

As for all networks supporting mobility, special functions are required for looking up the current position of a mobile terminal, for providing the moving terminal with a permanent address, and for ensuring security features such as privacy, authentication, or authorization. These and more functions are grouped under the term **location management**.

8.8.1 Requirements for location management

Several requirements for location management have been identified (Bhat, 1998b):

- **Transparency of mobility**: A user should not notice the location management function under normal operation. Any change of location should be performed without user activity. This puts certain constraints on the permissible time delay of the functions associated with location management. Furthermore, transparent roaming between different domains (private/private, private/public, public/public) should be possible. This may include roaming between networks based on different technologies using, for example, a dual mode terminal.

- **Security**: In order to provide a security level high enough to be accepted for mission-critical use (business, emergency etc.), a WATM system requires special features. All location and user information collected for location management and accounting should be protected against unauthorized disclosure. This protection is particularly important for roaming profiles which allow the precise tracking of single terminals. As the air interface is very simple to access, special access restrictions must be implemented to, e.g., keep out public users from private WATM networks. But users should also be able to determine the network their terminal is allowed to access. Essential security features include authentication of users and terminals, but also of access points. Additionally, encryption is necessary, at least between terminal and access point, but preferably end-to-end.

- **Efficiency and scalability**: Imagine WATM networks with millions of users like today's mobile phone networks. Every function and system involved in location management must be scalable and efficient. This includes distributed servers for location storage, accounting and authentication. Furthermore, the performance of all operations should be practically independent of network size, number of current connections and network load. Thus, clustering of switches and hierarchies of domains should be possible to increase the overall performance of the system by dividing the load. In contrast to many existing cellular networks, WATM should work with a more efficient, integrated signalling scheme. All signalling required for location management should therefore be incorporated into existing signalling mechanisms, e.g., by adding new information elements to existing messages. This allows for the utilization of the existing signalling mechanisms in the fixed ATM network which are efficient.

- **Identification**: Location management must provide the means to identify all entities of the network. Radio cells, WATM networks, terminals, and switches need unique identifiers and mechanisms to exchange identity information. This requirement also includes information for a terminal concerning its current location (home network or foreign network) and its current point of attachment. Furthermore, in addition to the permanent

ATM end system address (AESA), a terminal needs a routable temporary AESA as soon as it is outside its home network. This temporary AESA must be forwarded to the terminal's home location.

- **Inter-working and standards**: All location management functions must co-operate with existing ATM functions from the fixed network especially routing. Furthermore, location management in WATM has to be harmonized with other location management schemes, such as location management in current GSM networks, future UMTS networks, the Internet using Mobile IP, or Intranets with special features. This harmonization could for instance lead to a two-level location management if Mobile IP is used on top of WATM. All protocols used in WATM for database updates, registration etc. have to be standardized to permit mobility across provider network boundaries. However, inside an administrative domain proprietary enhancements and optimizations could be applied.

8.8.2 Procedures and entities

Several entities which support location management have been identified. The mobile terminal, which is wireless for the applications considered here (WMT), executes functions to initiate location updates and participates in authentication and privacy protocols. Many end-user mobility-supporting switches (EMAS) are necessary to identify connection setup messages destined for the WMTs and to invoke location resolution functions. Furthermore, EMASs redirect connections and some of them maintain location and authentication servers.

Location servers (LS) maintain a database containing the current AESA and the permanent AESA of a WMT. They also keep track of further service-specific parameters of a terminal and user, such as quality of service of connections. LSs may be part of an EMAS. An **authentication server (AUS)** maintains a secure database of authentication and privacy related information for each WMT. This also includes access rights and equipment identification.

Figure 8.17 illustrates registration and location update message flow after a WMT has moved to a new access point. The AP broadcasts a Broadcast_ID to identify the network, the current location, and radio transceiver. The WMT can now decide to associate with this AP if the access rights fit. The next step involves sending a registration message to the EMAS-E visited, which includes the address of the home EMAS and requests a temporary AESA. The visited EMAS-E now performs the request Loc_Update_Home to the home EMAS of the WMT. This request includes the authentication information and the current location of the WMT. The home EMAS then checks access rights and identity of the WMT by means of the message Auth_Req. If the Auth_Req_Reply signals that everything is ok, the home EMAS updates the home LS with the new location. The LS acknowledges together with the home EMAS. The visited EMAS-E returns a temporary AESA to the WMT in a Loc_Update_Reply.

The basic steps of a connection setup initiated by an arbitrary ATM terminal are depicted in Figure 8.18. This scenario comprises an arbitrary network (with

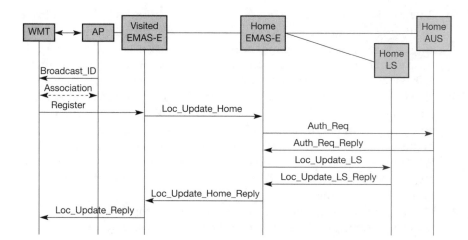

Figure 8.17
Registration and
location update

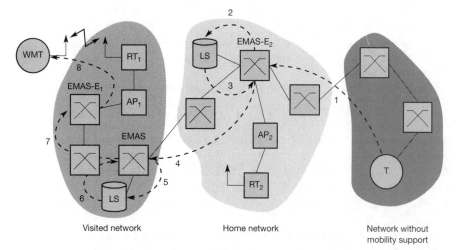

Figure 8.18
Connection setup for
a WMT in a foreign
network

Visited network   Home network   Network without
                                                mobility support

or without mobility support), the **home network** of a WMT, and the network currently visited. The home network is the network to which the WMT belongs according to its permanent address. The home network contains the EMAS-E to which all connections are routed for the WMT (in our example EMAS-E$_2$). All other networks are **foreign networks** for the WMT, the foreign network currently visited is the **visited network**. In this scenario, the following steps are required for localization of the WMT and connection setup:

1   Terminal T does not have any information about the mobility or the current location of the WMT. T only knows the permanent address of WMT and, thus, sets up a connection with WMT. The switch responsible for WMT (EMAS-E$_2$) detects the incoming connection setup.

2   Now EMAS-E$_2$ has to look up the current location of the WMT by sending a location request to the location server LS. LS has a mapping of permanent addresses to current foreign addresses of all WMTs it is responsible for. If several hierarchical look-up steps are needed, LS maps the permanent address to the EMAS in the visited network.

3   LS returns the current address of either the WMT or the EMAS responsible for further look-up. This hierarchical approach makes sense to avoid too frequent LS updates. Typically, a WMT remains in a certain area, thus it is highly probable that the WMT remains within the same network. If the WMT moves within this network, it is not necessary to inform the home LS. The WMT can still be reached by contacting the EMAS responsible for further look-up in the visited network.

4   EMAS-E$_2$ now redirects the incoming connection to the EMAS in the visited network. Redirecting can be accomplished without teardown, i.e., the connection setup is routed along a new path from EMAS-E$_2$. To optimize the route of a connection, partial teardown may be a solution. This means that some part of the connection will be released and a shorter connection can be chosen. This can reduce the effect of triangular routing (i.e., having a route for the connection starting at the terminal via EMAS-E$_2$ and ending at the WMT).

5   The EMAS responsible for the network currently visited can determine the location of the WMT in greater detail. Therefore, it issues a request to its LS. This EMAS may be an EMAS-E or EMAS-N.

6   The LS answers with the exact current location as represented in its database.

7   Now the connection setup can be forwarded to the EMAS-E$_1$, which is directly connected to the AP to which the WMT is also connected.

8   The final step is the connection setup to the WMT itself via the AP and RT.

To perform location update, registration, and connection setup, the entities of WATM need at least the following information:

- **WMT**: The permanent data stored in a WMT comprises the unique home address associated with the device, a key for terminal authentication, and a list of access rights. Temporary data are the current address of the device (assigned during registration) and the current radio transceiver the WMT is connected to. It has not yet been specified how much user specific information should be stored on the WMT. The location of the information might be a chip key (as for GSM) storing a user key and further user parameters (e.g., frequently used addresses).

- **LS**: In order to map the home address of a WMT to its current address, the LS in the home network needs a table including the current location status.

Furthermore, for each user a profile including access rights can be stored. Accounting and billing information for each user can either be stored by the LS or by a separate server.

- **AUS:** The AUS should store the home address for each WMT for identification (if the home address is used for this purpose) and a key which must match the one stored on the WMT for a successful authentication.
- **EMAS:** Each EMAS stores the address of its location server, as this address is needed for handling incoming connection setup requests. Furthermore, the address of an authentication server is required. If the EMAS is at the edge of a network (EMAS-E), then it can additionally store a list of terminals belonging to it (i.e., terminals currently registered and connected via an access point).

8.9 Addressing

Basic requirements for WATM addresses have been identified in Bhat (1998b):

- WATM should support all current formats of ATM end-system addresses (AESA), however, special structuring of addresses for mobile terminals can be applied.
- WMTs must have a permanent, i.e., location-invariant, address. This address is known by the WMT and can be used by other communication partners for contacting the WMT. Furthermore, this address has to correspond with a routable address from the 'home network', i.e., it has to be associated with an EMAS in the home network.
- The WMT must support the assignment of temporary, routable addresses during registration within a foreign network. The format of the temporary and permanent address may be different.

Based on these requirements, the WATM specification proposes a dual address assignment for WMTs. One address is the permanent, unique, location-invariant address based on the routable ATM address associated with an EMAS in the home network of the WMT. The other address is a routable address in the foreign network associated with the EMAS-E the WMT is currently connected to. An automatic mechanism should provide a temporary address for the WMT during registration.

8.10 Mobile quality of service

Quality of service (QoS) guarantees are one of the main advantages envisaged for WATM networks compared to, e.g., mobile IP working over packet radio networks. While the Internet protocol IP does not guarantee QoS, ATM networks do (at the cost of higher complexity). Thus, WATM networks should provide mobile QoS (M-QoS). M-QoS is composed of three different parts:

- **Wired QoS**: The infrastructure network needed for WATM has the same QoS properties as any wired ATM network. Typical traditional QoS parameters are link delay, cell delay variation, bandwidth, cell error rate etc.
- **Wireless QoS**: The QoS properties of the wireless part of a WATM network differ from those of the wired part. Again, link delay and error rate can be specified, but now error rate is typically some order of magnitude higher compared to, e.g., fibre optics. Additionally, channel reservation and multiplexing mechanisms at the air interface strongly influence cell delay variation.
- **Handover QoS**: A new set of QoS parameters is introduced by handover. Here, for example, handover blocking due to limited resources at target access points, cell loss during handover, or the speed of the whole handover procedure represent critical factors for QoS.

The WATM system has to map the QoS specified by an application onto these sets of QoS parameters at connection setup and has to check whether the QoS requested can be satisfied. However, applications will not specify single parameters in detail, but end-to-end requirements, such as delay or bandwidth. The WATM system must now map, e.g., end-to-end delay onto the cell delays on each segment, wired and wireless. To handle the complexity of such a system, WATM networks will initially only offer a set of different service classes to applications.

Additionally, applications must be adaptive to some degree to survive the effects of mobility, such as higher cell loss, delay variations etc. Applications could for example negotiate windows of QoS parameters in which they can adapt without breaking the connection.

A crucial point in maintaining QoS over time is QoS support in handover protocols. These protocols can support two different types of QoS during handover:

- **Hard handover QoS**: While the QoS with the current AP may be guaranteed due to the current availability of resources, no QoS guarantees are given after the handover. This is comparable to the traditional approach for, e.g., GSM networks with voice connections. If a terminal can set up a connection, the connection's quality is guaranteed. If there are not enough resources after handover (too many users are already in the target cell), the system cuts off the connection. This is the only possible solution if the applications and terminals cannot adapt to the new situation.
- **Soft handover QoS**: Even for the current wireless segment, only statistical QoS guarantees can be given, and in addition the applications have to adapt after the handover. This assumes adaptive applications and at least allows for some remaining QoS guarantees during, e.g., periods of congestion or strong interference.

If a terminal performs a handover to an access point which is low on resources, the following steps are possible: the terminal can close one or more connection(s) to free resources or the terminal can try to adapt the QoS of one or more connection(s). Furthermore, the AP can reject connections during the handover procedure because the WMT presents a list of connections to be handed over (see Figure 8.13).

8.11 Access point control protocol

As shown in Figure 8.10 through Figure 8.16, every AP exchanges a multitude of messages with the EMAS-E it is connected to. The protocol used for communication between these two entities is called the **access point control protocol (APCP)**. The main purpose of the APCP comprises reserving and releasing resources in the AP for connections (memory, radio frequencies etc.). Furthermore, a switch can prepare the AP for new connections and assist in handover via the APCP. The AP uses the protocol to inform the EMAS-E about newly associated WMTs.

The main reasons for the separation of AP and EMAS-E and a standardized interface in between the two are the following (compare also Figure 8.2 and Figure 8.7):

- All radio issues are kept separate from the switch. The switch only needs support for mobility and, thus, can also be used for mobility without wireless access.
- Signalling in the higher layers (e.g., ATM signalling) is independent from the signalling used for the AP, namely APCP. Thus, an AP could also be used for architectures without ATM signalling.
- Separation and standardized interfaces allow for multivendor solutions, i.e., switch and AP could come from different companies and, thus, end-users could benefit from higher flexibility and competitiveness.

Figure 8.19 shows the functional architecture of processes related to the APCP. The AP contains processes directly related to radio issues such as **wireless connection admission control (WCAC)** and **radio resource management (RRM)**. Additionally, the process **AP connection management (APCM)** handles the current connections. The switch comprises no wireless specific processes, but controls mobility. This is achieved using the four processes **resource management (RM)**, **call control (CC)**, **connection admission control (CAC)**, and **mobility management (MM)**.

The following messages are used for handover (see Figure 8.10 to Figure 8.16). Further messages have been specified as listed in Bhat (1998a):

Figure 8.19
APCP related functions in
the AP and EMAS-E

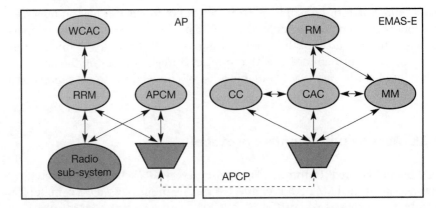

- **APCP_AssocReq**: The AP informs the switch about a new association with a WMT. In this context, association only refers to the establishment of a radio connection between the WMT and the AP. It may be the case that the EMAS-E requests the AP to disassociate the WMT, e.g., if the WMT is not authorized to access this AP or if registrations fails due to other reasons. This message needs at least the AESA of the WMT as a parameter.
- **APCP_AssocCnf**: The switch confirms an association to the AP. This message includes the WMT-AESA for identification and the ATM connection identifier used for the connection.
- **APCP_DisassocReq**: With this message, APs indicate that a WMT has left. This message includes at least the WMT-AESA.
- **APCP_DisassocCnf**: This message acknowledges APCP_DisassocReq and includes the WMT-AESA.
- **APCP_EnquiryReq**: An EMAS-E sends this message to reserve resources for a new connection at the AP. This message includes several parameters, such as the WMT-AESA, ATM connection identifier, and ATM traffic descriptors and QoS parameters for up and downlink (from and to the WMT).
- **APCP_EnquiryRes**: With this message, the AP can respond whether the requested resources are available or not. Message parameters include the WMT-AESA, the connection identifier, and the resources actually available.

8.12 Summary

This chapter has presented an overview of current standardization efforts in the WATM working group of the ATM Forum. WATM is the approach of extending the ATM scheme of connection-oriented communication with QoS provision to the wireless and mobile domain. The main difference between WATM and other approaches is the integration of a whole system into the specification. WATM specifies radio access, mobility management, handover schemes, mobile QoS, security etc.

Furthermore, the chapter has discussed the motivation behind WATM and has listed the services WATM should provide. These services build on many new functions required for mobility within the fixed network and on mobile and wireless terminals. As many problems in WATM are similar to those in other wireless networks, the ATM Forum tries to co-operate with other standardization bodies. For example, WATM can use BRAN technology as standardized by ETSI as radio access layer.

However, the main complexity of WATM lies within the functions and protocols needed for handover. In this context, several scenarios showing the messages, parameters, and entities involved in handover have been presented. The complexity of WATM is due to its ability to maintain QoS parameters for connections during handover and the connection-oriented paradigm of ATM. The consequences of these characteristics include the need for resource reservation, for checking for available resources at access points, and for rerouting of connections.

Since WATM is an integrated approach, issues like location management, security, and efficiency of the whole system have to be considered. In order to minimize overhead, WATM tries to harmonize the functions required with those available in fixed ATM.

Figure 8.20 shows other possible access scenarios for WATM. While this chapter has focused on the wireless access of mobile ATM terminals, several other

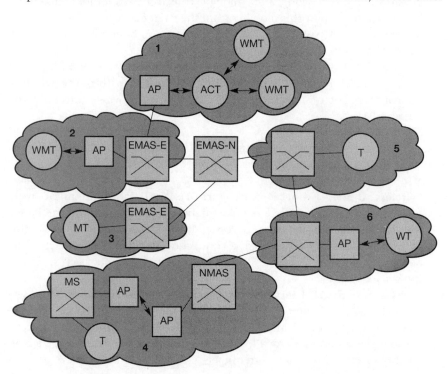

Figure 8.20
WATM reference model including further access scenarios

configurations are possible and are currently being discussed as explained in Bhat (1998b). As additional entities, Figure 8.20 shows the following components:

- **T (terminal)**: A standard ATM terminal offering ATM services defined for fixed ATM networks.
- **MT (mobile terminal)**: A standard ATM terminal with the additional capability of reconnecting after access point change. That is, the terminal can be moved between different access points within a certain domain.
- **WT (wireless terminal)**: This terminal is accessed via a wireless link, but the terminal itself is fixed, i.e., the terminal keeps its access point to the network.
- **WMT (wireless mobile terminal)**: The combination of a wireless and a mobile terminal results in the WMT. This is exactly the type of terminal presented throughout this chapter, as it has the ability of changing its access point and uses radio access.
- **AP (access point)**: Point of access to a network via a radio link as explained in this chapter.
- **EMAS (end-user mobility supporting ATM switch, -E: edge, -N: network)**: Switches with the support of end-user mobility, see 8.4.1.
- **NMAS (network mobility-supporting ATM switch)**: Not only terminals, but also a whole network can be mobile. Thus, certain additional functions are needed to support this mobility from the fixed network.
- **MS (mobile ATM switch)**: ATM switches can also be mobile and can use wireless access to another part of the ATM network.
- **ACT (ad hoc controller terminal)**: For the configuration of ad hoc networks, special terminal types might be required within the wireless network. These terminals could, for example, control wireless access without an AP.

Based on these entities, we can define several scenarios which should be supported by WATM if fully specified.

- **Wireless ad hoc ATM network (scenario 1)**: WMTs can communicate with each other without the need of a fixed network. Communication can be set up without any infrastructure. Access control can be accomplished via the ACT. If the ad hoc network needs a connection to a fixed network, this can be provided by means of an AP. This configuration has not been specified further yet.
- **Wireless mobile ATM terminals (scenario 2)**: The configuration discussed throughout this chapter is the wireless and mobile terminal accessing the fixed network via an AP. In this configuration, a WMT cannot communicate without the support provided by entities within the fixed network, such as an EMAS-E. This scenario is currently being specified in more detail.

- **Mobile ATM terminals (scenario 3)**: This configuration supports device portability and allows for simple network reconfiguration. Users can change the access points of their ATM equipment over time without the need for reconfiguration by hand. Again, this scenario need support through entities in the fixed network (e.g., EMAS-E).
- **Mobile ATM switches (scenario 4)**: An even more complex configuration comprises mobile switches using wireless access to other fixed ATM networks. Now entities supporting switch mobility are needed within the fixed network (NMAS). There are many applications for this scenario, e.g., networks in aircraft, trains, or ships. Within the mobile network either fixed, mobile, wireless, or mobile and wireless terminals can be used. This is the most complex configuration currently under discussion within an ATM environment.
- **Fixed ATM terminals (scenario 5)**: This configuration is the standard case which is already in use. Terminals and switches do not include capabilities for mobility or wireless access. This is also the reference configuration for applications which work on top of an ATM network. Thus, convergence layers have to hide the special characteristics of mobility and wireless access because no special applications should be required for the scenarios presented here.
- **Fixed wireless ATM terminals (scenario 6)**: To provide simple access to ATM networks without wiring, a fixed wireless link is the ideal solution. Many alternative carriers are using or planning to use this way of accessing customers as they do not own the wired infrastructure. This scenario does not require any changes or enhancements in the fixed network.

Up to now it has not been clear which technology or access scheme will be the most successful. There are many applications for every scenario shown; however, depending on the availability of services and market forces, one or the other scheme may be successful. From a technical point of view it is already quite clear that the combination of all scenarios, as shown in Figure 8.20, is one of the most complex communication systems, which is perhaps too ambitious to be realized in the near future. All configurations should be able to interact with existing cellular systems and Internet technology. Chakraborty (1998) discusses many problems that already arise when interworking with other narrowband networks like GSM, DECT, UMTS (see chapter 4) and standard TCP/IP networks.

8.13 Review exercises

1 Name reasons for the development of wireless ATM and find the institutions, companies, and organizations behind the standardization efforts. What is one of the main differences to Internet technologies from this point of view?

2 Compare ATM with TCP/IP and point out the main differences. Show the pros and cons of both approaches and discuss their influences on mobility and wireless access.

3 Which extensions are needed to support mobility and wireless access within an ATM environment?

4 What types of services for end-users are envisaged for WATM? Compare these services with the idea of wireless LANs as presented in chapter 7 and wireless telecommunication systems as discussed in chapter 4.

5 Recall the basic reference model of WATM. Which entities have been defined? Why does the specification separate the terminal from the wireless adapter?

6 What type of support for mobility and wireless access is needed in the fixed network? Show the influences of mobility support on the user and control plane respectively.

7 Why does WATM specify a separate APCP? What could be the reasons for separate APs?

8 What are the basic requirements for an RAL for WATM? Which layers have been identified within the RAL? Where is the QoS which should be provided by ATM reflected?

9 Which part of BRAN can be used for WATM? What other types of networks does BRAN specify and which higher layers can BRAN support?

10 Why is handover of major importance to WATM? Discuss the main requirements of handover and compare them to other wireless LANs/personal cellular networks and their handover scenarios.

11 What are the differences between slow fading of radio signals and sudden loss of radio connection in terms of handover? What are the problems associated with a sudden loss of the radio link?

12 Why does WATM only consider hard handover initially? What are the implications of this choice?

13 Compare the complexity, the entities involved, and the signalling overhead of the three basic handover scenarios presented.

14 Name some components of location management, their function, and outline why they are needed.

15 What are the functions of the registration procedure and why is registration needed in addition to handover?

16 Show the initial connection setup to a WMT in a foreign network. What is the motivation behind a hierarchy of location servers? How is connection setup accomplished in the home network?

17 Why is QoS so important in WATM networks? What different types of QoS should a WATM network support?

18 While this chapter mainly focuses on a scenario with WMTs and APs, additional scenarios are possible as shown in the summary. Find some more applications for each scenario and compare them in terms of their complexity. In your discussion, focus on the handover of a mobile ATM network, e.g., in an aircraft with connection via satellites.

19 Give some reasons for the success of WATM technology and try to find reasons which might hinder the success. Check out the current situation in this field with the help of the ATM Forum WWW server.

8.14 References

Acampora, A.(1996) 'Wireless ATM: a perspective on issues and prospects', *IEEE Personal Communications*, 3, (4), August.

Akyol, B. A.; Cox, D. C.(1996) 'Rerouting for handoff in a wireless ATM network', *IEEE Personal Communications*, 3, (5), October.

Anastasi, G.; Lenzini, L.; Mingozzi, E.; Hettich, A.; Krämling, A. (1998) 'MAC protocols for wideband wireless local access: evolution toward wireless ATM', *IEEE Personal Communications*, 5, (5).

ATM Forum (1996) *ATM traffic management specification version 4.0*, ATM Forum.

ATM Forum (1998) *Framework for dynamic COS discovery in Wireless ATM*, ATM98-0005, ATM Forum, February.

ATM Forum (1998) *Extension to backward COS discovery (BCD) approach*, ATM98-0231, ATM Forum, April.

Ayanoglu, E.; Eng, K. Y.; Karol, M. J.(1996) 'Wireless ATM: limits, challenges, and proposals', *IEEE Personal Communications*, 3, (4), August.

Barton, M.; Paine, R.; Chow, A.(1998) *Description of Wireless ATM Service Scenarios*, ATM Forum Contribution, July.

Bhat, R. R. (1998) *Draft baseline text for Wireless ATM Capability Set 1 Specification*, ATM Forum, BTD-WATM-01.09.

Bhat, R. R. (1998) *Wireless ATM Requirements Specification*, ATM Forum, RTD-WATM-01.02.

Chakraborty, S.S. (1998) 'The interworking approach for narrowband access to ATM transport-based multiservice mobile networks', *IEEE Personal Communications*, 5, (4).

ETSI (1997) *Radio Equipment and Systems (RES), High Performance Radio Local Area Networks (HIPERLAN), Requirements and architectures for wireless ATM access and interconnection*, European Telecommunication Standards Institute, TR 101 031 V1.1.1 (1997-07).

ETSI (1998a) *Broadband Radio Access Networks (BRAN): Inventory of broadband radio technologies and techniques*, European Telecommunication Standards Institute, TR 101 173 V1.1.1 (1998-05).

ETSI (1998b) *Broadband Radio Access Networks (BRAN): High Performance Radio Local Area Netowk (HIPERLAN) Type 1, Functional specification*, European Telecom- munication Standards Institute, EN 300 652 V1.2.1 (1998-07).

ETSI (1998c) *Broadband Radio Access Networks (BRAN): Requirements and architectures for broadband fixed radio access networks* (HIPERACCESS), European Telecommunication Standards Institute, TR 101 177 V1.1.1 (1998-05).

Händel, R.; Huber, N.; Schröder, S.(1994) *ATM Networks: concepts, protocols, applications*, Addison-Wesley.

Petras, D.; Krämling, A.(1997) 'Wireless ATM: Performance evaluation of a DAS++ MAC protocol with fast collision resolution by a probing algorithm', *International Journal on Wireless Information Networks*, 4, (4).

Rauhala, K. (1998) *Baseline Text for Wireless ATM specifications*, ATM Forum, BTD-WATM-01.07.

Rauhala, K. (1998) *Living list document of Wireless ATM working group*, ATM Forum, LTD-WATM-01.07.

Raychaudhuri, D.; Dellaverson, L. (1996) *Charter, scope and work plan for proposed wireless ATM working group*, ATM Forum Document, 96-0530.

Raychaudhuri, D.(1996) 'Wireless ATM networks: architecture, system design and prototyping', *IEEE Personal Communications*, vol. 3, no. 4, August.

Sanchez, J.; Martinez, R.; Marcellin, M. W. (1997) 'A survey of MAC protocols proposed for wireless ATM', *IEEE Network Magazine*, November/December.

Toh, C.-K. (1997) *Wireless ATM and ad hoc networks*, Kluwer Academic Publishers.

Umehira, M.; Nakura, M.; Sato, H.; Hashimoto, A. (1996) 'ATM wireless access for mobile multimedia: concept and architecture', *IEEE Personal Communications*, 3, (5), October.

Walke, B.; Petras, D.; Plassmann, D. (1996) 'Wireless ATM: air interface and network protocols of the mobile broadband system', *IEEE Personal Communications*, 3, (4), August.

Mobile network layer

9

This chapter introduces protocols and mechanisms developed for the network layer to support mobility. The most prominent example is Mobile IP, discussed in the first section, which adds mobility support to the Internet network layer protocol IP. While systems like GSM have been designed with mobility in mind from the very beginning, the Internet started at a time when no-one had a concept of mobile computers. Therefore, the Internet of today lacks mechanisms for the support of users travelling through the world. IP is the common base for thousands of applications and runs over dozens of different networks. This is the reason for supporting mobility at the IP layer; mobile phone systems, for example, cannot offer this type of mobility for heterogeneous networks.

Another kind of mobility, rather portability of equipment, is supported by DHCP presented in the second section. In former times computers did not change their location often. Today, due to laptops or notebooks, e.g., students show up at the university with their computers, want to plug them in or use wireless access. A network administrator does not want to configure dozens of computers every day or hand out a list of valid IP addresses, DNS servers, subnet prefixes, default routers etc. At this point the dynamic host configuration protocol (DHCP) sets in to support automatic configuration of computers.

The chapter concludes with a look onto ad hoc networks in combination with the network layer. How can routing be done in a dynamic network with permanent changes in connectivity? What if there are no dedicated routers or databases telling where a node currently is? The last section deals with some approaches offering routing by extending standard algorithms known from the Internet or utilizing knowledge of the current situation in the physical medium.

9.1 Mobile IP

The following gives an overview of Mobile IP, the extensions needed for the Internet to support the mobility of hosts. This chapter does not demonstrate all the minor details, but gives an overall view. An excellent reference is Perkins (1997) describing the development of mobile IP, all packet formats, mechanisms, discussions of the protocol and alternatives etc. in detail. The following requires some familiarity with Internet protocols, especially IP. A very good overview and detailed descriptions of Internet protocols is given in Stevens (1994).

9.1.1 Goals, assumptions, and requirements

As shown in chapter 1, mobile computing is clearly the paradigm of the future. The Internet is the network for global data communication with hundreds of millions of users. So why not simply use a mobile computer in the Internet?

The reason is quite simple: you will not receive a single packet as soon as you leave your home network, i.e., the network your computer is configured for, and reconnect your computer (wireless or wired) at another place. The reason for this is quite simple if you consider routing mechanisms in the Internet. A host sends an IP packet with the header containing a destination address besides other fields. The destination address not only determines the receiver of the packet, but also the physical subnet of the receiver. For example, the destination address 129.13.42.99 shows that the receiver must be connected to the physical subnet with the network prefix 129.13.42 (unless CIDR is used). Routers in the Internet now look at the destination addresses of incoming packets and forward them according to internal look-up tables. To avoid an explosion of routing tables, only prefixes are stored and further optimizations are applied. Otherwise a router would have to store the addresses of all computers in the Internet, which is obviously not feasible. As long as the receiver can be reached within its physical subnet, it gets the packets; as soon as it moves outside the subnet, no packet will reach it anymore. Thus, a host needs a so-called **topologically correct address**.

9.1.1.1 Quick 'Solutions'

One might think of a quick solution to this problem by assigning the computer a new, topologically correct IP address. So moving to a new location would also mean assigning a new address. Now the problem is that nobody knows of this new address. It is almost impossible to find a (mobile) host in the Internet which has just changed its address. Especially the domain name system (DNS) needs some time before it updates its internal tables necessary for the mapping of a logical name to an IP address. This approach does not work if the mobile node moves quite often. Furthermore, the Internet and DNS have not been built for frequent updates. Just imagine millions of nodes moving at the same time. DNS could never present a consistent view of names and addresses, for it uses caching to improve scalability. It is simply too expensive to update quickly.

Furthermore, there is a severe problem with higher layer protocols like TCP that rely on IP addresses. Changing the IP address while still having a TCP connection open means breaking the connection. A TCP connection can be identified by the tuple (source IP address, source port, destination IP address, destination port), also known as a **socket.** Therefore, a TCP connection cannot survive any address change. Breaking TCP connections is not an option, using programs like telnet would be impossible. Additionally, the mobile node would have to notify all communication partners about the new address.

Another approach is the creation of specific routes to the mobile node. Routers always choose the best-fitting prefix for the routing decision. If a router now has an entry for a prefix 129.13.42 and an address 129.13.42.99, it would choose the port associated with the latter for forwarding, if a packet with the destination address 129.13.42.99 comes in. While it is theoretically possible to change all routing tables all over the world to create specific routes to a mobile node, this does not scale at all with the number of nodes in the Internet. Routers are built for extremely fast forwarding, but not for fast updates of routing tables. While the first is done with special hardware support, the latter is typically a piece of software which cannot handle the burden of frequent updates. Furthermore, routers are the 'brains' of the Internet, holding the whole net together. No service provider or system administrator would allow changes to the routing tables, probably sacrificing stability, just for the mobility of individual users.

9.1.1.2 Requirements

Since the quick 'solutions' obviously did not work, a more general architecture had to be designed. Many field trials and proprietary systems finally led to mobile IP as a standard to enable mobility in the Internet. Several requirements accompanied the development of the standard:

- **Compatibility:** The installed base of Internet computers, i.e., computers running TCP/IP and connected to the Internet, is huge. A new standard cannot require changes for applications or network protocols already in use. People still want to use their favourite browser for WWW and do not change applications just for mobility. The same holds for operating systems. No-one would use another operating system only for mobility, so mobile IP has to be integrated into existing operating systems or at least work together with them. Routers within the Internet should not necessarily require other software. While it is possible to enhance the capabilities of some routers to support mobility, it is almost impossible to change all routers. Furthermore, mobile IP has to remain compatible to all lower layers used for the standard non-mobile IP. This means that mobile IP must not require special media or MAC/LLC protocols. So mobile IP has to use the same interfaces and mechanisms to access the lower layers as IP does. Finally, end-systems enhanced with a mobile IP implementation should still be able to communicate with fixed systems without mobile IP. Mobile IP has to ensure that users can still access all the other servers and systems in the Internet. But that also implies using the same address format and routing mechanisms.
- **Transparency:** Mobility should remain 'invisible' for many higher layer protocols and applications. Besides maybe noticing a lower bandwidth and some interruption in service, higher layers should continue to work even if

the mobile computer changed its point of attachment to the network. For TCP, for example, this means that the computer must keep its IP address as explained above. If the interruption of the connectivity does not take too long, TCP connections survive the change of the attachment point. Problems related to the performance of TCP are discussed in chapter 10. Clearly, many of today's applications have not been designed for use in mobile environments. Therefore, the only effects of mobility should be a higher delay and lower bandwidth. However, there are some applications for which it is better to be 'mobility aware'. Examples are cost-based routing or video compression. Knowing that it is currently possible to use different networks, the software could choose the cheapest one. Or if a video application knows that currently only a low bandwidth connection is available, it could use a different compression scheme. Therefore, additional mechanisms are necessary to inform these applications about mobility (Brewer, 1998).

- **Scalability and efficiency:** Introducing a new mechanism into the Internet must not jeopardize the efficiency of the network. Enhancing IP for mobility must not generate many new messages flooding the whole network. Furthermore, special care has to be taken considering the lower bandwidth of wireless links. Many mobile systems will have a wireless link to an attachment point. Therefore, only some additional packets should be necessary between a mobile system and a node in the network. Looking at the number of computers connected to the Internet and at the growth rates of mobile communication, it is clear that a myriad devices will participate in the Internet as mobile components. Just think of cars, trucks, mobile phones, every seat in every plane around the world etc. – many of them will have some IP implementation inside and move between different networks, thus requiring mobile IP. Therefore, it is indispensable for a mobile IP to be scalable over a large number of participants in the whole Internet, worldwide.
- **Security:** Mobility poses many security problems. A minimum requirement is the authentication of all messages related to the management of Mobile IP. It must be sure for the IP layer if it forwards a packet to a mobile host that this host really is the receiver of the packet. The IP layer can only guarantee that the IP address of the receiver is correct. There are no ways of preventing faked IP addresses or other attacks. According to Internet philosophy this is left to higher layers.

So the goal of a mobile IP can be summarized as 'supporting end-system mobility while maintaining scalability, efficiency, and compatibility in all respects with existing applications and Internet protocols'.

9.1.2 Entities and terminology

The following defines several entities and terms needed for understanding mobile IP as defined in RFC 2002 (Perkins, 1996a). Figure 9.1 illustrates an example scenario.

- **Mobile node (MN):** A mobile node is an end-system or router that can change its point of attachment to the Internet using mobile IP. The MN keeps its IP address and can continuously communicate with any other system in the Internet as long as link-layer connectivity is given. Mobile nodes are not necessarily small devices such as laptops with antennas or mobile phones; a router onboard an aircraft can be a powerful mobile node.
- **Correspondent node (CN):** At least one partner is needed for communication. In the following the CN represents this partner for the MN. The CN can be a fixed or mobile node.
- **Home network:** The home network is the subnet the MN belongs to with respect to its IP address. Within the home network no mobile IP support is needed.
- **Foreign network:** The foreign network is the current subnet the MN visits and which is not the home network.
- **Foreign agent (FA):** The FA can provide several services to the MN during its visit in the foreign network. The FA can have the COA (defined below), thus acting as tunnel endpoint and forwarding packets to the MN. Furthermore, the FA can be the default router for the MN. FAs can also provide security services for they belong to the foreign network as opposed to the MN only visiting. For mobile IP functioning, FAs are not necessarily needed. Typically, an FA is implemented on a router for the subnet the MN attaches to.
- **Care-of address (COA):** The COA defines the current location of the MN from an IP point of view. All IP packets sent to the MN are delivered to the COA, not directly to the IP address of the MN. Packet delivery toward the MN is done using a tunnel, as explained later. Therefore, to be more precise, the COA marks the tunnel endpoint, i.e., the address where packets exit the tunnel. There are two different possibilities for the location of the COA:
  - **Foreign agent COA:** The COA could be located at the FA, i.e., the COA is an IP address of the FA. Thus the FA is the tunnel end-point and forwards packets to the MN. Many MN using the FA can share this COA as common COA.
  - **Co-located COA:** The COA is called co-located if the MN temporarily acquired an additional IP address which acts as COA. This address is now topologically correct, and the tunnel endpoint is at the MN. Co-located addresses can be acquired using services such as DHCP (see section 9.2). One problem associated with this approach is the need for many additional addresses if many MNs request a COA. This is not always a good idea considering the scarcity of IPv4 addresses.
- **Home agent (HA):** The HA provides several services for the MN and is located in the home network. The tunnel for packets toward the MN starts at the HA. Furthermore, the HA maintains a location registry, i.e., it is informed of the MN's location by the current COA. Three alternatives for the implementation of an HA exist.

- The HA can be implemented on a router that is responsible for the home network. This is obviously the best position, because without optimizations to mobile IP, all packets for the MN have to go through the router anyway as explained later.
- If changing the router's software is not possible, the HA could also be implemented on an arbitrary node in the subnet. A disadvantage of this solution is the double crossing of the router by the packet if the MN is in a foreign network. A packet for the MN comes in via the router; the HA sends it through the tunnel which again crosses the router.
- Finally, a home network is not necessary at all. The HA could be again on the 'router' but this time only acting as a manager for MNs belonging to a virtual home network. All MNs are always in a foreign network with this solution.

The example network in Figure 9.1 shows the following situation: A CN is connected via a router to the Internet, as are the home network and the foreign network. The HA is implemented on the router connecting the home network with the Internet, an FA is implemented on the router to the foreign network. The MN is currently in the foreign network. The tunnel for packets toward the MN starts at the HA and ends at the FA, for the FA has the COA in this example.

9.1.3 IP packet delivery
Figure 9.2 illustrates packet delivery to and from the MN using the example network of Figure 9.1. A correspondent node CN wants to send an IP packet to the MN. One of the requirements of mobile IP was to support hiding the mobility of the MN. Therefore, CN does not need to know anything about the MN's current location and sends the packet as usual to the IP address of MN (step 1). This means that CN sends an IP packet with MN as destination address and CN as source address. The Internet, not having information on the current location of MN, routes the packet to the router responsible for the home network of MN. This is done using the standard routing mechanisms of the Internet.

Figure 9.1
Mobile IP example
network

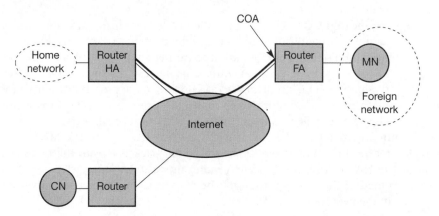

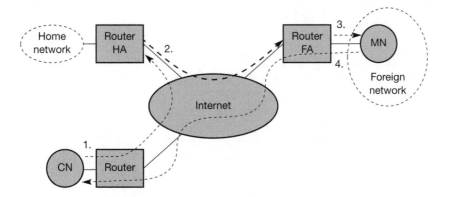

Figure 9.2
Packet delivery to and
from the mobile node

The HA now intercepts the packet, knowing that MN is currently not in its home network. Thus, the packet is not forwarded into the subnet as usual, but encapsulated and tunnelled to the COA. This is done by putting a new header in front of the old IP header showing the COA as new destination and HA as source of the encapsulated packet (step 2). (Tunnelling and encapsulation is described in more detail in section 9.1.6.) The foreign agent now decapsulates the packet, i.e., removes the additional header, and forwards the original packet with CN as source and MN as destination to the MN (step 3). Again, for the MN mobility is not visible. It receives the packet with the same sender and receiver address as it would have done in the home network.

At a first look, sending packets from the MN to the CN is much simpler, problems are discussed in section 9.1.8. The MN sends the packet as usual with its own fixed IP address as source and CN's address as destination (step 4). The router with the FA acts as default router and forwards the packet in the same way as it would do for any other node in the foreign network. As long as CN is a fixed node the remainder is in the fixed Internet as usual. If CN were also a mobile node residing in a foreign network, the same mechanisms as described in steps 1 through 3 would apply now in the other direction.

The following sections present some additional mechanisms needed for mobile IP to work, some enhancements to the protocol, and some efficiency and security problems.

9.1.4 Agent advertisement and discovery

One initial problem of an MN after moving is how to find a foreign agent. How does the MN discover at all that it has moved? For this, foreign agents and home agents advertise their presence periodically using special agent advertisement messages. These advertisement messages can be seen as a beacon broadcast into the subnet. For these advertisements Internet control message protocol (ICMP) messages according to RFC 1256 (Deering, 1991) are used with some mobility extensions. Routers in the fixed network implementing this standard also advertise their routing service periodically to the attached links.

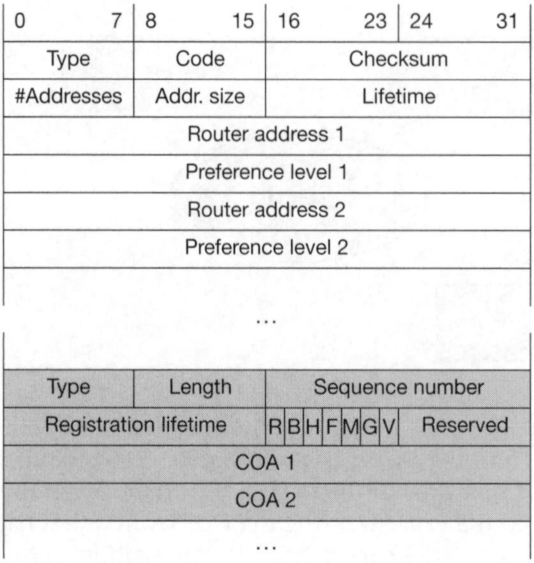

Figure 9.3

Agent advertisement
packet (RFC 1256 +
mobility extension)

0	7	8	15	16	23	24	31
Type		Code		Checksum			
#Addresses		Addr. size		Lifetime			
Router address 1							
Preference level 1							
Router address 2							
Preference level 2							

...

Type	Length	Sequence number	
Registration lifetime		R B H F M G V	Reserved
COA 1			
COA 2			

...

The agent advertisement packet according to RFC 1256 with the extension for mobility is shown in Figure 9.3. The upper part represents the ICMP packet while the lower part is the extension needed for mobility. Not shown in this figure are the fields necessary on lower layers for the agent advertisement. Clearly, mobile nodes must be reached with the appropriate link layer address. Moreover, the TTL field of the IP packet is set to 1 for all advertisements to avoid forwarding of advertisements. The IP destination address according to standard router advertisements can be either set to 224.0.0.1, which is the multicast address for all systems on a link (Deering, 1989), or to the broadcast address 255.255.255.255.

The fields in the ICMP part are defined as follows. The **type** is set to 9, the **code** can be 0, if the agent also routes traffic from non-mobile nodes, or 16, if it does not route anything other than mobile traffic. Foreign agents are at least required to forward packets from the mobile node. The number of addresses advertised with this packet is in **#addresses** while the **addresses** themselves follow as shown. **Lifetime** denotes the length of time this advertisement is valid. **Preference** levels for each address help a node to choose the router that is the most eager one to get a new node.

The difference compared with standard ICMP advertisements is seen in what follows after the router addresses. This extension for mobility has the following fields defined: **type** is set to 16, **length** depends on the number of COAs provided with the message and equals 6 + 4*(number of addresses). An agent furthermore shows the total number of advertisements sent since initialization in the **sequence number**. By the **registration lifetime** the agent can specify the maximum lifetime in seconds a node can request during registration as explained in section 9.1.5. The following bits specify the characteristics of an agent in detail. The **R** bit (registration) shows, if a registration with this agent is required rather than using a co-located COA at the MN. If the agent is currently too busy to accept new registrations it can set the **B** bit. The following two bits denote if the agent offers services as a home agent (**H**) or foreign agent (**F**) on the link where the advertisement has been sent. Bits M and G specify the method of encapsulation used for the tunnel as explained in section 9.1.6. While IP-in-IP encapsulation is the mandatory standard, **M** can specify minimal encapsulation and **G** generic routing encapsulation. The **V** bit finally can specify the use of header compression according to RFC 1144 (Jacobson, 1990). The following fields contain the **COAs** advertised. A foreign agent setting the F bit must at least advertise one COA. Further details and special extensions can be found in Perkins (1997).

A mobile node in a subnet can now receive agent advertisements from either its home agent or a foreign agent. This is one way for the MN to discover its location. If no agent advertisements are present and an MN has not received a COA by other means, e.g., DHCP as discussed in section 9.2, the mobile node must send agent solicitations. These solicitations again base on RFC 1256 for router solicitations. Certain care has to be taken that these solicitation messages do not flood the network, but basically an MN can search for an FA endlessly sending out solicitation messages. Discovering a new agent can be done anytime, not only if the MN is not connected to one. Consider the case that an MN is looking for a better connection while still sending via the old path. This is the case while moving through several cells of different wireless networks.

After these steps of advertisements and agent discovery the MN can now receive a COA, either one for an FA or a co-located COA. Furthermore, the MN knows its location (home network or foreign network) and the capabilities of the agent (if needed). The next step for the MN is the registration with the HA if the MN is in a foreign network as described in section 9.1.5.

Using a standard such as RFC 1256 for something different than the original purpose of router advertisements causes some problems. A quite obvious one is the minimum interval of three seconds between two advertisements. This makes absolute sense in wired networks because the topology changes rather slowly (it takes some time to replace dead routers etc.). However, in highly dynamic wireless networks with moving MNs and probably with applications requiring continuous packet streams, three seconds are too long. An MN would always have to wait at least three seconds before noticing that an agent is not reachable anymore. But maybe this advertisement has just been lost. Thus, to be sure to switch to another agent, an MN has to wait even longer. Issuing solicitations is no real solution for it unnecessarily floods the subnet.

9.1.5 Registration

After having received a COA, the MN has to register with the HA. The main purpose of the registration is to inform the HA of the current location for correct forwarding of packets. Registration can be done in two different ways depending on the location of the COA.

- If the COA is at the FA, registration is done as illustrated in Figure 9.4. The MN sends its registration request containing the COA (see Figure 9.6) to the FA which is forwarding the request to the HA. The HA now sets up a **mobility binding** containing the mobile node's home IP address and the current COA. Additionally, the mobility binding contains the lifetime of the registration which is negotiated during the registration process. Registration expires automatically after the lifetime and is deleted; therefore, an MN should reregister before expiration. This mechanism is necessary to avoid mobility bindings which are not used anymore. After setting up the mobility binding, the HA sends a reply message back to the FA which forwards it to the MN.
- If the COA is co-located, registration is simpler, as shown in Figure 9.5. The MN sends the request directly to the HA and vice versa. This, by the way, is also the registration procedure for MNs returning home into their home network. Here they also register directly with the HA.

For registration requests UDP packets are used. The IP source address of the packet is set to the interface address of the MN, the IP destination address is that of the FA or HA (depending on the location of the COA). The UDP destination port is set to 434. UDP is used for reasons of low overhead and better performance compared to TCP in wireless environments (see chapter 10). The fields relevant for mobile IP registration requests follow as UDP data (see Figure 9.6). The fields are defined as follows.

The first field **type** is set to 1 for a registration request. With the **S** bit an MN can specify if it wants the HA to retain prior mobility bindings. This allows for simultaneous bindings. The following bits denote the requested behaviour for packet forwarding. Setting the **B** bit generally indicates that an MN also wants to

Figure 9.4 (*Left*)
Registration of a mobile
node via the foreign
agent

Figure 9.5 (*Right*)
Direct registration of a
mobile node with the
home agent

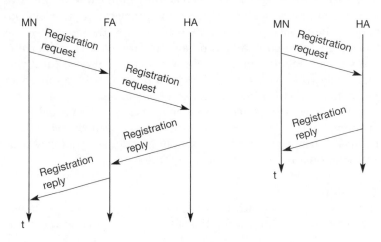

receive the broadcast packets which have been received by the HA in the home network. A more detailed description of how to filter broadcast messages which are not needed by the MN can be found in Perkins (1997). If an MN uses a co-located COA, it also takes care of the decapsulation at the tunnel endpoint. The **D** bit indicates this behaviour. As already defined for agent advertisements, the following bits **M**, **G**, and **V** denote the use of minimal encapsulation, generic routing encapsulation, and header compression respectively.

Lifetime denotes the validity of the registration in seconds. The **home address** is the fixed IP address of the MN, **home agent** is the IP address of the HA, and **COA** represents the tunnel endpoint. The 64 bit **identification** is generated by the MN to identify a request and match it with registration replies. Furthermore, this field is used for protection against replay attacks of registrations.

9.1.6 Tunnelling and encapsulation

The following describes the mechanisms used for forwarding packets between the HA and the COA, as shown in Figure 9.2, step 2. A **tunnel** establishes a virtual pipe for data packets between a tunnel entry and a tunnel endpoint. Packets entering a tunnel are forwarded inside the tunnel and leave the tunnel unchanged. Tunnelling, i.e., sending a packet through a tunnel, is achieved by using encapsulation.

Encapsulation is the mechanism of taking a packet consisting of packet header and data and putting it into the data part of a new packet. The reverse operation, taking a packet out of the data part of another packet, is called **decapsulation.** Encapsulation and decapsulation are the operations typically performed when a packet is transferred from a higher protocol layer to a lower layer or from a lower to a higher layer respectively. Here these functions are used within the same layer.

This mechanism is shown in Figure 9.7 and describes exactly what the HA at the tunnel entry does. The HA takes the original packet with the MN as destination, puts it into the data part of a new packet and sets the new IP header in such a way that the packet is routed to the COA. The new header is also called the **outer header** for obvious reasons. Additionally, there is an **inner header** which can be identical to the original header as this is the case for IP-in-IP encapsulation, or the inner header can be computed during encapsulation.

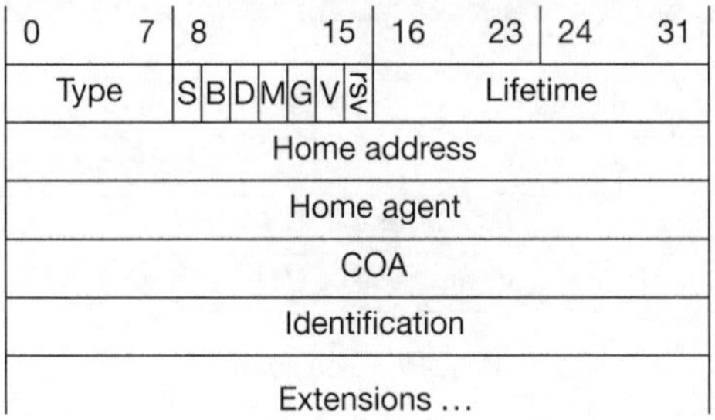

0	7	8	15	16	23	24	31
Type		S B D M G V rsv		Lifetime			
Home address							
Home agent							
COA							
Identification							
Extensions ...							

Figure 9.6
Registration request

Figure 9.7

IP encapsulation

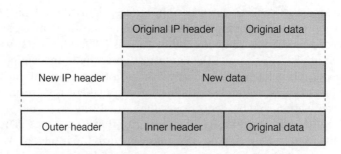

9.1.6.1 IP-in-IP encapsulation

There are different ways of performing the encapsulation needed for the tunnel between HA and COA. Mandatory for mobile IP is **IP-in-IP encapsulation** as specified in (Perkins, 1996b). Figure 9.8 shows a packet inside the tunnel. The fields follow the standard specification of the IP protocol as defined in RFC 791 (Postel, 1981). The fields of the outer header are set as follows. The version field **ver** is 4 for IP version 4, the Internet header length (**IHL**) denotes the length of the outer header in 32 bit words. **TOS** is just copied from the inner header, the **length** field covers the complete encapsulated packet. The fields up to TTL have no special meaning for mobile IP and are set according to RFC 791. **TTL** must be high enough so the packet can reach the tunnel endpoint. The next field, here denoted with **IP-in-IP**, is the type of the protocol used in the IP payload. Here this field is set to 4, the protocol type for IPv4 because again an IPv4 packet follows after this outer header. IP **checksum** is calculated as usual. The next fields are the tunnel entry as source address (the **IP address of the HA**) and the tunnel exit point as destination address (the **COA**).

If no options follow the outer header, the inner header starts with the same fields as just explained. This header remains almost unchanged during encapsu-

Figure 9.8

IP-in-IP encapsulation

Ver.	IHL	TOS		Length	
IP identification			Flags	Fragment offset	
TTL		IP-in-IP	IP checksum		
IP address of HA					
Care-of address of COA					
ver.	IHL	TOS		Length	
IP identification			Flags	fragment offset	
TTL		lay. 4 prot.	IP checksum		
IP address of CN					
IP address of MN					
TCP/UDP/ ... payload					

lation, thus showing the original sender CN and the receiver MN of the packet. The only change is TTL which is decremented by 1. This means that the whole tunnel is considered a single hop from the original packet's point of view. This is a very important feature of tunnelling for it allows the MN to behave as if it were attached to the home network. No matter how many real hops the packet has to take in the tunnel, it is just one (logical) hop away for the MN. Finally, the payload follows the two headers.

9.1.6.2 Minimal encapsulation

As seen with IP-in-IP encapsulation, several fields are redundant. For example, TOS is just copied, fragmentation often not needed etc. Therefore, **minimal encapsulation** as shown in Figure 9.9 is an optional encapsulation method for mobile IP. Again, the tunnel entry point and endpoint are specified. In this case, the field for the type of the following header contains the value 55 for the minimal encapsulation protocol. The inner header is different for minimal encapsulation. Still, the type of the following protocol and the address of the MN are needed. If the **S** bit is set, the original sender address of the CN is included. No field for fragmentation offset is left in the inner header and, therefore, minimal encapsulation does not work with already fragmented packets.

9.1.6.3 Generic routing encapsulation

While IP-in-IP encapsulation and minimal encapsulation work only for IP, the following encapsulation scheme also supports other network layer protocols in addition to IP. **Generic routing encapsulation** (GRE) allows the encapsulation of packets of one protocol suite into the payload portion of a packet of another protocol suite (Hanks, 1994). Figure 9.10 shows this procedure. The packet of one protocol suite with the original packet header and data is taken and a new GRE header is prepended. Together this forms the new data part of the new packet. Finally, the header of the second protocol suite is put in front.

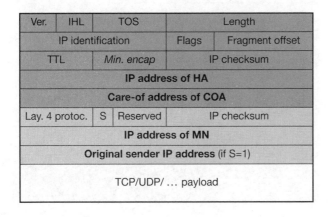

Figure 9.9
Minimal encapsulation

Ver.	IHL	TOS	Length		
IP identification			Flags	Fragment offset	
TTL		*Min. encap*	IP checksum		
IP address of HA					
Care-of address of COA					
Lay. 4 protoc.	S	Reserved	IP checksum		
IP address of MN					
Original sender IP address (if S=1)					
TCP/UDP/ ... payload					

Figure 9.10
Generic routing
encapsulation
(Hanks, 1994)

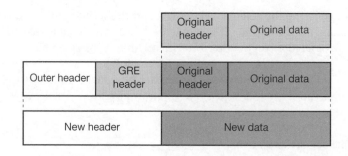

Figure 9.11 shows the fields of a packet inside the tunnel between home agent and COA using GRE as encapsulation scheme according to RFC 1701. The outer header is the standard IP header with HA as source address and COA as destination address. The protocol type used in this outer IP header is 47 for GRE. The other fields of the outer packet, such as TTL and TOS, may be copied from the original IP header. However, the TTL must be decremented by 1 when the packet is decapsulated to prevent indefinite forwarding.

The GRE header starts with several flags indicating if certain fields are present or not. A minimal GRE header uses only 4 bytes; nevertheless, GRE is flexible enough to include several mechanisms in its header. The **C** bit indicates if the checksum field is present and contains valid information. If C is set, the

Figure 9.11
Protocol fields for generic
routing encapsulation
(RFC 1701)

Ver.	IHL		TOS		Length			
IP identification					Flags	Fragment offset		
TTL			*GRE*		IP checksum			
IP address of HA								
Care-of address of COA								
C	R	K	S	s	rec.	rsv.	ver.	Protocol
checksum (optional)						offset (optional)		
Key (optional)								
Sequence number (optional)								
Routing (optional)								
Ver.	IHL		TOS		Length			
IP identification					Flags	Fragment offset		
TTL			Lay. 4 prot.		IP checksum			
IP address of CN								
IP address of MN								
TCP/UDP/... payload								

checksum field contains a valid IP checksum of the GRE header and the payload. The **R** bit indicates if the offset and routing fields are present and contain
valid information. The **offset** represents the offset in bytes for the first source
routing entry. The routing field, if present, has a variable length and contains
fields for source routing. If the C bit is set, the offset field is also present and,
vice versa, if the R bit is set, the checksum field must be present. The only
reason for this is to align the following fields to 4 bytes. The checksum field is
valid only if C is set, and the offset field is valid only if R is set respectively.

GRE also offers a **key** field which may be used for authentication. If this
field is present, the **K** bit is set. However, the authentication algorithms are not
further specified by GRE. The sequence number bit **S** indicates if the **sequence**
number field is present, if the **s** bit is set, strict source routing is used. Sequence
numbers may be used by a decapsulator to restore packet order. This can be
important, if a protocol guaranteeing in-order transmission is encapsulated and
transferred using a protocol which does not guarantee in-order delivery, e.g., IP.
Now the decapsulator at the tunnel exit must restore the sequence to maintain
the characteristic of the protocol.

The **recursion control** field (rec.) is an important field that additionally distinguishes GRE from IP-in-IP and minimal encapsulation. This field represents a
counter that shows the number of allowed recursive encapsulations. As soon as
a packet arrives at an encapsulator it checks whether this field equals zero. If the
field is not zero, additional encapsulation is allowed – the packet is encapsulated
and the field decremented by one. Otherwise the packet will most likely be dis-
carded. This mechanism prevents indefinite recursive encapsulation which
might happen with the other schemes if tunnels are set up improperly (e.g., several tunnels forming a loop). The default value of this field should be 0, thus
allowing only one level of encapsulation.

The following **reserved** fields must be zero and are ignored on reception. The
version field contains 0 for the GRE version. The following 2 byte **protocol** field
represents the protocol of the packet following the GRE header. Several values
have been defined, e.g., 0x6558 for transparent Ethernet bridging using a GRE
tunnel. In the case of a mobile IP tunnel, the protocol field contains 0x800 for IP.

The standard header of the original packet follows with the source address
of the correspondent node and the destination address of the mobile node.

9.1.7 Optimizations

Imagine the following scenario. A Japanese and a German meet at a conference
on Hawaii. Both want to use their laptops for exchanging data, both run mobile
IP for mobility support. Now recall Figure 9.2 and think of the way the packets
between both computers take.

If the Japanese sends a packet to the German, his computer sends the data to
the HA of the German, i.e., from Hawaii to Germany. The HA in Germany now
encapsulates the packets and tunnels them to the COA of the German laptop on
Hawaii. This means that although the computers might be only metres away, the

packets have to travel around the world! This inefficient behaviour of a non-optimized mobile IP is called **triangular routing**. The triangle is made of the three segments, CN to HA, HA to COA/MN, and MN back to CN.

With the basic mobile IP protocol all packets to the MN have to go through the HA. This can cause unnecessary overhead for the network between CN and HA, but also between HA and COA, depending on the current location of the MN. Furthermore, as the example shows, latency can increase dramatically. This is particularly unfortunate if MNs and HAs are separated by, e.g., transatlantic links.

One way to optimize the route is to inform the CN of the current location of the MN. The CN can thus learn the location by caching it in a **binding cache** which is a part of the local routing table for the CN. The appropriate entity to inform the CN of the location is the HA. The optimized mobile IP protocol needs four additional messages.

- **Binding request:** Any node that wants to know the current location of an MN can send a binding request to the HA. The HA can check if the MN has allowed dissemination of its current location. If the HA is allowed to reveal the location it sends back a binding update.
- **Binding update:** This message informs about the current location of an MN. The message contains the fixed IP address of the MN and the COA. The binding update can request an acknowledgement.
- **Binding acknowledgement:** If requested, a node returns this acknowledgement after receiving a binding update message.
- **Binding warning:** Finally, if a node decapsulates a packet for an MN, but it is not the current FA for this MN, this node sends a binding warning to the HA of the MN. The warning contains the IP address of the MN and the address of the node that has tried to send the packet to this MN. The HA should now send a binding update to the node that obviously has a wrong COA for the MN.

Figure 9.12 explains these additional four messages together with the case of an MN changing its FA. First of all, the CN can request the current location from the HA. If allowed by the MN, the HA returns the COA of the MN via an update message. The CN acknowledges this update message and stores the mobility binding. Now the CN can send its data directly to the current foreign agent FA_{old}. FA_{old} forwards the packets to the MN. This scenario shows a COA located at an FA. Encapsulation of data for tunnelling to the COA is now done by the CN, not the HA.

The MN might now change its location and register with a new foreign agent, FA_{new}. This registration is also forwarded to the HA to update its location database. Furthermore, FA_{new} informs FA_{old} about the new registration of MN. MN's registration message contains the address of FA_{old} for this purpose. Passing this information is achieved via an update message, which is acknowledged by FA_{old}. Registration replies are not shown in this scenario. Without the informa-

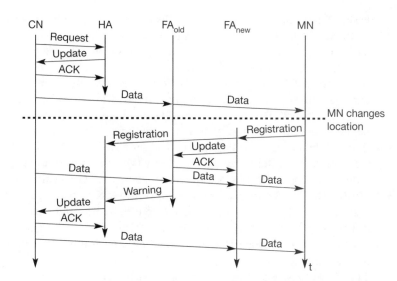

Figure 9.12
Change of the foreign
agent with the optimized
mobile IP

tion provided by the new FA, the old FA would not get to know anything about the new location of MN. In this case, CN surely does not know anything about the new location. Thus it still tunnels its packets for MN to the old FA, FA_{old}. This FA now notices packets with destination MN, but also knows that it is not the current FA of MN. FA_{old} might now forward these packets to the new COA of MN which is FA_{new} in this example. This forwarding of packets is another optimization of the basic Mobile IP providing **smooth handovers.** Without this optimization, all packets in transit would be lost while the MN moves from one FA to another. Especially with TCP as higher layer protocol this would result in severe performance degradation (see chapter 10).

In order to tell CN that it has a stale binding cache, FA_{old} sends a warning message to HA. HA now sends an update to CN to inform it about the new location. CN acknowledges this update. Now CN can send its packets directly to FA_{new}, thus, again avoiding triangular routing.

Unfortunately, this optimization of mobile IP to avoid triangular routing causes several security problems (e.g., tunnel hijacking) as discussed in Montenegro (1998).

9.1.8 Reverse tunnelling

At first glance, the return path from the MN to the CN shown in Figure 9.2 looks quite simple. The MN can directly send its packets to the CN as in any other standard IP situation. The destination address in the packets is that of CN. But there are several severe problems associated with this simple solution.

● **Firewalls:** Almost all companies and many other institutions secure their internal networks connected to the Internet with the help of a firewall.

Besides many other functions, firewalls can be set up to filter out malicious addresses from an administrator's point of view. Quite often firewalls only allow packets with topologically correct addresses to pass. However, MN still sends packets with its fixed IP address as source which is not topologically correct in a foreign network. Furthermore, firewalls often filter packets coming from outside containing a source address from computers of the internal network. This is done to avoid other computers that could use internal addresses and claim to be internal computers. However, this also implies that an MN cannot send a packet to a computer residing in its home network. Altogether, this means that not only the destination address matters for forwarding IP packets, but also the source address due to security concerns.

- **Multicast:** Reverse tunnels are needed for the MN to participate in a multicast group. While the nodes in the home network might participate in a multicast group, an MN in a foreign network cannot transmit multicast packets in a way that they emanate from its home network without a reverse tunnel.

- **TTL:** Consider an MN sending packets with a certain TTL while still in its home network. The TTL might be low enough so that no packet is transmitted outside a certain region. If the MN now moves to a foreign network, this TTL might be too low for the packets to reach the same nodes as before. Mobile IP is not transparent anymore if a user has to adjust TTL while moving. Therefore, a reverse tunnel is needed representing only one hop, no matter how many hops are really needed from the foreign to the home network.

All these considerations led to RFC 2344 (Montenegro, 1998) defining reverse tunnelling as extension to mobile IP. This RFC is backwards-compatible to mobile IP and defines topologically correct reverse tunnelling as necessary to handle the problems described above. Obviously, reverse tunnelling now creates a triangular routing problem in the reverse direction. All packets from an MN to a CN go through the HA. RFC 2344 does not offer a solution for this reverse triangular routing, because it is not clear if the CN can decapsulate packets. Remember that mobile IP should work together with all traditional, non-mobile IP nodes. Therefore, one cannot assume that a CN is able to be a tunnel endpoint.

Reverse tunnelling additionally raises several security issues which have been not solved up to now. For example, tunnels starting in the private network of a company and reaching out into the Internet could be hijacked and abused for sending packets through a firewall. Thus it is not clear if companies would allow for setting up tunnels through a firewall without further checking of packets. It is more likely that a company will set up a special virtual network for visiting mobile nodes outside the firewall with full connectivity to the Internet. This allows guests to use their mobile equipment, and at the same time today's security standards are maintained.

9.1.9 IPv6

While mobile IP was originally designed for IP version 4, IP version 6 (Deering, 1995) makes life much easier. Several mechanisms that had to be specified separately for mobility support come for free in IPv6 (Perkins, 1996d), (Johnson, 1998). One issue is security which is now a required feature for all IPv6 nodes. No special mechanisms as add-ons are needed for securing mobile IP registrations. Every IPv6 node masters address autoconfiguration, thus the mechanisms for acquiring a COA are already built into IPv6. Neighbour discovery as a mechanism mandatory for every node is also included in the specification, therefore, special foreign agents are no longer needed to advertise services. Combining the features of autoconfiguration and neighbour discovery means that every mobile node is able to create or obtain a topologically correct address for the current point of attachment.

Furthermore, every IPv6 node can send binding updates to another node, thus the MN can send its current COA to the CN and HA directly. These mechanisms are an integral part of IPv6. Besides that, a soft handover is possible with IPv6. The MN sends its new COA to the old router servicing the MN at the old COA, and the old router encapsulates all incoming packets for the MN and forwards them to the new COA.

Altogether, mobile IP in IPv6 networks requires fewer additional mechanisms from a CN, MN, and HA. The FA is not needed any more. A CN only has to be able to process binding updates, i.e., to create or to update an entry in the routing cache. The MN itself has to be able to decapsulate packets, to detect when it needs a new COA, and to determine when to send binding updates to the HA and CN. An HA must be able to encapsulate packets.

9.2 Dynamic host configuration protocol

The dynamic host configuration protocol (DHCP, RFC 2131, Drohms, 1997) is mainly used for the simplification of installation and maintenance of networked computers. If a new computer is connected to a network, DHCP can provide it with all necessary information for full system integration into the network, e.g., addresses of a DNS server and the default router, the subnet mask, the domain name, and an IP address. Especially the last capability, providing an IP address, makes DHCP very attractive for mobile IP as a source of care-of addresses. While the basic DHCP mechanisms are quite simple, many options are available as described in RFC 2132 (Alexander, 1997).

DHCP is based on a client/server model as shown in Figure 9.13. DHCP clients send a request to a server (DHCPDISCOVER in the example) to which the server responds. A client sends requests using MAC broadcasts. A DHCP relay might be needed to forward requests to a DHCP server.

A typical initialization of a DHCP client is shown in Figure 9.14. The figure shows one client and two servers. As described above, the client broad-

Figure 9.13
Basic DHCP configuration

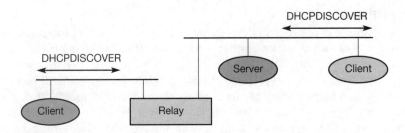

casts a DHCPDISCOVER into the subnet. There might be a relay to forward this broadcast. In the case shown, two servers receive this broadcast and determine the configuration they can offer to the client. One example for this could be a check of available IP addresses and choosing one for the client. Servers reply to the client's request with DHCPOFFER and offer a list of configuration parameters. Now the client can choose one of the offered configurations. The client in turn replies to the servers, accepting one of the configurations and rejecting the others using DHCPREQUEST. If a server receives a DHCPREQUEST with a rejection, it can free the reserved configuration for other possible clients. The server with the configuration accepted by the client now confirms the configuration with DHCPACK. This completes the initialization phase.

If a client leaves a subnet, it should release the configuration received by a server using DHCPRELEASE. Now the server can free the context stored for the client and offer the configuration again. The configuration a client gets from a server is only leased for a certain amount of time. Therefore, the client has to reconfirm the configuration from time to time. Otherwise the server will free

Figure 9.14
Client initialization via
DHCP

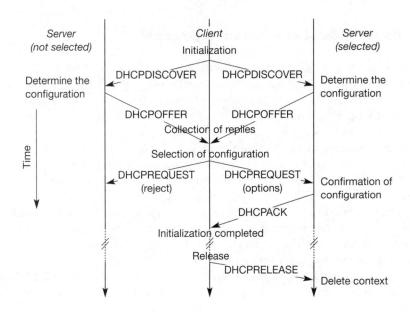

the configuration. This time-out of configuration helps in case of crashed nodes or nodes moved away without releasing the context.

DHCP is a good candidate for supporting the acquisition of care-of addresses for mobile nodes. The same holds for all other parameters needed, such as addresses of the default router, DNS servers, the timeserver etc. Therefore, a DHCP server should be located in the subnet of the access point of the mobile node, or at least a DHCP relay should provide forwarding of the messages.

Unfortunately, there are several problems related to the use of DHCP. One major issue is security. There has been no authentication of DHCP messages specified. This means that the mobile node cannot trust a DHCP server, and the DHCP server cannot trust the mobile node. Furthermore, there is no protocol for server-server configuration, i.e., one DHCP server cannot communicate with another DHCP server and exchange currently used configurations. Thus, configurations on servers have to be set up by hand. For example, address spaces that DHCP servers can use for clients have to be disjointed. An administrator has to take care that every DHCP server has its own address space for clients. This typically results in address space fragmentation.

9.3 Ad hoc networks

Mobility support described in sections 9.1 and 9.2 so far relies on the existence of at least some infrastructure. Mobile IP requires, e.g., a home agent, tunnels, and default routers. DHCP requires servers and broadcast capabilities of the medium reaching all participants or relays to servers. Cellular phone networks (see chapter 4) require base stations, infrastructure networks etc.

However, there are several situations where users of a network cannot rely on an infrastructure, the infrastructure is too expensive, or there is no infrastructure at all. In these situations ad hoc networks are the only choice. Examples for the use of ad hoc networks are:

- **Instant infrastructure:** Unplanned meetings, spontaneous interpersonal communications etc. cannot rely on any infrastructure. Infrastructures need planning and administration. It would take too long to set up this kind of infrastructure, therefore, ad hoc connectivity has to be set up.
- **Disaster relief:** Infrastructures typically break down in disaster areas. Hurricanes cut phone and power lines, floods destroy base stations, fires burn servers. Thus, emergency teams can only rely on an infrastructure they can set up themselves. No forward planning can be done, and the setup must be done extremely fast and reliably. The same applies to many military activities.
- **Remote areas:** Even if infrastructures could be planned ahead, it is sometimes too expensive to set up an infrastructure in sparsely populated areas. Depending on the communication pattern, ad hoc networks or satellite infrastructures can be a solution.

- **Effectiveness:** Services of existing infrastructures might be too expensive for certain applications. If, for example, only connection-oriented cellular networks exist, but an application sends only a small status information every other minute, a cheaper ad hoc packet-oriented network might be a better solution. Furthermore, registration procedures might take too long, and communication overhead might be too large with existing networks. Thus, application-tailored ad hoc networks can offer a better solution.

The reason for having a special section about ad hoc networks within a chapter about the network layer is that routing of data is one of the most difficult issues in ad hoc networks. General routing problems are discussed in section 9.3.1 while the sections following give some examples for routing algorithms suited to ad hoc networks. It has to be mentioned that routing functions sometimes also exist in layer 2, not only in the network layer (layer 3) of the reference model. HIPERLAN (see section 7.4), for example, offers forwarding/routing capabilities in layer 2 based on MAC addresses for ad hoc networks.

One of the first ad hoc wireless networks was the packet radio network started by ARPA in 1973. It allowed up to 138 nodes in the ad hoc network and used IP packets for data transport. This made an easy connection possible to the ARPAnet, the starting point of today's Internet. Twenty radio channels between 1718.4-1840 MHz were used offering 100 or 400 kbit/s. The system used DSSS with 128 or 32 chips/bit.

A variant of distance vector routing was used in this ad hoc network (Perlman, 1992). In this approach, each node sends a routing advertisement every 7.5 s. These advertisements contain a neighbour table with a list of link qualities to each neighbour. Each node updates the local routing table according to the distance vector algorithm based on these advertisements. Received packets also help to update the routing table. A sender now transmits a packet to its first hop neighbour using the local neighbour table. Each node forwards a packet received based on its own local neighbour table. Several enhancements to this simple scheme are needed to avoid routing loops and to reflect the possibly fast changing topology. The following sections discuss routing problems and enhanced routing mechanisms for ad hoc networks in more detail.

9.3.1 Routing

While in wireless networks with infrastructure support a base station always reaches all mobile nodes, this is not always the case in an ad hoc network. A destination node might be out of range of a source node transmitting packets. Thus, routing is needed to find a path between source and destination and to forward the packets appropriately. In wireless networks using an infrastructure, cells have been defined. Within a cell, the base station can reach all mobile nodes without routing via a broadcast. In the case of ad hoc networks, each node must be able to forward data for other nodes. This creates many additional problems discussed in the following.

Figure 9.15 gives a simple example of an ad hoc network. At a certain time t_1 the network topology might look as illustrated on the left side of the figure. Five nodes, N_1 to N_5, are connected depending on the current transmission characteristics between them. In this snapshot of the network, N_4 can receive N_1 over a good link, but N_1 receives N_4 only via a weak link. Thus, links do not necessarily have the same characteristics in both directions. Reasons for this are, e.g., different antenna characteristics or transmit power. N_1 cannot receive N_2 at all, N_2 receives a signal from N_1.

This situation can change quite fast as the snapshot at t_2 shows. N_1 cannot receive N_4 any longer, N_4 receives N_1 only via a weak link. But now N_1 has an asymmetric but bi-directional link to N_2 that did not exist before.

This very simple example already shows some fundamental differences between wired networks and ad hoc wireless networks related to routing.

- **Asymmetric links:** If node A receives a signal from node B this does not tell anything about the quality of the connection in the reverse direction. B might receive nothing, have a weak link, or even have a better link than the reverse direction. Thus, routing information collected for one direction is of almost no use for the other direction. However, many routing algorithms for wired networks rely on a symmetric scenario.
- **Redundant links:** Wired networks, too, have redundant links to survive link failures. However, there is only some redundancy in wired networks, which, additionally, is controlled by a network administrator. In ad hoc networks nobody controls redundancy, so there might be many redundant links up to the extreme of a completely meshed topology. Routing algorithms for wired networks can handle some redundancy, but a high redundancy can cause a large computational overhead for routing table updates.
- **Interference:** In wired networks links exist only where a wire exists, and connections are planned by network administrators. This is not the case for wireless ad hoc networks. Links come and go depending on transmission characteristics, one transmission might interfere with another one, and nodes might overhear transmissions of other nodes. Interference thus creates new problems by 'unplanned' links between nodes: if two close-by

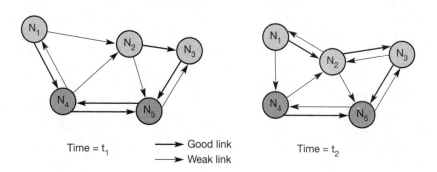

Time = t_1 → Good link   Time = t_2
             → Weak link

Figure 9.15
Example ad hoc network

nodes forward two transmissions, they might interfere and destroy each other. Interference might also help routing on the other hand. A node can learn the topology with the help of packets overheard.

● **Dynamic topology:** The greatest problem for routing arises from the highly dynamic topology. The mobile nodes might move as shown in Figure 9.15 or medium characteristics might change. This results in frequent changes in topology, so snapshots are valid only for a very short period of time. In ad hoc networks, routing tables must somehow reflect these frequent changes in topology, and routing algorithms have to be adapted. Routing algorithms used in wired networks would either react much too slowly or generate too many updates to reflect all changes in topology. Routing table updates in fixed networks, for example, take place every 30 seconds. This updating frequency might be too low to be useful for ad hoc networks. Furthermore, some algorithms rely on a complete picture of the whole network. While this works in wired networks where changes are rare, it fails completely in ad hoc networks. The topology changes during the distribution of the 'current' snapshot of the network, rendering the snapshot useless.

Let us go back to the example network in Figure 9.15 and assume that node N_1 wants to send data to N_3 and needs an acknowledgement. If N_1 had a complete overview of the network at time t_1, which is not always the case in ad hoc networks, it would choose the path N_1, N_2, N_3, for this requires only two hops (if we use hops as metric). Acknowledgements cannot take the same path, N_3 chooses N_3, N_5, N_4, N_1. This takes three hops and already shows that routing also strongly influences the function of higher layers. TCP, for example, makes round trip measurements assuming the same path in both directions. This is obviously wrong in the example shown, thus leading to misinterpretations of measurements and inefficiencies (see chapter 10).

Just a moment later, at time t_2, the topology has changed. Now N_3 cannot take the same path any longer to send acknowledgements back to N_1, while N_1 can still take the old path to N_3. Although already more complicated than fixed networks, this example still assumes that nodes can have a complete insight into the current situation. The optimal knowledge for every node would be a description of the current connectivity between all nodes, the expected traffic flows, capacities of all links, delay of each link, and the computing power of each node. While even in fixed networks traffic flows are not exactly predictable, for ad hoc networks link capacities are additionally unknown. The capacity of each link can change from 0 to the maximum of the transmission technology used. In real ad hoc networks no node knows all these factors, and establishing up-to-date snapshots of the network is almost impossible.

Ad hoc networks using mobile nodes face additional problems due to hardware limitations. Using the standard routing protocols with periodic updates wastes battery power without sending any user data and disables sleep modes. Furthermore, periodic updates waste bandwidth of the already scarce bandwidth resources of wireless links.

An additional problem not existing in wired networks is interference between two or more transmissions that do not use the same nodes for forwarding. If, for example, a second transmission from node N_4 to N_5 (see Figure 9.15) takes place at the same time as the transmission from N_1 to N_3, they could interfere. Interference could take place at N_2 which can receive signals from N_1 and N_4, or at N_5 receiving N_4 and N_2. If shielded correctly, there is no interference between two wires.

Considering all the additional difficulties in comparison to wired networks, the following observations concerning routing can be made for ad hoc networks with moving nodes:

- Traditional routing algorithms known from wired networks will not work efficiently (e.g., distance vector algorithms such as RIP (Hendrik, 1988), (Malkin, 1994) converge much too slowly) or fail completely (e.g., link state algorithms such as OSPF (Moy, 1994) exchange complete pictures of the network). These algorithms have not been designed with a highly dynamic topology, with asymmetric links, or with interference in mind.
- Routing in wireless ad hoc networks cannot rely on layer three knowledge alone. Information from lower layers concerning connectivity or interference can help routing algorithms to find a good path.
- Centralized approaches will not really work, for it takes too long to collect a current status and disseminate it again. Within this time the topology has already changed.
- Many nodes need routing capabilities. While there might be some without, at least one router has to be within the range of each node. Algorithms have to take care of the limited battery power of these nodes.
- The notion of a connection with certain characteristics cannot work properly. Ad hoc networks will work connectionless, for it is not possible to maintain a connection in a fast changing environment and to forward data following this connection. Nodes have to make local decisions for forwarding and send packets roughly toward the final destination.
- A last alternative to forward a packet across an unknown topology is flooding. This approach always works if the load is low, but it is very inefficient. A hop counter is needed in each packet to avoid looping, and the diameter of the ad hoc network, i.e., the maximum number of hops, should be known. (The number of nodes can be used as an upper bound.)
- Hierarchical clustering of nodes might help. If it is possible to identify certain groups of nodes belonging together, clusters can be established. While individual nodes might move faster, the whole cluster can be rather stationary. Thus routing between clusters might be simpler and less dynamic (see section 9.3.4).

The following sections give some examples for routing algorithms used in ad hoc networks and useful metrics that are different from the usual hop counting.

9.3.2 Destination sequence distance vector

Destination sequence distance vector (DSDV) routing is an enhancement to distance vector routing for ad hoc networks (Perkins, 1994). Distance vector routing is used as RIP in wired networks. It performs extremely poorly with certain network changes due to the count-to-infinity problem. Each node exchanges its neighbour table periodically with its neighbours. Thus, changes at one node in the network propagate slowly through the network (step by step with every exchange). The strategies to avoid this problem which are used in fixed networks (poisoned-reverse/split-horizon (Perlman, 1992)) do not help in the case of wireless ad hoc networks, due to the rapidly changing topology. Effects might be the creation of loops or unreachable regions within the network.

DSDV now adds two things to the distance vector algorithm:

- **Sequence numbers:** Each routing advertisement comes with a sequence number. Within ad hoc networks, advertisements may propagate along many paths. Sequence numbers help to apply the advertisements in correct order. This avoids loops that are likely with the unchanged distance vector algorithm.
- **Damping:** Transient changes in topology that are of short duration should not destabilize the routing mechanisms. Advertisements containing changes in the topology currently stored are therefore not disseminated further. A node waits with dissemination if these changes are most likely not yet stable. Waiting time depends on the time between the first and the best announcement of a path to a certain destination.

The routing table for N_1 in Figure 9.15 would be as shown in Table 9.1.

For each node N_1 stores the next hop toward this node, the metric (here number of hops), the sequence number of the last advertisement for this node, and the time at which the path has been installed first. Furthermore, the table contains flags and a settling time helping to decide when the path can be assumed stable. Router advertisements from N_1 now contain data from the first, third, and fourth column: destination address, metric, and sequence number. Besides being loop-free at all instants, DSDV has low memory requirements and a quick convergence via triggered updates.

Table 9.1

Part of a routing table for DSDV

Destination	next hop	metric	sequence no.	install time
N_1	N_1	0	S_1-321	T_4-001
N_2	N_2	1	S_2-218	T_4-001
N_3	N_2	2	S_3-043	T_4-002
N_4	N_4	1	S_4-092	T_4-001
N_5	N_4	2	S_5-163	T_4-002

9.3.3 Dynamic source routing

Imagine what happens in an ad hoc network where nodes exchange packets from time to time, i.e., the network is only lightly loaded, and DSDV or one of the traditional distance vector or link state algorithms is used for updating routing tables. Although only some user data has to be transmitted, the nodes exchange routing information to keep track of the topology. These algorithms maintain routes between all nodes, although maybe there is currently no data exchange at all. This causes unnecessary traffic and prevents nodes from saving battery power.

Dynamic source routing, therefore, divides the task of routing into two separate problems (Johnson, 1996):

- **Route discovery:** A node only tries to discover a route to a destination if it has to send something to this destination and there is currently no known route.
- **Route maintenance:** If a node is continuously sending packets via a route, it has to make sure that the route is held upright. As soon as a node detects problems with the current route, it has to find an alternative route.

The basic principle of source routing is also used in fixed networks, e.g. token rings. Dynamic source routing eliminates all periodic routing updates and works as follows.

If a node needs to discover a route, it broadcasts a route request with a unique identifier and the destination address as parameters. Any node that receives a route request does the following.

- If the node has already received the request (which is identified using the unique identifier), it drops the request packet.
- If the node recognizes its own address as the destination, the request has reached its target.
- Otherwise, the node appends its own address to a list of traversed hops in the packet and broadcasts this updated route request.

Using this approach, the route request collects a list of addresses representing a possible path on its way toward the destination. Thus, as soon as the request reaches the destination, it can return the request packet containing the list to the receiver using this list in reverse order. One condition for this is that the links work bi-directionally. If this is not the case, and the destination node does not currently maintain a route back to the initiator of the request, it has to start a route discovery by itself. The destination may receive several lists containing different paths from the initiator. It could return the best path, the first path, or several paths to offer the initiator a choice.

Applying route discovery to the example in Figure 9.15 for a route from N_1 to N_3 at time t_1 results in the following.

- N_1 broadcasts the request $((N_1)$, id = 42, target = $N_3)$, N_2 and N_4 receive this request.
- N_2 then broadcasts $((N_1, N_2)$, id = 42, target = $N_3)$, N_4 broadcasts $((N_1, N_4)$, id = 42, target = $N_3)$. N_3 and N_5 receive N_2's broadcast, N_1, N_2, and N_5 receive N_4's broadcast.
- N_3 recognizes itself as target, N_5 broadcasts $((N_1, N_2, N_5)$, id = 42, target = $N_3)$. N_3 and N_4 receive N_5's broadcast. N_1, N_2, and N_5 drop N_4's broadcast packet, for they all recognize an already received route request (and N_2's broadcast reached N_5 before N_4's did).
- N_4 drops N_5's broadcast, N_3 recognizes (N_1, N_2, N_5) as an alternate, but longer route.
- N_3 now has to return the path (N_1, N_2, N_3) to N_1. This is simple assuming symmetric links working in both directions. N_3 can forward the information using the list in reverse order.

The assumption of bi-directional links holds for many ad hoc networks. However, if links are not bi-directional, the scenario gets more complicated, and the algorithm has to be applied once again in the reverse direction, if the target currently does not maintain a path to the source of the route request.

- N_3 has to broadcast a route request $((N_3)$, id = 17, target = $N_1)$. Only N_5 receives this request.
- N_5 now broadcasts $((N_3, N_5)$, id=17, target=$N_1)$, N_3 and N_4 receive the broadcast.
- N_3 drops the request for it recognizes an already known id. N_4 broadcasts $((N_3, N_5, N_4)$, id = 17, target = $N_1)$, N_5, N_2, and N_1 receive the broadcast.
- N_5 drops the request packet, N_1 recognizes itself as target, and N_2 broadcasts $((N_3, N_5, N_4, N_2)$, id = 17, target = $N_1)$. N_3 and N_5 receive N_2's broadcast.
- N_3 and N_5 drop the request packet.

Now N_3 holds the list for a path from N_1 to N_3, (N_1, N_2, N_3), and N_1 knows the path from N_3 to N_1, (N_3, N_5, N_4, N_1). But still, N_1 does not know how to send data to N_3! The only solution is to send the list (N_1, N_2, N_3) with the broadcasts initiated by N_3 in the reverse direction. This example shows clearly how much simpler routing can be if links are symmetrical.

The basic algorithm for route discovery can be optimized in many ways.

- To avoid too many broadcasts, each route request could contain a counter. Every node rebroadcasting the request increments the counter by one. Knowing the maximum network diameter (take the number of nodes if nothing else is known), nodes can drop a request if the counter reaches this number.
- A node can cache path fragments from recent requests. These fragments can now be used to answer other route requests much faster (if they still reflect the topology!).

- A node can also update this cache from packet headers while forwarding other packets.
- If a node overhears transmissions from other nodes, it can also use this information for shortening routes.

After discovering a route, it has to be maintained as long as the node sends packets along this route. Depending on layer two mechanisms, different approaches can be taken:

- If the link layer uses an acknowledgement, as for example IEEE 802.11 does, the node can interpret this acknowledgement as an intact route.
- If possible, the node could also listen to the next node forwarding the packet, thus getting a passive acknowledgement.
- Furthermore, a node could request an explicit acknowledgement.

Again, this situation is complicated if links are not bi-directional. If a node detects connectivity problems, it has to inform the sender of a packet, thus initiating a new route discovery starting from the sender. Alternatively, the node could try to discover a new route by itself.

Thus, although dynamic source routing offers benefits compared to other algorithms by being much more bandwidth efficient, problems arise if the topology is highly dynamic and links are asymmetrical.

9.3.4 Hierarchical algorithms

Both routing algorithms, destination sequence distance vector and dynamic source routing only work for a smaller number of nodes and depend heavily on the mobility of nodes. For larger networks, clustering of nodes and using different routing algorithms between clusters and within clusters can be a solution. The motivation behind this approach is the locality property, meaning that if a cluster can be established, nodes typically remain within a cluster, only some change clusters. Thus, if the topology within a cluster changes, only nodes of the cluster have to be informed. Nodes of other clusters only need to know how to reach the cluster. The approach basically hides all the small details in clusters which are further away.

From time to time each node needs to get some information about the topology. Again, updates from clusters further away will be sent out less frequently compared to local updates. Clusters can be combined to super-clusters etc., that way building up a larger hierarchy. Using this approach, one or more nodes can act as clusterheads, representing a router for all traffic to/from the cluster. All nodes within the cluster and all other clusterheads use these as gateway for the cluster. Figure 9.16 shows an ad hoc network with interconnection to the Internet via a base station. This base station transfers data to and from the cluster heads. In this example, one cluster head acts as head of the super cluster as well, thus routing traffic to and from the super cluster.

Figure 9.16
Building hierarchies in
ad hoc networks

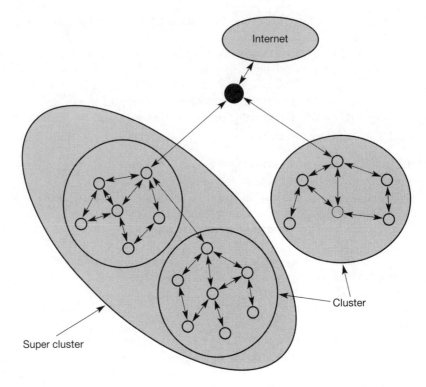

Super cluster

Cluster

9.3.5 Alternative metrics

The examples shown in this chapter always use the number of hops as routing metric. Although very simple, especially in wireless ad hoc networks, this is not always the best choice. Even for fixed networks, e.g., bandwidth can also be a factor for the routing metric. Due to the varying link quality and the fact that different transmissions can interfere, other metrics can be more useful.

One other metric, called **least interference routing** (LIR), takes possible interference into account. Figure 9.17 shows an ad hoc network topology. Sender S_1 wants to send a packet to receiver R_1, S_2 to R_2. Using the hop count as metric, S_1 could choose three different paths with three hops, which is also the minimum. Possible paths are (S_1, N_3, N_4, R_1), (S_1, N_3, N_2, R_1), and (S_1, N_1, N_2, R_1). S_2 would choose the only available path with only three hops (S_2, N_5, N_6, R_2). Taking interference into account, this picture changes. In order to calculate the possible interference of a path, each node calculates its possible interference. Interference is here defined as the number of neighbours that can overhear a transmission. Therefore, every node only needs local information to compute its interference.

In this example, the interference of node N_3 is 6, that of node N_4 is 5 etc. Calculating the costs of possible paths between S_1 and R_1 results in the following:

Figure 9.17
Example for least
interference routing

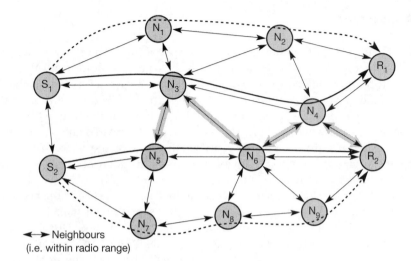

◄───► Neighbours
(i.e. within radio range)

$C_1 = cost(S_1, N_3, N_4, R_1) = 16$,
$C_2 = cost(S_1, N_3, N_2, R_1) = 15$,
and $C_3 = cost(S_1, N_1, N_2, R_1) = 12$.

All three paths have the same number of hops, but the last path has the lowest cost due to interference. Thus, S_1 chooses (S_1, N_1, N_2, R_1). S_2 also computes the cost of different paths, examples are $C_4 = cost(S_2, N_5, N_6, R_2) = 16$ and $C_5 = cost(S_2, N_7, N_8, N_9, R_2) = 15$. S_2 would, therefore, choose the path $(S_2, N_7, N_8, N_9, R_2)$, although this path has one hop more than the first one.

With both transmissions taking place at the same time, there would have been interference between them as shown in Figure 9.17. In this case, least interference routing helped to avoid interference. Taking only local decisions and not knowing what paths other transmissions take, this scheme can just lower the probability of interference. Interference can only be avoided if all senders know of all other transmissions (and the whole routing topology) and base routing on this knowledge.

Furthermore, routing can take several metrics into account at the same time and weigh them. Metrics could be the number of hops h, interference i, reliability r, error rate e etc. The cost of a path could then be determined as:

$$cost = \alpha h + \beta i + \gamma r + \delta e + \ldots$$

It is not at all easy (if possible at all) to choose the weights α, β, γ, δ,... to achieve the desired routing behaviour.

9.4 Summary

Mobility support on the network layer is of special importance, as the network layer holds together the huge Internet with the common protocol IP. Although based on possibly different wireless or wired technologies, all nodes of the network should be able to communicate. Therefore, mobile IP (an extension of the classical IP) has been designed which enables mobility in the Internet without changing existing wired systems. However, mobile IP leaves some points unresolved, especially if it comes to security, efficiency of the packet flow, and support for quality of service. Many of these issues are addressed in IP version 6 making working with mobility much simpler.

DHCP offers a fully automatic mechanism for a node to get all of the necessary information to be integrated into a network, thus supporting installation of new computers and the integration of mobile computers into networks. DHCP will be a major source of care-of addresses needed for mobile IP. But DHCP contains some problems, too, mainly the lack of security mechanisms and the non-existent server/server protocol requiring installations of DHCP servers by hand.

Finally, ad hoc networks offer a completely new way of setting up mobile communications if no infrastructure is available. In these networks routing is a major topic, for there is no base station that can reach all nodes via broadcast as in cellular networks. Traditional routing algorithms do not work well at all in the highly dynamic environment of ad hoc networks, therefore extensions of existing or completely new algorithms have to be applied. For larger groups of nodes only hierarchical approaches solve the routing problem, algorithms such as DSDV do not scale well. An important difference in wireless networks is the knowledge required about layer two characteristics. Information about interference and acknowledgements can help finding a good route.

Many questions of a mobile network layer are still open. It is important to see how the different approaches can be combined. For example, the extension of the foreign agent's capabilities allowing multiple hops to a mobile node could combine mobile IP with ad hoc networks. Recently more work has been done in the field of ad hoc networking in combination with mobile IP. The mobile ad hoc networking group (MANET) proposes new encapsulation mechanisms and routing protocols (Broch, 1998), (Corson, 1998), (Perkins, 1998), (Corson, 1999). Altogether, the network layer remains a large open and very interesting field for research.

9.5 Review exercises

1 Recall routing in fixed IP networks. Name the consequences and problems of using IP together with the standard routing protocols for mobile communications.

2 What could be quick 'solutions' and why do they not work?

3 Name the requirements for a mobile IP and justify them. Does mobile IP fulfil them all?

4 List the entities of mobile IP and describe data transfer from a mobile node to a fixed node and vice versa. Why and where is encapsulation needed?

5 How does registration on layer 3 of a mobile node work?

6 Show all the steps required for a handover from one foreign agent to another foreign agent including layer 2 and layer 3.

7 Explain packet flow if two mobile nodes communicate and both are in foreign networks. What additional routes do packets take if reverse tunnelling is required?

8 Explain how tunnelling works in general and especially for mobile IP using IP-in-IP, minimal, and generic routing encapsulation, respectively. Discuss the advantages and disadvantages of these three methods.

9 Name the inefficiencies of mobile IP regarding data forwarding from a correspondent node to a mobile node. What are optimizations and what additional problems do they cause?

10 What advantages does the use of IPv6 offer for mobility? Where are the entities of mobile IP now?

11 What are general problems of mobile IP regarding security and support of quality of service?

12 What is the basic purpose of DHCP? Name the entities of DHCP.

13 How can DHCP be used for mobility and support of mobile IP?

14 What are major open questions for DHCP?

15 Name the main differences between ad hoc networks and other networks. What advantages do ad hoc networks offer?

16 Why is routing in ad hoc networks complicated, what are the special challenges?

17 Recall the distance vector and link state routing algorithms for fixed networks. Why are both difficult to use in ad hoc networks?

18 What are the differences between destination sequence distance vector and the standard distance vector algorithm? Why is this extension needed?

19 How does dynamic source routing handle routing? What is the motivation behind dynamic source routing compared to other routing algorithms from fixed networks?

20 How does the symmetry of wireless links influence the routing algorithms proposed?

21 Think of ad hoc networks with faster moving nodes, e.g., cars in a city. What problems arise even for the routing algorithms adapted to ad hoc networks? What is the situation on highways?

9.6 References

Alexander, S.; Drohms, R. (1997) *DHCP options and BOOTP vendor extensions*, RFC 2132, March.

Brewer, E.A.; Katz, R.H.; Chawathe, Y.; Gribble, S.D.; Hodes, T.; Nguyen, G.; Stemm, M.; Henderson, T.; Amit, E.; Balakrishnan, H.; Fox, A.; Padmanabhan, V.; Seshan, S. (1998) 'A network architecture for heterogeneous mobile computing', *IEEE Personal Communications*, 5, (5).

Broch, J.; Johnson, D.B.; Maltz, D.A. (1998) *The dynamic source routing protocol for mobile ad hoc networks*, draft-ietf-manet-dsr-01.txt (work in progress), December.

Corson, S.; Macker, J. (1998) *Mobile Ad hoc Networking (MANET): Routing protocol performance issues and evaluation considerations*, draft-ietf-manet-issues-02.txt (work in progress), October.

Corson, S.; Papademetriou, S.; Papadopoulos, P.; Park, V.; Qayyum, A. (1999) *An Internet MANET Encapsulation Protocol (IMEP) specification*, draft-ietf-manet-imep-spec-01.txt (work in progress), February.

Deering, S. (1989) *Host extensions for IP multicasting*, RFC 1112, August.

Deering, S. (1991) *ICMP router discovery messages*, RFC 1256, September.

Deering, S.; Hinden, R. (1995) *Internet Protocol, version 6 (IPv6) Specification*, RFC 1883, December.

Drohms, R. (1997) *Dynamic Host Configuration Protocol*, RFC 2131, March.

Hanks, S.; Li, T.; Farinacci, D.; Traina, P. (1994) *Generic Routing Encapsulation (GRE)*, RFC 1701, October.

Hendrick, C. (1988) *Routing Information Protocol*, RFC 1058, June.

Jacobson, V. (1990) *Compressing TCP/IP headers for low-speed serial links*, RFC 1144, February.

Johnson, D.B.; Maltz, D.A. (1996) *Dynamic source routing in ad hoc wireless networks*, in: Mobile Computing (Imielinski/Korth), Kluwer Academic Publishers.

Johnson, D.B.; Perkins, C. (1998) *Mobility support in IPv6*, draft-ietf-mobileip-ipv6-07.txt (work in progress), November.

Malkin, G. (1994) *RIP version 2 carrying additional information*, RFC 1723, November.

Montenegro, G. (1998) *Reverse Tunneling for Mobile IP*, RFC 2344, May.

Moy, J. (1994) *OSPF version 2*, RFC 1583, March.

Perkins, C.; Bhagwat, P. (1994) *Highly dynamic Destination-Sequenced Distance Vector routing (DSDV) for mobile computers*, proceedings of ACM SIGCOMM.

Perkins, C. (1996a) *IP Mobility Support*, RFC 2002, October.

Perkins, C. (1996b) *IP Encapsulation within IP*, RFC 2003, October.

Perkins, C. (1996c) *Minimal Encapsulation within IP*, RFC 2004, October.

Perkins, C.; Johnson, D. B. (1996d) *Mobility support in IPv6*, proceedings of ACM Mobicom 96, November.

Perkins, C. (1997) *Mobile IP: Design Principles and Practice.* Addison Wesley Longman Publishing Company, Reading, Massachusetts, USA.

Perkins, C. (1998) *Mobile ad hoc networking terminology,* draft-ietf-manet-term-01.txt (work in progress), November.

Perlman, R. (1992) *Interconnections: Bridges and Routers,* Addison-Wesley Longman Publishing Company, Reading, Massachusetts, USA.

Postel, J. B. (1981) *Internet Protocol,* RFC 791, September.

Stevens, W. R. (1994) *TCP/IP Illustrated, Volume 1: The Protocols.* Addison Wesley Longman Publishing Company, Reading, Massachusetts, USA.

Mobile transport layer **10**

Supporting mobility only on lower layers up to the network layer is not enough to provide mobility support for applications as well. Most applications rely on a transport layer, such as TCP or UDP in the case of the Internet. Two functions of the transport layer in the Internet is checksumming over user data and multiplexing/demultiplexing of data from/to applications. While the network layer only addresses a host, ports in UDP or TCP allow addressing of dedicated applications. That is already all the connectionless UDP offers, thus, the following concentrates on TCP. While UDP works connectionless and does not give certain guarantees about reliable data delivery, TCP is much more complex and, therefore, needs special mechanisms to be useful in mobile environments. For UDP to work, mobility support in IP (such as mobile IP) is already enough.

The main difference between UDP and TCP is that TCP offers connections between two applications. Within a connection TCP can give certain guarantees, such as in-order delivery or reliable data transmission using retransmission techniques. Furthermore, TCP has built-in mechanisms to behave 'network friendly'. If, for example, TCP encounters packet loss, it assumes network internal congestion and slows down the transmission rate. This is also one of the main reasons to stay with protocols like TCP and not to choose the simpler UDP. UDP requires that applications handle reliability, in-order delivery etc. Furthermore, UDP does not behave network friendly, i.e., does not pull back in case of congestion.

The following section gives an overview of mechanisms within TCP that play an important role in using TCP for mobility. The main problem of many mechanisms is that they have been designed under assumptions completely different from those in mobile networks. Based on these problems, which can lead to a complete breakdown of TCP traffic, a set of solutions has been developed. Several solutions are presented in sections 10.2 to 10.8; each solution has its specific strengths and weaknesses.

10.1 Traditional TCP

This section highlights several mechanisms of the transmission control protocol (TCP) (Postel, 1981) that influence the efficiency of TCP in a mobile environment. A very detailed presentation of TCP is given in Stevens (1994).

10.1.1 Congestion control

A transport layer protocol such as TCP has been designed for fixed networks with fixed end-systems. Data transmission takes place using network adapters, fibre optics, copper wires, special hardware for routers etc. This hardware typically works without introducing transmission errors. Furthermore, if the software is mature enough, it will not drop packets or flip bits. Therefore, if a packet on its way from a sender to a receiver is lost in a fixed network, it is typically not because of hardware or software errors. Thus, the reason for a packet loss in a fixed network is very high is probably a temporary overload at some point of the transmission path, i.e., a state of congestion at some node.

Congestion may appear from time to time even in carefully designed networks. The packet buffers of a router are filled and the router cannot forward the packets fast enough because the sum of the input rates of packets destined for one output link is higher than the capacity of the output link. The only thing a router can do in this situation is to drop packets. A dropped packet is lost for the transmission, and the receiver notices a gap in the packet stream. Now the receiver does not directly tell the sender which packet is missing, but continues to acknowledge all in-sequence packets up to the missing one.

The sender notices the missing acknowledgement for the lost packet and assumes a packet loss due to congestion. Retransmitting the missing packet and continuing at full sending rate would now be unwise, for this might only increase congestion. Although it is not guaranteed that all packets of the TCP connection take the same way through the network, this assumption holds for most of the packets. To mitigate congestion, TCP slows down the transmission rate dramatically. All other TCP connections experiencing the same congestion do exactly the same, thus, the congestion is soon resolved. This co-operation of TCP connections in the Internet is one of the main reasons for the survival of the Internet as it is today. Using UDP is not a solution, because only in the beginning the throughput is higher compared to a TCP connection until everyone uses UDP. After that, congestion is the standard case and data transmission is less than predictable. Even under heavy load, TCP guarantees at least sharing of the bandwidth.

10.1.2 Slow start

TCP's reaction to a missing acknowledgement is quite drastic, but necessary to get rid of congestion fast enough. The behaviour TCP shows after the detection of congestion is called **slow start**.

The sender always calculates a **congestion window** for a receiver. Start size of the congestion window is one segment (TCP packet). Now the sender sends one packet and waits for acknowledgement. If this acknowledgement arrives, the sender increases the congestion window by one, now sending two packets (congestion window = 2). After arrival of the two corresponding acknowledgements, the sender again adds 2 to the congestion window, one for each of the acknowledgements. Now the congestion window equals 4. This scheme doubles the congestion window every time the acknowledgements come back, which takes one round trip time (RTT). This is called the exponential growth of the congestion window in the slow start mechanism.

It is too dangerous to double the congestion window each time because the steps might become too large. Therefore, the exponential growth stops at the **congestion threshold**. As soon as the congestion window reaches the congestion threshold, further increase of the transmission rate is only linear by adding 1 to the congestion window each time the acknowledgements come back.

Linear increase continues until a time-out at the sender occurs due to a missing acknowledgement, or until the sender detects a gap in transmitted data because of continuous acknowledgements for the same packet. In either case the sender sets the congestion threshold to half of the current congestion window. The congestion window itself is set to one segment and the sender starts sending a single segment. The exponential growth as described above starts once more up to the new congestion threshold, then the window grows in linear fashion.

10.1.3 Fast retransmit/fast recovery

These are two reasons, leading to a reduction of the congestion threshold, as mentioned before. One is a sender receiving continuous acknowledgements for the same packet. This informs the sender about two things. One is that the receiver got all packets up to the acknowledged packet in sequence. In TCP, a receiver sends acknowledgements only if it receives any packets from the sender. Thus, receiving acknowledgements from a receiver shows additionally that the receiver continuously receives something from the sender. Therefore, the gap in the packet stream is not due to severe congestion, but a simple packet loss due to a transmission error. The sender can now retransmit the missing packet(s) before the timer expires. This behaviour is called **fast retransmit**.

Furthermore, the receipt of acknowledgements shows that there is no congestion justifying a slow start. The sender can continue with the current congestion window. The sender performs a **fast recovery** from the packet loss. This mechanism can improve the efficiency of TCP dramatically.

The other reason for activating slow start mentioned in the last section was a time-out due to a missing acknowledgement. This is the only situation TCP using fast retransmit/fast recovery interprets as congestion in the network and activates the slow start mechanism.

10.1.4 Implications on mobility

While slow start is one of the most useful mechanisms in fixed networks, it drastically decreases the efficiency of TCP if used together with mobile receivers or senders. The reason for this is the use of slow start under the wrong assumptions. From a missing acknowledgement, slow start concludes a congestion situation. While this may also happen in networks with mobile and wireless end-systems, it is not the main reason for packet loss.

Error rates on wireless links are much higher compared to fixed fibre or copper links. Thus, packet loss is much more common and cannot always be compensated for by layer two retransmissions. Trying to retransmit on layer two could, for example, trigger TCP retransmission if it takes too long. Now layer two faces the problem of transmitting the same packet twice over a probably bad link. Detecting these duplicates on layer two is not an option, because more and more connections use end-to-end encryption, making it impossible to look into the packet.

Furthermore, mobility itself can cause packet loss. There are many situations where a soft handover from one access point to another is not possible for a mobile end-system. Using, for example, mobile IP, there could still be some packets in transit to the old foreign agent while the mobile node moves to the new foreign agent. It may now be the case that the old foreign agent cannot forward those packets to the new foreign agent or not even buffer the packets if disconnection of the mobile node takes too long. This packet loss has nothing to do with wireless access but is caused by the problems of rerouting traffic.

The TCP mechanism detecting missing acknowledgements via time-outs and concluding packet loss due to congestion cannot distinguish between the different causes. TCP reacts with slow start, which does not help in the case of transmission errors over wireless links and which does not really help during handover. This behaviour results in a severe performance degradation of an unchanged TCP if used together with wireless links or mobile nodes.

However, one cannot change TCP completely just to support mobile users or wireless links. The same arguments that were given to keep IP unchanged also apply for TCP. The installed base of computers using TCP is too large to be changed and, more important, mechanisms such as slow start keep the Internet operable. Every enhancement to TCP, therefore, has to remain compatible to the standard TCP and must not jeopardize the cautious behaviour of TCP in case of congestion.

10.2 Indirect TCP

Two competing insights led to the development of indirect TCP (I-TCP) (Bakre, 1995). One is that TCP performs poorly together with wireless links, the other is that TCP within the fixed network cannot be changed. Therefore, I-TCP segments a TCP connection into a fixed part and a wireless part. Figure 10.1 shows an example with a mobile host connected via a wireless link and an access point

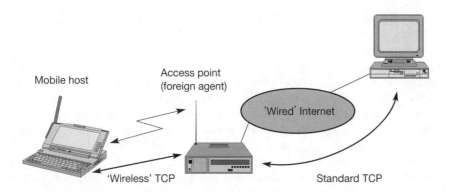

Figure 10.1
Indirect TCP segments
a TCP connection into
two parts

to the 'wired' Internet where the correspondent host resides. The correspondent node could also use wireless access. Then the following would also be applied to the access link of the correspondent host.

Between the fixed computer and the access point standard TCP is used. Thus, no computer in the Internet recognizes any changes to TCP. Instead of the mobile host, now the access point terminates the standard TCP connection, acting as a proxy. This means that the access point is now seen as the mobile host for the fixed host and as the fixed host for the mobile host. Between the access point and the mobile host, a special TCP, adapted to wireless links, is used. However, changing TCP for the wireless link is not a requirement. Even an unchanged TCP can benefit from the much shorter round trip time, thus starting retransmission much faster. A good place for segmenting the connection between mobile host and correspondent host is at the foreign agent of mobile IP. The foreign agent controls the mobility of the mobile host anyway and can also hand over the connection to the next foreign agent when the mobile host moves on. However, one can also imagine separating the TCP connections at a special server, e.g., at the entry point to a mobile phone network.

The correspondent host in the fixed network does not notice the wireless link or the segmentation of the connection. The foreign agent acts as a proxy and relays all data in both directions. If the correspondent host sends a packet, the foreign agent acknowledges this packet. Then the foreign agent tries to forward the packet to the mobile host. If the mobile host receives the packet, it acknowledges the packet. However, this acknowledgement is only used by the foreign agent. If a packet is lost on the wireless link due to a transmission error, the correspondent host would not notice this. However, the foreign agent tries to retransmit this packet locally to maintain reliable data transport.

Similarly, if the mobile host sends a packet, the foreign agent acknowledges this packet and tries to forward it to the correspondent host. If the packet is lost on the wireless link, the mobile hosts can notice this much faster due to the lower round trip time and can directly retransmit the packet. Packet loss in the wired network is now handled by the foreign agent.

I-TCP requires several actions as soon as a handover takes place. As Figure 10.2 demonstrates, not only the packets have to be redirected using, e.g., mobile IP. In the example shown, the access points act as proxies buffering packets for retransmission. After the handover, the old proxy must forward buffered data to the new proxy because it has already acknowledged the data. As explained in chapter 9, after registration with the new foreign agent, this new foreign agent can inform the old one about its location to enable packet forwarding. Besides buffer content, the sockets of the proxy, too, must migrate to the new foreign agent located in the access point. The socket reflects the current state of the TCP connection, i.e., sequence number, addresses, ports etc. No new connection may be established for the mobile host, and the correspondent host must not see any changes in connection state.

Several **advantages** come with I-TCP:

- I-TCP does not require any changes in the TCP protocol as used by the hosts in the fixed network or other hosts in a wireless network that do not use this optimization. Thus, all current optimizations for TCP still work between the foreign agent and the correspondent host.
- Due to the strict partitioning into two connections, transmission errors on the wireless link, i.e., lost packets, cannot propagate into the fixed network. Without partitioning, retransmission of lost packets would take place between mobile host and correspondent host across the whole network. Now only packets in sequence without gaps leave the foreign agent.
- It is always dangerous to introduce new mechanisms into a huge network such as the Internet without exactly knowing their behaviour. However,

Figure 10.2
Socket and state migration after handover of a mobile host

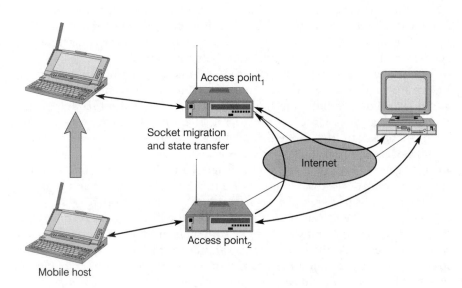

new mechanisms are needed to improve TCP performance (e.g., disabling slow start under certain circumstances), but with I-TCP only between the mobile host and the foreign agent. Different solutions can be tested or used at the same time without jeopardizing the stability of the Internet. Furthermore, optimization of these new mechanisms is quite simple because they only cover one single hop.

- The short delay between the mobile host and foreign agent can be determined and is independent of other traffic streams. Therefore, an optimized TCP can use precise time-outs to guarantee retransmission as fast as possible. Even standard TCP benefits from the short round trip time, thus recovering faster from packet loss.
- Partitioning into two connections also allows the use of a different transport layer protocol between the foreign agent and the mobile host or the use of compressed headers etc. The foreign agent can now act as a gateway to translate between the different protocols.

But the idea of segmentation in I-TCP also comes with some **disadvantages**:

- The loss of the end-to-end semantics of TCP might cause problems if the foreign agent partitioning the TCP connection crashes. If a sender receives an acknowledgement, it assumes that the receiver got the packet. Receiving an acknowledgement now only means (for the mobile host and a correspondent host) that the foreign agent received the packet. The correspondent node does not know anything about the partitioning, thus a crashing access node may also crash applications running on the correspondent node assuming reliable end-to-end delivery.
- In practical use, an increased handover latency may be much more problematic. All packets sent by the correspondent host are buffered by the foreign agent besides forwarding them to the mobile host (if the TCP connection is split at the foreign agent). The foreign agent removes a packet from the buffer as soon as the appropriate acknowledgement arrives. If the mobile host now performs a handover to another foreign agent, it takes a while before the old foreign agent can forward the buffered data to the new foreign agent. During this time more packets may arrive. All these packets have to be forwarded to the new foreign agent first before it can start forwarding the new packets redirected to it.
- The foreign agent must be a trusted entity because the TCP connections end at this point. If users apply end-to-end encryption, e.g., according to RFC 1827 (Atkinson, 1995), the foreign agent has to be integrated into all security mechanisms.

10.3 Snooping TCP

One of the drawbacks of I-TCP is the segmentation of the single TCP connection into two TCP connections, thereby losing the original end-to-end TCP semantic. The following TCP enhancement works completely transparently and leaves the TCP end-to-end connection intact. The main function of the enhancement is to buffer data close to the mobile host to perform fast local retransmission in case of packet loss. Again, a good place for the enhancement of TCP could be the foreign agent in the Mobile IP context (see Figure 10.3).

In this approach, the foreign agent buffers all packets with **destination mobile host** and additionally 'snoops' the packet flow in both directions to recognize acknowledgements (Balakrishnan, 1995), (Brewer, 1998). The reason for buffering packets toward the mobile node is to enable the foreign agent to perform a local retransmission in case of packet loss on the wireless link. The foreign agent buffers every packet until it receives an acknowledgement from the mobile host. If the foreign agent does not receive an acknowledgement from the mobile host within a certain amount of time, either the packet or the acknowledgement was lost. Alternatively, the foreign agent could receive a duplicate ACK also showing the loss of a packet. Now the foreign agent retransmits the packet directly from the buffer, thus performing a much faster retransmission compared to the correspondent host. The time out for acknowledgements can be set much shorter, for it reflects only the delay of one hop plus processing time.

To remain transparent, the foreign agent must not acknowledge data to the correspondent host. Doing so would make the correspondent host believe that the mobile host had received the data. This would violate the end-to-end semantic in case of a foreign agent failure. However, the foreign agent can filter the duplicate acknowledgements to avoid unnecessary retransmissions of data from the correspondent host. If the foreign agent now crashes, the time-out of the correspondent host still works and triggers a retransmission. Furthermore, the foreign agent may discard duplicates of packets already retransmitted locally and acknowledged by the mobile host. This avoids unnecessary traffic on the wireless link.

Data transfer from the mobile host with **destination correspondent host** works as follows. The foreign agent snoops into the packet stream to detect gaps in the sequence numbers of TCP. As soon as the foreign agent detects a missing packet, it returns a negative acknowledgement (NACK) to the mobile host. The

Figure 10.3
Snooping TCP as a
transparent TCP
extension

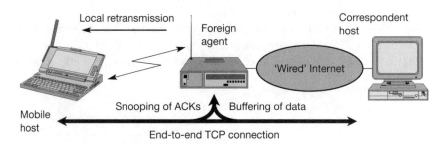

mobile host can now at once retransmit the missing packet. Reordering of packets is done automatically at the correspondent host by TCP.

Extending the functions of a foreign agent with a 'snooping' TCP has several **advantages:**

- A great advantage of this approach is the preservation of the end-to-end TCP semantic. No matter at what time the foreign agent crashes (if this is the location of the buffering and snooping mechanisms), neither the correspondent host nor the mobile host have an inconsistent view of the TCP connection as is possible with I-TCP. The approach automatically falls back to standard TCP if the enhancements stop working.
- No correspondent host needs to be changed, most of the enhancements are in the foreign agent. Supporting only the packet stream from the correspondent host to the mobile host does not even require changes in the mobile host.
- A nice effect of this approach is that it needs no handover of state as soon as the mobile host moves to another foreign agent. Assume there might still be data in the buffer not transferred to the next foreign agent. All that happens is a time-out at the correspondent host and retransmission of the packets, possibly already to the new care-of address.
- Furthermore, it does not matter if the next foreign agent uses the enhancement or not. If not, the approach automatically falls back to the standard solution. This is one of the problems of I-TCP, for the old foreign agent may have already signalled the correct receipt of data via acknowledgements to the correspondent host and now has to transfer these packets to the mobile host via the new foreign agent.

However, the simplicity of the scheme also results in some **disadvantages:**

- Snooping TCP does not isolate the behaviour of the wireless link as good as I-TCP. Assume for example that it takes some time until the foreign agent can successfully retransmit a packet from its buffer due to problems on the wireless link. Although the time-out in the foreign agent may be much shorter than the one of the correspondent host, after a while the time-out in the correspondent host triggers a retransmission. Thus, the problems on the wireless link are now visible also for the correspondent host and not fully isolated. The quality of the isolation snooping TCP offers strongly depends on the quality of the wireless link, time-out values, and further traffic characteristics.
- Using negative acknowledgements between the foreign agent and the mobile host assumes additional mechanisms on the mobile host. Thus, this approach is no longer transparent for arbitrary mobile hosts.
- Finally, all efforts for snooping and buffering data may be useless if certain encryption schemes are applied end-to-end between the correspondent host and mobile host. Using IP encapsulation security payload (RFC 1827, (Atkinson, 1995)) the TCP protocol header will be encrypted, thus snooping on the sequence numbers will not work any longer. Furthermore,

retransmitting data from the foreign agent may not work any longer because many security schemes prevent replay attacks – and retransmitting data from the foreign agent may be misinterpreted as replay.[26] Encrypting end-to-end is the way many applications go, therefore, it is not clear how this scheme could be used in the future.

10.4 Mobile TCP

Dropping packets due to a handover or higher bit error rates is not the only phenomenon of wireless links and mobility. Another is the occurrence of lengthy and/or frequent disconnections. For mobile users it happens quite often that they cannot connect at all. Examples are islands of wireless LANs inside buildings without coverage of the whole campus. What happens to standard TCP in the case of disconnection?

A TCP sender tries to retransmit data controlled by a retransmission timer that doubles with each unsuccessful retransmission attempt, up to a maximum of one minute. This means that the sender tries to retransmit an unacknowledged packet every minute and will give up after 12 retransmissions. What happens if connectivity is back again earlier? Even then, no data is successfully transmitted for a period of one minute! The retransmission time-out is still valid and the sender has to wait. Furthermore, the sender goes into slow-start because it assumes congestion.

What happens in the case of I-TCP if the mobile is disconnected? The proxy has to buffer more and more data, and thus, the longer the period of disconnection is, the more buffer is needed. Additionally, if a handover follows the disconnection, which is typical, even more state has to be transferred to the new proxy. The snooping approach also suffers from being disconnected. The mobile will not be able to send ACKs, thus, snooping cannot help in this situation.

The **M-TCP (mobile TCP)**[27] approach has the same goals as I-TCP and snooping TCP: to prevent the sender window from shrinking if bit errors or disconnection but not congestion cause current problems. M-TCP wants to improve overall throughput, to lower the delay, to maintain end-to-end semantics of TCP, and to provide a more efficient handover. Additionally, M-TCP is especially adapted to the problems arising from lengthy or frequent disconnections (Brown, 1997).

M-TCP splits the TCP connection into two parts as I-TCP does. An unmodified TCP is used on the standard host-**supervisory host (SH)** connection, while an optimized TCP is used on the SH-MH connection. The supervisory host is responsible for exchanging data between both parts similar to the proxy in I-TCP (see Figure 10.1). The M-TCP approach assumes a relatively low bit error rate on the wireless link. Therefore, it does not perform caching/retransmission of data via the SH. If a packet is lost on the wireless link, it has to be retransmitted by the original sender. This maintains the TCP end-to-end semantics.

The SH monitors all packets sent to the MH and ACKs returned from the MH. If the SH does not receive an ACK for some time, it assumes that the MH is disconnected. It then chokes the sender by setting the sender's window size to 0. Setting the window size to 0 forces the sender to go into **persistent mode**, i.e., the state of the sender will not change no matter how long the receiver is disconnected. This means that the sender will not try to retransmit data. As soon as the SH (either the old SH or a new SH) detects connectivity again, it reopens the window of the sender to the old value. Thus, the sender can continue sending at full speed. This mechanism does not require changes to the sender's TCP.

On the wireless side an adapted TCP is used that can recover from packet loss much faster. This modified TCP does not use slow start, thus, M-TCP needs a **bandwidth manager** to implement fair sharing over the wireless link.

The **advantages** of M-TCP are the following:

- M-TCP maintains the TCP end-to-end semantics. The SH does not send any ACK itself but forwards the ACKs from the MH.
- If the MH is disconnected, M-TCP avoids useless retransmissions, slow starts or breaking connections by simply shrinking the sender's window to 0.
- Since M-TCP does not buffer data in the SH as I-TCP does, it is not necessary to forward buffers to a new SH. Lost packets will be automatically retransmitted to the new SH.

The lack of buffers and changing TCP on the wireless part also has some **disadvantages:**

- As the SH does not act as proxy as in I-TCP, packet loss on the wireless link due to bit errors is propagated to the sender. M-TCP assumes low bit error rates, which is not always a valid assumption.
- A modified TCP on the wireless link not only requires modifications to the MH protocol software but also new network elements like the bandwidth manager.

10.5 Fast retransmit/fast recovery

As described in section 10.1.4, moving to a new foreign agent can cause packet loss or time out at mobile hosts or corresponding hosts. TCP concludes congestion and goes into slow start, although there is no congestion. Section 10.1.3 showed the mechanisms of fast recovery/fast retransmit a host can use after receiving duplicate acknowledgements, thus concluding a packet loss without congestion.

The idea presented by Caceres (1995) is to artificially force the fast retransmit behaviour on the mobile host and correspondent host side. As soon as the mobile host registers at a new foreign agent using mobile IP, it starts sending duplicated acknowledgements to correspondent hosts. The proposal is to send three duplicates. This forces the corresponding host to go into fast retransmit mode and not to start slow start, i.e., the correspondent host continues to send with the same rate it did before the mobile host moved to another foreign agent.

As the mobile host may also go into slow start after moving to a new foreign agent, this approach additionally puts the mobile host into fast retransmit. Thus, the mobile host retransmits all unacknowledged packets using the current congestion window size without going into slow start.

The **advantage** of this approach is its simplicity. Only minor changes in the mobile host's software already result in a performance increase. No foreign agent or correspondent host has to be changed.

One main **disadvantage** of this scheme is the insufficient isolation of packet losses. Forcing fast retransmission increases the efficiency, but retransmitted packets still have to cross the whole network between correspondent host and mobile host. Furthermore, if the handover from one foreign agent to another takes a longer time, the correspondent host will have started retransmission already. The approach focuses on loss due to handover, thus packet loss due to problems on the wireless link is not considered. Finally, this approach requires more co-operation between the mobile IP and TCP layer making it harder to change one without influencing the other.

10.6 Transmission/time-out freezing

While the approaches presented so far can handle short interruptions of the connection, either due to handover or transmission errors on the wireless link, some were designed for longer interruptions of transmission. Examples are the use of mobile hosts in a car driving into a tunnel, thus losing its connection to, e.g., a satellite (however, many tunnels and subways provide connectivity via a mobile phone), or a user moving into a cell with no capacity left over. In this case, the mobile phone system will interrupt the connection. The reaction of TCP, even with the enhancements of above, would be a disconnection after a time out.

Quite often, the MAC layer has already noticed connection problems, before the connection is actually interrupted from a TCP point of view. Additionally, the MAC layer knows the real reason for the interruption and does not assume congestion, as TCP would. Therefore, the MAC layer can inform the TCP layer of an upcoming loss of connection or that the current interruption is not caused by congestion. TCP can now stop sending and 'freezes' the current state of its congestion window and further timers. If the MAC layer notices the upcoming interruption early enough, mobile host and correspondent host can be informed. With a fast interruption of the wireless link, additional mechanisms in the access point are needed to inform the correspondent host of the reason for interruption. Otherwise, the correspondent host goes into slow start assuming congestion and finally breaks the connection.

As soon as the MAC layer detects connectivity again, it signals TCP that it can resume operation at exactly the same point where it had been forced to stop. For TCP time simply does not advance, and thus no timers expire.

The **advantage** of this approach is that it offers a way to resume TCP connections even after longer interruptions of the connectivity. Furthermore, it is independent of any other TCP mechanism, such as acknowledgements or sequence numbers, thus it may be used together with encrypted data. However there are some severe **disadvantages** of this scheme. Not only the software on the mobile host has to be changed. To be more effective, the correspondent host cannot remain unchanged. All mechanisms rely on the capability of the MAC layer to detect future interruptions. Finally, freezing the state of TCP does not help in case of some encryption schemes that use time-dependent random numbers. These schemes need resynchronization after interruption.

10.7 Selective retransmission

A very useful extension of TCP is the use of selective retransmission. TCP acknowledgements are cumulative, i.e., they acknowledge in-order receipt of packets up to a certain packet. If a single packet is lost, the sender has to retransmit everything starting from the lost packet (go-back-n retransmission). This obviously wastes bandwidth, not only in the mobile case, but in any network.

Using RFC 2018 (Mathis, 1996), TCP can indirectly request a selective retransmission of packets. The receiver can acknowledge single packets, not only trains of in-sequence packets. The sender can now precisely determine which packet is needed and can retransmit it.

The **advantage** of this approach is obvious: a sender retransmits only the lost packets. This lowers bandwidth requirements and helps especially in case of slow wireless links. The gain in efficiency is not restricted to wireless links and mobile environments. Using selective retransmission is also beneficial in all other networks. However, there might be the minor **disadvantage** of more complex software on the receiver side, because now more buffer is necessary to resequence data and to wait for gaps to be filled. But while memory sizes and CPU performance permanently increase, the bandwidth of the air interface remains almost the same. Therefore, the higher complexity is no real disadvantage any longer as it was in the early days of TCP.

10.8 Transaction oriented TCP

Assume an application running on the mobile host that sends a short request to a server from time to time, which respond with a short message. If the application requires reliable transport of the packets, it may use TCP (many applications of this kind use UDP and solve reliability on an higher, application-oriented layer).

Using TCP now requires several packets over the wireless link. First of all, TCP uses a three-way handshake to establish the connection. At least one packet is needed for transmission of the request, and finally TCP requires three more packets to close the connection via a three-way handshake. Assuming connections with a lot of traffic or with a long duration, this overhead is minimal. But in an example of only one data packet, TCP needs seven packets altogether.

This overhead led to the development of a transaction oriented TCP (T-TCP, RFC 1644 (Braden, 1994)). T-TCP can combine packets for connection establishment and connection release with user data packets. This can reduce the number of packets down to only two instead of seven.

The obvious **advantage** for certain applications is the reduction in the overhead which standard TCP has for connection setup and connection release. However, T-TCP is not the original TCP anymore, so it requires changes in the mobile host and all correspondent hosts, which certainly is a major **disadvantage.** This solution no longer hides mobility.

10.9 Summary

This chapter introduced the problems of TCP as a connection-oriented protocol in a mobile environment. The basic assumptions while designing the TCP have been completely different from the reality of using mobile hosts. Particularly, the mechanisms of TCP that make the protocol network-friendly and, thus, keep the Internet together, cause severe efficiency problems. TCP assumes a network congestion if acknowledgements do not arrive in time.

However, wireless links have much higher error rates compared to, e.g., a twisted pair or fibre optics, that way causing higher packet loss rates. Furthermore, mobility itself, i.e., the handover between different access points, can cause packet loss without any congestion in the network. In either case, TCP goes into a slow start state reducing its sending rate drastically.

Several solutions have been proposed to increase efficiency of TCP in mobile environments. Table 10.1 shows an overview of the mechanisms presented together with some advantages and disadvantages. The approaches are not all exclusive, but can be combined. Selective retransmission, for example, can be used together with the others and can even be applied to fixed networks.

An unchanged TCP faces even more problems when used over satellite links or in general links to a spacecraft (ranging from an LEO to interplanetary deep-space probes). The main problems are the extremely high RTT, error-prone links, limited link capacity, intermittent connectivity, and asymmetric channels (up to 1,000:1). Asymmetric channels with, for example, a high bandwidth from the spacecraft to ground control, limit throughput due to the limited capacity for the acknowledgements on the return path. (Durst, 1997) presents a set of TCP enhancements, primarily a **selective negative acknowledgement (SNACK)** option, that adapt TCP to the requirements in space communication. The set of

Approach	Mechanism	Advantages	Disadvantages
Indirect TCP	Splits TCP connection into two connections	Isolation of wireless link, simple	Loss of TCP semantics, higher latency at handover
Snooping TCP	'Snoops' data and acknowledgements, local retransmission	Transparent for end-to-end connection, MAC integration possible	Problematic with encryption, insufficient isolation of wireless link
M-TCP	Splits TCP connection, chokes sender via window size	Maintains end-to-end semantics, handles long term and frequent disconnections	Bad isolation of wireless link, processing overhead due to bandwidth management
Fast retransmit/ fast recovery	Avoids slow-start after roaming	Simple and efficient	Mixed layers, not transparent
Transmission/ time-out freezing	Freezes TCP state at disconnection, resumes after reconnection	Independent of content, works for longer interruptions	Changes in TCP required, MAC dependent
Selective retransmission	Retransmits only lost data	Very efficient	Slightly more complex receiver software, more buffer space needed
Transaction oriented TCP	Combines connection setup/release and data transmission	Efficient for certain applications	Changes in TCP required, not transparent

Table 10.1
Overview of several enhancements to TCP for mobility

protocols developed for space communication is known as **space communications protocol standards (SCPS)**, the extended TCP is called **SCPS-transport protocol (SCPS-TP)**.

As bandwidth is typically very limited in wireless environments, low protocol overhead is of particular importance. Using tunnelling schemes as in mobile

IP (see section 9.1) together with TCP, results in protocol headers of 60 byte in case of IPv4 and 100 byte for IPv6 due to the larger addresses. (Degermark, 1997) proposes a **header compression** scheme particularly suitable for error-prone links and multicast communication. Especially delay sensitive applications like, e.g., interactive games, with many small packets, benefit from small headers.

10.10 Review exercises

1   Compare the different types of transmission errors that can occur in wireless and wired networks. What additional role does mobility play?

2   What is the reaction of standard TCP in case of packet loss? In what situation does this reaction make sense and why is it quite often problematic in the case of wireless networks and mobility?

3   Can the problems using TCP be solved by replacing TCP with UDP? Where could this be useful and why is it quite often dangerous for network stability?

4   How and why does I-TCP isolate problems on the wireless link? What are the main drawbacks of this solution?

5   Show the interaction of mobile IP with standard TCP. Draw the packet flow from a fixed host to a mobile host via a foreign agent. Then a handover takes place. What are the following actions of mobile IP and how does TCP react?

6   Now show the required steps during handover for the solutions proposed in this chapter. What are the state and function of foreign agents, home agents, correspondent host, mobile host and care-of address before, during, and after handover? What information has to be transferred to which entity in order to maintain consistency for the TCP connection?

7   What are the influences of encryption on the proposed schemes? Consider for example IP security that can encrypt the payload, i.e., the TCP packet.

8   Name further optimizations of TCP regarding the protocol overhead which is important especially for narrow band connections.

10.11 References

Atkinson, R. (1995) *IP Encapsulating Security Payload (ESP)*, RFC 1827.

Bakre, A.; Badrinath, B. (1995) 'I-TCP: Indirect TCP for mobile hosts', proceedings of the 15th International Conference on Distributed Computing Systems (ICDCS), Vancouver, Canada.

Balakrishnan, H.; Seshan, S.; Katz, R.H. (1995) 'Improving reliable transport and handoff performance in cellular wireless networks', *Wireless Networks*, J.C. Baltzer, 1.

Braden, R. (1994) *T-TCP – TCP extensions for transactions functional specification*, RFC 1644.

Brewer, E.A.; Katz, R.H.; Chawathe, Y.; Gribble, S.D.; Hodes, T.; Nguyen, G.; Stemm, M.; Henderson, T.; Amit, E.; Balakrishnen, H.; Fox, A.; Padmanabhan, V.; Seshan, S. (1998) 'A network architecture for heterogeneous mobile computing', *IEEE Personal Communications*, 5, (5)

Brown, K.; Singh, S. (1997) 'M-TCP: TCP for mobile cellular networks', *ACM Computer Communications Review*, 27, (5).

Caceres, R.; Iftode, L. (1995) 'Improving the performance of reliable transport protocols in mobile computing environments', *IEEE Journal on Selected Areas in Communications,* 13, (5).

Degermark, M.; Engan, M.; Nordgren, B.; Pink, S. (1997) 'Low-loss TCP/IP header compression for wireless networks', *Wireless Networks*, J.C. Baltzer, no. 3.

Durst, R.C.; Miller, G.J., Travis, E.J. (1997) 'TCP extensions for space communications', *Wireless Networks,* J.C. Baltzer, no. 3.

Mathis, M.; Mahdavi, J.; Floyd, S.; Romanow, A. (1996) *TCP selective acknowledgement options*, RFC 2018.

Postel, J. (1981) *Transmission Control Protocol,* RFC 793.

Stevens, W. R. (1994) *TCP/IP Illustrated, Volume 1: The Protocols*. Addison Wesley Longman Publishing Company, Reading, Massachusetts, USA.

Support for mobility **11**

Transferring data from a sender to a single receiver or many receivers is not enough. Only applications make a communication network useful. However, to use well-known applications from fixed networks, some additional components are needed in a mobile and wireless communication system. Examples are file systems, data bases, security, accounting and billing mechanisms. As the plain hardware has to support user mobility, power consumption is an important issue.

This chapter focuses on two aspects, file systems and access to the **world wide web (WWW).** Some years ago, many research projects dealt with the problems of **distributed file systems.** Some focused on the support of mobile devices, low bandwidth wireless links, and disconnected operation. The main problem for distributed, loosely coupled file systems is the maintenance of consistency. Are all views on the file system the same? What happens if a disconnected user changes data? When and how should the system propagate changes to a user? Section 11.1 discusses several problems and presents some research projects.

However, the success of the WWW shifted the focus of many projects. Currently, a lot of research effort is put into the support of web browsing for mobile users as the web is the application driving the Internet. Thus, section 11.2 explains some basic properties of the web and presents the hypertext transfer protocol (HTTP) and hypertext markup language (HTML) in a short overview. For this section it is important to demonstrate the fundamental problems with HTTP and HTML if used in a mobile network with only low-bandwidth wireless access. The web has been designed for conventional computers and fixed networks. Several new system architectures try to alleviate these problems. These architectures are also good examples for client/server scenarios in wireless environments.

Section 11.3 presenting the **wireless application protocol (WAP)** is the main part of the chapter. WAP is a common effort of many companies and organizations to set up a framework for wireless and mobile web access using many different transport systems. Examples are GSM, GPRS, and UMTS as presented in chapter 4. WAP integrates several communication layers for security mechanisms, transaction-oriented protocols, and application support. In the current WWW these features are not an integral part but add-ons. Furthermore, WAP combines the telephone network and the Internet by integrating telephony applications into the web using its own wireless markup language (WML) and scripting language (WMLScript). Section 11.3 gives many examples. However, the reader should be aware that this is a very recent development and that new applications and mechanisms are still evolving.

11.1 File systems

The general goal of a file system is to support efficient, transparent, and consistent access to files, no matter where the client requesting files or the server(s) offering files are located. **Efficiency** is of special importance for wireless systems as the bandwidth is low and, thus, the protocol overhead and updating operations etc. should be kept at a minimum. **Transparency** addresses the problems of location-dependent views on a file system. In order to support mobility, the file system should provide identical views on directories, file names, access rights etc., independent of the current location. The main problem is **consistency** as section 11.1.1 illustrates in more detail.

General problems are the limited resources on portable devices and the low bandwidth of the wireless access. File systems cannot rely on large caches in the end-system or perform many updates via the wireless link. Furthermore, portable devices may be disconnected for a longer period of time. Hardware and software components of portable devices often do not follow standard computer architectures or operating systems respectively. Mobile phones, PDAs, and other devices have their own operating system, hardware, and application software. Portable devices are not as reliable as desktop systems or traditional file servers.

Standard file systems like network file system (NFS) are very inefficient, almost unusable in a mobile and wireless environment (Honeyman, 1995). Traditional file systems do not expect disconnection, low bandwidth connections, and high latencies. In order to support disconnected operation, the portable device may replicate files or single objects. This can be done in advance by pre-fetching or while fetching data (caching). The main problem is consistency of the copy with the original data. The following section presents some more problems and solutions regarding consistency.

11.1.1 Consistency
The basic problem for distributed file systems that allow replication of data for performance reasons is the consistency of replicated objects (files, parts of files, parts of a data structure etc.). What happens, for example, if two portable devices hold copies of the same object, then one device changes the value of the object and after that both devices read the value? Without further mechanisms one portable device reads an old value.

In order to avoid inconsistencies many traditional systems apply mechanisms to maintain a permanent consistent view for all users of a file system. This **strong consistency** is achieved by atomic updates similar to database systems. A writer of an object locks the object, changes the object, and unlocks the object after the change. If an object is locked, no other device can write the object. Cached objects are invalidated after a change. Maintaining strong consistency is not only very expensive in terms of exchanging updates via the wireless link, but sometimes even impossible. Assume a temporarily disconnected device with several objects in its cache. It is impossible to update the objects or invalidate them. Furthermore, locking the cached objects may not be visible to other users.

One solution is to forbid access to disconnected objects. This would basically prohibit any real application based on the file system. Thus, mobile systems have to use a **weak consistency** model for file systems. Weak consistency implies certain periods of inconsistency that have to be tolerated for performance reasons. However, the overall file system should still remain consistent and, thus, conflict resolution strategies are needed for reintegration. **Reintegration** is the process of merging objects from different users resulting in one consistent file system. A user could hold a copy of an object, disconnect from the network, change the object, and reconnect again. Then, the changed object has to be reintegrated. A **conflict** may occur, e.g., if an object has been changed by two users working with two copies. During reintegration the file system may notice that both copies differ, the conflict resolution strategy has to decide which copy to use or how to proceed. The system may detect conflicts based on time stamps, version numbering, comparison etc.

Assume, for example, that several people are writing an article. Each person is working on one section using his or her own laptop. As long as everyone stays within his or her section reintegration is simple. As soon as one person makes a copy of another section and starts changing, reintegration becomes difficult and is content-dependent. The examples in the following section show different solutions for file systems. These solutions vary in the granularity of caching and pre-fetching (files, directories, sub-trees, disk partitions), in the location of mobility support (fixed network and/or mobile computer), and in their conflict resolution strategies.

11.1.2 Examples
The predecessor of many distributed file systems that can be used for mobile operation is the Andrew file system (AFS, (Howard, 1988)). The following gives some examples of basic research systems.

11.1.2.1 Coda
Coda is the successor of AFS and offers two different types of replication: server replication and caching on clients. Disconnected clients work only on the cache, i.e., applications use only cached replicated files. Figure 11.1 shows the

Figure 11.1

Application, cache, and
server in Coda

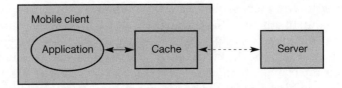

cache between an application and the server. Coda is a transparent extension of the client's cache manager.

In order to provide all necessary files for disconnected work, Coda offers extensive mechanisms for pre-fetching of files while still connected, called **hoarding** (Kistler, 1992). If the client is connected to the server with a strong connection (see Figure 11.2), hoarding transparently pre-fetches files currently used. This automatic data collection is necessary for it is impossible for a standard user to know all the files currently used. While standard programs and application data may be familiar to a user, he or she typically does not know anything about the numerous small system files needed in addition (e.g., profiles, shared libraries, drivers, fonts).

Furthermore, a user can pre-determine a list of files which Coda should explicitly pre-fetch. Additionally, a user can assign priorities to certain programs. Coda now decides on the current cache content using the list and a last recently used (LRU) strategy.

As soon as the client is disconnected, applications work on the replicates (see Figure 11.2, **emulating**). Coda follows an optimistic approach and, thus, allows read and write access to all files. The system keeps a record of changed files, but does not maintain a history of changes for each files. Thus, the cache always has only one replicate (possibly changed). After reconnection Coda compares the replicates with the files on the server as described in Kistler (1992). If Coda notices that two different users have changed a file, reintegration of this file fails and Coda saves the changed file as a copy on the server to allow for manual reintegration.

The optimistic approach of Coda is very coarse grained, working on whole files. The success of Coda relies on the fact that files in UNIX are seldom written by more than one user. Most files are just read, only some files are changed. Experiences with Coda showed that only 0.72 per cent of all file accesses resulted in write conflicts (Satyanarayanan, 1993). Considering only user files this is reduced to merely 0.3 per cent. However, this low conflict rate is not applicable to arbitrary shared files as used in, e.g., computer-supported cooperative work (CSCW). Therefore,

Figure 11.2

States of a client
in Coda

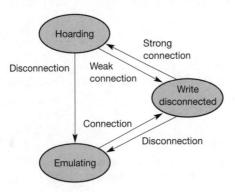

the tool application specific resolver (ASR) was developed to automate conflict resolution after failed reintegration (Kumar, 1993). A general problem of these tools is that they can only work after-the-fact. This means that the tools have to reconstruct a history of changes based on the replicate because Coda does not record every single change.

Another problem of Coda is the definition of a conflict. Coda detects only write conflicts, i.e., if two or more users change a file. Now consider two files f_1 and f_2. One client uses values from files f_1 and f_2 to calculate something and stores the result in file f_1. The other client uses values from files f_1 and f_2 to calculate something else and stores the result in file f_2. Coda would not detect any problem during reintegration of the files. However, the results may not reflect the correct values based on the files. The order of execution plays an important role. To solve this problem, a simple transaction mechanism was introduced into Coda as an option, the so-called isolation-only transactions (IOT, (Lu, 1994)). IOT allows to group certain operations and checks them for serial execution.

While in the beginning Coda simply distinguished the two states 'hoarding' while connected and 'emulating' while disconnected, later the loosely connected state **write disconnected** was integrated, too (see Figure 11.2, (Mummert, 1995)). If a client is only weakly connected, Coda decides if it is worthwhile to fetch a file via this connection or to let the user wait until a better connection is available. In other words, Coda models the patience of a user and weighs it against the cost of fetching the file required by the user.

Figure 11.2 illustrates the three states of a client in Coda. The client only performs hoarding while a strong connection to the server exists. If the connection breaks completely, the client goes into emulating and uses only the cached replicates. If the client loses the strong connection and only a weak connection remains, it does not perform hoarding, but decides if it should fetch the file in case of a cache miss considering user patience and file type. The weak connection, however, is not used for reintegration of files.

11.1.2.2 Little Work

The distributed file system Little Work is, like Coda, an extension of AFS (Huston, 1993), (Honeyman, 1995). Little Work only requires changes to the cache manager of the client and detects write conflicts during reintegration. Little Work has no specific tools for reintegration and offers no transaction service.

However, Little Work uses more client states to maintain consistency.

- **Connected:** The operation of the client is normal, i.e., no special mechanisms from Little Work are required. This mode needs a continuous high bandwidth as available in typical office environments using, e.g., a WLAN.
- **Partially connected:** If a client has only a lower bandwidth connection, but still the possibility to communicate continuously, the client is referred to as partially connected. Examples for this type of network are packet radio networks. These networks typically charge based on the amount of traffic

and not based on the duration of a connection. This client state allows to use cache consistency protocols similar to the normal state, but with a delayed write to the server to lower communication cost if the client changes the file again. This helps to avoid consistency problems, although no high-bandwidth connection is available.

- **Fetch only:** If there is only a network available that offers connections on demand, the client goes into the fetch only state. Example networks of this type are cellular networks such as GSM with costs per call. Now the client uses the replicates in the cache in an optimistic way, but fetches files via the communication link if they are not available in the cache. This enables a user to access all files of the server, but this also tries to minimize communication by working on replicates and reintegrate after reconnection using a continuously high bandwidth link.
- **Disconnected:** Finally, without any network the client is disconnected. Little Work now aborts if a cache miss occurs, otherwise replicates are used.

11.1.2.3 Ficus

In contrast to Coda, Ficus is a distributed file system which is not based on a client/server approach (Popek, 1990), (Heidemann, 1992). Ficus allows the optimistic use of replicates, detects write conflicts, and solves conflicts on directories. Ficus uses so-called **gossip protocols**, an idea many other systems took over later. A mobile computer does not necessarily need to have a direct connection to a server. With the help of other mobile computers it can propagate updates through the network until it reaches a fixed network and the server. Thus, changes on files propagate through the network step-by-step. Furthermore, Ficus tries to minimize the exchange of files that are valid only for a short time, e.g. temporary files. A critical issue for gossip protocols is how fast they propagate to the client that needs this information and how much unnecessary traffic it causes to propagate information to clients that are not interested.

11.1.2.4 MIo-NFS

The system mobile integration of NFS (MIo–NFS) is an extension of the Network File System (NFS, (Guedes, 1995)). In contrast to many other systems, MIo-NFS uses a pessimistic approach with tokens controlling access to files. Only the token-holder for a specific file may change this file. Thus, MIo-NFS avoids write conflicts. Read/write conflicts as discussed in 11.1.2.1 cannot be avoided. MIo-NFS supports three different modes:

- **Connected:** The server handles all access to files as usual.
- **Loosely connected:** Clients use local replicates, exchange tokens over the network, and update files via the network.
- **Disconnected:** The client uses only local replicates. Writing is only allowed if the client is token-holder.

11.2 World wide web

This section discusses some problems that web applications encounter when used in a mobile and wireless environment. The reader should be familiar with the basic concepts of the world wide web, its protocols (HTTP) and language (HTML). Section 11.3 presents a complete framework, the wireless application protocol (WAP), that handles many of the problems discussed here and, thus, this section serves as a basis for this framework. The approaches mentioned in this section are only discussed briefly in favour of a broader presentation of the WAP framework. The first two subsections give short overviews of HTTP and HTML together with their problems in wireless environments. Then, some approaches to improve HTML and HTTP are presented, most of them proprietary. The last subsection introduces different system architectures used for web access, each trying to improve the classic client/server scenario.

11.2.1 Hypertext transfer protocol

The **hypertext transfer protocol (HTTP)** is a stateless, lightweight, application-level protocol for data transfer between servers and clients (Berners-Lee, 1996). An HTTP **transaction** consists of an HTTP **request** issued by a client and an HTTP **response** from a server. Stateless means that all HTTP transactions are independent of each other. HTTP does not 'remember' any transaction, request, or response. This results in a very simple implementation without the need for complex state machines.

A simple request might proceed as follows. GET requests the source following next, here only / indicates the index file in the web root directory (index.html). Additionally, the protocol HTTP and version 1.0 is indicated. As this is not an introduction into HTTP the reader is referred to the extensive literature about the web and its protocols. But everyone can try this, just send the following to port 80 of your web server (using, e.g., telnet):

```
GET / HTTP/1.0
```

The server might answer with something similar to the following (the response):

```
HTTP/1.1 200 OK
Date: Fri, 06 Nov 1998 14:52:12 GMT
Server: Apache/1.3b5
Connection: close
Content-Type: text/html
<HTML>
<HEAD>
<TITLE>Institut f&uuml;r Telematik</TITLE>
</HEAD>
<BODY BGCOLOR="#ffffff">
```

```
<img src="icons/uni/faklogo_de.gif"
ALT=" [Universit&auml;t Karlsruhe, Fakult&auml;t f&uuml;r
Informatik] ">
...
```

The first line contains the status code (200) which shows that everything was ok (not the OK in the plain text, this is also sent with error codes indicating only that everything works). The HTTP header follows with information about date, time, server version, connection information, and type of the following content (the body of the response). Here the content is the (truncated) HTML code of the web page index.html in the root directory of the web server.

HTTP assumes a reliable underlying protocol, typically, TCP is used in the Internet. HTTP version 1.0 establishes a new connection for each request. Some enhancements have been integrated into HTTP version 1.1 (see section 11.2.3). This means, for example, if a web page contains five icons, two pictures, and some text, altogether eight TCP connections will be established – one for the pages itself including the text, five for fetching the icons, and two for the pictures. The typical **request method** of HTTP is GET as already shown, which returns the requested resource. This GET can become conditional if an If-Modified-Since is added to the header, which allows for fetching newer content. HTTP additionally makes it possible to request only the header without a body using the HEAD request. If a client wants to provide data to a function on a server it can use the POST method.

The server may answer with different **status codes**. Examples are the 200 from above indicating that the request has been accepted. Furthermore, a server can redirect a client to another location, it can show that user authentication is needed for a certain resource, that it refuses to fulfil the request, or that it is currently unable to handle the request.

HTTP also supports simple **caching** mechanisms. Caching is useful to avoid unnecessary retransmissions of content that has not changed since the last access. Caches may be located anywhere between a server and a client. Typically, each client maintains a cache locally to minimize delay when jumping back and forth on web pages. Caches can also exist for a whole company, university, region etc. Typically, the same pages will be accessed by many people. Therefore, it makes sense to cache those pages closer to the clients. Different header information supports caching. For example, one can assign an expiry date to a page. This means that an application must not cache this page beyond expiration. A no-cache entry in the header disables caching altogether. This may be useful for pages with dynamic content. Additional information regarding caching mechanisms in HTTP can be found in Berners-Lee (1996).

HTTP causes **many problems** already in fixed networks but even more in wireless networks.

- **Bandwidth and delay:** HTTP has not been designed with low bandwidth/high delay connections in mind. The original environment has been networked workstations running TCP/IP over wired networks with some Mbit/s bandwidth. HTTP protocol headers are quite large and redundant. Many information fields are transferred over and over again with each request because HTTP is stateless. Headers are readable for humans and transferred in plain ASCII. Furthermore, servers transfer content uncompressed, i.e., if applications do not compress content (as is the case for GIF or JPEG coded images), the server will not perform any compression. As TCP connections are typically used for each item on a web page (icons, images etc.), a huge overhead comes with each item. Think of a 50 byte large icon, then a TCP connection has to be established including a three-way-handshake, data transmission, and reliable disconnection. As pointed out in chapter 10, this may imply seven PDUs exchanged between client and server! TCP has not been designed for this transaction like a request/response scheme with only some data exchanged. As also shown in chapter 10, the slow-start mechanism built into TCP can cause additional problems. TCP may be too cautious in the beginning of a transmission, but before it can utilize the available bandwidth, the transmission is over. In other words, TCP typically never leaves the slow-start that way, causing unnecessary high delay. Another problem is caused by the DNS look-up, necessary for many items on a web page, reducing bandwidth and increasing delay even further. Each time a browser reads a hyperlink reference to a new sever it has to resolve the logical name into an IP address before fetching the item from the sever. This requires an additional request to a DNS server over the wireless link adding a round-trip time to the delay.

- **Caching:** Although useful in many cases, caching is quite often disabled by content providers. Many companies want to place advertisements on web pages and need a feedback, e.g., through the number of clicks on this page to estimate the number of potential customers. With a cache between a server and a client, companies cannot get realistic feedback. Either caches need additional mechanisms to create usage profiles or, which is most common, caching is disabled from the beginning using the `no-cache` keyword in the header. Network providers need someone to pay for pages and, therefore, follow this no-caching requirement from their customers. In this case users suffer by downloading the same content again and again from the server. Furthermore, many present-day pages contain dynamic objects that cannot be cached. Examples are access counters, time, date, or other customized items. This content changes over time or for each access; sometimes at least a part of a page is static and can be cached. Many of today's companies generate pages on demand which are customized for each customer (via CGI, ASP etc.). It is not possible to save a bookmark to a point further down the link hierarchy. Instead a user always has to enter the company's pages from the home page. Customization is saved in cookies.[28] This more or less prevents any caching because the names of links are also generated dynamically and the caching algorithms cannot detect access to the same content if the links differ. Additionally, even the homepages of companies are often created dynamically depending on the type of browser, client hardware, client location etc. Even if a cache could store some static content it is often impossible to merge this content with the dynamic remainder of a page. Mobility also quite often inhibits caching because the ways of accessing web servers change over time due to changing access points. However, caches at entry points of mobile networks may save some bandwidth and time. Many security mechanisms also inhibit caching. Authentication is often between a client and a server, not between a client and its cache. Keys for authentication have an associated time-out after which they are not valid anymore, thus caching content for this type of secured transactions is useless.

- **POSTing:** Sending content from a client to a server can cause additional problems if the client is currently disconnected. The POST request cannot be fulfilled in a disconnected state, thus a server could be simulated by accepting the posting via an additional process. But clearly this causes additional problems, e.g., if the real server does not accept the posting or if the server cannot accept the deferred posting.

11.2.2 Hypertext markup language

HTML is broadly used for describing the content of web pages in the world wide web (Raggett, 1998). No matter which version is used, they all share common properties: HTML was designed with standard desktop computers connected with a fixed wire to the Internet in mind. These computers share common properties, such as a relatively high performance (especially when compared to handheld devices), a colour high resolution display (24 bit true colour, 1,200×1,024 pixels is standard), mouse, sound system, and large hard disks.

What do standard handheld devices offer? Due to restrictions in power consumption and form (they should still be 'handheld'), these devices have rather small displays, often only black and white, with a low resolution, very limited user interfaces (touch screens, soft keyboards, voice commands etc.), and also low performance CPUs.

Furthermore, the network connection of desktop computers often consist of 100 Mbit/s LANs, some 6 Mbit/s ADSL connections, or at least a 64 kbit/s ISDN connection. Round-trip delays are in the range of some ms, probably a few 100 ms in transatlantic links. What do today's wireless connections offer in the wide area? 9,600 bit/s for standard GSM, about 100 kbit/s in the future with, e.g., GPRS. Round-trip delays are in the range of some seconds.

Web pages using the current HTML often ignore these differences in end-systems. Pages are designed primarily for a nice presentation of content, not for efficient transfer of this content. HTML itself offers almost no way of optimizing pages for different clients or different transmission technologies. But HTML is not the biggest problem when accessing web pages from wireless handheld clients.

Almost all of today's web pages, especially those of companies, are 'enriched' with special 'features', some using HTML, some not. These features include animated GIFs, Java Applets, Frames, ActiveX controls, multimedia content following different proprietary formats etc. Some of them can be interpreted directly by the client's browser, for some of them a special **plug-in** is needed. These additional content formats cause several problems. First of all, appropriate plug-ins are often only available for the most common computer platforms, not for those many handheld devices, each with its own operating system. If a plug-in was available, the browser would still have the problem of displaying, e.g., a true-colour video on a small black and white display, or displaying a GIF with many 'clickable' areas etc. Many web pages use exactly these GIFs for navigation. The user just has to click in the right area – but what if those GIFs cannot be displayed?

The approaches using content distillation or semantic compression might work with HTML, but those many additional plug-ins each need their own mechanism to translate them into a format useful for a wireless device with limited capabilities. Thus, without additional mechanisms and a more integrated approach, large high-resolution pictures would be transferred to a mobile phone with a low-resolution display causing high costs, because the user does not exactly know the consequences of following a link. Altogether, web pages typically ignore the heterogeneity of end-systems.

11.2.3 Some approaches that might help wireless access
The problems with HTTP and HTML are well-known and encouraged many different proprietary solutions, or better partial solutions. Some of the currently available efforts are:

- **Image scaling:** If a page contains a true colour, high-resolution picture, this picture can be scaled down to fewer colours, lower resolution, or finally to only the title of the picture. The user can then decide to download the picture separately. Furthermore, one can offer clipping, zooming, or detail studies to users if they are interested in a part of the picture.
- **Content transformation:** Many documents are only available in certain formats, e.g. Postscript or portable document format (PDF) (Adobe, 1999). Before transmitting such documents to a client without the appropriate reader, a special converter could translate this document into plain text (e.g. Fox, 1996a).
- **Content extraction/semantic compression:** Besides transforming the content, one could also extract, e.g., headlines or keywords from a document and present only those to a user (e.g. Bickmore, 1997). The user could then decide to download more related to a certain headline or keyword. One could also try to automatically generate an abstract from a given text. This semantic compression is, however, quite difficult for arbitrary text. Extracting headlines is simpler, but sometimes useless if HTML headlines are used for layout purposes and not for structuring a document.

- **Special languages and protocols:** Other approaches try to replace HTML and HTTP with other languages and protocols better adapted to a wireless environment. Examples are handheld device transport protocol (HDTP) and handheld device markup language (HDML) from Unwired Planet (King, 1997). Ideas from these proprietary solutions have been integrated into a broader approach (wireless application protocol) and will be discussed in the next section.
- **Push technologies:** Instead of pulling content from a server, the server could also push content to a client. This avoids the overhead of setting up connections for each item, but is useful only for some content, e.g. news, where users do not have to interact much.

Typically, many of these enhancements will be placed in the fixed network either integrated into the server or into a gateway between the fixed and the mobile network. These application gateways are already used to provide WWW content to users with mobile phones and comprise entities for compression, filtering, content extraction, and automatic adaptation to network characteristics. However, these proprietary approaches typically require enhancements to standard browsers and cannot really handle the broad range of heterogeneous devices. But also the standard transfer protocol for web content HTTP, has also been improved.

HTTP version 1.1 (RFC 2068 (Fielding, 1997)) offers several improvements:

- **Connection re-use:** Clients and servers can use the same TCP connection for several requests and responses. Furthermore, a client may send multiple requests at the beginning of a session, and the server can send all responses in the same order.
- **Caching enhancements:** A cache may now also store cacheable responses to reduce response time and bandwidth for future, equivalent responses. Caching tries to achieve semantic transparency, i.e., a cache should not affect client or server besides increasing the performance. The correctness of cached entries has therefore been enhanced. In order to fetch the most up-to-date appropriate version of an item, the item can be revalidated with the origin server, the entry can be considered as fresh enough, a warning can be included if the freshness has been violated, it can be shown that the item has not been modified etc. Web pages can contain further information about cacheability and semantic transparency. Furthermore, a special tag allows for the identification of content and helps to determine if two different URIs map to the same content. Several more tags determine if content is cacheable, cacheable in private caches only etc.
- **Miscellaneous:** HTTP/1.1 comprises further mechanisms to transfer compressed data, to check message integrity, to authenticate clients, proxies, and servers.

Some kind of state can be introduced into the stateless behaviour of HTTP by using **cookies** (Kristol, 1997). Cookies can set up a long-termed 'session' by storing state upon request. When a server requests storing a cookie on the client's side, this 'starts' the 'session'. Depending on server requirements, a cookie may reflect the current state of browsing, client capabilities, user profiles etc. A session is 'resumed' by returning a cookie to a server. Cookies may have additional attributes, such as a maximum age. However, this cookie mechanism is not really integrated into HTTP and cannot replace real sessions with mechanisms to suspend the session upon user request, to set-back to a certain state etc. Furthermore, many users feel uncomfortable using cookies because it is not obvious what exactly cookies store and what they reveal to servers.

11.2.4 System architectures

The classical underlying system architecture of the WWW is a client/server system. The client, a web browser running as an application on a computer, requests content from a server, the web server running on another computer. Without any enhancements, each click on a hyperlink initiates the transfer of the content the link points to (and possibly much more if the page contains further references – the browser fetches them automatically). The browser uses the protocol HTTP for transfer of content (see 11.2.1). Web pages are described using HTML (see 11.2.2) and many more (proprietary) formats.

As already discussed, caching is a major topic in the web client/server scenario. While caching is also useful for wired computers because it reduces the delay of displaying previously accessed pages, caching is the only way of supporting (partially) disconnected web browsers. Especially on mobile, wireless clients, network connection can be disrupted or quite often be of bad quality. Thus, the first enhancement was the integration of caching into web browsers. This is standard for all of today's browsers (e.g. Netscape, (1999), Microsoft, (1999)). Figure 11.3 shows a mobile client with a web browser running. This browser has an integrated caching mechanism as enhancement. This cache does not perform automatic pre-fetching of pages but stores already transferred content up to a certain limit. A user can then go 'offline' and still browse through the cached content (pages, pictures, multimedia objects etc.). Caching strategies are very simple. The user can for example determine if a check for updating is performed every time he or she accesses a page, only after restarting the browser, or not (i.e., a page has to be refreshed manually).

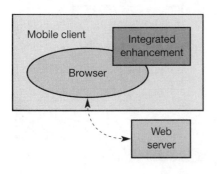
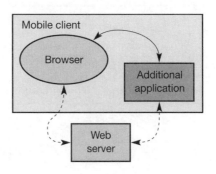

Figure 11.3 (*Left*) Integrated browser enhancement

Figure 11.4 (*Right*) Additional application supporting browsing

Figure 11.4 shows an architecture for an early approach to enhance web access for mobile clients. The initial WebWhacker, for example, is a companion application for the browser that supports pre-fetching of content, caching and disconnected service (BlueSquirrel, 1999). However, this approach is not transparent for a browser as there are now two different ways of accessing content (one directly to the web server, one via the additional application).

Thus, the typical enhancements for web browsing act as a transparent proxy as shown in Figure 11.5. The browser accesses the web server through the client proxy, i.e., the proxy acts as server for the browser and as client for the web server. The proxy can now pre-fetch and cache content according to many strategies. As soon as the client is disconnected, the proxy serves the content. Many approaches follow this scheme which is independent of the browser and, thus, allows other developments (e.g., Caubweb (LoVerso, 1997), TeleWeb (Schilit, 1996), Weblicator (Lotus, 1999), WebWhacker (BlueSquirrel, 1999)).

Example strategies for pre-fetching could be: all pages the current pages points to, all pages including those the pre-fetched pages point to (down to a certain level), pages but no pictures, all pages with the same keyword on the same server etc.

A proxy can also support a mobile client on the network side (see Figure 11.6). This network proxy can perform adaptive content transformation (e.g., semantic compression, headline extraction etc, see section 11.2.3) or pre-fetch and cache content. Pre-fetching and caching is useful in a wireless environment with a higher error probability. Similar to the enhancements for example I-TCP achieves (see chapter 10), splitting web access into a mobile and fixed part can improve overall system performance. For the web server the network proxy acts like any fixed browser with wired access. Disconnection of the mobile client does not influence the web server. Examples for this approach are TranSend (Fox, 1996a, 1996b), Digestor (Bickmore, 1997).

The benefits of client and network proxies can be combined, which results in a system architecture as illustrated in Figure 11.7. An example for this approach is WebExpress (Housel, 1996), (Floyd, 1998). Client proxy and network proxy can now interact better in pre-fetching and caching of data. The client proxy could, for example, inform the network proxy about user behav-

Figure 11.5 (*Left*)
Client proxy as browser support

Figure 11.6 (*Right*)
Network proxy as browser support

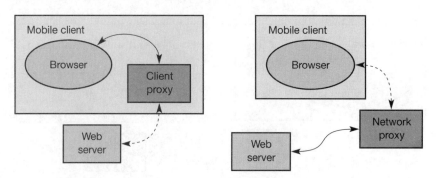

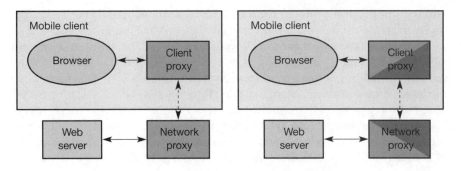

Figure 11.7 (*Left*)
Client and network proxy
as browser support

Figure 11.8 (*Right*)
Client and network proxy
with special transmission
protocol

iour, the network proxy can then pre-fetch pages according to this information. The whole approach is still transparent to the web server and the client browser.

You can even go one step further and implement a specialized network sub-system as shown in Figure 11.8. This solution has the same benefits as the previous one but now content transfer can be further optimized. Examples are online compression and replacement of transfer protocols, such as HTTP and TCP, with protocols better adapted to the mobility and wireless access of the client.

One example for such a system is Mowgli (Liljeberg, 1995), (Liljeberg, 1996). This system supports web access over cellular telephone networks, i.e., networks with low bandwidth and relatively high delay. The system not only replaces transport protocols but also performs additional content transformation needed for mobile phones. The browser still uses HTTP to the client proxy. The client proxy then uses a specialized transport service, the Mowgli data channel service, to the network proxy. Standard protocols are used to the web servers. Client and network proxy exchange their messages over long-lived Mowgli connections thus avoiding TCP's slow start and the one TCP connection per HTTP request behaviour.

Many other enhancements are possible. Examples are server extensions to provide content especially suited for wireless access and mobile, handheld clients. The following section presents a framework that includes many of the ideas discussed in the previous subsections: enhancements to HTML, support of different system architectures, and transfer protocols adapted to the requirements or mobile, wireless access.

11.3 Wireless application protocol

The growth of the Internet, Internet applications, and mobile communications led to many early proprietary solutions providing Internet services for mobile, wireless devices. Some of the problems these partial solutions face have been discussed in section 11.2 because the world wide web is the most important and fastest growing Internet application. To avoid many islands of incompatible solutions, e.g. special solutions for GSM, IS-136, or certain manufacturers, the

wireless application protocol forum (WAP Forum) was founded in June 1997 by Ericsson, Motorola, Nokia, and Unwired Planet (WAP Forum, 1998a.)

The basic objectives of the WAP Forum are to bring diverse Internet content (e.g., web pages, push services) and other data services (e.g., stock quotes) to digital cellular phones and other wireless, mobile terminals (e.g., PDAs, laptops). Moreover, a protocol suite should enable global wireless communication across different wireless network technologies, e.g., GSM, CDPD, UMTS etc. Therefore, the forum is embracing and extending existing standards and technologies of the Internet wherever possible and is creating a framework for the development of contents and applications that scale across a very wide range of wireless bearer networks and wireless device types.

All WAP Forum solutions must be:

- **interoperable**, i.e., allowing terminals and software from different vendors to communicate with networks from different providers,
- **scaleable**, i.e., protocols and services should scale with customer needs and number of customers,
- **efficient**, i.e., provision of QoS suited to the characteristics of the wireless and mobile networks,
- **reliable**, i.e., provision of a consistent and predictable platform for deploying services, and
- **secure**, i.e., preservation of the integrity of user data, protection of devices and services from security problems (WAP Forum, 1998a).

The WAP Forum has currently over 60 members from hardware manufacturers, software industry, computer and telecommunication companies and network providers. Several working groups have been established, the **WAP architecture working group** (ArchG: overall WAP architecture), the **WAP wireless protocol working group** (WPG: bearer-neutral transport protocols, WSP, WTP, WDP, WCMP), the **WAP wireless security working group** (WSG: WTLS), and the **WAP wireless application working group** (WAG: content formats, naming, etc., WAE, WML, WMLScript, WTA). Additional groups are under consideration (e.g., interoperability). The topics of these groups are discussed in the following sections. Additionally, several groups discuss the relationship of WAP to efforts in the World Wide Web Consortium (W3C (W3C, 1999)), the Internet Engineering Task Force (IETF (IETF, 1999)), European Telecommunications Standards Institute (ETSI (ETSI, 1999)), or the Bluetooth consortium (Bluetooth, 1999).

The WAP Forum published its first set of specifications in April 1998, version 1.0, covering many aspects of the whole architecture (WAP Forum, 1998a-r). This set of specifications forms the basis for the following sections. Section 11.3.1 presents the overall architecture of WAP and compares the WAP standardization with existing Internet protocols and applications, sections 11.3.2 to 11.3.9 discuss the components of the WAP architecture, while the last section, 11.3.10, presents example configurations.

11.3.1 Architecture

Figure 11.9 gives an overview of the WAP architecture, its protocols and components, and compares this architecture with the typical Internet architecture when using the world wide web (WAP Forum, 1998a).

The basis for transmission of data are different **bearer services**. WAP does not specify bearer services, but uses existing data services and will integrate further services. Examples are message services, such as short message service (SMS) of GSM, circuit-switched data, such as high-speed circuit switched data (HSCSD) in GSM, or packet switched data, such as general packet radio service (GPRS) in GSM. Many other bearers are supported, such as CDPD, IS-136, PHS. No special interface has been specified between the bearer service and the next higher layer, the **transport layer** with its **wireless datagram protocol (WDP)** and the additional **wireless control message protocol (WCMP)**, because the adaptation of these protocols are bearer-specific. The transport layer offers a bearer independent, consistent datagram-oriented service to the higher layers of the WAP architecture. Communication is done transparently over one of the available bearer services. The **transport layer service access point (T-SAP)** is the common interface to be used by higher layers independent of the underlying network. WDP and WCMP are discussed in more detail in section 11.3.2.

The next higher layer, the **security layer** with its **wireless transport layer security** protocol **WTLS** offers its service at the **security SAP (SEC-SAP)**. WTLS is based on the transport layer security (TLS, formerly SSL, secure sockets layer) already known from the WWW. But WTLS has been optimized for use in wireless networks with narrow-band channels. WTLS can offer data integrity, privacy, authentication, and denial-of-service protection and is presented in section 11.3.3.

The WAP **transaction layer** with its **wireless transaction protocol (WTP)** offers a lightweight transaction service at the **transaction SAP (TR-SAP)**. This

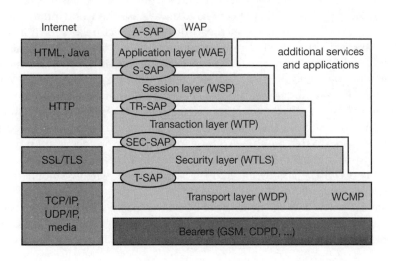

Figure 11.9
Components and interfaces of the WAP architecture

service efficiently provides reliable or unreliable requests and asynchronous transactions as explained in section 11.3.4. Tightly coupled to this layer is the next higher layer, if used for connection-oriented service as described in 11.3.5. The **session layer** with the **wireless session protocol (WSP)** currently offers two services at the **session-SAP (S-SAP)**, one connection-oriented and one connectionless if used directly on top of WDP. A special service for browsing the web (WSP/B) has been defined that offers HTTP/1.1 functionality, long-lived session state, session suspend and resume, session migration and other features needed for wireless, mobile access to the web.

Finally, on top of it all, the **application layer** with the **wireless application environment (WAE)** offers a framework for the integration of different WWW and mobile telephony applications. Therefore, it offers many protocols and services with special service access points as described in sections 11.3.6, 11.3.7, 11.3.8, and 11.3.9. The main issues here are scripting languages, special markup languages, interfaces to telephony applications, and many content formats adapted to the special requirements of small, handheld, wireless devices.

Figure 11.9 not only shows the overall WAP architecture but also its relation to the traditional Internet architecture for WWW applications. The WAP transport layer together with the bearers can be compared to the services offered by TCP or UDP over IP and different media in the Internet. If a bearer in the WAP architecture already offers IP services (e.g., GPRS, CDPD) then UDP is used as WDP. As already mentioned, the TLS/SSL layer of the Internet has also been adopted for the WAP architecture with some changes required for optimization. The functionality of the session and transaction layer can roughly be compared with the role of HTTP in the web architecture. However, HTTP does not offer all the additional mechanisms needed for efficient wireless, mobile access (e.g., session migration, suspend/resume). Finally, the application layer offers similar features as HTML and Java do. Again, special formats and features optimized for the wireless scenario have been defined and telephony access has been added.

WAP does not force all applications to always use the whole protocol architecture. Applications can use only a part of the architecture as shown in Figure 11.9. This means that, for example, if an application does not require security but the reliable transport of data, it can use a service of the transaction layer, and does not need the security layer. Simple applications can directly use WDP.

Different scenarios are possible for the integration of WAP components into existing wireless and fixed networks (see Figure 11.10). On the left side, different fixed networks, such as the traditional Internet and the public switched telephone network (PSTN), are shown. One cannot change protocols and services of these existing networks and, therefore, several new elements will be implemented between these networks and the WAP-enabled wireless, mobile devices in a wireless network on the right-hand side.

The current WWW in the Internet offers web pages with the help of HTML and web servers. To be able to browse these pages or additional pages with handheld devices, a wireless markup language (WML) has been defined in WAP.

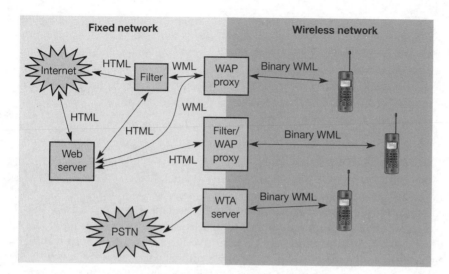

Figure 11.10
Examples for the integration of WAP components

Special filters within the fixed network can now translate HTML into WML, web servers can already provide pages in WML, or the gateways between the fixed and wireless network can translate HTML into WML. These gateways not only filter pages but act as proxies for web access, as explained in the following sections. For more efficient transmission, WML is additionally converted into binary WML.

In a similar way, a special gateway will be implemented to access traditional telephony services via binary WML. This wireless telephony application (WTA) server translates, e.g., signalling of the telephone network (incoming call etc.) into WML events displayed at the handheld device. It is important to notice the integrated view for the wireless client of all different services, telephony and web, via the WAE (see section 11.3.6).

11.3.2 Wireless datagram protocol

The **wireless datagram protocol (WDP)** operates on top of many different bearer services capable of carrying data. At the T-SAP WDP offers a consistent datagram transport service independent of the underlying bearer (WAP Forum, 1998b). The adaptation needed in the transport layer to offer this consistent service can differ much depending on the services of the bearer. The closer the bearer service is to IP, the smaller the adaptation can be. If the bearer already offers IP services, UDP (Postel, 1980) is used as WDP. Thus, WDP offers more or less the same services UDP does.

WDP offers **source** and **destination port numbers** used for multiplexing and demultiplexing of data respectively. The service primitive to send a datagram is **T-DUnitdata.req** with the **destination address (DA), destination port (DP), Source address (SA), source port (SP),** and **user data (UD)** as mandatory parameters (see Figure 11.11). Destination and source address are unique

Figure 11.11
WDP service primitives

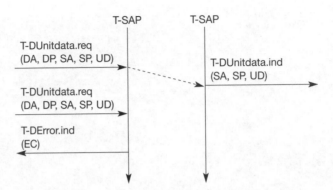

addresses for the receiver and sender of the user data. These could be MSISDNs (i.e., basically a telephone number), IP addresses, or any other unique identifiers. The **T-DUnitdata.ind** service primitive indicates the reception of data. Here destination address and port are only optional parameters.

If a higher layer requests a service the WDP cannot fulfil, this error is indicated with the **T-DError.ind** service primitive as shown in Figure 11.11. An **error code (EC)** is returned indicating the reason for the error to the higher layer. However, this primitive must not be used by the WDP to indicate problems with the bearer service, only for local problems, such as a user data size that is too large.

If any errors happen when WDP datagrams are sent from one WDP entity to another (e.g. the destination is unreachable, no application is listening to the specified destination port etc.), the **wireless control message protocol (WCMP)** provides error handling mechanisms for WDP (WAP Forum, 1998r) and should therefore be implemented. WCMP contains control messages that resemble the Internet control message protocol (ICMP (Postel, 1981b) for IPv4, (Conta, 1995) for IPv6) messages and can also be used for diagnostic and informational purposes. WCMP can be used by WDP nodes and gateways to report errors. However, WCMP error messages must not be sent as response to other WCMP error messages. In IP-based networks ICMP will be used as WCMP (e.g., CDPD, GPRS). Typical WCMP messages are **destination unreachable** (route, port, address unreachable), **parameter problem** (errors in the packet header), **message too big, reassembly failure**, or **echo request/reply**.

An additional **WDP management entity** supports WDP and provides information about changes in the environment which may impact on the correct operation of WDP. Important information is the current configuration of the device, currently available bearer services, processing and memory resources etc. Design and implementation of this management component is considered vendor-specific and, thus, outside the scope of WAP.

If the bearer already offers IP transmission, WDP (i.e., UDP in this case) relies on the segmentation and reassembly capabilities of the IP layer as specified in (Postel, 1981a). Otherwise, WDP has to include these capabilities, which is, e.g., necessary for the GSM SMS. The WAP specification provides many more adaptations to almost all bearer services currently available or planned for the future (WAP Forum, 1998q), (WAP Forum, 1998b).

11.3.3 Wireless transport layer security

If requested by an application, a security service, the **wireless transport layer security (WTLS)**, can be integrated into the WAP architecture on top of WDP as specified in (WAP Forum, 1998c). WTLS can provide different levels of security (for privacy, data integrity, and authentication) and has been optimized for low bandwidth, high delay bearer networks. Furthermore, WTLS takes into account the low processing power and very limited memory capacity of the mobile devices for cryptographic algorithms. WTLS supports datagram and connection-oriented transport layer protocols. New if compared to, e.g. GSM, is the security relation between two peers not only between the mobile device and the base station. WTLS took over many features and mechanisms from TLS (formerly SSL, secure sockets layer (Dierks, 1999)), but it has an optimized handshaking between the peers.

Before data can be exchanged via WTLS, a secure session has to be established. This session establishment consists of several steps; Figure 11.12 illustrates the sequence of service primitives needed for a so-called 'full handshake' (several optimizations are possible). The originator and the peer of the secure session can both interrupt session establishment any time, e.g., if the parameters proposed are not acceptable.

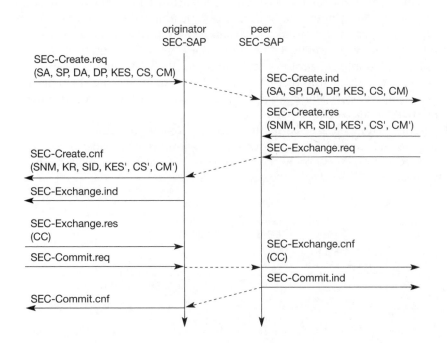

Figure 11.12
WTLS establishing a secure session

The first step is to initiate the session with the **SEC-Create** primitive. Parameters are **source address (SA)**, **source port (SP)** of the originator, **destination address (DA)**, **destination port (DP)** of the peer. Furthermore, the originator proposes a **key exchange suite (KES)** (e.g., RSA (Rivest, 1978), DH (Diffie, 1976), ECC (Certicom, 1999), a **cipher suite (CS)** (e.g., DES, IDEA (Schneier, 1996), and a **compression method (CM)** (currently not further specified). The peer answers with parameters for the **sequence number mode (SNM)**, the **key refresh** cycle **(KR)** (i.e., how often keys are refreshed within this secure session), the **session identifier (SID)** (which is unique with each peer), and the selected **key exchange suite (KES')**, **cipher suite (CS')**, **compression method (CM')**. The peer also issues a **SEC-Exchange** primitive. This indicates that the peer wishes to perform public-key authentication with the client, i.e., the peer requests a certificate from the originator.

The first step of the secure session creation, the negotiation of the security parameters and suites, is indicated on the originator's side, followed by the request for a certificate. The originator answers with its certificate and issues a **SEC-Commit.req** primitive. This primitive indicates that the handshake is completed for the originator's side and that the originator now wants to switch into the newly negotiated connection state. The certificate is delivered to the peer side and the SEC-Commit is indicated. The WTLS layer of the peer sends back a confirmation to the originator. This concludes the full handshake for secure session setup.

After setting up a secure connection between two peers, user data can be exchanged. This is done using the simple **SEC-Unitdata** primitive as shown in Figure 11.13. SEC-Unitdata has exactly the same function as T-DUnitdata on the WDP layer, namely it transfers a datagram between a sender and a receiver. Still this data transfer is unreliable, but now secure. This shows that WTLS can be easily plugged into the protocol stack on top of WDP. The higher layers simply use SEC-Unitdata instead of T-DUnitdata. Thus, parameters are the same here: **source address (SA)**, **source port (SP)**, **destination address (DA)**, **destination port (DP)**, and **user data (UD)**.

This section will discuss neither the security-related features of WTLS nor the pros and cons of different encryption algorithms. The reader is referred to the specification (WAP Forum, 1998c) and excellent cryptography literature e.g., (Schneier, 1996), (Kaufman, 1995).

Figure 11.13
WTLS datagram transfer

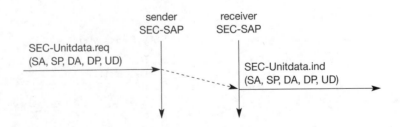

Although WTLS allows for different encryption mechanisms with different key lengths, it is quite clear that due to computing power on the handheld devices and export regulations in some countries, the encryption provided cannot be very strong. However, applications or users are free to put stronger encryption on top of the whole protocol stack if required (and allowed) – the appropriate algorithms *are* available worldwide.

Future work in the WTLS layer comprises consistent support for application level security (e.g. digital signatures) and different implementation classes with different capabilities to select from.

11.3.4 Wireless transaction protocol

The **wireless transaction protocol (WTP)** is on top of either WDP or, if security is required, WTLS (WAP Forum, 1998d). WTP has been designed to run on very thin clients, such as mobile phones. WTP offers several advantages to higher layers, including an improved reliability over datagram services, improved efficiency over connection-oriented services, and support for transaction-oriented services, such as web browsing. In this context, a transaction is defined as a request with its response, e.g. for a web page.

WTP offers many features to the higher layer. The basis are three **classes of transaction service** as explained in the following paragraphs. Class 0 provides unreliable message transfer without any result message. Class 1 and 2 provide reliable message transfer, class 1 without, class 2 with exactly one reliable result message (the typical request/response case). WTP achieves reliability using **duplicate removal**, **retransmission**, **acknowledgements** and unique **transaction identifiers.** No WTP-class requires any connection set-up or tear-down phase. This avoids unnecessary overhead on the communication link. WTP allows for **asynchronous transactions**, **abort of transactions**, **concatenation of messages**, and can **report success or failure** of reliable messages (e.g., a server cannot handle the request).

To be consistent with the specification, in the following the term **initiator** is used for a WTP entity initiating a transaction (a.k.a. client), and the term **responder** for the WTP entity responding to a transaction (a.k.a. server). The three service primitives offered by WTP are **TR-Invoke** to initiate a new transaction, **TR-Result** to send back the result of a previously initiated transaction, and **TR-Abort** to abort an existing transaction. The PDUs exchanged between two WTP entities for normal transactions are the **invoke PDU**, **ack PDU**, and **result PDU**. The use of the service primitives, the PDUs, and the associated parameters will be explained in the following together with the classes of transaction service.

A special feature of WTP is the ability to provide a **user acknowledgement** or, alternatively, an **automatic acknowledgement** by the WTP entity. If user acknowledgement is required, a WTP user has to confirm every message received by a WTP entity. Note that a user acknowledgement provides a stronger version of a confirmed service for it guarantees that the response comes from the user of the WTP and not the WTP entity itself. Examples will be given in the following.

11.3.4.1 WTP class 0

Class 0 offers an unreliable transaction service without a result message. The transaction is stateless and cannot be aborted. The service is requested with the **TR-Invoke.req** primitive as shown in Figure 11.14. Parameters are the **source address (SA)**, **source port (SP)**, **destination address (DA)**, **destination port (DP)** as already explained in section 11.3.2. Additionally, with the A flag the user of this service can determine, if the responder WTP entity should generate an **acknowledgement** or if a user acknowledgement should be used. The WTP layer will transmit the **user data (UD)** transparently to its destination. The class type C indicates here class 0. Finally, the transaction **handle H** provides a simple index to uniquely identify the transaction and is an alias for the tuple (SA, SP, DA, DP), i.e., a socket, with only local significance.

The WTP entity at the initiator sends an invoke PDU which the responder receives. The WTP entity at the responder then generates a **TR-Invoke.ind** primitive with the same parameters as on the initiator's side, except for H′ which is now the local handle for the transaction on the responder's side.

In this class the responder does not acknowledge the message and the initiator does not perform any retransmission. Although this resembles a simple datagram service, it is recommended to use WDP if only a datagram service is required. WTP class 0 augments the transaction service with a simple datagram like service for occasional use by higher layers.

11.3.4.2 WTP class 1

Class 1 offers a reliable transaction service but without a result message. Again, the initiator sends an invoke PDU after a **TR-Invoke.req** from a higher layer. This time class equals 1, and no user acknowledgement has been selected as shown in Figure 11.15. The responder signals the incoming invoke PDU via the

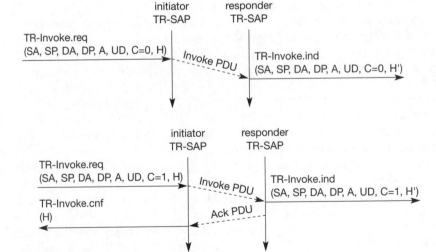

Figure 11.14
Basic transaction, WTP class 0

Figure 11.15
Basic transaction, WTP class 1, no user acknowledgement

TR-Invoke.ind primitive to the higher layer and acknowledges automatically without user intervention. The specification also allows the user on the responder's side to acknowledge, but this acknowledgement is not required. For the initiator the transaction ends with the reception of the acknowledgement, the responder keeps the transaction state for some time to be able to retransmit the acknowledgement if it receives the same invoke PDU again indicating a loss of the acknowledgement.

If a user of the WTP class 1 service on the initiator's side requests user acknowledgement on the responder's side, the sequence diagram looks as shown in Figure 11.16. Now the WTP entity on the responder's side does not send an acknowledgement automatically, but waits for the **TR-Invoke.res** service primitive from a user. This service primitive must have the appropriate local handle H' for identification of the right transaction. Now the WTP entity can send the ack PDU. A typical use for this transaction class are reliable push services.

11.3.4.3 WTP class 2

Finally, class 2 transaction service provides the classical reliable request/response transaction known from many client/server scenarios. Depending on user requirements many different scenarios are possible for initiator/responder interaction. Three examples are presented in the following.

Figure 11.17 shows the basic transaction of class 2 without user acknowledgement. Here a user on the initiator's side requests the service, the WTP entity sends the invoke PDU to the responder. The WTP entity on the responder's side indicates the request with the **TR-Invoke.ind** primitive to a user. The responder now waits for the processing of the request, the user on the responder's side can finally give the result UD* to the WTP entity on responder side using **TR-Result.req.** Now the **result PDU** can be sent back to the initiator, which implicitly acknowledges the invoke PDU. Thus, the initiator can indicate the successful transmission of the invoke message and the result with the two service primitives **TR-Invoke.cnf** and **TR-Result.ind.** A user may respond to this result with **TR-Result.res**, then an acknowledgement PDU is generated which finally triggers the **TR-Result.cnf** primitive on the responder's side.

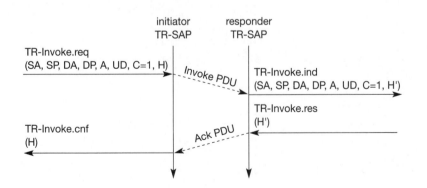

Figure 11.16
Basic transaction, WTP class 1, with user acknowledgement

Figure 11.17
Basic transaction, WTP
class 2,
no user
acknowledgement

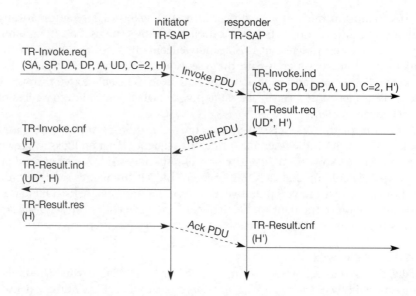

An even more reliable service can be provided using user acknowledgement as explained above. Now the time-sequence diagram looks different (see Figure 11.18). The user on the responder's side now explicitly responds to the Invoke PDU using the **TR-Invoke.res** primitive which triggers the **TR-Invoke.cnf** on the initiator's side via an **ack PDU**. And also the transmission of the result is a confirmed service as indicated by the next four service primitives. This service will likely be the most common in standard request/response scenarios as, e.g., distributed computing.

Figure 11.18
Basic transaction, WTP
class 2,
with user
acknowledgement

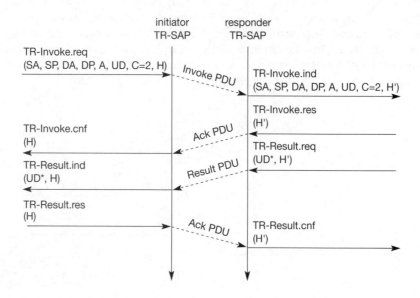

If the calculation of the result takes some more time, the responder can put the initiator on 'hold on' to prevent a retransmission of the invoke PDU because the initiator might assume packet loss if no result is sent back within a certain timeframe. This can be done as shown in Figure 11.19. After a time-out, the responder automatically generates an acknowledgement for the Invoke PDU. This shows the initiator that the responder is still alive and currently busy processing the request. After some more time the result PDU can be sent to the initiator as already explained.

WTP provides many more features not explained here, such as concatenation and separation of messages, asynchronous transactions with up to 2^{15} transactions outstanding, i.e., requested but without result up to now, and segmentation/reassembly of messages (WAP Forum, 1998d).

11.3.5 Wireless session protocol

The **wireless session protocol (WSP)** has been designed to function on top of the datagram service WDP or the transaction service WTP (WAP Forum, 1998e). For both types security can be inserted using the WTLS security layer if required. Basically, WSP provides a shared state between a client and a server to optimize content transfer. HTTP, a protocol WSP tries to replace within the wireless domain, is stateless, which already causes many problems in fixed networks (see 11.2.1). Many web content providers therefore use cookies to store some state on a client machine which is not an elegant solution (see 11.2.3). State is needed in web browsing, for example, to resume browsing in exactly the same context in which browsing has been suspended. This is an important feature for clients and servers. Client users can continue to work where they left the browser or when the network was interrupted, or users can get their customized environment every time they start the browser. Content providers can

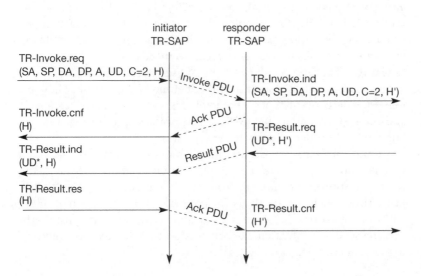

Figure 11.19
WTP class 2 transaction with 'hold on', no user acknowledgement

customize their pages to clients' needs and do not have to retransmit the same pages over and over again. WSP offers the following general features needed for content exchange between cooperating clients and servers:

- **Session management:** WSP introduces sessions that can be **established** from a client to a server and may be long lived. Sessions can also be **released** in an orderly manner. Important for mobile applications are the capabilities of **suspending** and **resuming** a session. Assume a mobile device being switched off – it would be useful for a user to be able to continue operation at exactly the point where the device was switched off. Session lifetime is independent of transport connection lifetime or continuous operation of a bearer network.
- **Capability negotiation:** Clients and servers can agree upon a common level of protocol functionality during session establishment. Example parameters to negotiate are: maximum client SDU size, maximum outstanding requests, protocol options, server SDU size.
- **Content encoding:** WSP also defines the efficient binary encoding for the content it transfers. WSP offers content typing and composite objects, as explained for web browsing.

While WSP is a general purpose session protocol, WAP has specified **wireless session protocol/browsing (WSP/B)** which comprises protocols and services most suited for browsing-type applications. In addition to the general features of WSP, WSP/B offers the following features adapted to web browsing:

- **HTTP/1.1 functionality:** WSP/B supports the functions HTTP/1.1 (Fielding, 1997) offers, such as extensible request/reply methods, composite objects, and content type negotiation. Basically, WSP/B is a binary form of HTTP/1.1. Thus, HTTP/1.1 content headers are used to define content type, character set encoding, languages etc., but binary encodings are defined for well-known headers to reduce protocol overheads.
- **Exchange of session headers:** Client and server can exchange request/reply headers that remain constant over the lifetime of the session. These headers may include content types, character sets, languages, device capabilities, and other static parameters. WSP/B will not interpret header information but passes all headers directly to service users.
- **Push and pull data transfer:** Pulling data from a server is the traditional mechanism of the web. This is also supported by WSP/B using the request/response mechanism from HTTP/1.1. Additionally, WSP/B supports three push mechanisms for data transfer: a confirmed data push within an existing session context, a non-confirmed data push within an existing session context, and a non-confirmed data push without an existing session context.

- **Asynchronous requests:** Optionally, WSP/B supports a client that can send multiple requests to a server simultaneously. This improves efficiency for the requests and replies can now be coalesced into fewer messages. Latency is also improved, for each result can be sent to the client as soon as it is available.

As already mentioned, WSP/B can run over the transaction service WTP or the datagram service WDP. The following shows several protocol sequences typical for session management, method invocation, and push services.

11.3.5.1 WSP/B over WTP

WSP/B uses the three service classes of WTP presented in section 11.3.4.1 to 11.3.4.3 as follows. Class 0 is used for unconfirmed push, session resume, and session management. Confirmed push uses class 1, method invocation, session resume, and session management class 2. The following time sequence charts will give some examples.

The first example (Figure 11.20) shows the session establishment of WSP/B using WTP class 2 transactions. With the **S-Connect.req** primitive a client can request a new session. Parameters are the **server address (SA)**, the **client address (CA)**, and the optional **client header (CH)** and **requested capabilities (RC)**. The session layer directly uses the addressing scheme of the layer below. TR-SAP and S-SAP can be directly mapped. A client header can comprise user-to-user information compatible with HTTP message headers according to Fielding (1997). These headers can be used, e.g., for caching if they are constant throughout the session. Interpretation is up to the user of this service. The capabilities are needed for the capability negotiation as listed in the features of WSP above.

WTP transfers the **connect PDU** to the server S-SAP where an **S-Connect.ind** primitive indicates a new session. Parameters are the same, but now the capabilities are mandatory. If the server accepts the new session it answers with an **S-Connect.res**, parameters are an optional **server header (SH)** with the same function as the client header and the **negotiated capabilities (NC)** needed for capability negotiation.

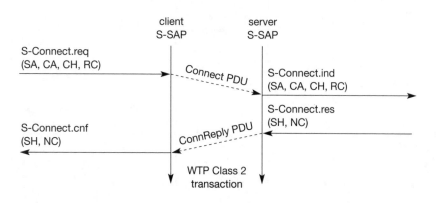

Figure 11.20
WSP/B session
establishment

WTP now transfers the **connreply PDU** back to the client, **S-Connect.cnf** confirms the session establishment and includes the **server header** (if present) and the **negotiated capabilities** from the server. WSP/B includes several procedures to refuse a session or to abort session establishment.

A very useful feature of WSP/B is shown in Figure 11.21, **session suspension** and **session resume**. If for example a client notices that it will soon be unavailable, e.g., the bearer network will be unavailable due to roaming to another network or the user switches off the device, the client can suspend the session. Session suspension will automatically abort all data transmission and freeze the current state of the session on the client and server side. A client suspends a session with **S-Suspend.req**, WTP transfers the **suspend PDU** to the server with a class 0 transaction, i.e., unconfirmed and unreliable. WSP/B will signal the suspension with **S-Suspend.ind** on the client and server side. The only parameter is the **reason R** for suspension. Reasons can be a user request or a suspension initiated by the service provider.

As also shown in Figure 11.21, a client can later resume a suspended session with **S-Resume.req**. Parameters are a **server address (SA)** and a **client address (CA).** If SA and CA are not the same as before suspending this session, it is the responsibility of the service user to map the addresses accordingly so that the same server instance will be contacted. Resuming a session is a confirmed operation.

Terminating a session is done by using the **S-Disconnect.req** service primitive (Figure 11.22). This primitive aborts all current method or push transactions used to transfer data. Disconnection is indicated on both sides using **S-Disconnect.ind.** The **reason R** for disconnection can be, e.g., network error, protocol error, peer request, congestion, maximum SDU size exceeded. S-

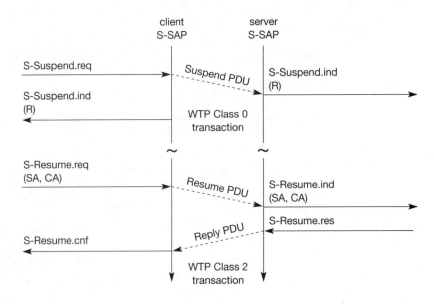

Figure 11.21
WSP/B session
suspension and
resume

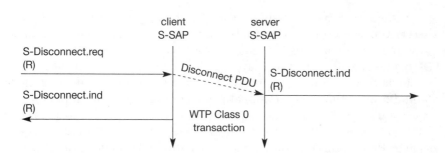

Figure 11.22
WSP/B session
termination

Disconnect. ind can also include parameters that redirect the session to another server where the session may continue.

The **S-MethodInvoke** primitive is used to request an operation to be executed by the server. The result, if any, is sent back using the **S-MethodResult** primitive (Figure 11.23). A client requests an operation with **S-MethodInvoke.req**. Parameters are the **client transaction identifier CTID** to distinguish between pending transactions, the **method M** identifying the requested operation at the server, and the **request URI** (Uniform Resource Identifier (Berners-Lee, 1994a) **RU**. URLs, such as http://www.xyz. int/ are examples of URIs (Berners-Lee, 1994b). Additional headers and bodies can be sent with this primitive.

The WTP class 2 transaction service now transports the **method PDU** to the server. A method PDU can be either a get PDU or a post PDU as defined in Fielding (1997). **Get PDUs** are used for HTTP/1.1 GET, OPTIONS, HEAD, DELETE and TRACE methods, and other methods that do not send content to the server. A **post PDU** is used for HTTP/1.1 POST and PUT and other methods that send content to the server.

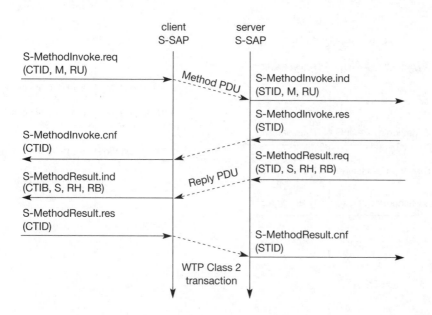

Figure 11.23
WSP/B completed
transaction

On the server's side, **S-MethodInvoke.ind** indicates the request. In this case a **server transaction identifier STID** distinguishes between pending transactions. The server confirms the request, now WSP/B does not generate a new PDU but relies on the lower WTP layer (see Figure 11.24 for more details).

Similarly, the result of the request is sent back to the client using the **S-MethodResult** primitive. Additional parameters are now the **status (S)**, the **response header (RH)**, and the **response body (RB).** Again, WSP/B stays close to HTTP/1.1 and so the Status S corresponds to the HTTP status codes in Fielding (1997). One famous example for a **status code** is **404**, indicating that the server could not find the web page specified in the request, typically a sign of an outdated bookmark or a lazy managed web server. But most of the time a server returns **200** indicating that everything is ok. Header and body, too, are equivalent to the HTTP header and body and, therefore, the response body typically carries the code of the web page if the status is 200.

WSP does not introduce PDUs or service primitives just for the sake of a symmetric and aesthetic protocol architecture. Figure 11.24 shows how WSP (thus also WSP/B) uses the underlying WTP services for its purposes. The **S-MethodInvoke.req** primitive triggers the **TR-Invoke.req** primitive, the parameters of the WSP layer are the user data of the WTP layer. Thus, the **invoke PDU** of the WTP layer carries the **method PDU** of the WSP layer inside. In contrast to a pure layered communication model here the lower WTP layer is involved in the semantics of the higher layer primitives and does not consider them as pure data only.

For the confirmation of its service primitives the WSP layer has none of its own PDUs but uses the **acknowledgement PDUs** of the WTP layer as shown. **S-**

Figure 11.24
WSP utilization of WTP
as lower layer

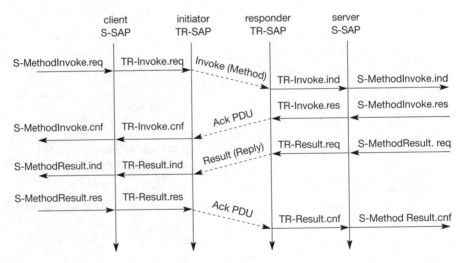

MethodInvoke.res triggers **TR-Invoke.res**, the **ack** PDU is transferred to the initiator, here **TR-Invoke.cnf** confirms the invoke service and triggers the **S-MethodInvoke.cnf** primitive which confirms the method invocation service. This mingling of layers saves a lot of redundant data flow but still allows a separation of the tasks between the two layers.

WSP does not provide any sequencing between different requests or restore any sequence between responses. Figure 11.25 shows four requests on the client's side (**S-MethodInvoke_i.req**). WSP may deliver them in any order on the server's side as indicated by **S-MethodInvoke_i.ind** (the confirmation primitives **S-MethodInvoke.res** and **S-MethodInvoke.cnf** have been omitted for clarity). Additionally, the user on the server's side may need different amounts of time for responding to the requests, e.g., if some requested data has to be fetched from disk while other data is already available in memory. Therefore, the responses **S-MethodResult_i.req** may be in arbitrary order, the WSP service only delivers them to the client S-SAP where they finally appear as **S-MethodResult_i.ind** completely independent of the original order of the requests.

Up to now all service primitives allowed the client to pull data from a server. With the help of push primitives a server can push data towards a client if allowed. The simplest push mechanism is the non-confirmed push as shown in Figure 11.26. The server sends unsolicited data with the **S-Push.req** primitive to the client. Parameters are the **push header (PH)** and the **push body (PB)**,

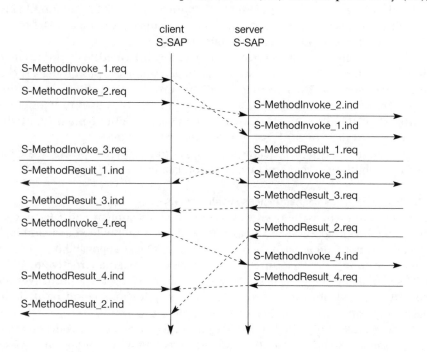

Figure 11.25
WSP/B
asynchronous,
unordered
requests

Figure 11.26
WSP/B
non-confirmed push

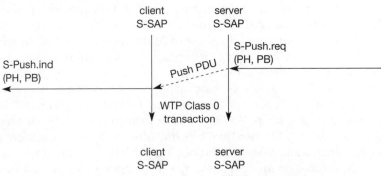

Figure 11.26
WSP/B
non-confirmed push

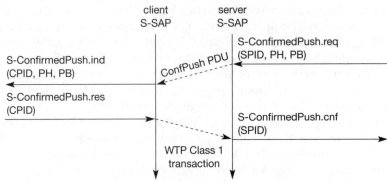

Figure 11.27
WSP/B confirmed push

again these are the header and the body known from HTTP. The unreliable, unconfirmed WTP class 0 transaction service transfers the **push PDU** to the client where **S-Push.ind** indicates the push event.

A more reliable push service offers the **S-ConfirmedPush** primitive as shown in Figure 11.27. Here the server has to determine the push using a **server push identifier (SPID)**. This helps to distinguish between different pending pushes. Now the reliable WTP class 1 transaction service is used to transfer the **confpush PDU** to the client. On the client's side a **client push identifier (CPID)** is used to distinguish between different pending pushes.

Additionally, WSP/B provides many ways to abort any operation such as session establishment, method invocation or data push.

11.3.5.2 WSP/B as connectionless session service

There are cases where the overhead of session establishment and release, confirmed method invocation and all associated states is simply too much and high reliability is not required. For these cases, WSP/B offers the possibility to run on top of the connectionless, unreliable WDP service. As an alternative to WDP, WTLS can always be used if security is required. The service primitives are directly mapped onto each other. Example applications could be periodic pushes of weather data from a remote sensor device to a client.

Figure 11.28 shows the three service primitives available for connectionless session service: **S-Unit-MethodInvoke.req** to request an operation on a server, **S-Unit-MethodResult.req** to return results to a client, and **S-Unit-Push.req** to

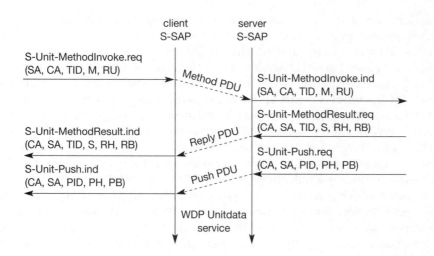

Figure 11.28
WSP/B as
connectionless
session service

push data onto a client. Transfer of the PDUs (**method, reply** and **push**) is done with the help of the standard unreliable datagram transfer service of WDP. Besides the **server address (SA)**, the **client address (CA)**, the **method (M)**, and the **request URI (RU)**, which have already been explained above, the user of the **S-Unit-MethodInvoke.req** primitive can determine a **transaction identifier (TID)** to distinguish between different transactions on the user level. TID is communicated transparently from service user to service user.

The function of the **S-Unit-MethodResult** primitive remains the same as explained above: the **status (S)**, **response header (RH)**, and **response body (RB)** represent the result of the operation. Finally, the **S-Unit-Push** primitive has the parameters **client address (CA)**, **server address (SA)**, **push identifier (PID)**, **push header (PH)**, and **push body (PB)**.

Although WSP already offers many services, specifies binary encodings for headers and content etc., there are many unsolved problems. Examples are the provisioning of QoS, i.e., how can certain quality parameters be applied to transactions and sessions, multicast support, i.e., how can a multicast session be created, or isochronous multimedia objects, i.e., the support of very strict time bounds for session services. Moreover, management of all services is still an open field.

11.3.6 Wireless application environment

The main idea behind the **wireless application environment (WAE)** is to create a general-purpose application environment based mainly on existing technologies and philosophies of the world wide web (WAP Forum, 1998g). This environment should allow service providers, software manufacturers, or hardware vendors to integrate their applications so they can reach a wide variety of different wireless platforms in an efficient way. However, WAE does not dictate or assume any specific man-machine-interface model, but allows for a variety of devices, each with its own capabilities and probably vendor-specific extras (i.e., each vendor can have its own look-and-feel). WAE has already integrated the following technologies and adapted them for use in a wireless environment with low power handheld devices. HTML (Raggett, 1998), JavaScript (Flanagan, 1997), and the handheld device markup language HDML (King, 1997) form the basis of the **wireless markup language (WML)** and the scripting language **WMLscript.** The exchange formats for business cards and phone books **vCard** (IMC, 1996a) and for calendars **vCalendar** (IMC, 1996b) have been included. **URLs** known from the web can be used. Furthermore, a wide range of mobile telecommunication technologies have been adopted and integrated into the **wireless telephony application (WTA)** (WAP Forum, 1998f).

Besides relying on mature and established technology, WAE has a focus on devices with very limited capabilities, narrow-band environments, and special security and access control features. The first phase of the WAE specification developed a whole application suite, especially for wireless clients as presented in the following sections. Future developments for the WAE will include extensions for more content formats, integration of further existing or emerging technologies, more server-side aspects, and the integration of intelligent telephone networks.

One global goal of the WAE is to minimize over-the-air traffic and resource consumption on the handheld device. This goal is also reflected in the logical model underlying WAE (Figure 11.29) showing some more details than the general overview in Figure 11.10. WAE adopts a model that closely follows the WWW model, but assumes additional gateways that can enhance transmission efficiency. A **client** issues an encoded request for an operation on a remote server. Encoding is necessary to minimize data sent over the air and to save resources on the handheld device as explained together with the languages WML and WMLscript.

Decoders in a **gateway** now translate this encoded request into a standard request as understood by the **origin servers.** This could be a request to get a web

Figure 11.29
WAE logical model

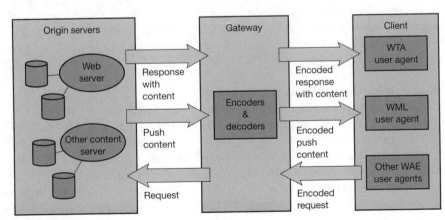

page or a request to set up a call. The gateway transfers this request to the appropriate origin server as if it came from a standard client. Origin servers could be standard web servers running HTTP and generating content using scripts, providing pages using a database, or applying any other (proprietary) technology. WAE does not specify any standard content generator or server, but assumes that the majority will follow the standard technology used in today's WWW.

The origin servers will respond to the request. The gateway now encodes the response and its content (if there is any) and transfers the encoded response with the content to the client. The WAE logical model does not only include this standard request/response scheme, but also push services. Then an origin server pushes content to the gateway. The gateway encodes the pushed content and transmits the encoded push content to the client.

Within a client several user agents can reside. User agents include such items as browsers, phonebooks, message editors etc. WAE does neither specify the number of user agents nor their functionality, but assumes a basic **WML user agent** that supports WML, WMLscript, or both (i.e., a 'WML browser'). Further domain-specific user agents with varying architectures can be implemented. Again, this is left to a vendor. However, one more user agent has been specified with its fundamental services, the **WTA user agent.** This user agent handles access to and interaction with mobile telephone features (such as call control). The basic languages WML and WMLScript, and the WTA will be described in the following three sections.

11.3.7 Wireless markup language

The **wireless markup language (WML)** (WAP Forum, 1998j) is based on the standard HTML (Raggett, 1998) known from the WWW and on HDML (King, 1997). WML is specified as an XML (W3C, 1998) document type. While designing WML, several constraints of wireless handheld devices had to be taken into account. First of all, the wireless link will always have only a very limited capacity compared to a wire. Furthermore, current handheld devices have small displays, limited user input facilities, limited memory, and only low performance computational resources.

WML follows a deck and card metaphor. A WML document is made up of multiple **cards.** Cards can be grouped together into a **deck.** A WML deck is similar to an HTML page, in that it is identified by an URL and is the unit of content transmission. A user navigates with the WML browser through a series of WML cards, reviews the contents, enters requested data, makes choices etc. The WML browser fetches decks as required from origin servers. These decks can be either static files on the server or they can be dynamically generated.

It is important to note that WML does not specify how the implementation of a WML browser has to interact with a user. Instead, WML describes the intent of interaction in an abstract manner. The user agent on a handheld device has to decide how to best present all elements of a card. This presentation depends much on the capabilities of the device.

WML includes several basic features:

- **Text and images:** WML gives, as do other mark-up languages, hints how text and images can be presented to a user. However, the exact presentation of data to a user is up to the user agent running on the handheld device. WML only provides a set of mark-up elements, such as emphasis elements (bold, italic, etc.) for text or tab columns for tabbing alignment.
- **User interaction:** WML supports different elements for user input. Examples are text entry controls for text or password entry, option selections, or controls for task invocation. Again, the user agent is free to choose how these inputs are implemented. They could be bound to, e.g., physical keys, soft keys, or voice input.
- **Navigation:** As with HTML browsers, WML offers a history mechanism with navigation through the browsing history, hyperlinks and other inter-card navigation elements.
- **Context management:** WML allows for saving the state between different decks without server interaction, i.e., variable state can last longer than a single deck, and so state can be shared across different decks. Cards can have parameters defined by using this state without access to the server over the narrow-band wireless channel.

The following paragraph gives a simple example of WML. After the keyword WML the first CARD is defined. This first card of the deck 'displays' a text after loading ('displaying' could also mean voice output etc.). As soon as a user activates the DO element (a button or voice command), the user agent displays the second card. On this second card the user can select one out of three pizza options. Depending on the choice of the user, PIZZA can have one of the values Mar, Fun, or Vul. Again, describing these options with WML does not automatically mean that these options are displayed as text. It could also be possible that the user agent reads the options through a voice output and the user answers through a voice input. WML only describes the intention of a choice.

```
<WML>
   <CARD>
    <DO TYPE="ACCEPT">
         <GO URL="#card_two"/>
    </DO>
    This is a simple first card!
    On the next you can choose ...
   </CARD>
   <CARD NAME="card_two">
    ... your favorite pizza:
    <SELECT KEY="PIZZA">
         <OPTION VALUE="Mar">
```

```
            Margherita</OPTION>
        <OPTION VALUE="Fun">Funghi
            </OPTION>
        <OPTION VALUE="Vul">Vulcano
            </OPTION>
    </SELECT>
    </CARD>
</WML>
```

WML may be encoded using a compact binary representation to save band-width on the wireless link. This compact representation is based on the binary XML content format as specified in WAP Forum (1998k). The binary coding of WML is only one special version of this format, the compact representation is valid in general for XML content. The compact format allows for transmission without loss of functionality or of semantic information. For example, the URL prefix http://, which is very common in URLs, will be coded as 4B. The keyword CARD with content and attributes following is coded as E9. The code for the SELECT keyword is 37 and OPTION is 35. These single byte codes are much more efficient than the plain text used in HTML.

11.3.8 WMLScript

WMLScript serves as a complement to WML and provides a general scripting capability in the WAP architecture (WAP Forum, 1998h). While all WML content is static, WMLScript offers several capabilities not supported by WML:

- **Validity check of user input:** before user input is sent to a server, WMLScript can check the validity and save bandwidth and latency in case of an error. Otherwise, the server has to perform all checks which always includes at least one round-trip time if problems occur.
- **Access to device facilities:** WMLScript offers functions to access hardware components and software functions of the device. On a phone a user could, e.g., make a phone call, access the address book, or send a message via the message service of the mobile phone.
- **Local user interaction:** Without introducing round-trip delays WMLScript can directly and locally interact with a user, show messages or prompt for input. Only, for example, the result of several interactions could be transmitted to a server.
- **Extensions to the device software:** With the help of WMLScript a device can be configured and new functionality can be added even after deployment. Users can download new software from vendors and, thus, upgrade their device easily.

WMLScript is based on JavaScript (Flanagan, 1997), but adapted to the wireless environment. This includes a small memory footprint of the simple WMLScript bytecode interpreter and an efficient over-the-air transport via a space efficient bytecode. A WMLScript compiler is used to generate this bytecode. This compiler may be located in a gateway (see Figure 11.29) or the origin servers store pre-compiled WMLScript bytecode.

Furthermore, WMLScript is event-based, i.e., a script may be invoked in response to certain user or environment events. WMLScript also has full access to the state model of WML, i.e., WMLScript can set and read WML variables.

WMLScript provides many features known from standard programming languages such as functions, expressions, or while, if, for, return etc. statements. The language is weakly-typed, i.e., any variable can contain any type (such as integer, float, string, boolean) – no explicit typing is necessary. WMLScript provides an automatic conversion between different types if possible. Parameters are always passed by value to functions.

Here is a simple example for some lines of WMLScript: the function pizza_test accepts one value as input. The local variable taste is initialized to the string 'unknown'. Then the script checks if the input parameter pizza_type has the value 'Mar'. If this is the case, taste is set to 'well... ', otherwise the script checks if the pizza_type is 'Vul'. If this is the case, taste is set to 'quite hot'. Finally, the current value of taste is returned as the value of the function pizza_test.

```
function pizza_test(pizza_type) {
    var taste = "unknown";
    if (pizza_type = "Mar") {
     taste = "well... ";
    }
    else {
     if (pizza_type = "Vul") {
          taste = "quite hot";
     };
    };
    return taste;
};
```

The WMLScript compiler can compile one or more such scripts into a **WMLScript compilation unit.** A handheld wireless device can now fetch such a compilation unit using standard protocols with HTTP semantics, such as WSP (see 11.3.5). Within a compilation unit a user can call a certain function using standard **URLs** with a **fragment anchor.** A fragment anchor is specified by the URL, a hash mark (#), and a fragment identifier. If the URL of the compilation unit of the example script was http://www.xyz.int/myscr, a user could call the script and pass the parameter 'Vul' via http://www.xyz.int/myscr#pizza_test('Vul').

The WAP Forum has specified several **standard libraries** for WMLScript (WAP Forum, 1998i). These libraries provide access to the core functionality of a

WAP client and, therefore, must be available in the client's scripting environment. One exception is the float library which is optional and only useful if a client can support floating point operations. The following six libraries have been defined so far:

- **Lang:** This library provides functions closely related to WMLScipt itself. Examples are `isInt` to check if a value could be converted into an integer or `float` to check if floating point operations are supported.
- **Float:** Many typical arithmetic floating-point operations are in this library (which is optional as mentioned before). Example functions are `round` for rounding a number and `sqrt` for calculating the square root of a given value.
- **String:** Many string manipulation functions are in this library. Examples are well-known functions such as `length` to return the length of a string or `subString` to return a sub-string of a given string. But this library also provides more advanced functions such as `find` to find a sub-string within a string or `squeeze` to replace several consecutive whitespaces with only one.
- **URL:** This library provides many functions for handling URLs with the syntax defined in Fielding (1995):

  ```
  <scheme>://<host>:<port>/<path>;<parameters>?<query>#
  <fragment>
  ```

for example http://www.xyz.int:8080/mypages;5;2?j=2&p=1#crd. The function `getPath` could now extract the path of this URL, i.e., 'mypages', `getQuery` has the query part 'j=2&p=1' as return value, and `getFragment` delivers the fragment used in the URL, i.e., 'crd'.

- **WMLBrowser:** This library provides several functions typical for a browser, such as `prev` to go back one card or `refresh` to update the context of the user interface. The function `go` loads the content provided as parameters:

  ```
  var my_card = "http://www.xyz.int/pizzamatic/apps.dck#
  start";
  var my_vars = "j=4&k=7";
  WMLBrowser.go(my_card, my_vars);
  ```

- **Dialogs:** For interaction with a user this library has been defined. An example function is `prompt` that displays a given message and prompts for user input.

11.3.9 Wireless telephony application

Browsing the web using the WML browser is only one application for a handheld device user. Additionally, a user still wants to make phone calls and access all the features of the mobile phone network as usual with a traditional mobile phone. This is where the **wireless telephony application (WTA)**, the **WTA user**

agent (as shown in Figure 11.29), and the **wireless telephony application interface WTAI** come in. WTA is a collection of telephony specific extensions for call and feature control mechanisms, merging data networks and voice networks (WAP Forum, 1998).

The WTA framework integrates advanced telephony services using a consistent user interface (e.g., the WML browser) and allows network operators to increase accessibility for various special services in their network. Furthermore, a network operator can reach more end-devices using WTA because this is integrated in the wireless application environment (WAE) which handles device specific characteristics and environments. But WTA should also enable third-party developers as well as network operators to create network-independent content that accesses the basic features of the bearer network. However, most of the WTA functionality is reserved for the network operators for security and stability reasons.

WTA extends the basic WAE application model in three ways:

- **Content push:** A WTA origin server can push content, i.e., WML decks, WMLScript to the client. This content can, e.g., enable the client to handle new network events that were unknown before. An example is given in Figure 11.31.
- **Handling of network events:** A device can have a table indicating how to react to certain events from the mobile network. Events could be an incoming call or text message. The device can look up how to react, e.g., look up in a private phonebook in order to map the incoming phone number onto a name.
- **Access to telephony functions:** Applications running on the client can access telephony functions from WML or WMLScript in a very simple way. Many functions are available in libraries for setting up calls, making phonebook entries etc.

These libraries have been defined in the WTAI specification (WAP Forum, 1998m) and allow for the creation of telephony applications using the WTA user agent. Library functions can be used from WML decks or WMLScript. The WTA user agent displays cards of a deck or executes a script, and receives events from the mobile network or content pushed from the WTA origin server.

Three classes of libraries have been defined:

- **Common network services:** This class contains libraries for services common to all mobile networks. The **call control** library contains, e.g., functions to set up calls, accept calls, and release calls. **Network text** contains functions to send, read, and delete text messages. **Phonebook** allows for the manipulation of the local phonebook entries (e.g. read, write, delete). Finally, the library **miscellaneous** contains, e.g., a function to indicate incoming data, e-mail, fax, or voice messages.

- **Network specific services:** Libraries in this class depend on the capabilities of the mobile network. Additionally, this class might contain operator-specific libraries.
- **Public services:** This class contains libraries with publicly available functions, i.e., functions third-party providers may use, not only network operators. One example is 'make call' to set up a phone call.

Functions in these libraries all follow the same syntax. For the use in WML, a URI is used (Berners-Lee, 1994a).

```
wtai://<library>/<function>;<parameters>;!<results>
```

The first parameter `<library>` indicates the name of the library, e.g., `cc` for WTACallControl, `wp` for WTAPublic. This is followed by the function name `<function>`, e.g., `sc` for 'setup call', `mc` for 'make call'. If required, parameters may follow. These could be phone numbers etc. Finally, one or more results could be returned. These results set variables in the user agent context.

Within a WML card the URI for calling a certain number could now be as follows:

```
wtai://wp/mc;07216086415
```

The same functions can also be used in WMLScript. Here calling a function follows the same scheme as calling any other function within WMLScript:

```
<returnvalue> = functionname(parameters);
```

The `returnvalue` may be needed if an application requires this value for further operation. The `functionname` is again derived from the name of the library and the name of the function within the library. Finally, one or more values can be passed to the function.

The same example for calling a number would now be:

```
WTAPublic.makeCall("07216086415");
```

The WTA architecture includes an elaborated **event handling** mechanism. Clients, i.e., WTA user agents, must be able to handle telephony-based events that are close to real time. This means that a reaction has to occur within certain strict time bounds. There are two ways events can reach the client. Either the operating system of the mobile device detects the event or the WTA server pushes an event to the client. The first case denotes a traditional event arriving at the device via the mobile phone network, which is then converted into a WTA event. The second event comes from a WTA server using the WSP push service.

No matter where the event comes from, the user agent has to first match this event to any existing **WML event binding** in the current context. If there is any binding with that event, the URL indicated must be loaded. This means that the event has just triggered loading a new card. If there is no such WML event binding, the event has to be tested for a match with the local **event table.** This table must indicate a new URL which has to be loaded in case of this event. Then the WTA user agent loads this new URL. This shows that events are always mapped to URLs.

If events are pushed from a WTA server, this server can push additional content that shows how to handle this event. If only this method is used (i.e., all events come from a WTA server and the mobile network also sends its events first to the server) then WTA events are used in the so-called **server-centric mode.** If the client handles events from the mobile network, while the server provides only, e.g., updates in event bindings, WTA events are used in the so-called **client-centric mode.** Those two extreme modes can now be combined in one architecture allowing an operator to choose the mode that fits best for each event.

An overview of the WTA logical architecture is given in Figure 11.30. The components shown are not all mandatory in this architecture, however, firewalls or other origin servers may be useful. The **client** is connected via a mobile network with a **WTA origin server**, other telephone networks (e.g., fixed PSTN), and a **WAP gateway.** Not shown here is a WML user agent running on the client or other user agents. The client may have voice and data connections over the mobile network. Other origin servers within the trusted domain may be connected via the WAP gateway. A firewall is useful to connect third-party origin servers outside the trusted domain.

Figure 11.30
WTA logical architecture

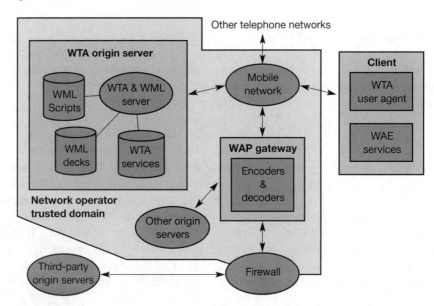

One difference between WTA origin servers and other servers besides security is the tighter control of QoS. A network operator knows exactly the latency, reliability, and capacity of its mobile network and, thus, can have more control over the behaviour of the services. Other servers, probably located in the Internet, may not be able to give as good QoS guarantees as the network operator. Similarly, the WTA user agent has a very rigid and real-time context management compared to the standard WML user agent used for browsing the web.

Figure 11.31 shows an exemplary interaction between a WTA client, a WTA server, the mobile network (with probably many more servers) and a voice box server. Someone might leave a message on a voice box server as indicated. This triggers a message from the voice box server to the WTA server which signifies that a new message has just arrived. The WTA server can then dynamically generate a new deck containing, e.g., references to all voice messages currently stored on the voice box server. It then pushes this deck to the WTA client.

The WTA client displays the new deck and the user can choose which voice message he or she wants to listen to. This request is sent back to the WTA server and the WTA client displays a new card to the user, e.g., showing a message such as 'please listen'. The WTA server translates the request for a specific voice message into a request for the voice box server to play the selected voice message. This request is now in a format suitable for the voice box server.

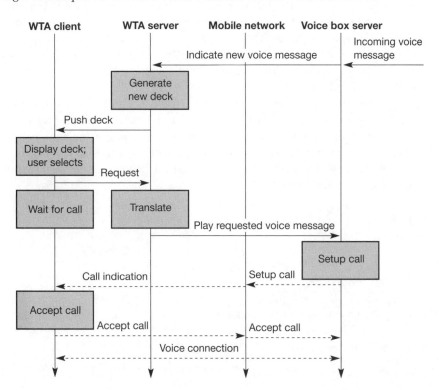

Figure 11.31
WTA example: voice message

The voice box server then sets up a call to the WTA client using standard call set-up procedures of the mobile phone network. The network indicates the call to the client and the call is answered automatically without user interaction since the client has been prepared for this event. The call is accepted and finally a voice connection is established between the voice box server and the WTA client. The dashed lines indicate the standard mobile network interaction not specific for WTA.

The following examples illustrate the integration of WTA, WTAI library calls, WML and WMLScript, and how authors can use the functions of WTA (WAP Forum, 1998m). Imagine you are watching a show on TV. At the end of the show you may vote for your personal champion. The traditional method is that each candidate gets an associated phone number and you have to dial the number – this is quite error prone if long numbers are used. Using WAP with WTA, the network operator could push a deck with several cards onto your handheld device and present a simple choice for voting as explained in the following paragraphs.

The first example consists of WML only and comprises two cards. The first card tells you to vote. If you accept, then the second card will be displayed. On this card, with the name voteChamp, you can choose between Mickey, Donald, and Pluto as champion. You do not have to dial a number but select directly the name of your champion. The variable voteNo will be set to the value (i.e., the phone number) associated with your champion. Now note the URL used after the user has accepted a choice. This URL tells the system to use the function sc (setup call) from the library cc (call control) in the WTAI. This function makes a call to the specified number (here voteNo) and keeps the call (indicated by the 1) even after the current context has been removed.

Altogether, this WML deck lets the user select a champion and then automatically calls the correct number. The user does not have to bother what the correct numbers are. A general problem of WML is the lack of dynamic behaviour. What happens in our example, if anything goes wrong with the call, e.g., the number is busy? To check for errors and report them to a user WMLScript has to be used in addition to WML.

```
<WML>
  <CARD>
    <DO TYPE="ACCEPT" TASK="GO"URL="#voteChamp"/>
    Please vote for your champion!
  </CARD>
  <CARD NAME="voteChamp">
    <DO TYPE="ACCEPT" TASK="GO"
        URL="wtai://cc/sc;$voteNo;1"/>
    Please choose:
```

```
    <SELECT KEY="voteNo">
      <OPTION VALUE="6086415">Mickey</OPTION>
      <OPTION VALUE="6086416">Donald</OPTION>
      <OPTION VALUE="6086417">Pluto</OPTION>
    </SELECT>
  </CARD>
</WML>
```

The following shows the same example, voting for a champion, but with WMLScript and WML for better error handling and reporting. Again, the network operator could push this code onto a handheld device. First of all, the function voteCall is defined. This function takes a number as input and then, in the second line, sets up a call to this number. Now the library function for setting up a call is used, WTACallControl.setup, not the URL as in the example before with just WML. Two values are passed to this function, the first is the phone number to dial and the second is again a value indicating to keep the call after the current context is removed. The advantage of using this function and not the URL is the simple handling of the return value, here stored in j.

Depending on the value of j, the next lines can prepare a message the WML browser can display to the user. The function to set up a call is specified in a way that a negative return value indicates an error. The value itself represents the WTAI error code. Predefined error codes are, for example, –5 for 'called part is busy', –6 for 'network is busy', or –7 for 'no answer' (i.e., the call setup timed out). If the return value is not negative, the variable Message of the browser is set to the string 'Called', the variable No to the value of Nr, i.e., the called number. Otherwise an error has occurred and Message is set to the string 'Error' and No is set to the error code stored in j.

Now a WML deck follows, similar to the first example, but with some important differences. Again, a text is displayed by the first deck. After accepting, the WML browser displays the choice of the three candidates as before. Again, the user can make a choice and the phone number associated with the candidate is stored in the variable voteNo. In this case no URL for the WTAI is loaded as in the example before, but the browser loads a URL pointing to a WMLscript. The WMLScript is located in the compilation unit script; the name of the script is voteCall. The value of the variable voteNo is passed to this function.

It is important to note that the control is now at the script. The second card does not forward control to the third card. In the example, this third card, which has to display a message, is called by the WMLScript function with the line WMLBrowser.go ("showResult"). This loads the card showResult in the WML browser. This third card displays some text and the values of the variables Message and No. These values have been set before in the WMLScript.

```
function voteCall(Nr) {
  var j = WTACallControl.setup(Nr,1);
  if (j>=0) {
    WMLBrowser.setVar("Message","Called");
    WMLBrowser.setVar("No", Nr);
  }
  else {
    WMLBrowser.setVar("Message","Error!");
    WMLBrowser.setVar("No", j);
  }
  WMLBrowser.go("showResult");
}


<WML>
  <CARD>

    <DO TYPE="ACCEPT" TASK="GO" URL="#voteChamp"/>
    Please vote for your champion!
  </CARD>
  <CARD NAME="voteChamp">
    <DO TYPE="ACCEPT" TASK="GO"
      URL="/script#voteCall($voteNo)"/>
    Please choose:
    <SELECT KEY="voteNo">
      <OPTION VALUE="6086415">Mickey</OPTION>
      <OPTION VALUE="6086416">Donald</OPTION>
      <OPTION VALUE="6086417">Pluto</OPTION>
    </SELECT>
  </CARD>
  <CARD NAME="showResult">
    Status of your call: $Message $No
  </CARD>
</WML>
```

This very simple example showed the interaction of WML and WMLScript together with the WTAI. Sure, error codes or phone numbers should not be displayed to a customer, but these codes and numbers should be translated into plain text with the help of WMLScript.

While WTAI is valid for many different mobile networks, the WAP Forum has specified several WTAI extensions valid only for specific networks. Currently, extensions have been defined for the Pacific Digital Cellular system (PDC, (WAP Forum, 1998n)), the Global System for Mobile

Communications (GSM, (WAP Forum, 1998o)), and the IS-136 TDMA cellular network (WAP Forum, 1998p). A typical GSM function is, for example, joining a multiparty call. Thus, the WTAI extension for GSM has the function `WTAGSM.multiparty` for WMLScript in its library and adds the URI `wtai://gsm/jm`.

11.3.10 Example stacks with WAP

After presenting different aspects of WAP, this last section deals once more with the scope of standardization efforts using sample configurations as shown in Figure 11.32. WAP tries to use existing technologies and philosophies as much as possible, mainly from the Internet. Thus, the simplest protocol stack, stack number 3, does not require new protocols or implementations. If an application needs only unreliable datagram service without security, WAP offers a way to use UDP if the bearer network provides IP service (as this is the case for, e.g. GPRS). Based on this very simple stack, more and more complex stacks can be configured by adding security with WTLS or a reliable transaction service with WTP. Applications for distributed computing such as CORBA could use this reliable data transfer service. Currently, these applications mostly use TCP. However, TCP might not be a good choice in a wireless mobile environment as demonstrated in chapter 10. WAP could provide an alternative solution.

The typical WAP application, i.e., a WAP user agent such as a WML or a WTA user agent, may require the full stack of protocols as shown in stack 1. These user agents run in the WAE and rely on, e.g., the WSP push service for pushing WTA events from a WTA server to the client.

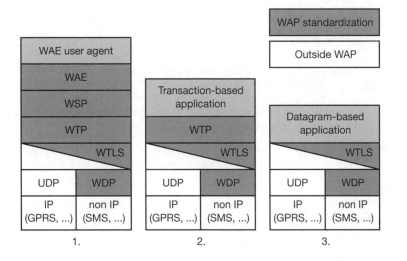

Figure 11.32
Sample protocol stack according to WAP

11.4 Summary

The application of the Internet attracting an ever growing number of people is the WWW. As chapters 1 and 4 show, wireless and mobile communication, especially in the wide area, has an increasing number of subscribers worldwide. Thus, it is only logical to combine both areas, WWW and mobile communications. This chapter dealt with several problems which the combination of the two areas causes, e.g., low available bandwidth in combination with inefficient protocols or HTML as a description language which is not adapted to the requirements of portable devices.

The major part of the chapter presented the WAP as a framework comprising several communication layers, a markup and scripting language, and a connection to the telephony network. This framework is still under development. However, many companies and organizations are supporting this approach. Important issues for all architectures and research projects supporting mobile web browsing are pre-fetching and caching of content (Jiang, 1998), content transformation and adaptation to the capabilities of portable devices (Brewer, 1998), (Fox, 1998), (Han, 1998), and using a browser while disconnected (Mazer, 1998).

The next step of the support for mobility is the provision of complete software frameworks for the development of new mobile applications. Examples are the Rover toolkit (Joseph, 1997) and MobiWare (Angin, 1998). Rover is a tool for building mobile-aware applications that are reliable in the presence of faults. MobiWare is a mobile middleware environment using CORBA and Java. This tool supports the creation of adaptive mobile networking applications with the help of open programmable interfaces.

11.5 Review exercises

1 Why is strong consistency of file systems problematic in a wireless and mobile environment? What are the alternatives?

2 How do conventional file systems react to disconnected systems? Try unplugging a computer that has mounted a file system via a network.

3 What advantages has the statelessness of HTTP? In what situations is state useful and how is it provided today? Where is long-term state stored, where short-term?

4 Which properties of HTTP waste bandwidth? What is the additional problem using HTTP/1.0 together with TCP?

5 How does caching improve access time and reduce bandwidth requirements? What are locations for a cache and their specific advantages?

6 What are problems of caches in real life? What type of content can be cached, which content causes problems? What are the additional problems with client mobility?

7 What discrepancies exist between the possibilities of HTML and the realities of wireless handheld devices? What are proposed solutions? What is the role of plug-ins today and how do they influence the usability of web pages?

8 Name mechanisms to improve web access for handheld devices. What is their common problem and what led finally to the development of WAP?

9 What are typical enhancements to the basic client/server architecture of the web? Reconsider these enhancements for a mobile wireless user with web access over a mobile phone network. What are efficient locations for the enhancements?

10 What are the primary goals of the WAP Forum efforts and how are they reflected in the WAP protocol architecture?

11 What migration paths does WAP offer for Internet and telephony applications and their protocols?

12 Is WDP a fixed protocol and why does WAP not define a SAP which WDP can use?

13 Why does WAP define its own security layer and does not rely on the security provided by the mobile phone network?

14 Name the advantages and disadvantages of user acknowledgements in WTP. What are typical applications for both cases?

15 Which WTP class reflects the typical web access best? How is unnecessary overhead avoided when using WSP on top of this class for web browsing?

16 What problems of HTTP can WSP solve? Why are these solutions especially needed in wireless mobile environments?

17 Why does WSP/B not put responses into the same order as the requests? Think, for example, of requests for different items on a web page.

18 What advantages does a connectionless session service offer compared to a simple datagram service?

19 What are the enhancements of WAE to the classic client/server model of the web? What are functions of this enhancement?

20 What is the fundamental difference of WML compared to HTML? Why is this difference important with respect to handheld devices? What is specified in addition to save bandwidth?

21 Why has a scripting language been added to WML? How can this language help saving bandwidth and reducing delay?

22   What are typical telephony events and how are they integrated into WAP? How can a user access features of mobile phones via the web browser?

23   What is the role of a WTA server? What are the different ways of integrating WTA servers into the WAP architecture?

11.6 References

Adobe (1999) http://www.adobe.com/.

Angin, O.; Campbell, A.T.; Kounavis, M.E.; Liao, R.R.F. (1998) 'The MobiWare toolkit: Programmable support for adaptive mobile networking', *IEEE Personal Communications*, 5, (4).

Berners-Lee, T. (1994a) *Universal Resource Identifiers in WWW, a unifying syntax for the expression of names and addresses of objects on the network as used in the world wide web*, RFC 1630.

Berners-Lee, T. (1994) *Uniform Resource Locators (URL)*, RFC 1738.

Berners-Lee, T.; Fielding, R.; Frystyk, H. (1996) *Hypertext Transfer Protocol – HTTP/1.0*, RFC1945.

Bickmore, T.; Schilit, B. (1997) 'Digestor: device independent access to the world wide web', proc. 6th International World Wide Web Conference, Santa Clara, CA, US.

Blue Squirrel Corporation (1999) *WebWhacker v3.2*, http://www.bluesquirrel. com/.

Bluetooth (1999) http://www.bluetooth. com/.

Brewer, E.A.; Katz, R.H.; Chawathe, Y.; Gribble, S.D.; Hodes, T.; Nguyen, G.; Stemm, M.; Henderson, T.; Amit, E.; Balakrishnen, H.; Fox, A.; Padmanabhan, V.; Seshan, S. (1998) 'A network architecture for heterogeneous mobile computing, *IEEE Personal Communications*, 5, (5).

Certicom Corporation (1999) http://www. certicom.com/.

Conta, A.; Deering, S. (1999) *Internet Control Message Protocol (ICMPv6) for the Internet Protocol Version 6*, RFC 1885.

Dierks, T.; Allen, C. (1999) *The TLS protocol version 1.0*, RFC 2246.

Diffie, W.; Hellman, M. (1976) 'New directions in cryptography', *IEEE Transactions on Information Theory*, 22, (6).

European Telecommunications Standards Institute (1999). http://www.etsi.org/.

Fielding, R. (1995) *Relative Uniform Resource Locators*, RFC 1808.

Fielding, R.; Gettys, J.; Mogul, J.; Frystyk, H.; Berners-Lee, T. (1997) *Hypertext Transfer Protocol – HTTP/1.1*, RFC 2068.

Flanagan, D. (1997) *JavaScript: the definitive guide*. O'Reilly.

Floyd, R.; Housel, B.; Tait, C. (1998) 'Mobile web access using eNetwork Web Express', *IEEE Personal Communications*, (5).

Fox, A.; Brewer, E. (1996) 'Reducing WWW latency and bandwidth requirements by real-time distillation', proc. 5th International World Wide Web Conference, Paris, France.

Fox, A.; Gribble, S.; Brewer, E.A.; Amir, E. (1998) 'Adapting to network and client variability via on-demand dynamic distillation', proc. ASPLOS'96, Cambridge, MA, USA.

Fox, A.; Gribble, S.D.; Chawathe, Y.; Brewer, E.A. (1998) 'Adapting to network and client variation using infrastructure proxies: Lessons and perspectives', *IEEE Personal Communications*, 5, (4).

Guedes, V.; Moura, F. (1995) 'Replica Control in Mio-NFS', proceedings of the ECOOP'95 Workshop on Mobility and Replication, Aarhus, Denmark, August.

Han, R.; Bhagwat, P.; LaMaire, R.; Mummert, T.; Perret, V.; Rubas, J. (1998) 'Dynamic adaptation in an image transcoding proxy for mobile web browsing', *IEEE Personal Communications*, 5, (6).

Heidemann, J.S.; Page, T.W., Guy, R.G.; Popek, G. J. (1992) 'Primarily disconnected operation: experiences with Ficus', proceedings of the 2nd Workshop on the Management of Replicated Data, Monterey, IEEE Computer Society Press, CA, USA, November.

Honeyman, P.; Huston, L. B. (1995) 'Communications and consistency in mobile file systems', *IEEE Personal Communications 2(6),* December.

Housel, B.; Lindquist, D. (1996) 'WebExpress: A system for optimizing web browsing in a wireless environment'. proc. ACM/IEEE MobiCom'96 conference, Rye, NY, USA.

Howard, J. H.; Kazar, M. L.; Menees, S. G.; Nichols, D. A.; Satyanarayanan, M.; Sidebotham, R. N., West, M. J. (1988) 'Scale and performance in a distributed file system', *ACM Transactions on Computer Systems*, 6(1), February.

Huston, L. B.; Honeyman, P. (1993) 'Disconnected operation for AFS', proceedings of USENIX Symposium on Mobile and Location-Independent Computing, Cambridge, MA, USA, August.

Internet Engineering Task Force (1999) http://www.ietf.org/.

Internet Mail Consortium (1996) *vCard – the electronic business card,* Internet Mail Consortium.

Internet Mail Consortium (1996) *vCalendar – the electronic calendaring and scheduling format,* Internet Mail Consortium.

Jiang, Z.; Kleinrock, L. (1998) 'Web prefetching in a mobile environment', *IEEE Personal Communications,* vol. 5, no. 5.

Joseph, A.D.; Kaashoek, M.F. (1997) 'Building reliable mobile-aware applications using the Rover toolkit', *Wireless Networks*, J.C. Baltzer, 3.

Kaufman, C.; Perlman, R.; Speciner, M. (1995) *Network security – private communication in a public world,* Prentice Hall.

King, P.; Hyland, T. (1997) *Handheld device markup language specification.* Unwired Planet.

Kistler, J. J.; Satyanarayanan, M. (1992) 'Disconnected operation in the Coda file system', *ACM Transactions on Computer Systems,* 10(1), February.

Kristol, D.; Montulli, L. (1997) *HTTP state management mechanism,* RFC 2109.

Kumar, P.; Satyanarayanan, M. (1993) 'Supporting application-specific resolution in an optimistically replicated file system', proceedings of 4th Workshop on Workstation Operating Systems, Napa, CA, USA, October.

Liljeberg, M.; Alanko, T., Kojo, M.; Laamanen, H.; Raatikainen, K. (1995) 'Optimizing world wide web for weakly connected mobile workstations: An indirect approach', proc. 2nd International Workshop on Services in Distributed and Networked Environments, SDNE'95, Whistler, B.C., Canada.

Liljeberg, M.; Helin, H.; Kojo, M.; Raatikainen, K.: Mowgli WWW (1996) 'Improved usability of WWW in mobile WAN environments', proc. IEEE Global Internet 1996, London, England.

Lotus Corporation (1999) *Weblicator 1.03,* http://www.lotus.com/.

LoVerso, J.; Mazer, M. (1997) 'Caubweb: detaching the web with Tcl', proc. 5th Annual USENIX Tcl/Tk Workshop, Boston, MA, USA.

Lu, Q.; Satyanarayanan, M. (1994) 'Isolation-only transactions for mobile computing', *Operation Systems Review,* 28(2), April.

Mazer, M.S.; Brooks, C.L. (1998) 'Writing the web while disconnected', *IEEE Personal Communications,* 5, (5).

Microsoft Corporation (1999) *Microsoft Internet Explorer,* http://www.microsoft.com/.

Mummert, L. B.; Ebling, M. R., Satyanarayanan, M. (1995) 'Exploiting weak connectivity for mobile file access', proceedings of the 15th Symposium on Operating System Principles, Copper Mountain Resort, CO, USA, December.

Netscape Corporation (1999) *Netscape Communicator,* http://www.netscape.com/.

Popek, G. J.; Guy, R. G.; Page, T. W. (1990) 'Replication in the Ficus distributed file system', proceedings of the Workshop on the Management of Replicated Data, Los Alamitos, IEEE Computer Society Press, CA, USA, November.

Postel, J. (1980) *User Datagram Protocol,* RFC 768.

Postel, J. (1981a) *Internet Protocol,* RFC 791.

Postel, J. (1981b) *Internet Control Message Protocol,* RFC 792.

Raggett, D.; LeHors, A.; Jacobs, I. (1998) *HTML 4.0 specification,* W3C recommendation, REC-html40-19980424.

Rivest, R.; Shamir, A.; Adleman, L. (1978) 'A method for obtaining digital signatures and public-key cryptosystems', *Communications of the ACM,* 21, (2).

Satyanarayanan, M.; Kistler, J. J.; Mummert, L. B.; Ebling, M. R.; Kumar, P.; Lu, Q. (1993) 'Experiences with disconnected operation in a mobile computing environment', proceedings of USENIX Symposium on Mobile and Location-Independent Computing, Cambridge, MA, USA, August.

Schilit, B.; Douglis, F.; Kristol, D.M.; Krzyzanowski, P.; Sienicki, J.; Trotter, J.A. (1996) 'TeleWeb: loosely connected access to the world wide web', proc. 5th International World Wide Web Conference, Paris, France.

Schneier, B. (1996) *Applied cryptography second edition: Protocols, Algorithms and source code in C.* John Wiley & Sons.

World Wide Web Consortium (1998) *Extensible Markup Language (XML) 1.0 Specification,* W3C recommendation, REC-xml-19980210.

World Wide Web Consortium (1999) http:// www.w3c.org/.

WAP Forum (1998a) *Wireless application protocol architecture specification,* WAP Forum, http://www.wapforum.org/, April.

WAPForum (1998b) *Wireless datagram protocol specification,* WAP Forum, http://www. wapforum.org/, April.

WAP Forum (1998c) *Wireless transport layer security protocol,* WAP Forum, http://www. wapforum.org/, April.

WAP Forum (1998d) *Wireless transaction protocol specification,* WAP Forum, http://www. wapforum.org/, April.

WAP Forum (1998e) *Wireless session protocol specification,* WAP Forum, http://www. wapforum.org/, April.

WAP Forum (1998f) *Wireless application environment specification,* WAP Forum, http:// www.wapforum.org/, April.

WAP Forum (1998g) *Wireless application environment overview,* WAP Forum, http:// www.wapforum.org/, April.

WAP Forum (1998h) *WMLscript language specification,* WAP Forum, http://www. wapforum.org/, April.

WAP Forum (1998i) *WMLscript standard libraries specification,* WAP Forum, http:// www.wapforum.org/, April.

WAP Forum (1998j) *Wireless markup language specification,* WAP Forum, http://www. wapforum.org/, April.

WAP Forum (1998k) *Binary XML content format specification,* WAP Forum, http:// www.wapforum.org/, April.

WAP Forum (1998l) *Wireless telephony application specification,* WAP Forum, http://www. wapforum.org/, April.

WAP Forum (1998m) *Wireless telephony application interface specification,* WAP Forum, http://www.wapforum.org/, April.

WAP Forum (1998n) *Wireless telephony application interface specification,* PDC specific addendum, WAP Forum, http://www. wapforum.org/, April.

WAP Forum (1998o) *Wireless telephony application interface specification,* GSM specific addendum, WAP Forum, http://www. wapforum.org/.

WAP Forum (1998p) *Wireless telephony application interface specification,* IS-136 specific addendum, WAP Forum, http://www. wapforum.org/.

WAP Forum (1998q) *WAP over GSM USSD specification,* WAP Forum, http://www. wapforum.org/.

WAP Forum (1998r) *Wireless control message protocol specification,* WAP Forum, http:// www. wapforum.org/.

Wireless Application Protocol Forum (1998s) http://www. wapforum.org/.

Notes

1 Apart from the term 'portable', several other terms are used when speaking about devices (e.g., 'mobile' in the case of 'mobile phone'). This book mainly distinguishes between wireless access to a network and mobility of a user with a device as key characteristics.

2 Actually, this is already done within the phone network, your phone just handles the signalling.

3 Putting a mainframe on a truck does not really make it a mobile device.

4 Chapter 4 will present more features of modern mobile phone systems, including the growing demand for bandwidth to use typical Internet applications via the mobile 'phone'.

5 This was done in Karlsruhe, Germany, at the location of today's University of Karlsruhe (http://www.uni-karlsruhe.de/) where the author teaches Mobile Communications.

6 Roaming here means a seamless handover of a telephone call from one network provider to another while crossing national boundaries.

7 Note that the book does not describe analog systems.

8 As always, predictions for the future should be treated cautiously.

9 Sudden changes in phase cause high frequencies, an undesired side-effect.

10 These sequences should have a low cross-correlation. More details are given in section 3.5.

11 This example could also be n dimensional.

12 Clearly, this is not a good code, for it is much too short. Here, coding is only done per bit, a much longer code could also stretch over many bits.

13 All systems presented here are digital, for older analog systems such as the US AMPS (advanced mobile phone system) the reader is referred to, e.g., Goodman (1997).

14 UMTS is Europe's and Japan's proposal for the next generation mobile and wireless system within the ITU IMT-2000 framework.

15 More information about channels can be found in Goodman (1997) and ETSI (1993a).

16 In other types of documentation, this number is also called 'Mobile Subscriber ISDN Number' or 'Mobile Station ISDN Number'. Even the original ETSI standards use different wordings for the same acronym.

17 Here, a discrepancy exists between ITU-T standards and ETSI's GSM. MS can denote mobile station or mobile subscriber. Typically, almost all MS in GSM refer to subscribers, as identifiers are not dependent on the station, but on the subscriber identity (stored in the SIM).

18 Strictly speaking, the name 'data link control' for the upper part of layer two is wrong in this architecture. According to the OSI reference model, the data link control (layer two) comprises the logical link control (layer 2b) and the medium access control (layer 2a).

19 Formerly known as trans European trunked radio, but worldwide marketing is better without 'Europe' in the name (see DECT).

20 This speed is a problem, as currently only DAB can provide higher bit rates at high speeds.

21 As the focus of this book is in data transmission, the reader is referred to ETSI (1997a)

for more details about audio coding, audio transmission, multiplexing etc.

22 Bluetooth is a direct translation of the name Blåtand, a Danish Viking king from the early middle ages.

23 Bhat (1998a) uses MT as acronym for a wireless mobile ATM terminal. However, this use does not seem to be consistent with the fact that the document also mentions mobile terminals (i.e., without radio access) and clearly distinguishes between mobility and wireless access. Therefore, this book uses the more consistent term WMT.

24 Bhat (1998a) distinguishes between radio ports as logical points of wireless access for a WMT and radio transceivers as the device sending and receiving radio signals. However, as there may be a radio transceiver associated with each radio port, only the acronym RT is used here, as this distinction is not important for understanding the basic principles of WATM.

25 A splitting point is a switch where an incoming connection is split into two or more outgoing connections.

26 In this context the foreign agent is also called 'snoop proxy'.

27 The reader should be aware that mobile TCP does not have the same status as mobile IP, which is an Internet RFC.

28 Usually, a cookie is represented as an entry in a file that stores user specific information for web servers on the client side. A company can store information in a cookie and retrieve this information as soon as the user visits the company's web pages again.

29 This is *not* the 'International Standards Organization' or the 'International Standardization Organization' or whatever some authors write. ISO is not an acronym, but is derived from the Greek word *isos* which means equal as used (as prefix) in isometric, isomorphic etc. (http://www.iso.ch/).

Appendix – Acronyms

AAL	ATM Adaptation Layer
ABR	Available BitRate
ACF	Association Control Function
ACID	Atomicity, Consistency, Isolation, Durability
ACK	ACKnowledgement
ACL	Asynchronous Connectionless Link
ACT	Ad-hoc Controller Terminal
ADA	Alias DA
ADSL	Asymmetric Digital Subscriber Line
AESA	ATM End System Address
AFS	Andrew File System
AGCH	Access Grant CHannel
AIB	Alias Information Base
AID	Acknowledgement IDentifier
AIDCS	AID CheckSum
AK-HCPDU	AcKnowledgement HCPDU
AM	Amplitude Modulation
AMES	ATM Mobility Extension Service
AMPS	Advanced Mobile Phone System
ANSI	American National Standards Institute
AP	Access Point
APCF	AP Control Function
APCM	AP Connection Management
APCP	AP Control Protocol
ARIB	Association of Radio Industries and Broadcasting
ARQ	Automatic Repeat reQuest
ARQN	ARQ sequence Number
ASA	Alias SA
ASCII	American Standard Code for Information Interchange
ASK	Amplitude Shift Keying
ASP	Active Server Page
Assoc	Association
ATIM	Ad-hoc TIM

ATM	Asynchronous Transfer Mode
ATMC	ATM Connection function
AuC	Authentication Centre
AUS	AUthentication Server
Auth	Authentication
BCA	Borrowing Channel Allocation
BCCH	Broadcast CCH
BCH	Bose-Chaudhuri-Hocquenghem
BER	Bit Error Rate
BFSK	Binary FSK
B-ISDN	Broadband ISDN
BLI	Block Length Indicator
BLIR	Block Length Indicator Replica
BLIRCS	BLIR CheckSum
BMP	BitMaP
BPSK	Binary PSK
BRAN	Broadband Radio Access Networks
BSC	Base Station Controller
BSS	Base Station (Sub)system
BSS	Basic Service Set
BSSAP	BSS Application Part
BSSGP	BSS GPRS Protocol
BTS	Base Transceiver Station
BTSM	BTS Management
BW	BackWard
CAC	Channel Access Control
CAC	Connection Admission Control
CAMEL	Customized Application for Mobile Enhanced Logic
CATV	Community Antenna Television
CBR	Constant BitRate
CC	Call Control
CC	Country Code
CCA	Clear Channel Assessment
CCCH	Common CCH
CCF	Call control and Connection Function
CCH	Control CHannel
CCIR	Consultative Committee for International Radiocommunication
CD	Compact Disc
CDM	Code Division Multiplexing
CDMA	Code Division Multiple Access
CDPD	Cellular Digital Packet Data
CDV	Cell Delay Variation
CEPT	European Conference for Posts and Telecommunications

CGI	Common Gateway Interface
CIDR	Classless InterDomain Routing
CIF	Common Interleaved Frame
CKSN	Ciphering Key Sequence Number
CLMS	Connectionless Message Service
CM	Call Management
CN	Core Network
CN	Correspondent Node
Cnf	Confirmation
COA	Care-Of Address
Codec	Coder/decoder
COFDM	Coded OFDM
COMS	Connection Oriented Message Service
CORBA	Common Object Request Broker Architecture
COS	Cross Over Switch
CPM	Continuous Phase Modulation
CPU	Central Processing Unit
CRC	Cyclic Redundancy Check
CS	CheckSum
CSCW	Computer Supported Cooperative Work
CSMA	Carrier Sense Multiple Access
CSMA/CA	CSMA with Collision Avoidance
CSMA/CD	CSMA with Collision Detection
CT	Cordless Telephone
CTS	Clear To Send
CU	Capacity Unit
CVSD	Continuous Variable Slope Delta
CW	Contention Window
DA	Destination Address
DAB	Digital Audio Broadcasting
DAMA	Demand Assigned Multiple Access
D-AMPS	Digital-AMPS
DBPSK	Differential Binary PSK
DC	Direct Current
DCA	Dynamic Channel Allocation
DCCH	Dedicated CCH
DCF	Distributed Coordination Function
DCS	Digital Cellular System
DDIB	Duplicate Detection Information Base
DECT	Digital Enhanced Cordless Telecommunications
DFWMAC	Distributed Foundation Wireless MAC
DH	Diffie, Hellman
DHCP	Dynamic Host Configuration Protocol
DIFS	DCF IFS

Disassoc	Disassociation
DLC	Data Link Control
DNS	Domain Name System
DPCCH	Dedicated Physical Control CHannel
DPCH	Dedicated Physical CHannel
DPDCH	Dedicated Physical Data CHannel
DQPSK	Differential QPSK
DS	Distribution System
DSDV	Destination Sequence Distance Vector
DSL	Digital Subscriber Loop
DSMA	Digital Sense Multiple Access
DSSS	Direct Sequence Spread Spectrum
DT-HCPDU	DaTa-HCPDU
DTIM	Delivery TIM
DTMF	Dual Tone Multiple Frequency
DVB	Digital Video Broadcasting
DVB-C	DVB-Cable
DVB-S	DVB-Satellite
DVB-T	DVB-Terrestrial
DVD	Digital Versatile Disk
DVTR	Digital Video Tape Recorder
ECDH	Elliptic Curve Diffie Hellman
EDGE	Enhanced Data rates for GSM Evolution
EDTV	Enhanced Definition TV
EHF	Extremely High Frequency
EIR	Equipment Identity Register
EIRP	Equivalent Isotropically Radiated Power
EIT	Event Information Table
EMAS	End-user Mobility-supporting ATM Switch
EMAS-E	EMAS-Edge
EMAS-N	EMAS-Network
ESS	Extended Service Set
ETSI	European Telecommunications Standards Institute
EY-NPMA	Elimination-Yield Non-preemptive Priority Multiple Access
FA	Foreign Agent
FACCH	Fast Associated Dedicated CCH
FCA	Fixed Channel Allocation
FCCH	Frequency Correction CHannel
FDD	Frequency Division Duplex
FDM	Frequency Division Multiplexing
FDMA	Frequency Division Multiple Access
FEC	Forward Error Correction
FHSS	Frequency Hopping Spread Spectrum
FIB	Fast Information Block

FIC	Fast Information Channel
FM	Frequency Modulation
FPLMTS	Future Public Land Mobile Telecommunication System
FR	Frame Relay
FSK	Frequency Shift Keying
FT	Fixed Radio Termination
FW	ForWard
GEO	Geostationary (or Geosynchronous) Earth Orbit
GFSK	Gaussian FSK
GGSN	Gateway GSN
GIF	Graphics Interchange Format
GMM	Global Multimedia Mobility
GMSC	Gateway MSC
GMSK	Gaussian MSK
GP	Guard Period
GPRS	General Packet Radio Service
GPS	Global Positioning System
GR	GPRS Register
GRE	Generic Routing Encapsulation
GSM	Groupe Spéciale Mobile, Global System for Mobile communications
GSN	GPRS Support Node
GTP	GPRS Tunnelling Protocol
GWL	GateWay Link
HA	Home Agent
HBR	High Bit-Rate
HC	HIPERLAN CAC
HCPDU	HIPERLAN CAC PDU
HCQoS	HIPERLAN CAC QoS
HCSAP	HIPERLAN CAC SAP
HCSDU	HIPERLAN CAC SDU
HDA	Hashed Destination HCSAP Address
HDACS	HDA CheckSum
HDB	Home Data Base
HDLC	High level Data Link Control
HDML	Handheld Device Markup Language
HDTP	Handheld Device Transport Protocol
HDTV	High Definition TV
HEC	Header Error Check
HEO	Highly Elliptical Orbit
HF	High Frequency
HI	HBR-part Indicator
HIB	Hello Information Base
HID	HIPERLAN IDentifier

HIPERLAN	High-PERformance LAN
HLR	Home Location Register
HM	HIPERLAN MAC
HMPDU	HIPERLAN MAC PDU
HMQoS	HIPERLAN MAC QoS
HO	HandOver
HO-HMPDU	HellO-HMPDU
HP	HIPERLAN PHY
HSCSD	High Speed Circuit Switched Data
HTML	HyperText Markup Language
HTTP	HyperText Transfer Protocol
ICMP	Internet Control Message Protocol
ICO	Intermediate Circular Orbit
ID	IDentifier
IEEE	Institute of Electrical and Electronics Engineers
IETF	Internet Engineering Task Force
IFS	Inter Frame Spacing
ILR	Interworking Location Register
IMEI	International Mobile Equipment Identity
IMF	Identity Management Function
IMSI	International Mobile Subscriber Identity
IMT	International Mobile Telecommunications
IN	Intelligent Network
IOT	Isolation Only Transactions
IP	Internet Protocol
IR	InfraRed
IrDA	Infrared Data Association
IS	Interim Standard
ISDN	Integrated Services Digital Network
ISI	InterSymbol Interference
ISL	Inter Satellite Link
ISM	Industrial, Scientific, Medical
ISMA	Inhibit Sense Multiple Access
ISO	International Organization for Standardization[29]
I-TCP	Indirect TCP
ITU	International Telecommunication Union
ITU-R	ITU Radiocommunication sector
ITU-T	ITU Telecommunication sector
IV	Initialization Vector
IWF	InterWorking Function
JCT	Japanese Cordless Telephone
JDC	Japanese Digital Cellular
JPEG	Joint Photographic Experts Group
KID	Key IDentifier

LA	Location Area
LAI	Location Area Identification
LAN	Local Area Network
LAPC	Link Access Procedure for the C-Plane
LAPD	Link Access Procedure for the D-channel
LAPD$_m$	LAPD for mobile
LBR	Low Bit-Rate
LC	Link Controller
LED	Light Emitting Diode
LEO	Low Earth Orbit
LF	Low Frequency
LI	Length Indicator
LIR	Least Interference Routing
LLC	Logical Link Control
LM	Link Manager
LMP	Link Manager Protocol
Loc	Location
LOS	Line-Of-Sight
LRU	Last Recently Used
LS	Location Server
MAC	Medium Access Control
MACA	Multiple Access with Collision Avoidance
MATM	Mobile ATM
MBS	Mobile Broadband System
MCC	Mobile Country Code
MCI	Multiplex Configuration Information
MCM	MultiCarrier Modulation
MEO	Medium Earth Orbit
MF	Medium Frequency
MH	Mobile Host
MHEG	Multimedia and Hypermedia information coding Experts Group
MIB	Management Information Base
ML	MSDU Lifetime
MM	Mobility Management
MMF	Mobility Management Function
MN	Mobile Node
MNC	Mobile Network Code
MOC	Mobile Originated Call
MOT	Multimedia Object Transfer
MPEG	Moving Pictures Expert Group
M-QoS	Mobile QoS
MS	Mobile Station
MS	Mobile Switch
MSAP	MAC SAP

MSC	Mobile (Services) Switching Centre
MSC	Mobile Switch Controller
MSC	Main Service Channel
MSDU	MAC SDU
MSIN	Mobile Subscriber Identification Number
MSISDN	Mobile [Station (International)|Subscriber] ISDN Number
MSK	Minimum Shift Keying
MSRN	Mobile [Station|Subscriber] Roaming Number
MT	Mobile Termination
MTC	Mobile Terminated Call
M-TCP	Mobile TCP
MTSA	Mobile Terminal Security Agent
MUL	Mobile User Link
NA-TDMA	North American-TDMA
NAV	Net Allocation Vector
NDC	National Destination Code
NFS	Network File System
NIB	Neighbour Information Base
NIT	Network Information Table
NMAS	Network Mobility-supporting ATM Switch
NMT	Nordic Mobile Telephone
NNI	Network-to-Network Interface
NNI+M	NNI+Mobility
NRL	Normalized Residual HMPDU Lifetime
NSA	Network Security Agent
NSS	Network and Switching Subsystem
NTSC	National Television Standards Committee
OFDM	Orthogonal FDM
OMC	Operation and Maintenance Centre
OSI	Open Systems Interconnection
OSS	Operation Subsystem
PACS	Personal Access Communications System
PACS-UB	PACS-Unlicensed Band
PAD	PADding
PAD	Program Associated Data
PAL	Phase Alternating Line
PC	Personal Computer
PCF	Point Coordination Function
PCH	Paging Channel
PCM	Pulse Code Modulation
PCS	Personal Cellular System
PCS	Personal Communications Service
PDA	Personal Digital Assistant
PDC	Pacific Digital Cellular

PDF	Portable Document Format
PDN	Public Data Network
PDO	Packet Data Optimized
PDTCH	Packet Data TCH
PDU	Protocol Data Unit
PHS	Personal Handyphone System
PHY	PHYsical layer
PIFS	PCF IFS
PIN	Personal Identity Number
PLCP	Physical Layer Convergence Protocol
PLI	Padding Length Indicator
PLL	Phase Lock Loop
PLMN	Public Land Mobile Network
PLW	PLCP-PDU Length Word
PM	Phase Modulation
PMD	Physical Medium Dependent
POTS	Plain Old Telephone Service
PPM	Pulse Position Modulation
PRACH	Physical Random Access Channel
PRMA	Packet Reservation Multiple Access
PS	Power Saving
PSF	PLCP Signalling Field
PSK	Phase Shift Keying
PSN	PDU Sequence Number
PSPDN	Public Switched Packet Data Network
PSTN	Public Switched Telephone Network
PT	Portable radio Termination
PTM	Point-to-Multipoint
PTP	Point-to-Point
PTP-CLNS	PTP-ConnectionLess Network Service
PTP-CONS	PTP-Connection Oriented Network Service
PUK	PIN Unblocking Key
QAM	Quadrature AM
QoS	Quality of Service
QPSK	Quadrature PSK
RA	Receiver Address
RACH	Random Access Channel
RAL	Radio Access Layer
RAND	Random number
Req	Request
Res	Response
RFC	Request For Comments
RIB	Route Information Base
RIP	Routing Information Protocol

RL	Residual Lifetime
RLC	Radio Link Control
RLP	Radio Link Protocol
RM	Resource Management
RNS	Radio Network Subsystem
ROM	Read Only Memory
RR	Radio Resource
RRC	Radio Resource Control
RRM	Radio Resource Management
RSA	Rivest, Shamir, Adleman
RSS	Radio SubSystem
RT	Radio Transceiver
RTR	Radio Transmission and Reception
RTS	Request To Send
RTT	Radio Transmission Technologies
RTT	Round Trip Time
SA	Source Address
SAAL	Signalling AAL
SACCH	Slow Associated Dedicated CCH
SAMA	Spread Aloha Multiple Access
SAP	Service Access Point
SATM	Satellite ATM Services
SC	Sanity Check
SC	Synchronization Channel
SCF	Service Control Function
SCH	Synchronization Channel
SCO	Synchronous Connection-Oriented link
SCPS	Space Communications Protocol Standards
SCPAS-TP	SCPS-Transport Protocol
SDCCH	Stand-alone Dedicated CCH
SDM	Space Division Multiplexing
SDMA	Space Division Multiple Access
SDT	Service Description Table
SDTV	Standard Definition TV
SDU	Service Data Unit
SEC-SAP	Security SAP
SEQN	SEQuence Number
SFD	Start Frame Delimiter
SFN	Single Frequency Network
SGSN	Serving GSN
SH	Supervisory Host
SHF	Super High Frequency
SIFS	Short IFS
SIG	Signalling

SIM	Subscriber Identity Module
SMRIB	Source Multipoint Relay Information Base
SMS	Short Message Service
SN	Subscriber Number
SNACK	Selective Negative ACKnowledgement
SNAP	Sub-Network Access Protocol
SNDCP	Subnetwork Dependent Convergence Protocol
SRES	Signed Response
SS	Supplementary Service
SS7	Signalling System No. 7
S-SAP	Session-SAP
SSL	Secure Sockets Layer
STA	STAtion
SUMR	Satellite User Mapping Register
SW	Short Wave
SwMI	Switching and Management Infrastructure
T	Terminal
TA	Transmitter Address
TCH	Traffic CHannel
TCH/F	TCH Full rate
TCH/FS	TCH/F Speech
TCH/H	TCH Half rate
TCH/HS	TCH/H Speech
TC-HMPDU	Topology Control-HMPDU
TCP	Transmission Control Protocol
TD-CDMA	Time Division-CDMA
TDD	Time Division Duplex
TDM	Time Division Multiplexing
TDMA	Time Division Multiple Access
TDT	Time and Data Table
TE	Terminal
TETRA	Terrestrial Trunked Radio
TFI	Transport Format Identifier
TFTS	Terrestrial Flight Telephone System
TI	Type Indicator
TIB	Topology Information Base
TIM	Traffic Indication Map
TINA	Telecommunication Information Networking Architecture
TLLI	Temporary Logical Link Identity
TLS	Transport Layer Security
TM	Traffic Management
TMN	Telecommunication Management Network
TMSI	Temporary Mobile Subscriber Identity
TOS	Type Of Service

TPC	Transmit Power Control
TR-SAP	Transaction SAP
T-SAP	Transport SAP
TSF	Timing Synchronization Function
T-TCP	Transaction TCP
TTC	Telecommunications Technology Council
TTL	Time To Live
TV	TeleVision
UBR	Unspecified BitRate
UD	User Data
UDP	User Datagram Protocol
UE	User Equipment
UHF	Ultra High Frequency
UIM	User Identification Module
UMTS	Universal Mobile Telecommunications System
UN	United Nations
UNI	User-to-Network Interface
UNI+M	UNI+Mobility
UP	User Priority
UPT	Universal Personal Telecommunications
URI	Uniform Resource Identifier
UTRA	UMTS Terrestrial Radio Access
UTRAN	UTRA Network
UWC	Universal Wireless Communications
V+D	Voice and Data
VAD	Voice Activity Detection
VBR	Variable BitRate
VBR-nrt	VBR non real-time
VBR-rt	VBR real-time
VC	Virtual Circuit
VCC	Visitor Country Code
VDB	Visitor Data Base
VHE	Virtual Home Environment
VHF	Very High Frequency
VLF	Very Low Frequency
VLR	Visitor Location Register
VNDC	Visitor National Destination Code
W3C	World Wide Web Consortium
WAE	Wireless Application Environment
WAN	Wide Area Network
WAP	Wireless Application Protocol
WATM	Wireless ATM
WCAC	Wireless Connection Admission Control
W-CDMA	Wideband-CDMA

WCMP	Wireless Control Message Protocol
W-CTRL	Wireless ConTRoL
WDP	Wireless Datagram Protocol
WLAN	Wireless LAN
WLL	Wireless Local Loop
WML	Wireless Markup Language
WMLScript	Wireless Markup Language Script
WMT	Wireless Mobile Terminal
WPAN	Wireless Personal Area Network
WP-CDMA	Wideband Packet-CDMA
WRC	World Radio Conference
WSP	Wireless Session Protocol
WSP/B	Wireless Session Protocol/Browsing
WTA	Wireless Telephony Application
WTAI	Wireless Telephony Application Interface
WTLS	Wireless Transport Layer Security
WTP	Wireless Transaction Protocol
WWW	World Wide Web
XML	eXtensible Markup Language
XOR	eXclusive OR

Index